Christian infighting is a play of Satan. He wants to keep us busy fighting our own, so that we don't unite together to fight against the real enemy and his demonic powers. *Quenching the Spirit* attempts to give a necessary other side for some who have been consistently shot at by pen and mouth. May the truth set us free so we can begin to love and forgive one another.

Rita M. Bennett, president
Christian Renewal Association Inc.
Edmonds, Washington

William DeArteaga's book is for believers who have received the Holy Spirit and for our brethren who were taught to believe that orthodoxy precludes present-day gifts and miracles. This has deprived them — and others — of a God-given privilege. *Quenching the Spirit* is what the church of Jesus Christ desperately needs to hear. Now.

Charles E. Blake, bishop
West Angeles Church of God in Christ
Los Angeles, California

Quenching the Spirit defuses our innate fear of changing the way we respond to the revelation of God. Long overdue, it challenges us to reassess — without prejudice — the charismatic approach to worship and to reevaluate Christian service without insisting on sameness.

Judson Cornwall, author
Phoenix, Arizona

The gospel is not only in word, but in power. From day one, it was intended to be demonstrated. God did not just talk; He acted. Jesus preached, taught and healed, and He commanded His disciples to do the same. Praise God that *Quenching the Spirit* exalts Jesus for His miracles of compassion on hurting people.

Billy Joe Daugherty, pastor
Victory Christian Center
Tulsa, Oklahoma

D0377524

Satan's deception during a move of God is both subtle and powerful because the devil's disguise is a religious spirit. He cloaks his activity by honoring what God *has* done, while fighting what God *is* doing. Brother DeArteaga thoroughly exposes this stronghold of pharisaical religion.

Francis Frangipane, senior pastor
River of Life Ministries
Cedar Rapids, Iowa

Too often we are pushed toward an extreme position on our beliefs when we are attacked in an extreme way. DeArteaga has done a great favor for "Spirit-filled life" believers. He has experienced the anointing of God and presents a scholarly case. What a great combination!

Charles Green, pastor
Faith Church
New Orleans, Louisiana

In the midst of some reputable voices hurling broad-sweeping attacks against the charismatic movement, here comes a disciplined, honest, analytical, historical and theological response. The unfortunate indictment against the charismatic movement now has a response to balance it! It's a must to read *Quenching the Spirit*.

Ronn Haus, president
United Christian Broadcasting Network
Concord, California

We charismatics can certainly claim to have been bad-mouthed, sadly, by many of our fellow believers because we have contended for certain truths which have been neglected by the church over the years.

However, none of us can claim to have all the truth, and we should all be wary of casting the first stone. I believe the biblical way to judge is on the fruit that is borne. I pray *Quenching the Spirit* will bring balance and, hopefully, restore some unity among Christians.

Ray McCauley, pastor and founder
Rhema Ministries
South Africa

It was necessary for someone to respond to the negative things that have been said concerning the charismatic movement. *Quenching the Spirit* was written in the proper spirit by a man with good credentials.

Paul Paino, founder
Calvary Temple
Fort Wayne, Indiana

I personally thank Creation House for publishing this tremendous book by William DeArteaga.

My response to *Quenching the Spirit* is enthusiastic! This book meets a great need and could save hundreds of thousands from ending up in the quicksands of an unscriptural and biased reaction to what God is doing.

I pray for all to see in their hearts how the Pentecostal and charismatic moves of the Holy Spirit will make Jesus so much more real to them.

Oral Roberts
Oral Roberts University
Tulsa, Oklahoma

As a member of a pioneering family in charismatic renewal, I rejoice in this balanced and scholarly response to what has often been unbalanced and unsound criticism. William DeArteaga accurately identifies the real issues and puts the debate on solid ground historically and biblically.

R. Loren Sandford, senior pastor
New Song Fellowship
Thornton, Colorado

I think it's great that we have someone to come to the defense of the scriptural supernatural. We need signs and wonders to confirm the Word!

Karl D. Strader, pastor
Carpenter's Home Church
Lakeland, Florida

One of the most disturbing facts about Christianity is that very few Christians ever advance beyond their first revelation. They find it impossible to receive and accept new truth that God reveals. This happened in the New Testament with the Lord Jesus and the Pharisees. I am thankful that *Quenching the Spirit* faces this critical situation within the body of Christ. May many come to know the truth that will set them free from traditionalism.

Lester Sumrall
Lester Sumrall Evangelistic Association (LeSea)
South Bend, Indiana

In *Quenching the Spirit*, William DeArteaga summarizes and answers twenty centuries of criticism against spiritual renewal movements. From the ancient Pharisees through Benjamin Warfield to Dave Hunt, this book offers a new way of defending Pentecostals and charismatics from their harshest critics. A must-read book for those who are looking for solid answers.

Vinson Synan, Dean
School of Divinity
Regent University
Virginia Beach, Virginia

.: is a most fitting time for *Quenching the Spirit* to be read by all believers who truly are seeking truth. The church must be refocused from who is telling the truth to *who* is the truth. Seeing Jesus as the truth eliminates debate with and judgment of one another.

Fear, resulting from ignorance of truth, often encourages us to cease what is important and to focus on the unimportant. *Quenching the Spirit* truly enables us to separate the holy from the profane. DeArteaga has written a masterpiece — don't miss it!

Iverna Tompkins
Iverna Tompkins Ministries
Phoenix, Arizona

QUENCHING THE
SPIRIT

*Discover the REAL Spirit Behind
the Charismatic Controversy*

William DeArteaga

**CREATION
HOUSE**
BOOKS ABOUT SPIRIT-LED LIVING
ORLANDO, FLORIDA

Creation House
Strang Communications Company
600 Rinehart Road
Lake Mary, 32746
(407) 333-3132

First edition:
First printing, July 1992
Second printing, September 1992

Second edition:
First printing, May 1996

ACKNOWLEDGMENTS

THE WRITER OF ECCLESIASTES WARNED millennia ago: "Of making many books there is no end, and much study wearies the body" (Eccl. 12:12, NIV). A glance at the notes at the end of the book will show that this work was not thrown together quickly. I owe a special debt of gratitude to Carolyn, my wife, for helping me complete this work. She has understood that the Lord called me to be a scribe of the kingdom (Matt. 13:52) and to work for His glory regardless of the time and effort involved.

I also owe much to my home fellowship friends and the prayer and praise fellowship that I lead at St. Jude's Episcopal Church, Marietta, Georgia. Many a time I pled for their prayer support when I had a difficult chapter to write. On one occasion I told them I was writing on quantum physics and revelation, and they didn't even ask why it was difficult. The plea over another "very difficult chapter" became a standing joke among my friends, and we rejoiced greatly when the last such chapter was finished. Only those who have experienced the power of the prayer of the righteous (James 5:16) will understand how much this book owes to their heavenly intercessions.

I should also like to thank Walter Walker and Deborah Poulalion, my editors at Creation House, for their patience with my text and for their many excellent suggestions.

Special thanks go to two fine Christian scholars who helped me update and correct the chapters on E. W. Kenyon. They are Dr. Dale Simmons of Bethel College (Indiana) and the irrepressible Geir Lie, a Norwegian scholar whose meticulous and persistent scholarship has unearthed long lost documents pertaining to Kenyon's ministry.

CONTENTS

Part IV
From Quantum Physics to Faith

Part V
From Reproof to Pharisaism

Part VI
Conclusions

FOREWORD

STRANGE AS IT MAY SEEM, a tragic fact in the history of Christianity is that the blessings of God have often become an occasion for discord and division in the church. If we allow him to do so, the devil will use any phase of divine revelation to divide believers. For example, look at the bitter disputes in the past over the issue of the Lord's supper, questions pertaining to the Lord's return or problems raised by the doctrine of God's sovereign grace. In more recent years the quarrel has been over matters concerning the ministry of the Holy Spirit, with the gifts of the Spirit prominent among subjects of disagreement.

Millions of Christians have testified to discovering a deeper spiritual life through the experience known as the baptism in the Holy Spirit. Their testimonies include not only descriptions of a greater intimacy with Christ but also claims of the manifestation of spiritual gifts and the working of miracles. However, not everyone is willing to concede that such phenomena are indeed the product of divine activity — in spite of the evident sincerity of such believers, the obvious results of their enthusiastic witness and the biblical evidence supporting the experiences they claim. As a result, acrid criticism has been aimed at participants in the so-called renewal movement with most of the opposition coming from conservative evangelical Christians who profess to believe the Bible.

How can we account for this raging battle in which the saints are so busy taking snipes at one another that they give scant attention to Satan, their common enemy? In this book William DeArteaga places much of the responsibility on critics who maintain a pharisaic intolerance that is foreign to the Spirit of Christ. In reviewing significant spiritual awakenings in church history, DeArteaga describes the attitudes and tactics of censurers who, in the name of orthodoxy, have sought to quell the work of the Spirit, thus repeating the errors of biblical Pharisees.

The primary basis for such opposition, DeArteaga charges, is a cessationist position that relegates spiritual gifts and commonplace miracles to only the apostolic age, regarding such phenomena as a sort of double portion to get the church off to a good start. The author's efforts have been well spent if this book succeeds in persuading cessationists, those who believe miracles and spiritual gifts have ceased, to honestly evaluate their position in light of both biblical and historical testimony.

Such a self-examination, with a sincere effort to put aside traditional prejudices ingrained in me from Sunday school through seminary, led to a change in my own position years ago. Could it be that modern pharisaic faultfinders seek to tone down the first-century fervor because it makes their own pale, churchly religiosity look drearily pitiful in comparison? Or is God so unwise that He would begin a work by raising high hopes and expectations that He never intended to fulfill?

The historical review in this book reveals how anything out of the ordinary disturbs the correctness of a stiff and starched orthodoxy that excuses its anemic condition by confining such power to the early church with the threadbare conclusion that the age of miracles has passed. In reality, the day of miracles has not passed; it is simply that for many people the day of miraculous faith has passed.

Sad to say, Pentecost is on the church calendar, but too often it is not the church's condition. Consequently, many churches live on a memory. I think God must prefer an overexuberant faith that He must hold in rein somewhat to a pallid orthodoxy that rigidly intones the words but really does not believe them. It surely must be easier to restrain a fanatic than resurrect a corpse.

Jerry Horner, Th.D.
Professor of New Testament
Oral Roberts University
April 1996

PREFACE

I WOULD LIKE TO DESCRIBE a little about my background by explaining how *Quenching the Spirit* was conceived and written.

In 1985 I was preparing a book on the charismatic renewal and the history of inner healing. In August of that year, Dave Hunt's book *The Seduction of Christianity* was released. I and many others in the renewal movement were distressed by its inaccurate and unjust assault on the charismatic renewal. I immediately saw the book as an example of Christian Pharisaism. Its attack on the renewal exemplified the same type of resistance that Jesus encountered from first-century Pharisees who were trying to protect their traditional theology and practice.

I first became aware of the Pharisee phenomenon when I was an undergraduate at Fordham University twenty years ago. I read books by Catholic theologians who labored to depict Christian Pharisees as legalists, who exhibited rigid morals without mercy. When I became a charismatic Christian, I came to understand that there was also a deeper level to the Christian Pharisee — that of opposing the move of the Holy Spirit.

Within a year of the release of *The Seduction of Christianity* I had produced a book-length response to Hunt's work. Sections of that manuscript were published in the anthology *The Church Divided* (South Plainfield, N.J.: Bridge Publishing, 1986).

Then 1988 saw the publication of *A Different Gospel* by D. R.

McConnell. McConnell's work was not a spectacular best-seller like *Seduction*. It was moderate in tone, a scholarly "pastor's book," but it offered a formidable challenge to the integrity of the charismatic renewal. In particular, McConnell showed that many concepts from the Word-Faith movement were influenced by teachers who had been involved in varying degrees with New Thought and Christian Science, two of the cults in America in the late 1800s. McConnell's thesis was expanded in Hank Hannegraaff's best-selling book, *Christianity in Crisis*. Both McConnell and Hannegraaff misunderstood American Christian history because they did not take into account the influence of the orthodox Faith-Cure movement, which I'll describe.

I was uniquely equipped to approach this challenge because of my own spiritual life. In my search for God from 1974 to about 1980, I surveyed much of the metaphysical literature available. The grace of God led me out of that environment and enabled me to see that though elements of truth existed there, they were surrounded by and imbedded in Gnostic heresies. I am thankful that what little I wrote during that period was not widely distributed. Some Christians may be surprised by my unusual route to biblical faith and Christian scholarship. Yet because of that path I was made aware of the indispensable need for discernment in spiritual experiences, a major theme of this book.

History shows that the Lord uses many different ways to bring His children into the kingdom. Evangelicals quickly and easily recognize the pattern set by Martin Luther. In a sudden flash of grace and illumination, Luther renounced his efforts at earning salvation and pursued a Christian life solidly established on the basis of grace. On the other hand, Augustine was raised in a pious household, but as a young man he experimented with various pagan philosophies and cults before returning to Christianity.

Naturally, Augustine's writings show a masterful command of the dangers of heresy. Thus, through his wasted years of theological confusion, the Lord gave him insight into heresy, an important contribution he could pass on to the church. In the same way, I am hopeful that the Lord can now use my research and writing to help others in the body of Christ to discern truth from error, enabling them to reject what is false while holding on to that which is good and of God.

William DeArteaga
Smyrna, Georgia
April 1996

INTRODUCTION

Rejoice always; pray without ceasing; in everything
give thanks for this is God's will for you in Christ Jesus.
Do not quench the Spirit; do not despise prophetic utterances.
But examine everything carefully; hold fast to that
which is good; abstain from every form of evil.
1 Thessalonians 5:16-22

A T THE BEGINNING OF THIS century, unfortunately, an overwhelming majority of Christians believed that only the first-century church was empowered with the gifts of the Holy Spirit. Because most assumed that such spiritual empowering passed away with the twelve apostles, the early church could not serve as a true example for believers today. For centuries this assumption molded the traditional theologies of the church. Thus the few Christians who ministered healing or exercised the gifts of the Spirit were accused of heresy or even of practicing witchcraft.

God loved the church so much that He would not allow it to remain in this error, no matter how satisfied most Christians felt about their theology or how content they were with formal religion. The Holy Spirit has continued to act upon the church, pulling, shoving and pestering it to bring to "remembrance" what Jesus said about the Great Commission and spiritual empowerment for service (John 14:26; Mark 16:17-18).

The church in the last 150 years has experienced an expansion of ministry power and missionary effectiveness not seen since the first centuries.[1] As a result, Christians have begun to behave as if the book of Acts were a practical model of the living church. In the process certain graced individuals adjusted their "given" theologies and made some changes which would allow the release of long-suppressed spiritual gifts. Some researchers predict that in the future the majority of the world's Christians will belong to churches that accept and practice the gifts of the Holy Spirit as normal in Christian life.[2]

However, these changes have not come without cost or opposition. One of the recent attacks on the theology and practice of spiritual gifts has come from Hank Hanegraaff in *Christianity in Crisis*. This book caused quite a stir in evangelical and charismatic circles, but Hanegraaff is not alone in his opposition. As often as the Holy Spirit has given a fresh outpouring, certain people have lined up to discredit and malign the movement. Every revival has its critics.

This book performs the unpleasant task of documenting resistance to the unexpected, and often unwelcomed, movings of the Holy Spirit. We shall also examine opposition to the more biblically accurate and Spirit-empowered practices and theologies that resulted. Ironically, influential churchmen led this resistance, sincerely believing they were protecting the orthodox faith.

We are not suggesting that resistance to theological change is always mistaken. In fact Scripture warns the believer to be vigilant against "every wind of doctrine" and false teachings. The problem lies in discerning prophet from charlatan and authentic biblical insight from passing fashion.

Errors in discernment can have the gravest consequences for the Christian community. For example, in recent years many mainline churches have accepted the idea that homosexuality is not a sin but a God-given orientation. Such a position does violence to Scripture and weakens the authority and spiritual power of the entire Christian church. In this case the church leadership has not resisted enough.

On the other hand, when churchmen resist the prompting of the Holy Spirit, other unfortunate consequences result. The community is diverted from the purpose of God and eventually falls prey to some form of religiosity or legalism. To this type of resistance we give the biblical name Pharisaism. The major part of this work involves studying both the biblical and modern manifestations of Pharisaism. We will see throughout history how Pharisaism has attempted to quench the Spirit and has labeled as heretics those who have led the way in rediscovering biblical and spiritual truth.

ONE

The Longevity
of the Pharisees

———————

A PHARISEE IS A DEEPLY religious person who, among other things, staunchly asserts and defends the status quo with regard to tradition, order and consensus orthodoxy. I use the term *consensus orthodoxy* throughout this book to refer to the theological interpretations accepted by most religious people of the day.

Most often the Pharisee practices religion conscientiously to the point of legalism, but this is not the most serious error in spirituality. Rather the Pharisee exaggerates the traditions and truths of consensus orthodoxy in order to oppose any new work of the Holy Spirit. Ultimately then a Pharisee opposes the work of God from within the church. As we shall see, the Bible defines Pharisaism as a heresy.

In Scripture, the Greek word that is translated as heresy is *hairesis*, and it simply means sects. From the way *hairesis* is used in the epistles, we can conclude that certain sects have beliefs and ways of spirituality that are deeply destructive and not just theologically mistaken. In Peter's second letter these groups are called "destructive heresies" (2 Pet. 2:1). These destructive heresies take a person out of spiritual fellowship with the body of Christ.[1]

The New Testament points to two sects that were indeed spiritually deadly. These should be considered as the biblical type or pattern of true heresy. One was the Gnosticism that plagued the churches founded by Paul.[2] The other was Pharisaism.

The early Gnostics believed, among other things, that the created world was evil and in opposition to the world of the spirit, which was therefore good. As a result, the Gnostic way of spirituality accepts visions, prophecies and spiritual experiences without any restraint. In effect, the Gnostics do not discern between the activities of lower, demonic spirits and the inspiration of the Holy Spirit.

Pharisaism deals with spiritual experiences exactly opposite to the way Gnosticism does. Unlike the Gnostics, the Pharisees restrict the flow of spiritual experiences until religion becomes a purely intellectual and theological exercise, and the Spirit is quenched.

Gnosticism has been a recurring heresy throughout all of church history, and from the time of Irenaeus, bishop of Lyons (A.D. 130-200), it has been a much studied form of counterfeit spirituality.* Pharisaism has not been studied extensively until recently (though Acts 15:5 and Colossians 2:18-23 show clearly that it continued to be a problem in the Jerusalem church and churches founded by Paul).[3]

Pharisaism in Scriptural Context

The twenty-third chapter of Matthew contains Jesus' strongest denouncement of the Pharisees. Here Jesus was functioning in His role as prophet, one sent from God to reprove evil. All the characteristics that we associate with the Pharisees — hypocrisy, legalism, the reduction of scriptural interpretation to nitpicking — were exposed by Jesus' sharp words.

The characteristics that Jesus denounced were but the end product of a long theological and spiritual process. One has to look carefully to the Scriptures to understand why the Pharisees arrived at this sorry state of spiritual life. We then can see that the Pharisees had certain assumptions about themselves and certain expectations that placed them in fundamental opposition to Jesus.

Heresy is commonly understood as being a belief system which is contrary to truth. However, Pharisaism was heretical in spite of its theological correctness. Jesus made this point at the beginning of Matthew 23 when he said that Pharisees "seated themselves in the chair of Moses" (v. 2). This means they were the inheritors of Moses' learning, just as a chair of philosophy is passed by one scholar to another in a

---

* Dave Hunt, with whom I will cross theological swords often in this work, produced a fine book describing many of the current manifestations of Gnosticism: *The Cult Explosion* (Eugene, Oreg.: Harvest House, 1980).

university. In other words, something other than the Pharisees' specific theology caused their destructiveness to the kingdom of God.

The Pharisees' real problem came from two sources. First, they drastically overvalued the role of theology in spiritual life; they made theological correctness the chief religious virtue. Somewhere in that process the primary command to love God and mankind was subordinated to correct theology. Second, they had a man-given confidence in their theological traditions as being the perfect interpretation of Scripture. They falsely placed their theology, referred to as the traditions of the elders, on the same level as Scripture.

For example, the Pharisees were grievously offended by Jesus and His disciples for not washing before eating (Matt. 15:2-6). As good an idea as this was, washing before meals was not part of the Mosaic law; but the Pharisees had become so attached to their tradition that it became the basis of their offense at Jesus. They mistook the instrument of understanding of Scripture for Scripture itself.

Two centuries after Christ, the traditions of the elders referred to in the Gospels were put into writing in the Jewish Talmud, the official commentary for the Scriptures. It would be fair to say that the main issue of contention between Jesus and the Pharisees was the relationship between the Torah (the first five books of the Bible) and the Talmud (the Pharisees' theological commentaries). In a broad sense, the Torah represented the inspired Word of God while the Talmud referred to theological commentaries.

The Pharisees valued the Talmud as equally important to the Torah in regard to daily life. Jesus held no such confusion. The Torah was eternal, the Word of God. The Talmud, on the other hand, was man's interpretation that needed continual reevaluation in the light of the eternal Word.

Though Jesus kept the Law of Moses (Torah) perfectly[*], it seems as if He made a point of violating the traditions of the elders on a regular basis. Jesus came to bring new revelation and understanding to what the Torah really meant, but the Pharisees were stuck in their consensus orthodoxy and wound up in opposition to the move of the Spirit.

Judging by Origins

Because of this confusion and the Pharisees' love of rabbinical

---

[*] The exception to this was Jesus' declaration that all foods were pure, therefore negating the Mosaic dietary laws (Mark 7:19).

discourses, faith became intellectualized. Faith, defined by the Old Testament patriarchs as *trust* in God and *expectancy* in His provision, began to be understood as adherence to theological and ritual positions (acceptance of the Talmud). The center of faith moved from the heart to the head. A sign of this was the way the Pharisees bombarded Jesus with theological questions.

As a natural result of their intellectualism, the Pharisees split into factions among themselves. Divisions occur whenever the intellect is enthroned as the measure of spirituality — not because spiritual gifts are exercised, as many charge. The principal factions were the schools of Hillel and Shammai. Gamaliel, mentioned twice in Acts, was a disciple of Hillel and a noted teacher in his own right (Acts 5:34-40 and 22:3).

Pride of scholarship and intellect led the Pharisees to assume that all spiritual issues should be evaluated by solely theological means (knowledge of the Talmud). True discernment, however, is an activity of the Holy Spirit within man, in conjunction with intellectual and theological concepts.

The Pharisees evaluated religious questions and spiritual phenomena on the basis of authoritative opinion rather than spiritual discernment. Again, Scripture was confused with traditional opinion (Talmud). The principal point of judgment came to the question, what were the *origins* and *pedigree* of the person or opinion? Did the person manifesting spiritual power, such as healing or exorcism, have the right to that power by nature of his training and association with the proper rabbinical school?

In Jesus' cleansing of the temple, for example, the principal concern was Jesus' *authority* for the act, not the justice of the act itself. The temple did need cleansing of its hucksters, but Jesus didn't seem to have the rabbinical credentials for it (Mark 11:27-33).

Eventually the Pharisees' suspicion of spiritual phenomena became so intense that they began to assume that all unknown spiritual phenomena were dangerous.[4] For example, consider what happened to Peter and John after a lame man was healed (Acts 4:1-22). They were dragged before the Sanhedrin to be prosecuted, and the question they were asked was: "By what power or by what name did you do this?" (v. 7). Peter answered their challenge with great wisdom and boldness, declaring that his authority came through Jesus.

The members of the Sanhedrin were astonished by the courage and wisdom of the apostles, since they were "uneducated, common men" (v. 13, RSV). In other words, Peter and John did not belong to a rabbinical school. The members of the Sanhedrin assumed that only they themselves, trained in their own schools, could interpret Scripture correctly or have direct power or revelations from God.

In this context we can understand the Pharisees' difficulty with John the Baptist. The general populace credited him as a prophet, yet he was not a Pharisee. Who and what was he? Jesus made use of their confusion when He responded to their challenge of His authority (Matt. 21:23-27).

Ironically, the Pharisees had been on the cutting edge of Judaism in opposing apostasy and paganism under the reign of a pagan Greek government during the first and second century B.C. They assumed that their theological traditions, which served well in discerning against Greek paganism, placed them in spiritual descent with the great prophets of the past. They also expected Judaism to develop and flower along lines they had already charted. The Messiah would thus be a super-Pharisee who would resolve all their disputes by His brilliant interpretations.

The Pharisees' Flawed System of Discernment

Rather than affirm the Pharisees' expectations and assumptions, the true Messiah overturned them with the same firmness that He used on the money changers at the temple. The Pharisees were galled by Jesus' understanding of spiritual accountability, discernment and evaluation. He completely short-circuited their Talmudic system of theological controversies, rabbinical authority, proper origins and pedigrees. Jesus declared that spiritual questions must be evaluated by their *fruit* (Matt. 7:15-18).

By His rejection of the Talmud, Jesus did not mean that Scripture should be ignored. Rather He was pointing out the errors that man makes when interpreting God's message. The Pharisees developed the Talmud as an attempt to provide rules for situations not covered explicitly in Scripture. This practice is known as "fencing" (making overly restrictive rules to keep people away from the possibility of sinning). The most extreme form of fencing developed in the Jewish tradition was the kosher rules of food that go beyond the Mosaic code, as in, for example, providing separate plates for dairy and meat items.

Jesus, on the other hand, knew that such fences were man-made and subject to adjustment. Jesus affirmed that discernment is by fruit, not tradition (Talmud) — both in spiritual experiences and for conduct in areas of life where Scripture is not specific. John the Baptist had already raised the fruit question in regard to the Pharisees who came to him seeking baptism (Matt. 3:8-10). Jesus made the fruit criterion central to authentic discernment for His disciples. He instructed them: "Beware of the false prophets, who come to you in sheep's clothing, but inwardly are ravenous wolves. You will know them by their fruits. Grapes are not gathered from thorn bushes, nor figs from thistles, are they?" (Matt. 7:15-16).

The contrast between the Christian view of spiritual accountability and discernment on the one hand (fruit) and the Pharisees' view on the other (origins) is summarized dramatically in the case of the man healed of blindness from birth (John 9). When the Pharisees questioned the man and then his parents, they were not concerned with the fruit of the incident (that is, that the man had his sight restored), but rather the origins and pedigree of the healer. They wanted to know what rabbinical school Jesus came from that authorized Him to do spiritual works. The Pharisees declared, "We are disciples of Moses. We know that God has spoken to Moses; but as for this man [Jesus], we do not know where He is from" (vv. 28-29).

Jesus' injunction to judge the fruit of spiritual phenomena was extended by the Holy Spirit in Paul's epistles. His writings developed the concept of testing discernment, which would identify whether spiritual phenomena was from God or another source. Paul wrote: "And this I pray, that your love may abound still more and more in real knowledge and all discernment, so that you may approve the things that are excellent, in order to be sincere and blameless until the day of Christ" (Phil. 1:9-10.)

Paul is talking about discernment but not discernment of spirits. The discernment in this passage is associated with knowledge, and its purpose is to test and accept what is excellent. This is repeated in 1 Thessalonians: "Do not quench the Spirit, do not despise prophesying, but test everything; hold fast what is good, abstain from every form of evil" (5:19-22, RSV). Paul thus instructs his readers to test new things by attending to their fruits, which was Jesus' viewpoint (see also Gal. 5:19-23).

Paul further clarified the concept of testing by fruit by indicating that spiritual phenomena from God had certain characteristics which he named "fruit of the Spirit." "But the fruit of the Spirit is love, joy, peace, patience, kindness, goodness, faithfulness, gentleness, self-control; against such things there is no law" (Gal. 5:22-23). All of this went against the understanding of the Pharisees, who assumed that all phenomena could be judged by rigorous attention to their origins and their adherence to consensus interpretation (Talmud).

Even though the concept of testing discernment has not always been recognized, it is a major element of Scripture. The Holy Spirit knew that in the two-thousand-year history of Christianity, the church would face issues and develop procedures not directly mentioned in the Bible but still of God. For example, in the eighteenth century the institution of Sunday school was invented. After much argumentation and testing of its fruit the church found it excellent and adopted it.

Similarly, the evangelical ritual of the altar call, developed during nineteenth-century revivals, stirred much controversy. Some claimed that calling for a decision for Jesus was a violation of God's sovereign right to save and to damn. The altar call is now well accepted.[5]

However, the fruit criterion should only be used to test those things within the possibility of scriptural validity. Things plainly contrary to Scripture cannot be tested by their fruits. For example, a person cannot test adultery and unwarranted divorce and believe those things are not sin because they produced the good fruit of a new, happier family. That is delusion. The original adultery was sin regardless of the subsequent feelings or even of the new children produced. Similarly some spiritualists can perform healings by calling on demonic spirits. The good fruit of healing comes at the cost of contradicting God's command against sorcery. It brings satanic bondage and is temporary at best.

The Pharisees' Distorted Faith

Jesus' ministry attacked and challenged the Pharisees' distorted definition of faith. Jesus, in word and deed, reminded all who would listen that the primary meaning of faith was a trust-expectancy relationship with God. God would provide for the needs of the believer, deliver the afflicted from the kingdom of Satan, and do great and mighty works of power. Jesus understood that faith came from a direct relationship with God rather than the theology and rituals learned in rabbinical schools.[5]

This did not mean that Jesus disdained theological knowledge and doctrine. Rather, in the total faith equation that He taught His disciples, faith-expectancy and trust in God were critically important, while Talmudic doctrines (theological commentaries) were of secondary importance.

Scripture clearly demonstrates the importance of faith over doctrine in two incidents, the exorcism of the daughter of the Canaanite woman (Matt. 15:21-28) and the healing of the centurion's servant (Matt. 8:5-13). In each instance the healing or exorcism was done through the proxy faith of the seekers and at long distance. In both cases the seekers had incorrect theology, according to religious leaders. Yet despite their pagan beliefs, both had tremendous faith-expectancy that God used to grant their requests for healing through Jesus.

We cannot conclude that Jesus was affirming by silence the pagan doctrines of either seeker. Rather He praised and affirmed their faith-expectancy as a spiritual virtue and example for others. The right theology would come later through their relationship with Him.

A Hellish Spiritual Inheritance

The Pharisees' self-evaluation was that they were on the forefront of what God was doing for Israel; Jesus' judgment of them was considerably different:

> Woe to you, scribes and Pharisees, hypocrites! For you build tombs of the prophets and adorn the monuments of the righteous, and say, 'If we had been living in the days of our fathers, we would not have been partners with them in shedding the blood of the prophets.' Consequently you bear witness against yourselves, that you are sons of those who murdered the prophets. Fill up then the measure of the guilt of your fathers. You serpents, you brood of vipers, how shall you escape the sentence of hell? (Matt. 23:29-33).

Jesus' argumentation needs some clarification. He was talking about *acquired spiritual inheritance*, a concept not often discussed in theology. He said that because the Pharisees opposed the Holy Spirit in that generation (that is, in His person and His teachings), they had allied themselves with those who had opposed the prophets (and the Holy Spirit in the prophets) in former generations. Thus although they believed themselves to be the protectors of orthodoxy, the Pharisees were really the opponents of the Holy Spirit.

Jesus' revelation on spiritual inheritance warns every generation that present attitudes opposing the work of the Holy Spirit place a person in the hellish spiritual inheritance of the prophet murderers. Believers must be willing and able to discern the work of the Holy Spirit for contemporary times.

Stephen, speaking under the influence of the Holy Spirit, repeated this same concept in the closing words of his defense before the Sanhedrin. The court of the Sanhedrin was divided between Pharisees and Sadducees. The Sadducees were gentlemen philosophers who did not believe in the spiritual world of angels or the afterlife (while the Pharisees believed in those things). Yet both groups stood in profound opposition to the Holy Spirit and to the ministry of Jesus. Stephen said:

> You men who are stiff-necked and uncircumcised in heart and ears are always resisting the Holy Spirit; you are doing just as your fathers did. Which one of the prophets did your fathers not persecute? And they killed those who had previously announced the coming of the Righteous One, whose betrayers and murderers you have now become; you who received the law as ordained by angels, and yet did not keep it (Acts 7:51-53).[6]

The Sin Against the Holy Spirit

The Pharisees responded to Jesus' ministry and warnings of their dead spiritual state by accusing Him of sorcery. The accusation had a certain logic to it given their assumptions. Jesus worked miracles, yet neither He nor His disciples came from the established rabbinical schools.

Ultimately, they explicitly accused Jesus of casting out demons by the power of Beelzebub (Matt. 12:24). Jesus answered by pointing out that the demonic kingdom would not cast out itself and that the good fruit of His exorcisms was a sign that His ministry was from God (Matt. 12:25-29). Significantly, through this false accusation of sorcery, Jesus defines the unforgivable sin against the Holy Spirit:

> And whoever shall speak a word against the Son of Man, it shall be forgiven him; but whoever shall speak against the Holy Spirit, it shall not be forgiven him, either in this age, or in the age to come (Matt. 12:32).

There is a critical issue here. Certainly witchcraft and sorcery are serious sins, and when identified they must be denounced. Certain acts of sorcery make the spiritual activities of lesser spirits look like part of the work of the Holy Spirit, as in spiritualism, for example. In this sense spiritualism is a sin of discernment, a serious sin which must be confessed and can be forgiven.

However, the opposite sin of discernment, claiming that the works of the Holy Spirit are really the product of demonic activity, calling something sorcery when it is in fact from God, is more than a serious sin; it is *unforgivable*. Regardless of how one interprets this text, this alone should make the accusation of sorcery for an unknown or unusual spiritual phenomenon something that a Christian makes reluctantly and only after much study and many prayers for discernment. Judgment of any healing or exorcism as demonic especially warrants caution.

Finally, the Pharisees, in conjunction with the chief priests and Sadducees, conspired to eliminate the "sorcerer" Jesus by bringing false witnesses against Him. Again we can understand the logic of their actions by looking at their assumptions. Notice their thought processes when Jesus raised Lazarus from the dead, which was one of His most powerful and public miracles (John 11:45-53). The fact could not be denied. But they were convinced that this act, like His other miracles, were works of sorcery. They feared also that the people were deluded and would follow Jesus in a rebellion against them and the Romans. This would result in the destruction of the limited independence of Israel.

Therefore any means to stop Him, including false testimony (a direct sin against the eighth commandment), would be both politically expedient and spiritually acceptable in view of the dangers of the moment. When Jesus' trial took place, a group of Pharisee-directed false witnesses brought lying and conflicting charges against Jesus (Mark 14:56). Thus Pharisaism, which had spent its energies and historical development in seeking elaborate ways of honoring all of the commandments and statutes of the law, wound up breaking them in the crudest of ways.

Christian Pharisaism in the New Testament Church

Most Christians are unaware that Pharisaism continued to be a problem in the Jewish-Christian church of Jerusalem. In Acts those Christians who had been Pharisees objected to Paul's practice of excusing Gentile converts from circumcision and freeing them from the ritual laws of Judaism (15:5ff). Although they were overruled, this attitude reappeared when Paul had to confront Peter who was trying to please the "men from James" (that is, the Christians from Jerusalem) by refusing to eat with Gentile Christians (Gal. 2:11-14).

The theology of Jewish-Christian Pharisees survived well until the third century through the Ebonite sect. This group of Jewish-Christians believed in Jesus as the Messiah but rejected Paul's writings.[7]

Even though the church in Jerusalem was obviously plagued with

Christian Pharisees, the Pharisees in the churches founded by Paul made a more important contribution to the understanding of Pharisaism as a continuing heresy in the church. A careful reading of the Corinthian letters and the letter to the Galatians reveals that some of the Christians in those communities spontaneously drifted into a form of Pharisaism which Paul had to reprove forcefully.

For example, the church at Corinth had already fallen into theological contention over the teachings of the early Christian leaders, Paul, Apollos and Cephas (1 Cor. 1:10-18). Apparently the Corinthian Christians were judging each other on the basis of factional theological viewpoints. A primitive "Christian Talmud" had formed within a decade of the start of the church!

Paul reprimands the Corinthians for this and counters with the assertion that Christians are free from all such man-inspired judgments but must remain attentive to Scripture ("what is written").

> Therefore do not go on passing judgment before the time, but wait until the Lord comes who will both bring to light the things hidden in the darkness and disclose the motives of men's hearts; and then each man's praise will come to him from God. Now these things, brethren, I have figuratively applied to myself and Apollos for your sakes, that in us you might learn not to exceed what is written, in order that no one of you might become arrogant in behalf of one against the other (1 Cor. 4:5-6).

The very next item on Paul's agenda is the assertion that the immoral stepson be judged and excommunicated (5:1). This seems like a contradiction, but it reaffirms Jesus' basic insight that the moral law (Torah) has eternal validity, but human commentaries (Talmud) are not and cannot be a basis of judgment.

In part 1 of this book we will examine the struggle between the Torah and the Talmud in the widespread revival of the eighteenth century known as the Great Awakening.

PART I

The Great Awakening as a "Messy" Revival

TWO

Stirrings of the Spirit
in the Great Awakening

I N OCTOBER 1741 THE Rev. Samuel Johnson, acting dean of Yale
College, wrote an anxious letter to a friend in England. Johnson was
suspicious of a revival then sweeping New England, led by the itinerant preacher George Whitefield:

> But this new enthusiasm, in consequence of Whitefield's
> preaching through the country and his disciples', has got
> great footing in the College [Yale]...Many of the scholars
> have been possessed of it, and two of this year's candidates
> were denied their degrees for their disorderly and restless en-
> deavors to propagate it...We have now prevailing among us
> the most odd and unaccountable enthusiasm than perhaps ob-
> tained in any age or nation. For not only the minds of many
> people are at once struck with prodigious distresses upon
> their hearing the hideous outcries of our itinerant preachers,
> but even their bodies are frequently in a moment affected
> with the strangest convulsions and involuntary agitations and
> cramps, which also have sometimes happened to those who
> came as mere spectators....[1]

The meetings that Johnson described in such negative terms were
part of the Great Awakening, considered as the first and certainly the

most important revival in American history. The Great Awakening (1740 – 1744) forever blessed and changed the course of American history. It influenced, enlivened and refreshed the Protestant churches in the still weak and dependent colonies. With the Great Awakening came a new boldness in lay ministry and prayer. A generation-long decline in church membership was reversed, and tens of thousands of new converts were brought into the churches.

Most important, the Great Awakening established a new and revolutionary pattern of mass evangelization that became the hallmark of American Christianity. The pattern included preachers who were freed from the stifling demands of formal, theological sermons and allowed to proclaim a clear message of repentance and conversion. Without the innovations of the Great Awakening such preachers as Billy Sunday or Billy Graham could not have carried out their ministries.

The fruits of the Great Awakening were not restricted to prayer and preaching. The churches influenced by it developed new outreaches and missionary activities. For example, Awakening preachers made the first systematic attempts in the colonies to evangelize African-Americans. This was also considered revolutionary, and it stirred up much controversy even in the colony of New York.[2]

Unfortunately, along with the Great Awakening came the "great opposition." After an initial period of goodwill and support, most of the clergy turned against the Awakening as a dangerous deviation from sound doctrine. Within a few years of its greatest successes, the revival was discredited as mere emotionalism and then quenched as a serious movement.

Interestingly, there are major points of similarity between the present renewal and the original American revival. Both movements were characterized by ecstatic spiritual experiences and unusual physical reactions to the power of the Holy Spirit. Being "slain in the Spirit," as charismatics would call it today, was quite common in the Awakening. In both revivals participants reported they had seen visions and felt that God had actually spoken to them. In both the Great Awakening and the charismatic renewal, many among the clergy disdained and discredited such claims.

On the negative side, both revivals were accompanied by numerous excesses and a general lack of wisdom and discernment. The spontaneity of spiritual awakening violated the traditional order of worship. Self-righteousness, divisiveness and criticism of the established churches and their leaders emerged in both revivals.

Precursors of the Great Awakening

The Awakening was part of a greater move of the Spirit that manifested in three main revivals in different countries and with different theologies. In the American colonies, the major revival preachers were all Calvinists. But in Germany the revival was conducted within Pietist theology, which focused more on personal religious experience, as well as Lutheran theology. In Great Britain the revival was mixed in its theology, with a strong Calvinist element but also with the new Wesleyan theology that later became Methodism.[3] Wesley's theology directly contradicted the predestination of Calvinism.

As early as 1720 to 1726 there was a revival among Dutch Reformed churches (Calvinist) in New Jersey. The leader of this revival was Theodore Frelinghuysen. Although Dutch-born and educated in Calvinism, he spent a year in Germany where he learned about German Pietism. Pietism originated as a lay reform movement within the German Lutheran churches. Its stress on personal devotion and morality challenged the current focus on doctrine and scholasticism. Frelinghuysen was called to a Dutch Reformed congregation in New Jersey and brought with him the Pietist innovations of private prayer meetings (currently called home groups) and lay helpers to assist the pastor in ministry.

Frelinghuysen preached a simple message of repentance and salvation. For this he was much criticized by more "proper" ministers who believed sermons should have more theological substance. Eventually, however, his preaching and leadership bore fruit in a general revival of the churches in his area. The Pietist practices he introduced became standard among the colonial revivalists of all denominations.

Meanwhile, William Tennent, a Presbyterian pastor in Pennsylvania, established the Log College on the frontier where young men were trained in evangelization and personal piety. His son Gilbert was its most famous graduate. The school operated from 1726 to 1746, and its graduates were to become important itinerant evangelists of the coming Great Awakening.

From 1734 to 1736 there was a local revival among the Puritan (again Calvinist) churches of the Connecticut River Valley centering in Northampton, Massachusetts. This revival was triggered by the preaching of a young, philosophically inclined pastor, Jonathan Edwards.

However, it was the Anglican evangelist George Whitefield who united the various sparks of revival into the Great Awakening. He cooperated with the local revival leaders and urged them to spread their work. Whitefield had met the Wesley brothers while a student at Oxford and was greatly influenced by their devotion and evangelical spirit. In 1737 he came to Georgia for a brief tour as an evangelist. Whitefield was later to separate from the Wesley brothers on the issue of predestination. Whitefield remained a rigorous Calvinist to the end of his life, but he always held the Wesleys in love and esteem.[4]

Back in Great Britain, Whitefield did evangelization all through Scotland, Wales and England. Like the Wesley brothers, he learned that open-air preaching could be more effective than proper church meetings. He also acquired a reputation as an evangelical radical, who used emotional delivery (called "enthusiasm") to bring his audiences to conviction. That was not considered proper or dignified.

In 1739 Whitefield left for his second tour of the colonies. This tour, from 1739 to 1741, produced the greatest number of conversions and is usually identified as the catalyst of the Great Awakening. The Awakening reached its peak in about 1742 but declined rapidly after that. When Jonathan Edwards wrote his now classic *Religious Affections* in 1746, he cited the Awakening as a past event.

Theological Setting During the Great Awakening

At the time of the Great Awakening, many of the churches in both Great Britain and the colonies were demoralized and lethargic due to the influence of deism among the educated clergy. Deism was the belief that God was the creator of the universe but was distant and not concerned with everyday events in the lives of human beings. As unbiblical as this was, it was a natural position for those persons who had no encounters with faith-filled, answered prayer or spiritual experiences. For men such as Benjamin Franklin and Voltaire, leaders of the Enlightenment, deism became a well-defined philosophy.

For most others deism was more of an attitude that attached itself to existing theologies. Many churchgoers lived moral, godly lives and subscribed to all the statements of the traditional theology but had no experience of God's grace. This form of Christian life had earlier become acceptable in Puritan theology as the "halfway covenant." It allowed the children and grandchildren of the Puritan founders to enter into church membership (and political rights) without a discernible conversion experience.

Ironically, many who were influenced by deism often held strongly to traditional theology (or orthodoxy), using it as a substitute for a personal experience of grace and conversion. They often defended the conventional order of worship and other church practices against the newer forms of preaching and worship as if they were major doctrinal issues.

In the period of the Great Awakening, deism had become attached to Arminianism. As a theological opinion Arminianism was not a heresy; it was rather a deviation from traditional Calvinism. The Arminian view recognized the individual's role in accepting God's gift of salvation. However, most of the leaders of the Awakening sincerely believed that Arminianism was *the* great heresy of the age because it did not mesh with Calvin's predestination, and they often preached against it. With historical perspective we can see that this was a false issue. The real enemy was not Arminianism but the deist elements who claimed to be within the Arminianism tradition.

The Wesleyan revival in England and the Lutheran Pietist revival were Arminian in terms of traditional Calvinist theology, but the Holy Spirit operated as well in that theological environment as it did in the Calvinist colonies. In fact, most evangelicals today would be Arminian when compared to the terms of original Calvinism.

Unfortunately, pure Calvinist theology could not interpret the spiritual experiences that were to accompany the Great Awakening. This struggle produced one of the legacies of the Great Awakening, a method devised to discern a move of the Holy Spirit, provided by America's greatest theologian, Jonathan Edwards.

Jonathan Edwards (1703 – 1758)[5]

Jonathan Edwards was born into a pious Christian family of eleven children, where he was the only son (four older sisters and six younger). His father was the minister to the small Puritan town of East Windsor, Connecticut. His mother was the daughter of Solomon Stoddard, the most important and powerful minister in all of New England. As a child Edwards saw two periods of revival in his grandfather's church.

His education was Bible-directed and pious, but also attentive to the classic Latin and Greek studies demanded in the era. Very early he developed an awe of nature and an appreciation, encouraged by Puritan theology, that nature's laws were a reflection of God's glory. Edwards left his home to enter Collegiate School (later called Yale College) in 1716.

Yale had been set up in competition with Harvard College because many devout Puritans felt that Harvard was losing its original piety and turning toward deism. (Their suspicions were well founded. Harvard became deist and solidly Unitarian before the turn of the century.) At

Yale Edwards studied biblical languages, Greek and Latin literature, logic, natural philosophy (science) and newer philosophies of the era.

Edwards Discovers Locke[6]

In college Edwards discovered the writings of the English philosopher John Locke (1632 – 1704), especially his famous *Essay Concerning Human Understanding*. A disciple and biographer of Edwards, Samuel Hopkins, wrote of Edwards's discovery of Locke:

> In the second year at college, and thirteenth of his age, he read Locke on the human understanding, with great delight and profit. His uncommon genius, by which he was, as it were by nature, formed for closeness of thought and deep penetration, now began to exercise and discover itself. Taking that book into his hand, upon some occasion, not long before his death, he said to some of his select friends, who were then with him, that he was beyond expression entertained and pleased with it, when he read it in his youth at college; that he was as much engaged and had more satisfaction and pleasure in studying it, than the most greedy miser in gathering up handfuls of silver and gold from some new discovered treasure.[7]

Locke's *Essay Concerning Human Understanding* dealt with the problem of how ideas are formed and how the mind relates complex ideas to understanding. Locke understood that emotions, images and ideas interacted in the mind to influence the will. This was a more modern and realistic way of understanding the mind than the "faculties" psychology that was popular at the time.

During the Middle Ages Catholic theologians developed a faculties scheme of understanding the mind and its relation to the human soul.[8] This modified an older pattern developed by the Greek philosopher Aristotle. Faculties psychology came in several varieties. Some divided the mind into vegetative, sensitive and intellectual souls to take into account that the body automatically did certain things, such as digestion and breathing, without thinking.

In all forms of faculties psychology the intellect was given not only the highest status but rulership over the other areas of the mind and soul. The intellectual soul included the abilities for reasoning, for willing and for conscience. The sensitive soul, which was *under* the intellectual soul, included the abilities of common sense, memory and imagination.

This scheme had the indirect and unintended result of placing a low value on the function of imagination, little comprehending its role in creative thinking. Faculties theories of the mind were no longer defendable after Locke and the later development of modern psychology. However, their assumptions have remained embedded in certain forms of Christian theology.

Locke intended to clarify language and make it possible for mankind to think and speak with clear ideas, thereby avoiding ambiguity or misunderstandings. His ideal was to separate the emotions from reason as far as possible. Locke and many of his generation were horrified by the recently ended Thirty Years War which pitted Catholic against Protestant. Locke believed that if clear ideas prevailed and emotions were checked such wars would not occur again.

The irony of Edwards's discovery and subsequent use of Locke's philosophy is that Edwards used Locke's analysis to achieve the opposite of what Locke intended. Because Edwards was biblically centered, he knew that the separation of emotions from reason was not possible or even desirable. (Those who have watched the *Star Trek* series on TV can see the result of this separation in the character of Mr. Spock. That unfortunate hybrid creature cannot experience emotions and must make every decision on purely logical grounds.)

The Christian mind should operate as the biblically defined heart — the union of will, ideas and emotions under grace. For Edwards, Locke clarified the processes by which the human mind operated. Certainly the formation of clear ideas was important in clarifying goals and avoiding irrationality, but Edwards correctly understood that emotions and imagination were legitimate and not to be suppressed. Ultimately Edwards's psychology was both more realistic than and far superior to Locke's.

Edwards's Conversion

Edwards's genius for academic matters was evident to all, and he remained at Yale to complete a master's degree. During his graduate studies (1721) he had a profound conversion experience which reoriented his life. Of that experience he wrote:

The first instance that I remember of that sort of inward,

sweet delight in God and divine things that I have lived much in since, was on reading those words [1 Tim. 1:17]: "Now unto the King eternal, immortal, invisible, the only wise God, be honour and glory for ever and ever, Amen." As I read the words, there came into my soul, and was as it were diffused through it, a sense of the glory of the Divine Being; a new sense, quite different from anything I ever experienced before. Never any words of Scripture seemed to me as these words did...After this my sense of divine things gradually increased, and became more and more lively...God's excellency, his wisdom, his purity and love seemed to appear in every thing; in the sun, moon, and stars; in the clouds, and blue sky; in the grass, flowers, trees; in the water, and all nature which used greatly to fix my mind. I often used to sit and view the moon for continuance, and in the day, spent much time in viewing the clouds and sky, to behold the sweet glory of God in these things...I had vehement longings of soul after God and Christ, and after more holiness, wherewith my heart seemed to be full, and ready to break....[9]

His experience of God was significant because it did not fit the Puritan understanding of conversion, which was more intellectual and less experiential. This caused him much distress at the time, although his experience was entirely Christian. However, the conflict prepared him to understand that God sometimes moves in unexpected ways.

Edwards in the Pulpit

His first pastorate was in a Presbyterian church in New York which had experienced a split between its pastor and congregation. After helping bring a reconciliation and the return of the original pastor, Edwards accepted a call (1726) to assist his maternal grandfather, the famous Solomon Stoddard, in Northampton, Massachusetts. Within two years Stoddard died and young Edwards assumed pastoral direction of the relatively large and influential congregation.

In the course of his Northampton pastorate, Edwards discovered that many of his congregation had not experienced true conversion. Most had become satisfied with the halfway covenant and centered their lives on cultivating their own prosperity. Edwards determined to change this state of affairs. He set out to preach repentance and conversion through his understanding of Locke. Edwards's preaching not only mobilized the intellect, but also the imagination and emotions to move his congregation to desire a saving knowledge of Jesus.

In the following sermon excerpt Edwards incited the listeners' imaginations to form a clear idea of hell to move their wills to desire salvation. Though his imagery was vivid, his style of delivery was unemotional, almost deadpan:

> But to help your conception, imagine yourself cast into a fiery oven, all of a glowing heat, or into the midst of a glowing brick-kiln, or of a great furnace, where your pain would be as much greater than that occasioned by accidentally touching a coal of fire, as the heat is greater. Imagine also that your body were to lie there for a quarter of an hour, full of fire, as full within and without as a bright coal of fire, all the while full of quick sense; what horror would you feel at the entrance of such a furnace! And how long would that quarter of an hour seem to you! If it were to be measured by a glass, how long would the glass seem to be running! And after you had endured it for one minute, how overbearing would it be to you to think that you had it to endure the other fourteen!
>
> But what would be the effect on your soul, if you knew you must lie there enduring that torment to the full for twenty-four hours! And how much greater would be the effect, if you knew you must endure it for a whole year; and how vastly greater still, if you knew you must endure it for a thousand years! O then, how would your heart sink, if you thought, if you knew, that you must bear it forever and ever![10]

This was a radical departure from the preaching of his era where, under the influence of faculties psychology, preaching was aimed at informing the listener's intellect of the gospel, not in creating images or stirring the emotions.

Revival in Northampton

Toward the end of 1734, revival broke out in the church Edwards pastored in Northampton and its surrounding villages, a precursor of the Great Awakening to come. By the time the revival subsided about two years later some three hundred persons had been converted. Edwards related the news of the revival in a letter to a pastor in Boston. Edwards was urged to write a more detailed description of the revival, and he reworked his letter for publication. The full account of the Northampton revival was published in London in 1737 as *A Faithful Narrative of the Surprising Work of God in the Conversion of Many Hundred Souls in Northampton.*

Edwards described conversion experiences in his congregation in terms familiar to the Puritan-Calvinist leaders of his day.[11] First the person was stirred to initial conviction by some sermon, neighbor's discussion or even a passing word. Then he or she would seek the Scriptures and find not relief but a deeper sense of conviction. This would lead to a crisis of despair where the person understood that prayers, Bible reading and religious activities were useless to assure salvation. Then final assurance came as the seeker rested in the confidence of Jesus' atoning blood. (At this point in history the concept of the altar call to consolidate the conversion process had not been developed. That was the task of Charles Finney and other nineteenth-century evangelists.)

A Faithful Narrative was capped by several case studies of conversion. One study focused on a woman, Abigail Hutchison, dying from a wasting sickness. She was an unmarried woman of nominal Puritan religious practices. On hearing a remark by her brother about the need for saving conversion she began to search the Scriptures. After the normal pattern of conviction and despair she came to a final assurance in Christ.

However, Abigail's conversion produced both a new mental state and some unusual physical manifestations of that state.

> Her mind was so swallowed up with a sense of the glory of God's truth and other perfections, that she said it seemed as though her life was going...Soon after this she went to a private religious meeting, and her mind was full of a sense and view of the glory of God all the time; and when the exercise was ended, some asked her concerning what she had experienced; and she began to give them an account; but as she was relating it, it revived such a sense of the same things that her strength failed; and they were obliged to take her and lay her on the bed.[12]

At the time Abigail's prostration was seen as an emotional overload. Recent studies by charismatic theologians would suggest that such faintings were a sign of the activity of the Holy Spirit. They are called

37

being slain in the Spirit, or resting in the Spirit.[13] This phenomenon was quite common to the later Great Awakening, and it was the very thing which evoked the most derision among the Awakening's critics. *A Faithful Narrative* thus included material that was familiar to the reader — the conversion cycle — and material that was unfamiliar — the phenomenon of revival, or "exercises," as Edwards termed them.

The Decline of the Northampton Revival

Edwards ended *A Faithful Narrative* on a word of caution. The revival at Northampton was dampened when a well-respected gentleman committed suicide. He had begun the process of conviction but stayed in despair, not feeling the release of assurance for more than a year. His suicide caused scandal and discouragement.

Edwards said the revival was also dampened by some persons in the community whom he believed had gone in dangerous and extreme directions. One man from the nearby village of South Hadley suffered from the "enthusiastic delusion" of believing that laymen were capable of ministering to others. He counseled another person who was suffering melancholy and actually prayed with him. This was considered a reserved duty of the ordained clergy at the time and out of proper church order. Further the same individual believed that in the coming revival the gifts of the Spirit would be released again. Edwards counseled with this person and helped him see his "errors," though not before much scandal had been given to the revival.

Edwards believed that the combination of the suicide and enthusiasms grieved the Spirit:

> After these things the instances of conversion were rare here in comparison of what they had before been...and the Spirit of God not long after this time, appeared very sensibly withdrawing from all parts of the country.[14]

From 1736 to 1740 Edwards tried in vain to reset the fires of revival in Northampton. He reminded the congregation of the glory days and even preached some of his old sermons, but to no avail. Those who had been converted continued in their Christian lives, but the time of new harvest was over. It did not return until the coming of the Anglican evangelist George Whitefield.

The Great Awakening in New England

In September 1739 George Whitefield came to the American colonies for a preaching tour. His reputation as a revivalist preceded him. Many expected that revival would come to the colonies as it had already come to England. That is exactly what happened. Whitefield spent forty-five days in America, traveling from South Carolina to Maine, preaching in forty towns and giving ninety-seven sermons. He accomplished an amazing tour given travel conditions at the time.

Whitefield was welcomed by both laypeople and pastors. He received invitations to preach from practically every church on his itinerary. Often even the biggest churches could not accommodate the crowds. No matter, Whitefield took to preaching in the open air, as he had done in Wales. In that way he preached to thousands at a time. Benjamin Franklin, later prominent in the American Revolution, was his personal friend (and printer). Franklin described Whitefield's preaching in Philadelphia:

> The multitudes of all sects and denominations that attended his sermons were enormous, and it was a matter of speculation to me, who was one of the number, to observe the extraordinary influence of his oratory on his hearers, and how they admired and respected him, notwithstanding his common abuse of them, by assuring them they were naturally *half beasts and half devils*. It was wonderful to see the change soon made in the manners of our inhabitants. From being thoughtless or indifferent about religion, it seemed as if all the world were growing religious, so that one could not walk through the town in an evening without hearing psalms sung in different families of every street.[15]

Whitefield accepted an invitation to preach in Edwards's church, and he spent three days in Northampton preaching to overflowing audiences. When Whitefield left, Edwards was able to maintain the revival in Northampton. The number of conversions that flooded in surpassed the earlier Northampton revival from 1734 to 1736. Edwards organized private meetings in imitation of the pastor Frelinghuysen's New Jersey revival. He also established special services for the youth, among whom there was a rich harvest. Edwards described the progress of revival in a letter to a pastor friend in Boston:

Many of the young people and children that were professors [already converted] appeared to be overcome with a sense of the greatness and glory of divine things...and many others at the same time were overcome with distress about their sinful and miserable state and condition; so that the whole room was full of nothing but outcries, faintings and such like. Others soon heard of it, in several parts of town, and came to them; and what they saw and heard there was greatly affecting to them; so that many of them were overpowered in like manner; and it continued thus for some hours; the time being spent in prayer, singing, counseling and conferring. There seemed to be a consequent happy effect of that meeting to several particular persons, and in the state of religion in the town in general.[16]

While Edwards was preaching in other pulpits in 1741, he invited Samuel Buell, a licensed preacher and graduate from Yale, to preach at Northampton. The revival flared again under Buell's spirited preaching, but the accompanying "enthusiasm" started to get out of hand.

There were some instances of persons lying in a sort of trance, remaining for perhaps a whole twenty-four hours motionless, and with their senses locked up; but in the meantime under strong imaginations, as though they went to heaven, and had there a vision of glorious and delightful objects. But when the people were raised to this height, Satan took the advantage, and his interposition in many instances soon became very apparent; and a great deal of caution and pains were found necessary to keep the people, many of them from running wild.[17]

Edwards brought moderation and discernment to the situation with his pastoral skills. In imitation of Nehemiah and Ezra, he gathered a general assembly of the people of Northampton and reinstated the covenant with God that the founding Puritans had established on their arrival. This channeled the people's spiritual energies and emotions toward specific activities and attitudes. Northampton became a changed community, with a presence of piety, charity and devotion felt even by passing travelers.

Extremism in the Great Awakening

However, few pastors in colonial America had the knowledge and discerning wisdom of Edwards. In fact the Great Awakening in many other places outside Northampton turned extremist, and even ugly. Many preachers attempted to follow Whitefield's preaching style and itinerant ministry. Few, however, had his education (or anointing), and excesses in preaching and emotional manifestations went unchecked. Two individuals have long been cited by historians as examples of these extremists, Gilbert Tennent (1703 – 1764) and James Davenport (1716 – 1757).

Gilbert Tennent had been trained in evangelism by his father in the Log College and had a generally successful ministry as itinerant revivalist. He raised the ire of the clergy when his messages became critical of the established churches. He suggested that lay believers be allowed to move their church memberships to wherever they wished if they found their pastors to be spiritually dry or unconverted. These opinions were considered radical and dangerous in New England where all but the larger towns had *one* established, tax-supported church.

Perhaps more radical still was his opinion of the clergy. He preached that many ordained pastors were unconverted hypocrites and secret Arminians. (Arminianism was considered questionable theology in colonial America, a suspicion intensified because of the deists who claimed to hold to its tenets.)

The colonies had a real problem with an unconverted clergy leaning toward deism. Whitefield himself confronted the issue because he knew that deism was taking its toll on the clergy in America as it was in the British Isles. Whitefield was certain that the low state of the church was principally because of clergy who disguised their spiritual deadness with sound doctrine. He declared that ministers can "preach the gospel of Christ no further than we have experienced the power of it in our own hearts."[18]

But Tennent went further than Whitefield and suggested that *self-appointed laymen* inquire into the spiritual state of their pastors and reject those who were suspect. Naturally such views were considered a breach of sound theology and a threat to church order. Church order was indeed disrupted because the Puritan (Congregational) church professed that believers had the authority to dismiss their pastors. Many pastors who at first had taken a positive position on the Awakening now turned against the revival. By 1742 Tennent saw the destructiveness of his preaching emphasis and publicly repented, but the revival had already suffered great damage.

More damaging and more extreme than Tennent was James Davenport. By most accounts Davenport was an insecure and unstable person in spite of the fact that he had been educated in a pious household, graduated from Yale and ordained as a pastor. He witnessed one of Whitefield's sermons and was captivated by his emotional preaching. He felt a call on his own life to set out as an itinerant revivalist.

Davenport believed he had the gift to discern the spiritual state of an individual clergyman, whether he was converted or unsaved. As he toured from town to town he summoned the clergy to give their conversion witness before him for his judgment. Naturally, most clergy refused. Davenport automatically judged and condemned those as unbelievers. He brought further ridicule to the Awakening when he initiated a public bonfire in New London to burn secular books and those of deist authors.

Discernment During the Awakening

Jonathan Edwards was appalled by these developments and set about defending the Awakening from its own extremists. He was scheduled to give a commencement sermon at Yale, and he took the opportunity to gather his thoughts on the discernment problems of the Awakening. The sermon was published as *The Distinguishing Marks of a Work of the Spirit of God* and appeared late in 1741.

Edwards began his address by citing 1 John 4:1, "Beloved, believe not every spirit, but try the spirits whether they are of God: because many false prophets are gone out into the world" (KJV). He then proceeded to apply biblical principles of discernment to the Awakening. Edwards had to wage a two-front campaign on behalf of the revival. He had to counter the extremists who believed everything in the revival was from God; therefore, the more spectacle, the better. He also had to persuade the traditionalists that in spite of abuses much of the Awakening was from the Spirit of God.

Edwards graciously admitted to the Awakening's critics that there were serious flaws in the public manifestations of the revival. In his usual systematic way he categorized nine major faults. Among these were that Awakening preachers dwelt too much on God's wrath, that some sudden converts later behaved scandalously, that serious errors in judgment and even satanic ideas intermingled with the emotional outbursts of the revival, and that revival meetings often produced unseemly bodily manifestations.

By bodily manifestations Edwards was referring to the way individuals in congregations would respond as they sensed the power of the Holy Spirit. This issue would recur in many revivals. The basic conflict is this: The Holy Spirit acts *on* the spirit of man, but the energies and manifestation of this divine activity are expressed *through* the soul. Often these expressions include behaviors which are born out of that person's culture. These are open to suggestions and subconscious elements that do not come from the Holy Spirit.

A good example is what happened when the Pentecostal revival of the 1900s hit the people of the Appalachian Mountains. The Christians there experienced the power of the Holy Spirit, and they had few inhibitions about how they displayed their experience of that power because most of them were unrefined and unconcerned with social etiquette. For them there was nothing wrong with falling on the floor and shouting. Proper Christians dismissed that as emotionalism and hysteria, and derided these early Pentecostals as "holy rollers." In the more recent charismatic renewal of the 1970s the same power of the Holy Spirit fell, but the manifestations were more subdued because it occurred among more sophisticated congregations.[19] Ironically, in the Toronto Blessing, Christians have become so used to the manifestations and so thankful for the fruit that they often unabashedly receive from the Spirit regardless of the "exercises," as Jonathan Edwards would call them.

Even though Edwards did not really understand the physical manifestations issue, he at least saw its virtues despite its problems. He argued that the temporary "enthusiasm," even in its unseemly form, was incidental to the true move of God. Edwards said the authenticity of God's hand in the Awakening was proven by five "sure, distinguishing, scripture evidences." These evidences were that a true revival:

1. raises the esteem of Jesus in the community, proclaiming Him as Scripture depicts Him, Son of God and Savior.[20]

2. works against the kingdom of Satan, which encourages sin and worldly lusts.[21]

3. stimulates "a greater regard for the Holy Scriptures, and establishes them more in their truth and divinity...."[22]

4. is marked by a spirit of truth.[23]

5. manifests a renewed love of God and of man.[24]

Edwards was asking his listeners to discern the Awakening by distinguishing enthusiastic behaviors from ultimate spiritual fruit. He understood that this discernment was difficult for his audience, who unlike himself clung to faculties psychology and believed that human reason alone was the ultimate test of sound theology. In his concluding section Edwards exhorted his listeners not to oppose the Spirit of God in the Awakening for that would be to commit the unpardonable sin (Matt. 12:22-32).

> Whether what has been said in this discourse be enough to convince all that have heard it, that the work that is now carried on in the land, is the work of God, or not, yet I hope that for the future, they will at least hearken to the caution of Gamaliel that has been now mentioned; for the future not to oppose it, or say anything against it...lest they should be found to be opposers of the Holy Ghost. There is no kind of sin so hurtful and dangerous to the souls of men, as those that are committed against the Holy Ghost....
>
> A time when the Holy Spirit is much poured out, and men's lusts, lukewarmness and hypocrisy reproached by its powerful operations, is the most likely time of any whatsoever, for this sin to be committed...Those that maliciously oppose and reproach this work, and call it the work of the Devil, want but one thing of the unpardonable sin, and that is doing it against inward conviction. And though some are so prudent, as not openly to oppose and reproach the work, yet 'tis to be feared, at this day when the Lord is going forth so gloriously against his enemies, that many that are silent and inactive, especially ministers, will bring that curse of the angel of the Lord upon themselves, Judg. 5:23: "Curse ye Meroz, said the angel of the Lord: curse ye bitterly the inhabitants thereof, because they came not to the help of the Lord, to the help of the Lord against the mighty."[25]

It was too late; the warning went unheeded. By 1742 a majority of the New England clergy had determined that the Great Awakening was merely a widespread epidemic of enthusiasm (emotionalism) and what was needed was a return to sound theology. They soon found a brilliant champion for that point of view in the pastor of the oldest and most prestigious church in Boston, the Rev. Charles Chauncy.

THREE

The Great Awakening Quenched

Charles Chauncy (1705 – 1787)[1]

C HARLES CHAUNCY BROUGHT TOGETHER ALL of the doubts, criticisms and fears about the Awakening into a single-minded assault. His social position among the Boston clergy made him particularly effective in his mission of discrediting the Great Awakening. Chauncy was called to be the associate pastor of First Church of Boston (Congregational) in 1727 and remained there until his death in 1787. First Church was the oldest, largest and most prestigious church in Boston. It was nicknamed "Old Brick," which became Chauncy's nickname as well in his later years.

Chauncy's father was a merchant who died when Charles was but five years old. His mother raised him and managed to send him to Harvard for a divinity degree. He was a meticulous scholar and completed a master's degree before assuming his pastoral duties. Chauncy considered himself perfectly orthodox; but, of the modern, liberal theological opinions, he tended toward the new Arminianism.

Unlike Edwards, Chauncy was perfectly satisfied with the assumptions of faculties psychology. Its stress on the intellect and the role of reason in traditional theology fit Chauncy perfectly. He had limited artistic imagination and was ill at ease with poetry. In fact, he once expressed a desire for a prose translation of Milton's *Paradise Lost* so that he might understand it.[2]

Chauncy was a person of extremely regular habits. A friend described his daily routine:

> [Chauncy] was remarkably temperate in his diet and exercise. At twelve o'clock he took one pinch of snuff, and only one in twenty-four hours. At one o'clock, he dined on one dish of plain, wholesome food, and after dinner he took one glass of wine, and one pipe of tobacco, and only one in twenty-four hours. And he was equally methodical in his exercise, which consisted chiefly or wholly of walking.[3]

The Traditional Fear of Enthusiasm

As a young assistant pastor Chauncy was open to the possibility of revival when the Great Awakening began. He had actually prayed for a revival of the kind that had occurred with Edwards in Northampton from 1734 to 1736. Several of his closest ministerial friends had written laudatory prefaces to the Boston edition of Edwards's book describing the revival.

Yet from the beginning Chauncy felt ill at ease with the emotions he saw manifest in the Awakening. The Boston papers had covered the progress of the Awakening as Whitefield preached in the middle and Southern colonies. They also noted the other itinerant revivalists who had recently begun their ministries. Though generally favorable to the Awakening, the reports described some of the disputes that the revivalists had with the established clergy, including their sometimes uninvited invasions of ministers' territories to preach. Included in the reports were vivid descriptions of the physical manifestations and enthusiastic behavior of revival crowds.

For a Harvard-educated minister such as Chauncy the most troubling aspect of the Awakening was its enthusiasm. To the orthodox Protestants of the eighteenth century, enthusiasm meant much more than simply overemotionalism. It carried connotations of heresy and delusion. The Reformers had originally protested against the abuses of Catholic spirituality which included a nondiscerning acceptance of visions, trances and other spiritual phenomena. To counter the Catholic abuses, the Reformers affirmed a faith based on Scripture and limited spiritual experiences (see chapter 7).

The two centuries of Protestant history since the Reformation seemed to verify the original suspicions about enthusiasm. Many of the post-Reformation revivals had tended to become overly emotional and lose contact with biblical restraints. That happened in the Anabaptist movement (an early form of the Baptists) and in Quakerism.

Most colonials had heard of the French Huguenots who had come to England in 1706. The Huguenots were well respected in England for their resistance to Catholic persecution. However, these refugees belonged to a group which had rediscovered the gift of prophecy (and its abuse). They soon fell into undiscerned prophecy, visions and attempts to resurrect the dead. Some Huguenots fell into gross immorality and incest, and the whole movement was discredited.[4]

In 1742 an anonymous pamphlet appeared in Boston reviewing the dangers of enthusiasm. It was titled *The Wonderful Narrative, or a Faithful Account of the French Prophets, Their Agitations, Extasies [sic], and Inspirations*... and recounted in gory detail the history of Huguenot prophets. The intent was to draw an analogy between the excesses of Huguenots and current religious practices:

> It is a STRONG PRESUMPTION therefore against any, that they have *strange Fire* working in them, when they are seized with SWOONINGS, and have bodily Representations of those Things, which are *spiritually* to be discerned, because these *Sights* have been common among *Enthusiasts* of all Sorts, but seldom or never among *solid* Christians. In the Beginning of the Reformation, there were Swarms of those, who pretended to these *extraordinary* Matters; but they were always esteemed a Clog to the Reformation, and a disgrace of it: Nor are VISIONS and TRANCES more common any where, than among *Papists*; The lives of their Saints...are filled with Relations in this Kind.[5]

The First Charges Against the Awakening

Even before the publication of the pamphlet, Chauncy had turned against the Awakening. Whitefield had come to Boston in 1740, and Tennent followed the next year. The forceful emotionalism of Whitefield and Tennent led Chauncy to equate revivalism with irrationality and enthusiasm. Chauncy was particularly distressed at the extemporaneous style of preaching, which seemed to him an act of presumption (a presumption that God would provide the sermon even though the pastor didn't prepare). Pastors of the era, including Edwards, prepared carefully, wrote out their sermons and read them to their congregations. Chauncy's were particularly well researched and meticulously written.

As the Great Awakening spread, many congregations became dissatisfied with their deist pastors and in some cases removed them. This happened to one of Chauncy's friends, the Rev. Samuel Osborn. Chauncy believed a grave injustice had been done to a sincere servant of God. The fact is that many in the Boston clergy were indeed tending toward deism, as subsequent history was to show.

Whitefield's revival campaign in Boston (1740) was a tremendous success. Practically every pulpit in the city had been offered to him, including Chauncy's First Church. Whitefield preached outside when the crowds could not be contained in the largest churches and ended his tour with an open-air meeting of more than twenty thousand persons. When Whitefield left Boston, the town had been spiritually shaken and revived to a degree never experienced before.

Unfortunately in the spring of 1741 Whitefield's journal account of his tour of New England appeared in print. It was an embarrassment to the pro-Awakening party, for Whitefield's candid thoughts on the dangers of the unconverted clergy seemed to condemn the very pastors who first supported him. Many, including Chauncy, felt insulted and betrayed.

The insult gave Chauncy the courage to give his first public sermon against the Awakening in the summer of 1741. It was a critique of the revivalists' overemphasis on sudden and dramatic conversion experiences. Chauncy rightly noted that the feeling of conversion was not as definite a mark of conversion as a changed and sanctified life.

Besides the problem with extemporaneous preaching, other innovations of the Awakening bothered Chauncy and other ministers. The new phenomenon of lay preachers ("exhorters") was particularly controversial. Many exhorters believed they had a "call" from God to preach and were doing so without formal education. The established clergy perceived this as a threat.

The publication of Edwards's *Distinguishing Marks* triggered in Chauncy a period of critical reflection on the Awakening. By then the field was filled with untrained exhorters and second-string evangelists. Many were encouraging crowds to manifest groans and other signs of distress as indispensable signs of the Spirit's activities.

Chauncy took aim at the new rash of physical manifestation in a sermon titled "The Outpouring of the Holy Ghost." It reasserted the conventional understanding of the work of the Spirit in conviction of sin. Chauncy said the Spirit was to encourage gospel faith and change men into "new creatures" — without external manifestations.

Thus Chauncy was contrasting the new measures of the Awakening with the proper theological interpretations agreed upon by the religious leaders of the day. This consensus orthodoxy* was used to condemn the emotional sermons, itinerant preachers and the physical manifestations of conviction and conversion during the Awakening.

While granting that some people had been converted and saved and that some good had come from the Awakening, Chauncy lamented that its chief effects were disorder and confusion:

> Alas! what unchristian heats and animosities are there in many places, to the dividing and breaking in pieces of churches and towns? What spirit of rash, censorious, uncharitable judging prevails too generally all over the land?...What prejudices are there in the minds of too many people against *standing ministry*, tho' perhaps as faithful a one as any part of the world is favour'd with? And how general is the disposition they discover to flock after every *weak* and *illiterate* EXHORTER, to the contempt of their *pastors*?...How heated are the imaginations of a great many, and into what excesses do they betray them?[6]

In truth by this time opinions on the Awakening had divided both clergy and public. The supporters of the revival were dubbed the "New Lights" and the opponents "Old Lights." The 1742 Massachusetts convention of the Congregational clergy became a battleground for debate on the Awakening. The Old Lights saw in Chauncy the boldest spokesman and gathered in his home for conversations and exchanges of information on developments and instances of abuses in the Awakening.

---

*   Consensus orthodoxy is dangerous because its doctrine is accepted on the merits of current popularity rather than biblical accuracy. In contrast, I use the word *orthodoxy* alone to signify doctrine that *is* consistent with the Scriptures. As Paul warns, on earth we only know "in part" (1 Cor. 13:12), and thus, all biblical orthodoxy may never be possessed by any one individual or denomination. This should keep us humble before those we believe to be in error.

Chauncy Turns From Critic to Opposer

The final stroke for Chauncy came through a personal encounter with the infamous James Davenport. This most eccentric of the itinerants had come to Boston in June 1742. By this time even the ministers who supported the Awakening did not want him in town. Davenport promptly denounced several ministers as unconverted. In response the Boston ministers' association censured him. Davenport retaliated with a general denunciation of the Boston clergy. The truth was, however, that many of the clergy were still committed to the cause of revival.

Davenport quickly discovered that the principal opposer was Chauncy, and he did what had been his custom. He went to Chauncy's home, uninvited, and challenged Chauncy to give an account of his soul's state for Davenport's judgment. Chauncy turned the tables and gave Davenport a tongue lashing for his presumption and enthusiasm.

> I beg, *Sir*, you would take warning! Whatever you may think of your self, you certainly have a *heated imagination.* 'Tis too evident to be denied, that you often take the *motions of your own mind*, for *divine communications*...if you deal with me as you have done with much better men, I may expect to be called a poor, carnal, unconverted wretch. But I assure you beforehand, I esteem it a *very* small thing to be judged by your Judgement; and the rather, because I *certainly know*, you are ignorant of my state towards GOD.

Chauncy ended his encounter with Davenport by adding:

> However you act towards me, I presume not to *judge you. To your own master you stand, or fall.* I have taken notice only of *that* in you, which is *visible* to the world; And tho' I have, and do condemn it, as what is opposite to the plain laws of GOD; yet, I pronounce no sentence respecting *your state.* GOD knows how far you may be under the power of a *disturbed imagination*, and will make all the favourable allowances your case will admit of: I desire to do so also, and would hope the best concerning you.[7]

Chauncy garnered great benefit from this encounter. He wrote an open letter to Davenport describing the affair and repeating his arguments. This affirmed Chauncy's leadership of the Old Lights and further discredited the Awakening.

Chauncy then moved to the offensive. He was thoroughly convinced that the Awakening was a serious threat to rational Christianity and believed if it went unchecked it would lead to anarchy of the type experienced by the Munster Anabaptists, a radical Reformation sect which fell into ethical error. He penned a much tougher criticism of the Awakening in the form of a long letter. It was published in Scotland and copies were sent back and circulated in the colonies. The thrust of the letter was that the Awakening was producing far more harm than good.

> 'Tis scarce imaginable what Excesses and Extravagancies People were running into, and even encouraged in; being told such Things were Arguments of the *extraordinary Presence of the Holy Ghost* with them. The same houses of Worship were scarce emptied Night nor Day for a Week together, and unheard of Instances of supposed Religion were carried on in them, some would be *praying*, some *exhorting*, some *singing*, some *clapping their Hands*, some *laughing*, some *crying*, some *shrieking and roaring out*; and so invincibly set were they in these Ways, especially when encouraged by any Ministers (as was too often the Case), that it was a vain Thing to argue with them, to shew them the Indecency of such Behavior; and whoever indeed made an Attempt this Way, might be sure aforehand of being called an *Opposer* of the *Spirit*, and a *Child of the Devil*.[8]

The meticulous scholar of Harvard did not stop with one letter. He spent much of 1742 and 1743 in correspondence with like-minded pastors all over the colonies, compiling a dossier of extremist revivalist activities. Chauncy became the editor, and his home a clearinghouse, of the anti-Awakening literature of the colonies. Other opposers sought his advice and ceded to his judgment and editorial opinions.

Edwards had challenged the audience at the Yale commencement address to go to the outlying towns and villages and see for themselves what the Great Awakening was accomplishing. Chauncy decided to do just that. In the summer and fall of 1742 he went on an arduous three-hundred-mile circuit that covered New England, New Jersey and New York. He talked to pastors, especially fellow Harvard graduates, and observed the revival firsthand.

When he returned home to recuperate he had a vast amount of material, both from his tour and from the letters he had solicited. During the winter of 1742 to 1743, he had obtained either the proofs or an early copy of Edwards's new work on the revival, *Some Thoughts Concerning Revival*. Chauncy read the work carefully and understood its potential for encouraging and extending the progress of the Awakening.

The Deception of Selective Collections

Chauncy's *Seasonable Thoughts on the State of Religion in New England* was composed as a point-by-point refutation of Edwards's *Some Thoughts Concerning Revival*. It was released in the fall of 1743 and became an instant best-seller. In fact it had been subscribed to by a major part of the Boston establishment. It outsold all other books on the Awakening by a large margin.

Seasonable Thoughts was a compendium of every abuse and mistake, unruly meeting and exaggerated event Chauncy could find. It was a caricature of the Great Awakening, not a history.[9] The colonial historian of Connecticut, Benjamin Trumbull (1735-1820), had a low opinion of Chauncy's work. Trumbull believed that Chauncy had gathered evidence carelessly and principally from the opponents of the Awakening. Trumbull, on the other hand, lived for years in the communities affected by the revival and knew of the positive long-term effects of the Awakening.[10]

Seasonable Thoughts ensured the defeat of the Awakening. Using the assumptions of Calvinist theology and faculties psychology (that is, Mr. Spock's logic), Chauncy "proved" to his contemporary ministers what they wanted to hear: the Awakening was all enthusiasm and no Spirit. Ministers could rest secure in their pulpits and feel confident that the new measures were a passing fad.

Edwards knew from the reception of the book that he was beaten and the revival was over. Both Harvard and Yale, outraged by the negative comments in Whitefield's journals and by other accusations of the itinerants, passed strong resolutions against enthusiasm and the Awakening. Edwards was not welcomed back for further commencement sermons.

Edwards did rework — one last time — the arguments on behalf of revival and presented them as a sermon series at Northampton. Several years later they were published as *A Treatise Concerning Religious*

Affections. It sold slowly with only one printing occurring during Edwards's lifetime. It took several generations to recognize it as a classic on discernment and psychology of spiritual experiences.

Chauncy was the man of the hour, the hero of "reasonable" Christianity. Immediately after publication of *Seasonable Thoughts* he began organizing a resistance campaign to Whitefield's forthcoming tour of the colonies. His effort was successful. When Whitefield arrived in 1744 practically all of the pulpits were closed to him, and the wind had gone out of the Awakening. Revival was not to be rekindled again until after the American Revolution a generation later.

Chauncy and Edwards After the Great Awakening

Among the many ironies of the Great Awakening controversy, the greatest is that of the later course of Charles Chauncy's life. The defender of consensus orthodoxy became one of the founding theologians of Unitarianism, the American deistic cult. Toward the end of his long life he released a work titled *Salvation for All Men* (1783). It advocated universal salvation — the very opposite of Calvinism. The liberal ministers and congregations who were displeased with Calvinism and had rejected the Awakening readily accepted Chauncy's doctrine of universal salvation.

Here lies the true fruit of Chauncy's opposition to the Awakening. These same congregations quickly discarded the trinity as an unintelligible doctrine. A theology of the Spirit is difficult to maintain if one rejects the presence of the Holy Spirit during revival when His work is most manifest. The third Person of the trinity becomes a doctrine without verification and easily reasoned away.

Edwards's story is altogether different. After the ebb of the Awakening he experienced increasing difficulties with his congregation at Northampton. The issue was of the administration of the Lord's supper. The congregation wanted to maintain their tradition of open communion, but Edwards believed that communion was a sacrament reserved for professed Christians only. After much contention he was deposed of his pastorate in 1750.

Edwards then accepted a call from the frontier town of Stockbridge, Massachusetts, where he ministered to a mixed congregation of Indians and white settlers. Far from the tensions and politics of Boston and Northampton he spent seven years as a pastor and writer. There he produced some of the greatest masterpieces of American theology, including works on such issues as freedom of the will and original sin.

In the fall of 1757 Edwards received a call to become president of Princeton. When he arrived in the area there was a threat of a smallpox outbreak. To set an example, he was one of the first to volunteer to be inoculated. The vaccine at the time was crude, randomly killing one in a hundred of those inoculated. Edwards became gravely ill with the vaccine and after a month's struggle became one of those it killed.

An Invitation to Pentecost — Looking Back on the Great Awakening

Time often gives wisdom and perspective to spiritual matters. Chauncy is no longer considered as the hero who saved the colonists from outbursts of enthusiasm. Even liberal scholars, who have little understanding of the spiritual world, side with Edwards on the Awakening. Chauncy is seen as a religious bureaucrat who defended the status quo without comprehending the deeper issues of revival. Chauncy was competent enough to impress his contemporaries, but his writings, given the growth in psychology and spiritual understanding since then, seem superficial and mean-spirited.[11]

Edwards had a prophetic insight into the importance of the Awakening in the midst of the period of its greatest abuses.

> If God intends this great revival of religion to be the dawning, or a forerunner of an happy state of his church on earth, it may be an instance of the divine wisdom, in the beginning of it, to suffer so many irregularities and errors in conduct, to which he knew men, in their present weak state, were most exposed, under great religious affections and when animated with great zeal. For it will be very likely to be of excellent benefit to his church, in the continuance and progress of the work afterwards: their experience in the first setting out of the mischievous consequences of these errors, and smarting for them in the beginning, may be an happy defense to them afterwards, for many generations, from these errors, which otherwise they might continually be exposed to.[12]

Interestingly, the critics of the Awakening would have described the norms in much of the church today as extremism. Lay ministry and lay evangelists (exhorters) are now part of every evangelical and charismatic church. The laity carry on functions of public worship, prayer and ministry that would have astounded even the radical itinerants of the Awakening.

Chauncy's indignant descriptions of revival prayer meetings sound hysterical. His use of pejorative words, such as *disorder* and *indecent*, merely reflect his shortsightedness. By reading between the lines one could also describe the meetings as faith-filled and lively. Similar scenes have recurred in later revivals to the point where only a snobbish minority would find them offensive.

Even Edwards did not discern the full potential for revival that had occurred in Northampton. Recall the unnamed saint of South Hadley who believed in the restoration of the gifts of the Spirit (see chapter 2). From the perspective of the consensus orthodoxy of the times the man was deluded and an enthusiast. From the modern perspective he was prophetically correct.

It seems much of what was defined as extremism, even by some of the Awakening defenders, was really an invitation by the Holy Spirit to further renewal and spiritual power. Christians as a whole, and certainly the clergy, were not ready to receive that invitation.

Cambuslang and Cane Ridge: Opposed and Unapposed Revivals

That revivals can be destroyed by human opposition is demonstrated by comparing the revival at Cambuslang, Scotland, to the revival at Cane Ridge, Tennessee. These two events, separated by an ocean and almost six decades, were so similar that they might be considered as a single revival with an interruption.[13] The Cambuslang revival occurred in 1742 five miles outside of Glasgow during the time the Great Awakening was at its height. The revival at Cambuslang was opposed by religious critics, and it faded quickly. The Cane Ridge revival began in a village on the Kentucky frontier in 1801; it had general support, and revival spread to all parts of the nation.

Both revivals came about during Presbyterian communion services, which were reverently called "the sacrament." At that time Presbyterians celebrated the sacrament only once a year at the local church. This special service was preceded by several days of fasting, preaching and corporate repentance.

Expectancy had been fanned by news of the Great Awakening in America. Jonathan Edwards's *Faithful Narrative,* which first appeared in 1737, had been widely circulating in Scotland. The local preacher, William McCulloch, read Edwards's narrative from the pulpit and in imitation of Edwards began to preach repentance and conversion, thereby preparing his congregation for revival. The sacrament held in Cambuslang in 1741 was carried out with special fervor.[14] The "fallings" (resting in the Spirit) manifested. By the end of 1741 his community was in revival, and many conversions had taken place.

The next summer's sacrament at Cambuslang was highly anticipated. People came from all over the United Kingdom, and the crowd numbered in the thousands. George Whitefield was in Scotland following his recent colonial tour and joined the event. He preached on multiple occasions and served the Lord's supper along with more than twenty other ministers. McCulloch recounted: "While he [Whitefield] was serving some of the tables he appeared to be so filled with the love of God, as to be in a kind of ecstasy..."[15]

The sacrament was so powerfully affective that in an unprecedented move the Cambuslang church elders called for a *second* sacrament in August. Again the crowds came from all over the United Kingdom. At both sacraments much phenomenon manifested. Hundreds experienced the fallings, but there were also prophetic utterances and much laughter, groaning and moaning.

These phenomena, or "exercises" as Edwards called them, caused scandal and opposition. Numerous visiting clergy, including many from the universities, came only to observe. Many of them turned critical. Ministers who took part in the sacraments were ridiculed as inducing "enthusiasm," and other critics even termed the revival "demonic."[16] Although similar phenomena were happening in America, opposition was so strong among a majority of the clergy in Scotland that the next year the sacrament had little impact. Outlying villages and towns were touched for several years by revival, but there was never another sacrament in Scotland like the two at Cambuslang of 1742. For decades the believers who participated in it, and the ministers who served it, would pray for another revival "as as Cambuslang."

That prayer was answered almost sixty years later, but not in Scotland. The 1801 revival in Cane Ridge, Kentucky, was similar to Cambuslang in two ways. It arose from a Presbyterian "sacrament," and it was the end product of the small, local revivals of previous years.

America in the post-Revolutionary War era had reached a low point in its spiritual life. Deism, not Christianity, was the predominant religion, and the frontier was a particularly uncivilized place hostile to the church. Several Presbyterian ministers had emigrated from Scotland to serve the Scots and Scotch-Irish on the frontier. They began praying for revival and organizing concerts of prayer for revival among local churches.

In 1797 a Presbyterian pastor, James McGready, noted for his emotional preaching, led three small congregations in Logan County, Kentucky, into revival. That was temporarily quenched by skeptical local clergy who derided the "enthusiastic" phenomenon, particularly the fallings. But in the summer of 1799 another wave of revival hit McGready's ministry as he was joined by his brother, a Methodist preacher. By 1800 their sacraments all became revivals, and the revival spread to other denominations, particularly Baptist and Methodist churches in the frontier.

By the summer of 1801 expectancy was at an all-time high on the frontier. When McGready announced the sacrament for the first week of August at the meeting house in the village of Cane Ridge, more than ten thousand people came. This was astonishing to its organizers, for it was a gigantic figure for a frontier event. About 140 wagons camped close together to form an instant town, and many came with small tents. It was America's first large "camp meeting." Practically everyone in the state came; all social levels were represented, from the governor to hundreds of slaves.

Significantly, and unlike Cambuslang, there were no disdaining ministers or influential deist aristocrats ready to ridicule the event. That was fortunate, for many who attended were indeed greatly exercised by the Spirit. The historian of Cane Ridge, Paul Conkin, who exhaustively examined the eyewitness records, noted the large numbers of persons who experienced the fallings, and added:

> Almost as prominent as falling were various bodily movements. Convulsive motions dated at least from early Scottish communions, and after Cane Ridge would become known, collectively and misleadingly, as the "jerks." The term concealed the diversity of such motions, including rhythmic dancing. More conventional shouts and groans joined with a near babble of speech, some incoherent, some later distinguished as holy laughter or singing.[17]

The revival fire spread to all parts of the nation, including the more sophisticated Atlantic coast, ebbing only after 1805. Some historians claim that it continued even into the 1830s. The camp meeting became an established revival tool of American Christianity among evangelical churches, especially the Baptists and Methodists.[18]

This move of the Spirit, called by historians the Second Great Awakening, destroyed deism as a major threat to American Christianity and established evangelical Christianity as normative Protestantism. A similar revival could have swept Scotland after 1742. However, Cane Ridge had a key advantage: the opposition was weak and the university theologians were far away.

Lessons Learned From These Revivals

The issues raised in the Great Awakening, the Edwards/Chauncy controversy, and Cambuslang are perennial whenever the Holy Spirit moves in revival. It is a fact that revivals are messy by nature. That is, the Holy Spirit moves within a human environment that is always molded by human sin, including encumbering religious traditions and demonic presences. Thus the manifestations of the Holy Spirit are imperfect and contaminated because of human sinfulness, flawed human institutions, theology and practices. This even happened in New Testament times.

Paul's Corinthian congregation was among the most Spirit-filled and the most unruly and contentious *at the same time*. This messy church was experiencing both revival and disorder. Yet the Spirit did not depart because of disorder. On the contrary, the Spirit continued to operate in the Corinthian church, although abuses of the Spirit's gifts were common, and Paul was forced to establish a pattern for order and discernment.

This is especially clear in regard to the gifts of prophecy and tongues (1 Cor. 13–14). For instance, Paul spent much time defining the right way to use gift of tongues and how to avoid abusing it. He also carefully warned his congregation not to forbid tongues. Similarly in 1 Thessalonians 5:20 Paul warns Christians not to despise prophecy. In other words, the gifts are worth having despite the worst of abuses. Paul's writings show that abuses do not end the manifestations of the Spirit, though they make their reception and discernment more difficult.

Here we must examine Paul's important distinction between reproof, which he gave, and condemnation or "despising," which he warned against. Biblical reproof is always specific and affirms a potential for restoration of an authentic pattern. Condemnation, such as "all prophecy is nonsense" or Chauncy's accusation that the Awakening was nothing but enthusiasm, is not godly but destructive. Condemnation grieves the Spirit and wounds the congregation.

Note that in the book of Revelation (chapter 2) Jesus begins each of His reproofs to the seven churches in a positive way. This implies that restoration is possible after the specific evil or fault is eliminated. Condemnation, however, does not function in that way. Chauncy did not want a reproved and cleansed Awakening (which is what Edwards wanted). Chauncy wanted decency, a quiet church and restored ministerial authority and prestige. He wanted an end to the new measures that threatened his security and his sense of proper religion.

Both human opposition of and demonic influence in revivals can be limited by cultivating spiritual discernment and mature spiritual leadership. Discernment in turn depends on a foundation of discernment in community tradition and theology. Here Edwards was at a tremendous disadvantage. He had no readily available theology of discernment, although he did read the earlier Puritan writing that described the occasional unusual visions and experiences associated with personal conversion. This literature was an advance over traditional Calvinism but little help in discerning the phenomena of mass revivals.[19] For reasons we will explain in chapter 6, the Reformers rejected the need for discernment when they threw out the whole of Catholic mystical theology.

Although discernment is principally a spiritual function, it is based on certain biblical principles which must be taught publicly. In its most basic form such a theology must accept that the Holy Spirit can operate in the current age and that the Spirit's operations can be discerned from the surrounding noise of psychic and demonic interference.

In spite of Edwards's own theories, it seems that the Great Awakening was not quenched because of its extremists. It was quenched because of the condemnation of its opponents. This condemnation demoralized the supporters and marred the faith of the public to the point where they no longer welcomed the presence of the Spirit. This seems the best explanation of why the Whitefield revival of 1744 failed.

This is not to say that revivals end only because of criticism and opposition. All revivals contain an element of God's sovereignty that the human mind cannot fully comprehend. Some revivals fade out because the Spirit, for sovereign reasons, ceases to be poured out. This seems to have happened to the charismatic renewal of the late 1970s. By 1980 that fresh outpouring had ended though few wanted to admit it.*

However, it seems that every time there is a revival and God moves in a new and different way (as He does in every true revival), many in the religious establishment find themselves in opposition. The New Testament describes these kind of people who embody the condemnation and opposition to the presence of the Holy Spirit that Chauncy personified so well. They were a group of men who were religiously devout, well educated and scripturally knowledgeable — the Pharisees. Pharisaism opposes the work of the Spirit in the name of consensus orthodoxy. In the rest of this book we will see that Pharisaism recurs whenever there is revival.

In part 2 we turn to a specific examination of how the spirit of Pharisaism afflicted the church in the post-New Testament era.

---

* On the other hand, Richard Lovelace, the contemporary authority on revivals, believes that authentic revival is *begun by the sovereign work of God, but sustained* only if the revived community goes beyond personal piety and to the area of social action and concern.[20]

PART II

The Church Robbed of Power

FOUR

Spiritual Gifts in the Early Church

Healing and Exorcism in the First Centuries

THE DOCUMENTS NOW AVAILABLE SHOW that the church in the first centuries had a powerful ministry of healing and exorcism that mirrored Jesus' public ministry. Yet by the year 500 that ministry was a mere shadow of its original status. It is also absolutely clear that at no time in church history did this ministry end completely.[1]

One of the many witnesses to the healing and exorcism ministry of the early church was Irenaeus, bishop of Lyons, France (130 – 200):

> Those who are in truth His disciples, receiving grace from Him, do in His name perform miracles, so as to promote the welfare of other men, according to the gift which each one has received from Him. For some do certainly and truly drive out devils, so that those who have thus been cleansed from evil spirits frequently both believe in Christ and join themselves to the Church...others still, heal the sick by laying their hands upon them, and they are made whole.[2]

This "healing-and-exorcism-as-evangelization" has been rediscovered and much publicized in recent years as *power evangelism*.[3] It is in harmony with New Testament practice. Jesus healed those who came to Him, risking that some would not fully recognize Him as Lord (Luke 17:11-19). Likewise, Paul used his gift of healing to attract people to the gospel before preaching (Acts 28:8-9).

The Gifts of the Spirit in the Early Church

The earliest theology about the gifts of the Spirit was formed by what could be gleaned from the experience of the church and from hints in the Old Testament. The effects of the Holy Spirit as described in Isaiah 11:2 were particularly influential: "And the Spirit of the Lord will rest on Him, the spirit of wisdom and understanding, the spirit of counsel and strength, the spirit of knowledge and the fear of the Lord."

The writings of Justin Martyr (100 – 165), one of the earliest apologists of the church, show how the early church attempted to understand its experience of the gifts of the Spirit in Isaiah's terms.

> [Christians] are also receiving gifts, each as he is worthy, illuminated through the name of this Christ. For one receives the spirit of understanding, another of counsel, another of strength, another of healing, another of foreknowledge, another of teaching, and another of the fear of God.[4]

Note that Justin incorrectly associated the gifts of the Spirit with worthiness. This misunderstanding, that the gifts of the Spirit were to be spiritually earned, might be termed the "Galatian bewitchment." Paul warned his Galatian congregation of falling into a similar error:

> You foolish Galatians, who has bewitched you...This is the only thing I want to find out from you: did you receive the Spirit by the works of the Law, or by hearing with faith? Are you so foolish? Having begun by the Spirit, are you now being perfected by the flesh? (Gal. 3:1-3).

The Institutional Church and the Decline of the Gifts

Even from the day of Pentecost, forces in the world have discouraged the full manifestations of the gifts of the Spirit. Recent studies have examined the decline of the gift of prophecy in the first centuries of church history. As the church hierarchy became established, the bishops took over the functions of the charismatically gifted lay prophets. Keep in mind that the function of prophecy in the New Testament is different from the Old Testament forthtelling and foretelling. The main function of New Testament prophecy is "edification and exhortation and consolation" (1 Cor. 14:3). Edification, exhortation and consolation became increasingly the reserved duties of the priests and bishops, as were sermons and other pastoring activities. As the responsibilities of the bishops increased, prophetic utterances given by a charismatically gifted person became a threat to the duties of the clergy. Eventually laypersons were shut off from the prophetic ministry altogether.[5]

The same decline occurred in the gift of healing. The Catholic ritual (sacrament) of anointing the sick took healing out of lay hands and institutionalized it. What was originally a commission for every believer (Mark 16:18) became restricted to clergy.[6]

The Montanist Controversy

Another major event in the early church's experience encouraged the suppression of the gifts of the Spirit. It was the rise and fall of the Montanist revival. The Montanists began about the year 175 and spread throughout many areas of the Roman Empire. They were a Pentecostal element within the church which stressed the gift of prophecy (1 Cor. 14) and moral uprightness. At the beginning they were perfectly orthodox. In fact Tertullian, one of the foundational theologians of the early church, was a Montanist. Unfortunately the Montanists drifted into nondiscerned and undisciplined prophecies. They separated from the church and set up their own hierarchy. Like many later sects, the Montanist prophets predicted the date and place of the second coming. When it did not happen, the sect self-destructed with increasingly radical and unscriptural prophecies.[7]

All of this soured the church toward manifestations of prophecy or the other gifts of the Spirit; but this the wrong conclusion. Rather than suppressing all prophecy, the church needed a better understanding of discernment. Had the original prophets been reproved and given pastoral direction at an early stage of their ministry, the Montanist revival might have survived as a positive event in church history.

Formation of Doctrine

Another obstacle to the full development of the gifts in the early church was doctrinal in nature. The theology of the trinity had developed from the struggles against Gnostic heresies. Although this was a positive development, it had an unintended negative by-product. The pastoral elements of the Christian's life in the Spirit, the gifts of the Spirit, were subordinated to the theological concerns. The theology focused on questions about the nature of the trinity and the personhood of Christ and of the Holy Spirit rather than on daily living in the Spirit. That essential element of good theology, the connection between Scripture and present spiritual experience, was greatly weakened.

A recent history of the doctrine of the Holy Spirit was written by Alasdair Heron. The theology of the gifts of the Spirit is discussed only in the chapters on modern Pentecostalism. This represents Christian literature throughout the centuries: the person and work of the Holy Spirit have been given much attention, but the gifts of the Spirit were given little notice until about seventy years ago.[8]

The first five centuries of the Christian era were also the centuries when the great doctrines of the church were formulated in the creeds and councils. Again this had both positive and negative consequences. Certainly the doctrinal definitions helped identify heresy with greater ease. However, the unintended consequence was a shift in the understanding of faith away from faith-expectancy to faith-doctrine.

The definition of a Christian increasingly became more a matter of who intellectually conformed to the creeds and councils and less a matter of who trusted in God and Jesus and could heal the sick, cast out demons or do the other mighty works of discipleship. Unintentionally the church was following the route of the Pharisees in eliminating faith-expectancy for the sake of faith-doctrine.

The Mirage of the Desert[9]

In the fourth century there arose a form of Christian covenant community in the Egyptian and Palestinian desert that was to have far-reaching influence in the history of Christendom. The monks and nuns who came to these communities wished to separate themselves from the immorality of the Roman Empire and live in a totally Christian setting. They developed a lifestyle centered on constant prayer and self-denial, believing themselves to be in the tradition of Elijah and John the Baptist.

At the beginning the desert monks were gifted in healing and exorcism. Unfortunately Desert Christianity was captivated by the philosophy of the times and adopted many Stoic and neo-Platonic ideals.

65

Among these ideals was the concept that pain and illness were to be accepted bravely (stoically). In fact several Scripture verses supported this, such as Paul's "thorn in the flesh" (2 Cor. 12:7). In addition it is central to the Christian Scriptures that every believer take up a cross and share the sufferings of Christ (2 Cor. 1:5-7; Phil. 3:10).

However, they made an absolute connection between the sufferings brought on by illness and the believer's sharing of Christ's sufferings. This concept of illness as redemptive suffering subordinated the many Scripture passages which showed that illness was brought on by demonic oppression and an evil to be dispersed by the church's ministry (Luke 13:16, for example). Therefore, these monks were still willing to pray for outsiders, but they were not anxious to receive healing prayer for themselves. One of the great healer monks, Benjamin of Nitria, suffered a long and painful illness from dropsy but refused healing prayers so that he might partake of the sufferings of Christ.[10]

In essence, the monks inverted the Scripture, making the normative biblical attitude toward healing the exception, and the exception (redemptive suffering), the normative. This type of inversion of Scripture was passed on to subsequent Christian theology. It was to become the perfect alibi for those Christian communities that lost their faith-expectancy for healing prayer because all illness could then be assumed to be from the Lord and for the purpose of redemptive suffering.[11]

Asceticism and Humility Versus the Gifts of the Spirit

Even more of a distortion of Scripture was found in the monks' idea that holiness was to be acquired through asceticism. That is, the monks believed that the perfect Christian life included constant fasting and self-punishments. This was the "Galatian bewitchment" in its extreme form.

Athanasius (296 – 373), bishop of Alexandria and defender of Trinitarian theology, wrote a biography of the founder of Egyptian monasticism, St. Anthony. There he lauds Anthony for his stern ascetical practices, including the fact that he never bathed or washed his feet.[12] This strange view was part of an overreaction to the immorality of the Roman public bath system where sexual activity was rampant.

Early in his Christian life, Anthony heard 1 Corinthians 9:27, "But I buffet my body and make it my slave, lest possibly, after I have preached to others, I myself should be disqualified." This made a tremendous impression on him, and for twenty years he lived as a hermit in prayer and constant fasting and mortification. After his season of prayer he emerged to a more public life with several gifts of the Spirit, including discernment of spirits and healing. People from all over Egypt came to him with their sick and possessed. At times, as in Jesus' healing of the Phoenician woman's daughter, Anthony ministered exorcism through the parent's faith rather than a direct prayer over the possessed child.[13]

Anthony warned his fellow monks not to be puffed up with pride because of their spiritual gifts — a valid point.[14] However, this warning, that spiritual gifts can endanger the monk's humility and prayer life, became a central theme of subsequent monastic literature. Thus the gifts of the Spirit were seen as tools to be used infrequently because they were a danger to the person's holiness. This teaching overruled Paul's admonition that Christians should desire and use the spiritual gifts (1 Cor. 14:1) and Jesus' command that works of the believers were to be a form of public light to the world (Matt. 5:15-16).

A false opposition was created between humility and the gifts of the Spirit. It was no longer considered proper to do what the lay ministers did in the times of Irenaeus, which was to heal and cast out demons as evangelization. A theology had been created which made any form of power evangelism, to use today's vocabulary, impossible.

Through the writings and influence of John Cassian (cir. 360 – 435), the patterns of the Desert Fathers became the ideal for the Western church. Cassian summed up what he had learned in the desert monasteries about the use of the gifts of the Spirit: "When they did possess them by the grace of the Holy Spirit they would never use them, unless perhaps extreme and unavoidable necessity drove them to do so."[15]

More than a thousand years later, the theology of avoiding the gifts was codified by the Spanish mystic, St. John of the Cross (1542 – 1591). He was given the title "Doctor of the Church," which affirms him as a foundational theologian of the Catholic church. Like the Desert Fathers, he believed that any spiritual manifestations, such as visions or gifts of healing, endangered the believer's quest for spiritual perfection.[16] This led to other delusions; for example, that the goal of Christian prayer life was individual perfection and that this perfection was somehow in conflict with the public ministry of the gifts of the Spirit. This was a tragic misunderstanding of Scripture because 1 Peter 4:10 clearly declares that the gifts of the

Spirit are for the community: "As each one has received a special gift, employ it in serving one another, as good stewards of the manifold grace of God."[17]

Prevailing Prayer and Love, Not Asceticism

What made the confusion between true holiness and asceticism so long-standing was that it could, like so many errors, be justified by Scripture. Fasting was certainly a major factor in the prayer life taught in both Old and New Testaments. The believer is urged in several New Testament verses to share the sufferings of Christ (for example, 2 Cor. 1:6-7; 1 Pet. 4:13), something that modern Christians tend to ignore. Paul did urge bodily discipline and did encourage celibacy as a superior form of Christian life which allows the believer to give undivided attention to serving the Lord (1 Cor. 7).

Yet the way the desert monks put this together was exaggerated and unbalanced.[18] Within this theological tradition there was a confusion of factors which disguised the sources of both its errors and successes. Many of the monks and nuns who went through the spiritual disciplines of constant prayer and ascetical practices did experience some of the gifts of the Spirit ("graces," as they were called). It was difficult to argue against a theology that worked in guiding persons toward great personal holiness and love. This is especially true in a society, such as medieval Christendom, where the spiritual authorities had the power of life and death in enforcing their consensus orthodoxy.

Only by comparison with other religions that practice asceticism, such as Buddhism, can we see that what produced holiness and the gifts of the Spirit in Christians was their intense prayer life and devotion to the person of Jesus, not their severe asceticism. The medieval monks and nuns were baptized in the Holy Spirit the difficult way, through persistent, laborious prayer, also known as prevailing prayer, much in the manner of the Old Testament prophets (Matt. 11:12). God was not confirming their theology; rather He gave them blessings out of His love in spite of their imperfect theology.

Documents of the period make it clear that many Catholic saints did in fact receive the baptism of the Spirit.[19] This conclusion was supported by Vinson Synan, who was the assistant general superintendent to the Pentecostal Holiness Church and a man brought up to believe that the Catholic church was the "whore of Babylon." After a careful study of medieval Catholic literature, Synan pointed out that prevailingprayer was the normal way of receiving the baptism of the Spirit until very recent times. Further, Synan suggested that persons who went through this process more highly cherished the gifts and used them with more discretion than contemporary charismatics or Pentecostals.[20]

Lest the reader believe that the Galatian bewitchment (receiving gifts of the Spirit by works) is a unique characteristic of Catholic theology, it is well to remember that similar confusions have taken place within Protestantism. In the 1860s a Protestant devotional movement arose among Methodists and evangelicals termed the "Holiness" movement (see chapter 9). It was made up of Christians who were dissatisfied with the lax state of religious commitment among America's Protestants. Although the movement began as a great "faith-alone" revival, part of their program was to live by a code of morals above the rest, as in refusing the use of all alcohol, tobacco, dancing and makeup and jewelry for women. Most of the early Pentecostal leaders came from this Holiness tradition.[21]

Pentecostals came to believe that a person who wished to receive the baptism of the Holy Spirit had to renounce the worldly life-style and adopt the Holiness code. They were utterly astounded by the charismatic renewal. Here were thousands of persons who received the Spirit without accepting the Holiness code; for example, women wore makeup and heels, and some people smoked and still drank wine. What we had among the Pentecostals was a confusion of factors similar to the confusion of the Desert Fathers (though not as severe or long lasting). The early Pentecostals had received the baptism of the Holy Spirit because they had desired it, prayed for it and had the faith to receive it, not because of their specific Holiness code. God blesses believers with the gifts of His Spirit not because their theology is perfect but because of their commitment to Jesus.

Summary

The gifts of the Spirit in the early church did not long survive in their fullness for several reasons. Normal institutional developments tended to subdue charismatic gifts in laymen while priests and bishops acquired increasing power and duties.

The traditions of the Desert Fathers became a Talmud for Catholic theology. Unbiblical extremism in asceticism and humility diminished the role of the gifts of the Spirit in believers' lives. The gifts were seen as valid but dangerous to the Christian's "perfection." The monks of the desert had shown Christendom how to achieve heroic heights of piety but at the cost of serving the world with the power of the Holy Spirit. Thus by the beginning of the Middle Ages the gifts of the Spirit were only infrequently practiced and most often by the clergy. Chapter 5 describes in more detail errors that arose in the doctrine of healing, including petitioning the saints and belief in the power of relics to heal.

FIVE

Truth and Error in the Catholic Ministry of Healing

St. Augustine of Hippo (354 – 430)

THE MOST IMPORTANT FIGURE IN the formation of the theology of healing (and non-healing) was St. Augustine, bishop of Hippo in North Africa. Augustine not only sketched what became orthodox Catholic theology, but his writings were read extensively by Martin Luther, John Calvin and other Reformers. Many of his theological viewpoints were passed on to Protestantism through the Reformers, especially his understanding of salvation by grace. Unfortunately, he made several key errors in the theology of healing that were accepted by later Catholic and Protestant theologians.

Augustine was raised as a Christian but educated in the classical learning of his day and showed special talents in literature and philosophy. As a young man he explored the non-Christian cults and settled into the Manachaean religion (Gnostic) and into a sexually permissive life. Providentially, he experienced a dramatic conversion and returned to the religion of his childhood.

Augustine dedicated all of his classical learning and talents as a writer to the service of Christianity. His participation in non-Christian religions gave him a background with which to appreciate the truth of biblical revelation and the deceitfulness of heresy. Significantly, the majority of his works were concerned with combatting the various heresies and cults of the times.

He made many original contributions to Christian theology, including his massive work on the trinity, which became the reference point for Western orthodoxy on this topic. Unfortunately, Augustine followed the earlier tradition and understood the gifts of the Spirit in terms of

Isaiah 11:2, which does not include healing, instead of as they are defined in 1 Corinthians 12. In his work *The Lord's Sermon on the Mount*, he drew parallels between the gifts of the Spirit according to Isaiah and the beatitudes of the Sermon on the Mount.[1] This work did much to define the Catholic view of the gifts of the Spirit.

Augustine's Theology of Healing[2]

Augustine's early writings dismissed the ministry of healing as improper to Christian life. In one of his first books, *On the True Religion*, he wrote in reference to the gospel accounts of healing and miracles:

> "These miracles were not allowed to last until our times lest the soul [of the believer] ever seek visible things and the human race grow cold because of familiarity with those things whose novelty enkindled it."[3]

Similarly, in another early work Augustine reasoned that the gospel miracles were performed to give Jesus the public authority that was necessary to convince the multitude.[4] This implied that more philosophical or spiritual Christians had no need of miraculous evidence.

This system of spiritual reasoning is called cessationism; that is, the belief that miracles and the healing ministry ceased after biblical times.* Most often cessationism was coupled with the idea that God's miraculous activity was a temporary intrusion into the normal world. The purpose of miracles was to authenticate the authority of an Old Testament prophet or Jesus and His apostles. Missing in the cessationist theology of miracles is an understanding of healing as a sign of God's compassion or the miraculous as a mark of the kingdom (see Mark 8:2; Luke 9:1-2).

The idea of cessationism originated before Augustine. In fact it can be traced to Jewish rabbinical commentaries that preceded the Christian era. Some rabbis had been concerned that since the times of Haggai, Zechariah and Malachi there had not been an authentic prophet in Israel. Several ideas were proposed to explain why this was so, such as the lack of piety among the population. In the first century Christian writers used this rabbinical speculation to assert that the Holy Spirit had been withdrawn from the Jews and passed on to the Christians.[5] By the third

---

* Although the pronunciation is very similiar, the word *cessationism* is distinct from the word *secessionism*, which is derived from the verb *to secede*.

century a few Christian apologists were using cessationism as an explanation for the apparent rarity of healing miracles in the Christian community. Augustine adopted this view as a new Christian and maintained
it most of his Christian life.

About six years before he died Augustine rejected cessationism. This
was due to a dramatic healing he witnessed. The case involved a young
man afflicted by epilepsy and miraculously healed at the beginning of
an Easter service at his church. That caused him to investigate other
reports of healings.[6]

By the time he came to write his last works, *City of God* and *The
Retractions*, he enthusiastically affirmed the continued healing ministry
of the church. *The Retractions* was written when Augustine was nearing
death, and he decided to correct his earlier writings. His ability to be
critical of his earlier mistakes was a mark of his profound humility.

In *The Retractions* he explained that miracles were still common in
the Christian community although he had not seen some of the more
spectacular miracles of the apostolic age, such as people healed by the
mere shadow of an apostle (Acts 5:15):

> But what I said is not to be so interpreted that no miracles are
> believed to be performed in the name of Christ at the present
> time. For, when I wrote that book *On the True Religion*, I
> myself had recently learned that a blind man had been re-
> stored to sight in Milan...and I know about some others, so
> numerous even in these times, that we cannot know about all
> of them nor enumerate those we know.[7]

Augustine's final theology of healing is found in *The City of God*,
completed four years before his death. He describes the healing ministry that flowered in his diocese after his acceptance of healing prayer.
From his personal experience he came to understand how cessationism
crept into Christian writings: Christians were shy about telling of their
own healings. According to Augustine, although everyone knew of the
gospel accounts of healing, few heard of their own neighbors' healings.

As bishop he determined to remedy this and insisted that persons
miraculously healed give a witness in church. Two years before he
wrote the *City of God* he began a record of healing miracles within his
diocese. In that short time seventy healings were recorded.

Augustine only wrote about those healings he could personally verify. Several occurred during the administration of baptism, including

complete healings from a hernia and gout. A young man was saved from the prospect of agonizingly painful rectal surgery by the fervent prayers of his family and the priests of his district. In another case a woman with advanced breast cancer had a dream in which she was told to go to the next baptismal service and have a newly baptized person pray for her. She did so and was instantly healed of the cancer.[8]

Augustine believed in the healing power of relics to evoke the intercessory prayers of martyred saints. This type of petition was the major element in his theology of healing. In several churches of North Africa the remains of Stephen, the martyr of Acts 7, were believed to have been interred. Augustine verified that persons within his diocese had been healed through prayers at these shrines.

The modern reader, especially one of the evangelical persuasion, would find several elements of Augustine's theology to be superstitious or more pagan than Christian. It is true that Augustine's theology of relics and healing shrines falls short of the ministry commissioned by Jesus. Yet his theology was not totally unbiblical. Certainly other elements of his theology of healing are entirely valid and have recurred whenever the Christian healing ministry has been restored.

Healing Through Sacraments

Among the valid discoveries that Augustine made was the coupling of healing prayer with the sacraments. Already theologians prior to him had wrestled with the concept of the sacraments and had identified two chief Christian sacraments, baptism and the Lord's supper. It was generally understood that these rites were special acts whereby God's covenant promises, graces and power were appropriated in the life of the individual Christian. Therefore the grace of Christian baptism would be powerful enough to produce effects besides the spiritual. The modern Christian healing movement confirms what Augustine learned centuries ago, that healing is often a by-product of baptism. The ministry of healing through the routine sacramental ministry of the church has been developed in recent decades by Catholic and Episcopalian writers and is an effective and ongoing ministry of those churches today.[9]

Matter and Spiritual Power

Sacraments are characterized by the use of material means, such as water or bread, to execute the covenant. This is derived from the biblical revelation that God made the earth and everything in it "good" (Gen. 1) and that eventually all the earth will be sanctified (Rev. 21:1). This perspective on the material world is radically different from Gnosticism. Gnosticism purported that all matter was the creation of one of the rebellious gods, and no possible good could be associated with it.

Part of the biblical understanding of sacrament involves the ability of matter to carry with it spiritual power. Many passages of Scripture show this clearly, especially in reference to cloth and clothing. A good example is God's instruction to Ezekiel about the rite of the temple, specifically about the duties of the priests as they enter and exit the sanctuary.

> And it shall be that when they enter at the gates of the inner court, they shall be clothed with linen garments...And when they go out into the outer court, into the outer court to the people, they shall put off their garments in which they have been ministering and lay them in the holy chambers; then they shall put on other garments that they may not transmit holiness to the people with their garments (Ezek. 44:17,19).

The fact that touching can release spiritual power to heal is repeated in the well-known New Testament story of the woman with the issue of blood (Luke 8:42-48). This passage shows that many people were brushing against Jesus; yet the woman's need and her faith-expectancy which released His healing power from His clothing. Also, in Acts 19:11-12 Paul's aprons and handkerchiefs retained so much of God's power that they were taken to the sick for healing and exorcism.

Augustine's belief in the healing power of Stephen's bones and the later cult of relics came from overgeneralization of a passage found in 2 Kings. In that passage Elisha the prophet had died, and his bones lay exposed in a pit. A burial party passed by but was suddenly attacked by raiders; the body of the dead man was thrown into Elisha's tomb. When the body hit the prophet's bones, the man came back to life (2 Kin. 13:20-21). Somehow, Elisha's bones had retained God's power, and this power was discharged as the body of the dead man touched it. Augustine assumed that the bones of Stephen would have similar healing qualities.

Augustine's Belief in Relics

From a purely biblical perspective Augustine's assumption was possible. However, a flaw in his thinking allowed a valid biblical truth — that matter can carry a healing energy — to be demonized. The word *demonization* is used here in Paul Tillich's sense of the tendency to elevate certain partial truths to exaggerated absolutes.[10] The error had to do with the philosophical assumptions undergirding Augustine's thinking.

Classical Greek philosophy, which formed the base upon which early Christian theology was constructed, had difficulty assimilating the concept of spiritual power. The main concern of the Greek philosophers was how things were similar (the problem of universals). Permanence was considered more important than change. The central concept of Plato's philosophy was his ideal "forms," and that of Aristotle was the concept of "essence." Earlier Greek philosophers, such as Hereclitus, understood change and energy but were out of fashion in Augustine's day (these were the pre-Socratics).[11]

Augustine, as a philosophically trained gentleman, carried the prejudices of classical Greek philosophy into his theology. The changeless and eternal were "good," while the temporary and changeable tended to debase the good. When he read about the healing power of Peter's aprons or Elisha's bones, he understood them as being holy in "essence" and "form." This would be a permanent characteristic given to matter by its association with a holy person. He did not understand that the healings resulted from temporary spiritual power which would eventually be discharged. Even today the Catholics define relics as "objects sanctified by contact with his (the saint's) body."[12]

Ironically, the original Greek text of the Scripture, written in the non-philosophical commercial Greek of the era, possessed an entirely adequate language for spiritual power. The word used by New Testament authors for the energies of God was *dunamis*, which simply means power. While Christian theology dedicated much thinking to God's personhood and the complications of the trinity (all eternal characteristics of God), it developed no theology for God's *dunamis*. An adequate theology of grace should have dealt with *dunamis*, but this did not happen either. The exception is some of the later literature from the Greek Orthodox church which examined the "divine energies" as part of the experience of mystical prayer.[13]

The concept of God's *dunamis* was so neglected in subsequent Western theology that the translators of the King James Version of the Bible used the word *virtue* for *dunamis* (for example, Luke 6:19). It seemed to them that it would be crude to say that Jesus felt power leaving Him when He was touched by the crowd, so they moralized it to say virtue.

Augustine also missed a cue when he did not pursue the fact that newly baptized Christians had healing authority, as he discovered in the case of the woman with breast cancer. Had he followed this lead it might have revealed to him that the gift of healing is a gift of grace, not of works. This revelation could have ended the long prevalence of the Galatian bewitchment which was to reign in Catholic theology until recent times (Gal. 3).

Thus Augustine's theology of healing was a mix of truth, exaggeration and error. Some healings were accomplished, but his belief in the permanent holiness of relics and shrines certainly undermined the healing ministries of the layperson, the laying on of hands or anointing with oil with faith-expectancy.

Healing in the Middle Ages

With some unbiblical aspects of Augustine's theology as a guide, the ministry of healing did not fare well in the development of the Catholic sacraments during the Middle Ages. The ministry of healing declined through a series of changes similar to the process that James Ash identified for the decline of the charismatic gift of prophecy (see previous chapter). It became ritualized and changed from a ministry among charismatic lay people to a priestly duty.

Healing was divided into two parts: 1) anointing with oil (extreme unction), which was assigned the favored status of a sacrament, and 2) exorcism, which was never recognized as a sacrament but was simply called a rite. Both were reserved for the ordained priesthood. The division into anointing and exorcism had some practical value, although if one studies the Gospel accounts of the ministry of Jesus, that type of division was not apparent. Rather Jesus healed the afflicted by either curing an illness or commanding an evil spirit to leave, depending on the situation.

Augustine's theology was elaborated into a cult of relics and pilgrimages. Many readers who studied *Canterbury Tales* in English 101 may remember Chaucer's description of the Pardoner. A pardoner was a traveling clerical official who sold forgiveness for punishment in the afterlife due to sin (this punishment was exacted in purgatory). Chaucer's Pardoner carried bottles of pigs' bones and bits of rags which he claimed to be relics of great saints. He hypocritically told church audiences that those bones and rags would heal all of their ailments as well as those of their animals.

What happened to the rite of anointing with oil for healing was especially tragic. The early church clearly understood the passage in James 5:14-16 as a commission to pray for healing in association with the forgiveness of sins. During the first centuries of the church's existence much healing was done in this way in spite of the general decline in the manifestations of the gifts of the Spirit. However, by the eighth and ninth centuries, anointing with oil was no longer practiced as a part of healing prayer. It was transformed into a rite of "happy death." When the priest would perform last rites for a terminally ill person, he would anoint the person with oil during the final sacrament, called extreme unction. With all sins confessed, the person would not have to suffer in purgatory when he died but could go directly to heaven. Thereby, the church overrode the biblical intention of anointing with oil, which was physical healing *plus* forgiveness for the sins that may have brought on the illness (James 5:15).[14]

James's association between illness and sin is not an idiosyncrasy in Scripture. It represents a continuity of revelation from both the Old Testament (Ps. 31:9-10) and the ministry of Jesus (John 5:5-14). Like most profound truths, the association between sin and sickness can be demonized into an absolute, as in the Eastern concept of *karma.** Scripture warns against such rashness; the story of Job shows that illness can be brought about by factors not related to personal sin. Similarly, Jesus warned His disciples against assuming that a man was born blind because he or his parents sinned (John 9:3). The total biblical revelation is suggestive, not absolute. Some illness is the fruit of personal sin, but some is not. However, when the Catholic church developed two distinct sacraments, confession and extreme unction, this biblical association between illness and sin was further weakened.

Biblical Warning Against Excessive Sacramentalism

The Catholic church never understood the eternal message of the warnings from Old Testament prophets against the misuse of the Old Testament sacraments. Several of the prophets had spoken of the misuse of the temple ritual of sacrifice and repentance. This was emphasized by Isaiah who warned that the God-ordained rites of the temple worship became no more than magic when performed without proper attitude of

---

* Karma is the belief that a person decides his destiny by what he does. For example, if a man lives like an animal, he will be reincarnated in the body of an animal.

heart or willingness to obey God's basic demands for justice. In a biting passage he equates acts of the temple ritual with acts of Canaanite witchcraft:

> But he who kills an ox is like one who slays a man; he who sacrifices a lamb is like the one who breaks a dog's neck; he who offers a grain offering is like one who offers swine's blood; he who burns incense is like the one who blesses an idol. As they have chosen their own ways, and their soul delights in their abominations (Is. 66:3).

By the end of the Middle Ages the Catholic healing ministry had solidified into its classical form. The traditions of Desert Christianity had produced a double bind on the Catholic. If a Catholic felt he had a ministry of healing, he should not exercise it because it was a threat to his humility. If he exercised it, he was not humble, and therefore his ministry was not valid.

Far safer to a person's humility was healing prayer through the intercession of the saints and Mary. If the saints produced a healing miracle it would not endanger the humility of the petitioner. Unfortunately, as the Protestant critique pointed out, this was both unbiblical and perilously close to spiritualism.[15] Indirect petition through the saints also made it difficult for the Christian to exercise direct faith-expectancy. The prayer of petition, though certainly a valid form of Christian prayer, was not the prayer of faith that Jesus urged upon the disciples (Matt. 17:20).

St. Thomas Aquinas and Christian Materialism[16]

The Catholic theology of healing and how it fit in with the gifts of the Spirit was further complicated by the writings of St. Thomas Aquinas (1224 – 1274). Practically all of Christian theology written before him was based on Platonic or neo-Platonic philosophy (a later and more mystical form of Platonism). Augustine was, for example, a Christian neo-Platonist. These philosophies were idealist insofar as they affirmed supremacy of thought and mind over the material world.

Starting in the ninth century the writings of Aristotle began to be introduced into Christian Europe. Aristotle was the materialist and realist of the ancient world. He assumed that the human mind had no direct effect on matter. He also believed that the only path to reliable knowledge was through the five senses, then through the application of reason to the evidence of the senses. By implication, spiritual experiences do not qualify as reliable knowledge.

Aristotle meticulously applied his theory of knowledge to many areas, such as biology, logic and politics. His writings became a compendium of the scientific knowledge for the ancient world. When Aristotle's writings were rediscovered, they awed the medieval intellectuals and became the rage within the universities because they showed a range and depth of knowledge unknown in Europe. At the same time his materialist viewpoint was rightly seen as a threat to the Christian faith. In a stroke of creative genius, St. Thomas accepted most of Aristotle's philosophical assumptions, modified them and converted them into servants for Catholic theology.

St. Thomas's Christian materialism understood the world as divided between the natural material creation and the supernatural order of God, angels and spirits. It is important to note this vocabulary does not exist in Scripture. There is no Greek phrase for *supernatural.* The Bible recognizes a material and a spiritual dimension of creation, but they are not two creations. In St. Thomas's Christian materialism the interaction between the natural and supernatural was a special event. In the New Testament, interaction between the spiritual and material was as common as praying in tongues, giving a prophetic utterance or laying hands on the ill and praying for healing.

St. Thomas also accepted Aristotle's philosophical realism. He certainly credited God with the power to create and command matter, but he accepted the assumption that the human mind did not directly influence matter. As applied to faith, this view fit medieval Catholic practice perfectly. Petitionary prayer, then, did not depend on the direct faith-expectancy of the believer, but on the intercessory power of the saints and the virgin (who functioned in the supernatural realm). God then intervened and interrupted the material world with a supernatural act.

Within a hundred years of his death, St. Thomas had become the predominant theologian of the Catholic church, and through him Aristotle's materialism was established within Christian theology. This did not have an immediate effect on the church's healing ministry or the gifts of the Spirit because those had been damaged in the previous centuries. Nor did the theology in any way change Catholic prayer practice, even in its more mystical traditions of the religious orders, because St. Thomas recognized these as part of the supernatural aspect of the church. But his teaching rationalized earlier errors into a solid and logically impeccable theology. Ironically, his Christian materialism was to influence Protestant theology more profoundly than it did Catholic practice (see next chapter).

The Catholic Experience Verification

Whatever its faults, and there were many, Catholic theology did resist Augustine's original cessationism. It maintained a belief in the continuous (if rare) manifestation of miracles, healing and the gifts of the Spirit. This was superior to the Protestant position which denied them all (see next chapter). Catholics maintained what might be termed an "experience hermeneutic" in regard to the Bible; that is, there was a cycle of verification between the Bible and experience. Current experiences in the miraculous verified biblical accounts of miracles, and biblical accounts of the miraculous fed expectancy for miracles.

The problem with the Catholic experience hermeneutic lay in the area of discernment.[17] The medieval public believed every story of the miraculous without separating rumor and myth from fact, or psychic energies from truly spiritual events. This mix of myth and authentic miracle is seen, for instance, in St. Bonaventura's *Life of St. Francis*. This biography of the beloved saint records healing miracles performed by St. Francis that are entirely probable side by side with myths, such as sheep coming and kneeling in front of an altar.

Augustine's wise policy of recording the healings of the local congregation was perverted to the public reading of fantastic and exaggerated saints' tales during mass. Among the clergy there developed a sense that the pious believer must have legends and that these must not be disturbed lest their faith in God also be weakened. For the great majority of Catholic clergy discernment was not a high priority. Tragically, this attitude lasted until recent times.

Let me give a personal example. In the 1950s, when in parochial school, I received a second-grade reader about the lives of the saints. Among the saints described was the knight St. George. Pictures and text portray him as slaying the dragon, rescuing the maiden and being a perfect Christian knight.

Obviously, both the writer of that child's book and the bishop who stamped it with his *imprimatur* (declaration of orthodoxy) knew there were no such things as dragons. Yet they felt the tradition of George was "venerable" and good, and so it was presented along with other valid tales of saints' miracles.[*] The nuns did not stop to consider how destructive this mix of myth and truth would be. As we grew older some of us concluded that "not all" the saints' tales were true. By high school there was much cynicism, and by college most of us assumed *none* of the saints' tales was true.

Understandably, Calvin and the Reformers dismissed the reports of saints' miracles as so much superstition. This was unfortunate, for just as the Reformation was gaining strength, groups of Catholic clerics were developing techniques of historical verification and discernment with which to separate myth from valid spiritual phenomena. A start was made by the Benedictine monks during the Middle Ages. Then the Bollandists, a group of Jesuits based in Belgium, made further progress.

Significantly, the Bollandists experienced much opposition from the Catholic hierarchy. They got into trouble for proving that the Carmelite order of nuns was founded in the Middle Ages and not by the prophet Elijah, as the pious myth told. This infuriated the nuns, who then pressed for the dissolution of the Bollandists.[19]

By the time the Bollandists were producing substantial results, Catholic scholarship was being ignored by the intellectuals of Europe. The age of the Enlightenment had arrived, and anti-Christian deists like Voltaire simply used the *critical* half of Bollandists' findings to attack Christianity and to prove that saints' tales were myths. They ignored the other segment of the findings which proved valid spiritual events had continued throughout history.[20]

Protestant theologians considered any Catholic literature as from an enemy and simply ignored the Bollandists' findings. The situation was aggravated as Catholics claimed that the continued miracles performed by their saints proved that the Catholic church was the one true church. Protestant theologians concluded that miracles were impossible among Catholics because of their nonbiblical theology. Both sides missed the mark: Catholic miracles were not a verification of Catholic theology but rather the result of the saint's devotion to God, his prayer life and faith-expectancy that miracles would happen.

The Reformation provided reproof for several serious errors in Catholic theology. At the same time, a brilliant theologian, John Calvin, laid the groundwork for weaknesses in Protestant theology as well.

** Francis Schaeffer rightly notes that children should *never* be given false religious instruction that ultimately will have to be untaught.[18]

SIX

The Reformers Overreact to Catholic Error

Cessationism as Doctrine

WHEN MARTIN LUTHER, AN AUGUSTINIAN monk, nailed his Ninety-Five Theses on the church door in Wittenburg (1517), Catholicism was in a quagmire. Its believers were plagued by ignorance and superstitions, and its theology was wounded by unbiblical traditions. Unfortunately the Reformers' dream of restructuring the church along biblical lines was more difficult than they imagined.

All of the first generation of Reformers were taught Catholic theology as young men. In attempting to mold the new Reformed theology they incorporated the philosophical assumptions of Catholicism, specifically the Christian materialism of Thomas Aquinas.[1] While accepting St. Thomas's philosophical assumptions, they criticized Catholic theology for being overly mystical *and* overly scholastic. They judged it as overly mystical with regard to prayer and pastoral concerns and overly scholastic when it came to basic doctrines (that is, concerned with speculations that were beyond biblical evidence).

In reacting against Catholic scholasticism both Luther and Calvin turned to Augustine for their inspiration and were rewarded by rediscovering Augustine's insights into salvation by grace. Yet they read Augustine selectively and critically. Augustine's general theology was accepted, while his discoveries about healing prayer were rejected as the source of the Catholic abuses they knew so well.

Augustine's early cessationist theology seemed to fit the Reformers' goals of cleansing the church. If healing and the gifts of the Spirit belonged only to the apostolic church, then the corrupt practices of pilgrimages, relic worship and the like were the natural result of attempting to move in the spiritual life without God's grace.

Calvin's Development of Radical Cessationism

Martin Luther was the first of the Reformers to resurrect Augustine's cessationist theory. However, it was John Calvin (1509 – 1564), the great systematic theologian and Protestant leader of Geneva, Switzerland, who converted cessationism from a debatable theory into a basic doctrine.[2] Calvin argued many times in his writings against *any* continued ministry of healing or of the miraculous:

> But that gift of healing, like the rest of the miracles, which the Lord willed to be brought forth for a time, has vanished away in order to make the new preaching of the gospel marvelous forever. Therefore, even if we grant to the full that anointing [for the sick] was a sacrament of those powers which were then administered by the hands of the apostles, it has nothing to do with us, to whom the administering of such powers has not been committed.[3]

As part of his cessationism Calvin ridiculed the Catholic sacrament of extreme unction as a useless, man-invented ritual:

> And for what greater reason do they [the Catholics] make a sacrament out of this unction than out of all the other symbols mentioned to us in Scripture?...Why is not clay made of spittle and dust a sacrament? But the others (they reply) were individual examples, while this was commanded by James. That is, James spoke for that same time when the church still enjoyed such a blessing of God. Indeed, they affirm that the same force is still in their anointing, but we experience otherwise....
>
> James wishes all sick persons to be anointed (James 5:14); these fellows [the Catholic priests] smear with their grease

not the sick but half-dead corpses when they are already drawing their last breath, or (as they say), *in extremis.* If in their sacrament they have a powerful medicine with which to alleviate the agony of diseases, or at least to bring some comfort to the soul, it is cruel of them never to heal in time. James would have the sick man anointed by the elders of the church; these men allow only a priestling as anointer.[4]

In regard to the other gifts of the Spirit, such as prophecy and the gifts of the word of wisdom and knowledge, Calvin was again negative in the absolute. Actually, there is not a single direct statement about the gifts of the Spirit in his *Institutes.* Instead he used the phrase "evident powers" of the Spirit to indicate the original apostolic gifts described in Acts. What he had to say about the cessation of the evident powers is gleaned from his discussion of the Catholic sacrament of confirmation, where a Catholic bishop lays hands on the person for the intention of receiving the gifts of the Spirit:

> If this ministry which the apostles then carried out still remained in the church, the laying on of hands would also have to be kept. But since that grace has ceased to be given, what purpose does the laying on of hands serve?...In what respect, then, will these actors [Catholic bishops] say they are following the apostles? They should have brought it about with the laying on of hands, in order that the evident power of the Holy Spirit might be immediately expressed. This they do not accomplish.[5]

These passages reflect both the truth and tragedy of the Reformation. Calvin's critical observations are true, and today even Catholic theologians would agree with many of them. Yet Calvin could not see past the problem to the Bible's original intention. There is no evidence that Calvin ever attempted a simple laying on of hands or an anointing with oil in faith for healing. He assumed the theology of cessationism to be correct, and from that untested assumption developed his doctrine. That doctrine doomed Protestantism to a long period of healing powerlessness.

Radical Cessationism

Calvin extended cessationism from Augustine's early understanding that healing and miracles were no longer operative to a broader concept that practically no spiritual experiences were proper for the current age. This expansion happened for several reasons. Calvin was anxious that Protestantism not follow the Catholic mystical tradition of spirituality. Like healing prayer, Catholic contemplative prayer had become debased to a point where many monks and nuns were confusing the frequency of spiritual experiences with progress in the spiritual life (similar to the Gnostic acceptance of all spiritual experience as good). Combined with the asceticism of the Desert Fathers this produced a form of spirituality that at times lacked discernment and even common sense.[6] (The anti-gifts theology of St. John of the Cross discussed in chapter 4 was developed partially to combat the same abuses that concerned Calvin.)

At the same time Calvin accepted the contemporary Catholic philosophy pertaining to the mind and soul. This was the Christian materialism of St. Thomas Aquinas which stressed the role of the five physical senses and which we saw as faculties psychology of colonial America (part 1).[7] In deference to Catholic mystical tradition St. Thomas had accepted the spiritual abilities (faculties) of the soul and the "graces of prayer" (Catholic terminology for the gifts of the Spirit).

On the contrary, Calvin felt no need to give legitimacy to the spiritual giftings of individuals or the Catholic understanding of the graces of prayer. Calvin's purposes of discrediting the Catholic mystical tradition were better served by completely denying the spiritual gifts and accepting the five senses and reason as the only reliable way to know truth.

Thus for Calvin the only manner in which one could discern God's will and voice was in the reading of Scripture and through the inner witness of the spirit. In fact, practically the only spiritual experience permitted to Christians by Calvin's cessationism was the experience of being converted. Experiences such as revelatory dreams and visions were reserved for biblical persona only.

By default, the conversion experience became the center of the Christian's life. Witnessing about it became an item of major importance in Calvinist and eventually in evangelical churches. This led in its extreme form to the tragic developments in New England Puritanism, in which church membership became smaller and smaller because conversion testimonies had to fit the mold of the traditional conviction-salvation experience.[8] We have already seen how this led to the halfway covenant of New England theology with which Jonathan Edwards had to contend.

Calvin's expanded cessationism unintentionally destroyed the capacity for spiritual discernment in Reformed Protestantism. That is because discernment implies that some spiritual experiences (visions, prophecies and so forth) can be from the Lord, whereas others may be from demonic or fleshly sources. In Reformed theology no present-day spiritual experiences such as visions or prophecies would be of the Lord, so that such experiences were either delusions (enthusiasm) or entrapments from the devil. One can even further appreciate the originality of Jonathan Edwards, who developed the first Protestant literature on discernment as a by-product of his defense of the Awakening.

The tragedy of Calvin's attempt to reform medieval Catholicism was that in negating Catholic quasi-Gnosticism (the overestimation of spiritual experiences), he fell into quasi-Pharisaism (the premature rejection of most spiritual experiences).

Calvinism as Protestant Scholasticism

Within a hundred years of Luther's break with Catholicism, the Protestant world had fallen into entrenched theological elaborations. Protestant historians call it the era of Protestant scholasticism.[9] Calvinist theologians elaborated cessationism to some surprising conclusions. For one, it was asserted that, after the resurrection of Jesus, demons were banished from the earth. Therefore exorcism, like healing, was a papist superstition and unnecessary in the current age.

Incredibly, some Calvinist theologians also claimed that evangelization among the heathen was also an apostolic gift which ceased after biblical times. This missionary cessationism delayed large-scale missionary activity from the Reformed churches for almost a century and a half. The great evangelical missionary societies which did such tremendous work in the nineteenth and twentieth centuries were formed in the 1800s, *not* in the 1650s or 1700s. It took that long to shake off this most lamentable extension of cessationism.[10]

There were scattered and heroic exceptions to this. Jonathan Edwards, David Brainard and other Puritans ministered to the Indians of America, but in comparison to Catholic efforts the record of orthodox Calvinism on missions is poor prior to the 1850s.

Echoes of this missionary cessationism can even be found in some churches today. When my wife was counseling in a small town in northern Georgia she had a conversation with the local Baptist preacher. He was well read in Calvin's *Institutes*. When she asked him about his church's evangelical outreach he carefully explained that they did none, for that is presuming that man can do God's sovereign work!

Not surprisingly, the process that Catholicism had earlier undergone in changing the meaning of faith from faith-expectancy to faith-doctrine was repeated in Protestantism. By the nineteenth century one of the key phrases in the literature of evangelical Protestantism was "sound doctrine"; that is, the attempt to verify one's position as a Christian by accepting correct creeds. Those believers who did make breakthroughs in spiritual experiences were under suspicion as heretical, such as members of the Pietist movement of Germany.

Faith Without Analogous Experiences

Protestants settled for what might be called a cessationist hermeneutic; they said miracles happened in biblical times, but those miracles can only be verified by the faith in the biblical records, not present-day experiences. This avoided the myth-making of Catholicism (Francis's kneeling sheep and the like) but at a terrible cost. Cessationism robbed Protestants of an important means of biblical verification: analogous spiritual events. Protestant theologians expected the public to believe every miraculous event in the Bible but to reject any present-day evidence for the miraculous as false. This is counter-analogous. It is contrary to the way people normally think, which is from the known to the unknown, and from partial knowledge to fuller knowledge.[11]

Cessationist theologians often justified their counter-analogous hermeneutic by citing Jesus' reproof to Thomas for not believing in His resurrection: "Blessed are they who did not see, and yet believed" (John 20:29). Thomas's "not seeing" was connected to not seeing or believing in miracles for *today*. Thomas's "yet believing" affirmed the cessationists' belief that miracles had occurred at one time. However, Thomas did witness many of Jesus' miracles, including several resuscitations from the dead. Actually Thomas was reproved because he would not *extend* his faith after having much analogous evidence of Christ's power and authority.

The importance of analogies in faith is demonstrated by an article in the *British Medical Journal* by Dr. Rex Gardner, gynecologist and medical missionary. The doctor meticulously researched the writing of Venerable Bede (673 – 735), the monk-historian of the early English church. He compared Bede's reports of healing miracles with similar cases of healing prayer in his own ministry and of other medical missionaries.[12] Gardner found parallels in his own experiences in Africa for healings from severe construction accidents and "hopeless and fatal" diseases found in reports by Bede. On the contemporary mission field, he was also able to get follow-up information and verification for the healings. As a medical doctor his analysis was especially impressive as he could authoritatively declare which healing cases were recoveries outside the realm of natural possibility.

As far as Dr. Gardner could tell from modern verified experiences in healing prayer, nothing in Bede's accounts was improbable or more miraculous than what is ministered through the faith-filled prayers of contemporary Christians. He concluded that modern historians have been biased by materialist assumptions in dividing Bede's work into "good history," such as when Bede recorded the political and social events of this time, and "religious myths," such as when Bede recorded healing miracles within the Anglo-Celtic community.

Dr. Gardner's article is an encouragement to any Christian who reads it. A known healing in the present verifies by analogy an unknown healing in the past. It is all based on analogous verification between events in the past and the present. That type of encouragement and verification is impossible when either biblical events or miracles of the early church are interpreted with the cessationist hermeneutic. Just how damaging the cessationist hermeneutic has been to Christendom will be discussed next.

SEVEN

The Fall of
Christianity in Europe

Cessationism and the Enlightenment

THE DOCTRINE OF CESSATIONISM HAD tragic consequences that are only now coming to light, the most serious of which was the decline and fall of Protestantism in Northern Europe. This happened as the Reformed churches attempted to maintain their faithfulness to the gospel but denied the need for spiritual experiences or miraculous acts (such as healing), even though these were intrinsic to biblical spirituality. Reformed Protestantism eventually became a ghost-like faith because of the lack of support from any analogous experience.[1]

The cessationist hermeneutic made Protestant theology easy prey for Enlightenment intellectuals who were looking for ways of discrediting Christianity and freeing mankind from the "shackles" of revealed religion. A generation of skeptical philosophers and critics exposed the weakness of cessationism by bringing it to its logical conclusion: Since no miracles are observable in the present, none took place in the past.

The Scottish philosopher David Hume (1711 – 1776) summed up decades of anti-miraculous polemics in his famous book, *An Enquiry Concerning Human Understanding*. Hume's discussion of miracles was inferior to, and dependent on, an earlier work written by the Anglican deist and priest Conyers Middleton, *A Free Enquiry into Miraculous*

Powers (1748). However, Hume's book became much more influential.[2]

Hume's *An Enquiry Concerning Human Understanding* was a major turning point in European history. It banished any residual belief in the miraculous from European secular thought. After its publication, intellectuals could not easily or publicly declare belief in miracles.[3]

Hume well understood the importance of analogies in human thought. In his writings he used the logic of analogy in equating the Gospel miracles with the folktales of old, such as those recounted by the ancient Greek historian Herodotus. He had mixed outlandish tales of monsters, omens and the like with valid historical events.

> *It is strange*, a judicious reader is apt to say, upon the perusal of these wonderful historians, *that such prodigious events never happen in our days.* But it is nothing strange, I hope, that men should lie in all ages.[4]

Hume's famous attack on miracles provoked a heated response from Christian intellectuals. Protestant theologians attempted to pick apart his logic. They stressed that observation and experience are not universally truthful, as experience never determines with certainty the whole range of reality. One Christian writer cited the true story of the first Dutch ambassador to Siam to illustrate this point. It seems that the ambassador was recounting Dutch history to the king of Siam when the ambassador told of a winter battle in which soldiers crossed a frozen river. At that point the king, who had never seen ice or snow, became incensed. He shouted that solid water was not possible, concluded that nothing that the ambassador had told him was true and threw him out of court.[5]

It was wonderful that Christians made the point that experience does not determine all truth. But note that Hume's Protestant critics granted him the central assumption that no miracles could be observed in the present. Cessationist theology guaranteed that no observations of miracles would even be attempted by the pious Christian. No analogous evidence, as was in Rex Gardner's article (see previous chapter), could be brought to bear against Hume's argument.

After Hume and other Enlightenment thinkers had challenged Christianity on the miraculous, European Protestantism separated into two camps. One was the theological conservatives (evangelicals) who maintained the cessationist hermeneutic at all cost. The other was that of the liberals, like Friedrich Schleiermacher, who attempted to accommodate the gospel to Hume's logic. Schleiermacher decided that Calvin's acceptance of the miracle accounts in Scripture was improper for enlightened believers, and a more radical method of biblical interpretation developed, the "myth hermeneutic." In this interpretation the miracles in the Bible were seen as fables or myths that had deep meaning but never occurred historically.

The contemporary biblical scholar and theologian Rudolf Bultmann popularized this attitude toward biblical interpretation and called it "demythologizing." But all the elements of it were present in liberal theology a century before he was born. The illogical and circular nature of the myth hermeneutic is seen in Bultmann's attitude to modern healing. When questioned about the public healing ministry of Johann Blumhardt, he called it a "legend" and an "abomination" to Protestantism.[6]

Blumhardt was a German pastor who discovered he had a healing gift in spite of the theology he had been taught. In the 1840s he established a healing house, a place where persons could come for healing prayer. His institution was under close scrutiny by government officials, skeptics and Christians alike. No one denied that many healings took place, though the materialists believed they were only psychosomatic cures.[7] Bultmann illustrated the blindness of the myth hermeneutic when he called this ministry a "legend." Miracles *never* happen; no evidence for miracles in the present will be investigated or entertained, period.

In the course of two centuries liberal theology ran its tragic course of attempting to save the gospel by accommodating to the assumptions of the Enlightenment and became instead a destroyer of biblical faith. Without belief in the miracle accounts in Scripture, the claims of Jesus as Son of God could not be upheld. Yet the New Testament miracles of Jesus were difficult to accept without the analogies of present-day miracles.

Very early the evangelicals rightly saw that accommodating liberal theology to the Enlightenment through the myth hermeneutic was a Trojan horse to biblical faith. However, because evangelical scholars could not and would not point to any contemporary miracles or gifts of the Spirit, their witness against the myth hermeneutic was mostly ineffective. Further, by not dealing convincingly with the serious issues raised by Hume, the evangelicals paid the price of losing the intellectual classes. Evangelicals gradually came to be seen as anti-intellectual and antiscientific.*

---

* There were some notable exceptions, as in the churchmen of the Princeton

By and large the liberals won control of the mainline seminaries, both in Europe and in America. These became faithless institutions controlled by a new class of Sadducees. They had neither faith-expectancy nor faith-doctrine but lived as gentlemen scholars propagating worldly philosophies in the guise of theology.[8] The "death of God" theology of the 1960s, a popular form of demythologizing, was only one of the apostate theologies that formed the faith of mainline seminarians.

In America the case of Andover Seminary is a particularly tragic example of this. Andover was founded in 1807 specifically as an orthodox reaction to liberal and Unitarian inroads at Harvard. The faculty at Andover was forced to subscribe to a statement of orthodoxy as a way of ensuring that liberalism would not sneak in as it had at Harvard. After the 1860s, however, the statement of orthodoxy became less and less effective in stemming the logic of liberal theology and higher biblical criticism (the myth hermeneutic). Eventually Andover became the most liberal of Northern seminaries and was absorbed into its old enemy Harvard.[9] What happened at Andover is a case study of the futility of attempting to maintain orthodoxy in the face of articulate philosophies without analogies to verify the biblical record.

The cessationism-to-faithlessness process was especially dramatic in Europe. It eventually left that continent, once the center of Christianity, in the spiritual darkness of the "post-Christian era."[10] In this post-Christian era, which began in the early twentieth century in Europe, the overwhelming majority of people no longer believe in a personal God. The popular contemporary American Calvinist theologian Dave Hunt (see chapter 21) recently visited Northern Europe and lamented how corrupt and pagan the heartland of the Reformation had become. He had not the slightest clue that the cessationism central to Calvinism and to his own theology had anything to do with Protestant Europe's spiritual decline.[11]

The famous Catholic historian Hilaire Belloc had a better perspective and decades ago commented on the Protestant decline. He correctly ascribed it to the influence of Calvinism (cessationism) on Northern European civilization. In an understandable overstatement he called Calvinism a "failed heresy." His point was that although Calvinism was effective in critiquing Catholicism, it could not by itself maintain the gospel faith.[12]

---

theology who attempted to reconcile science and revelation in the nineteenth century and the work of Francis Schaeffer in our own time.[13]

This is confirmed by what we saw in the Great Awakening. The revivalist party had rejected Calvin's cessationism and affirmed the role of spiritual experiences in the life of the believer. The opposers such as Chauncy (though Arminian in regard to free will) held to Calvin's radical cessationism and won the battle against the Awakening but lost the war of faith less than a generation later as many slid into deism and Unitarianism.

That the cessationism-to-faithlessness process did not go as far or as quickly in America was mostly because of God's grace in pouring on America several waves of revival that followed the pattern of the Great Awakening. America also received large numbers of Quakers, Moravians, Pietists and other non-Calvinist Protestant refugees. These were the very denominations which had an appreciation for the experiential dimension of Christianity and never fully accepted cessationism. Similarly, the Methodists, the most influential denomination of America in the nineteenth century, were an experiential, almost charismatic, denomination until the beginning of the twentieth century.

The Natural Law in Christian Theology[14]

When Christian theology embraces neither the miraculous nor natural law, it no longer has anything to do with this life. It is totally otherworldly. As Christian Europe became secular and then pagan, many of its biblically based beliefs weakened. Among these beliefs were the ideas of natural theology and natural law. Natural theology refers to those things that man knows about God and morality by reason and conscience only (as opposed to biblical revelation). Natural law is made of those moral principles which can be discerned as operating in society beyond and above formal law-giving institutions.

Early Greek philosophers discovered the concept of natural law as the first step of philosophy. For if all the forces of nature are at the capricious pleasure of gods, as is believed in many primitive religions, then no systematic investigation of nature is possible. Early Greek thinkers first sought to understand nature as autonomous and lawful and then went on to distinguish eternal, unchangeable moral rules from those that are man-made and temporary.

By the time of Christ, Stoic philosophers (both Greek and Roman) had developed a sophisticated theory about natural law. Although the boundaries of natural law were fuzzy, customary moral ideas such as respect for elders were considered a part of the natural law. Paul, a master of the Mosaic law, also adopted elements of the Greek concept of natural law at some point of his education. The similarities between certain passages in the letters of Paul and Stoic philosophy are so striking that in the Middle Ages a legend sprang up of correspondence between Paul and Seneca, the great Spanish Stoic.

It is in the letter to the Romans that Paul expressed the idea of natural law and natural theology most clearly. Natural theology is defined by Paul as those ideas placed within man:

> For the wrath of God is revealed from heaven against all...who suppress the truth in unrighteousness, because that which is known about God is evident within them; for God made it evident to them. For since the creation of the world His invisible attributes, His eternal power and divine nature, have been clearly seen, being understood through what has been made....
>
> For when Gentiles who do not have the Law [of Moses] do instinctively the things of the Law...they show the work of the Law written in their hearts, their conscience bearing witness, and their thoughts alternately accusing or else defending them (Rom. 1:18-20; 2:14-15).

Paul's "graced borrowing" of Stoic natural law formed the basis of much of the legal and theological thought of the Middle Ages. St. Thomas Aquinas made natural law and natural theology the centerpiece of his theology. But the highest point of natural theology was reached three hundred years after St. Thomas in the work of a Spanish Jesuit, Francis Suarez (1548 – 1617). Unfortunately, Suarez and other Catholic theologians went far beyond the suggestions of Scripture and pushed both natural law and natural theology beyond reasonableness. It was claimed that practically every Christian doctrine, such as the incarnation, could either be proved or confirmed by natural theology. This seemed pious, but in reality such a theology slighted the role of faith based on Scripture as the foundation of Christianity.

The Death of Natural Law

As long as the Christianity of the day was culturally and politically dominant, the exaggerated concept of natural law could be accepted. However, when European culture turned secular and anti-Christian, the frail logical structure of Catholic natural theology was exposed and ridiculed. Again, David Hume, who had so effectively ridiculed miracles, led the assault on natural theology and natural law. But this time the mortal blow was struck by Immanuel Kant (1724 – 1804), perhaps the greatest philosopher of modern times. Kant was not anti-Christian, as other Enlightenment philosophers were. Rather he had a passion for truth and could not tolerate logical exaggerations.

Kant believed that man's conscience and sense of moral obligations were the greatest proof of God's existence, but beyond that little could be proved of God or of the spiritual world. This was quite reasonable in view of the cessationism that Kant and his contemporaries were taught as orthodox Christian belief.[15] (One wonders what he would have thought of natural theology had he lived to see a Pentecostal healing revival.) In any case Kant's writings did for natural law and natural theology what Hume did for the miraculous; it made them unacceptable to the European educated classes.

Kant's influence on Christian theology worked its way, much like Hume's, from the universities down. Suarez's textbook of natural theology, *Disputationes Metaphysical*, had been influential in both Catholic and Protestant Europe for much of the seventeenth and eighteenth centuries. But after the writings of Hume and Kant natural theology and natural law were steadily abandoned. By the end of the nineteenth century one had to look long and hard for a Protestant theologian who would write about either topic.

Thus the Christian religion was confirmed and sealed as purely an other-worldly doctrine. The educated Protestant, cleric or layperson did not know how to pray for healing, cast out demons or believe for the miraculous intervention of God in his life. The theologians did not have even enough confidence to proclaim any form of natural theology or natural law that related to earth life. The cynics, including Karl Marx, labeled Christianity as "pie in the sky," for it promised heaven but could do no apparent earthly work.

As the Enlightenment drew to a close, European philosophers began the long, futile search for moral anchorage. The philosopher Nietzsche proclaimed at the end of the nineteenth century, "God is dead!" He meant that in the spiritual aridity of cessationism and Christian materialism, most people no longer really believed in God.

Nietzsche gave the most influential analysis of the times. But the major philosophical alternative to Christianity was given by the philosopher G. W. F. Hegel (1770 – 1831) in the form of a counterfeit Holy

Spirit called the "spirit of history." With Hegel's philosophy a person could align himself with the direction of history (that is, correct politics) and fulfill his moral destiny. This gave a sense to the individual that earth life was meaningful and his role important, a perfect counterfeit spirituality. The spirit of history became a substitute for both the guidance of natural law and the experience of the Holy Spirit.

In the twentieth century mankind has suffered grievously from Hegel's counterfeit religion. Hegelian philosophy wed to Nietzschean philosophy led to Fascism and Nazism (the Hegelian right). United to radical economic thought, it produced Marxism (the Hegelian left).[16]

Scottish "Common Sense" Realism[17]

One branch of Protestant theology, centered in Scotland, mightily resisted both Hume's skepticism and, later, Hegel's counterfeit spirit of history. It was based on a philosophical school of thought called "Scottish common sense realism." Scottish realism understood the world to be totally independent and separate from the mind of man, but man's mind could understand it through common sense.

The union of Christian theology to this form of philosophy succeeded in delaying the spread of German demythologizing and Hegelian philosophy in Great Britain and America for almost a century. Through Scottish realism the belief in the miracles of the New Testament were protected. Unfortunately this philosophy also strengthened and justified the theology of cessationism.

Scottish common sense realism (or Scottish realism for short) arose as a philosophical counter to the skepticism of Enlightenment philosophers. Hume, for example, was skeptical not only of miracles, but of ordinary knowledge. A person following Hume's philosophy would be left with the conclusion that *nothing* is known for certain. At the same time another English philosopher (and unlike Hume a sincere Christian), the Anglican bishop George Berkeley (1688 – 1753), developed a radical idealist philosophy which pictured the universe as composed of little more than human and divine thoughts.

For the educated Christian these were confusing times. Unlike our current era, the core education was in philosophy, so what philosophers said became quickly influential in Christendom. The philosophies of Hume and Berkeley left little room for a real world created by God that could be known with any degree of reliability.

Into this chaotic situation came a group of philosophers and educators from the Scottish universities who seemed to restore sanity to knowing and believing. The major figures of Scottish realism did most of their writing in the latter part of the eighteenth century. Although there were several varieties of Scottish realism, most of its adherents had a common set of beliefs.[18]

Because man could understand the material world through common sense, the Scottish realists had great enthusiasm for the natural sciences, such as astronomy and physics, as a way of acquiring solid knowledge. This was tempered by a belief that science, philosophy and all good thinking should be done with a minimum of hypotheses. They believed that general rules, or even scientific laws, should be derived only from clear evidence (empiricism.) The heroes of Scottish realism were in fact two Englishmen, Francis Bacon and Sir Isaac Newton, one considered the founder and the other the great practitioner of scientific thinking.

Scottish realists recognized intuition as legitimate, but the key to solid, reliable knowledge was an empiricism which trusted the five physical senses. Naturally, spiritual experiences were unimportant and deceptive since they did not come through the five physical senses. In this aspect the Scottish realists consciously imitated the philosophy of St. Thomas Aquinas. Scottish realism was both thoroughly materialistic and philosophically realist.

Scottish realism was quickly drafted to the defense of Protestant theology. Theologians could again trust in reason and observation without having to cede to the skepticism of Hume or the fantasies of Berkeley. The reliance on the five senses and the distrust of spiritual experiences fit perfectly the prejudices of evangelical cessationism. The Christian could lead a perfectly normal Protestant life by relying on the five senses, avoiding mystical (spiritual) experiences and using common sense to evaluate sound doctrine. The Christian who lived this way felt that this type of life was both biblical (at least for his dispensation) and in harmony with the latest scientific theology.

Scottish Realism as Consensus Orthodoxy

Scottish realism spread quickly and became part of the consensus orthodoxy of evangelical Protestantism by the 1850s.[19] It was introduced into America when John Witherspoon was called from Scotland to become president of Princeton (1768).[20] He dismissed several idealist teachers (ones who supported Bishop Berkeley) and established Scottish realism as the orthodoxy at Princeton. This was the origin of the Princeton School of theology, which was basically Calvinist, of which Benjamin B. Warfield was the last and most distinguished practitioner. One could say that Princeton theology was Calvinism updated with the language and assumptions of Scottish realism.[21]

From the 1800s well into the 1870s most American seminaries taught some form of Scottish common sense realism as the basis of orthodox theology. Liberal seminaries began incorporating other philosophies (such as in Hegelian idealism) after mid-century, but evangelical seminaries continued with Scottish realism until much later. In fact it might be said that Scottish realism continues to be the undergirding philosophy of many evangelical institutions today.

In spite of its positive points as the tool of evangelical theology, Scottish realism eventually proved to have serious destructive aspects also.[22] Ominously, the earliest founders of Scottish realism had opposed the Great Awakening because the religious experiences that came with revival seemed to have nothing to do with the rational use of the senses.[23] In part 3 we will see that churchmen and theologians schooled in Scottish realism ridiculed and destroyed a new revival which rediscovered the healing ministry of the church. But before we examine that revival we need to see how the Calvinist cessationism went through its last restructuring and became dispensationalism.

EIGHT

The Rise of Dispensationalism

John Darby's Dispensationalism

The Plymouth Brethren

CALVIN'S RADICAL CESSATIONISM REACHED ITS most popular expression in a small but influential evangelical denomination called the Plymouth Brethren. The Brethren were founded in the 1830s in Ireland and England at a time when the established church, the Anglican church, was at a spiritual low point. The church had allowed the growth of abuses such as the renting of church pews, with high prices and status going to the front rows. At the same time many of the clergy were adopting quite a few of the elements of the liberal deist theology which had resulted in Unitarianism in America.

An evangelical wing throughout the Anglican church resisted this spiritual decline. Part of that resistance came from devout Christians in the Dublin area who began a separate Bible study. By 1827 they were celebrating the Lord's supper independently of Anglican services. These initial services were open to persons of different denominations and seen as a sign of the true unity of the body of Christ.

These Bible studies spread and soon became known as the Plymouth Brethren because of their strong presence in that English city. The earliest adherents stressed simplicity of life and disregard for the deep social divisions of contemporary society. A. N. Groves, the founder, was a socially prominent dentist with a substantial income, but he gave it all up to minister to the poor and became a missionary to India.

John N. Darby

The predominant theologian of the Brethren was John Nelson Darby (1800 – 1882).* While attending an Anglican seminary, Darby began to evangelize the poor and ignorant Catholic peasants. He became enraged by the Anglican spiritual insensitivity and brutal social policy which attempted to persecute Catholics into conversion. He separated from Anglicanism and joined the Plymouth Brethren in Dublin.

Darby rejected the theological heritage of the Church of England. As other members of the fellowship had done, he sought inspiration from Calvin. Darby not only became the denomination's most influential theologian, but its most important church planter. By the time of his death in 1882 he had founded more than one thousand Brethren congregations in the British Isles, North America and Europe.

Darby's Theology

Darby's intense study of biblical prophecy led him to several substantial discoveries. He saw that the Old Testament promises of the Jewish kingdom were still unfulfilled and had to be realized before Christ's return. Therefore a new Jewish earthly kingdom would soon be established. He made this prediction a century before the establishment of the state of Israel. Darby's insight helped reverse Christianity's long standing anti-Semitism and prepared many evangelicals throughout the world to support and welcome the state of Israel.

Unfortunately Darby's theology was also shaped by his bitter experiences with the Church of England. His idea of what the "true" church should be was a point-by-point negation of the Anglican church. For him, true Christian fellowship (he did not like the word *church*) was a small gathering, ideally no more than thirty members, who worshipped by the direction of the Spirit. There would be no ordained clergy, no seminaries and little concern for church buildings.

He also believed that the true church would always be a small group of believers, called out of the world and perpetually persecuted. The

---

*   Darby has not fared well at the hand of church historians, Brethren and non-Brethren, in spite of the fact that he was immensely influential in his lifetime.[1]

true church could not be influential in the secular world, such as in politics or social legislation. Its function was to call persons *out* of the world, not to transform the world. Only the church of the antichrist would be large and politically powerful (for example, Anglican, Catholic, Lutheran). He saw the established churches as being so corrupt as to be beyond the possibility of reform and renewal. His famous phrase for the state of the church was "the church in ruins."[*]

It was also Darby's innovation to stress the doctrine of the rapture of the church. This element of Scripture had received insignificant attention before his writings. The rapture fit in with his other theological views perfectly. The true, small and persecuted church would soon be raptured while the apostate church of the antichrist would suffer the coming wrath of God in a period of tribulation (a pretribulation rapture). This eschatology (theology of the end times) was a form of premillennialism.[**]

Darby was so sure of his biblical interpretations that, like the Seventh-Day Adventists of the same era, he ventured to give an exact date for the rapture — 1842. In spite of its nonoccurrence, the pretribulation rapture of the church and premillennialism continued to be central to his theology. This particular eschatology was then considered unorthodox, but today it is the majority opinion among evangelicals.

Dispensationalism

The most significant element of Darby's theology was his elaborate division of the ages of mankind into distinct spiritual eras. In each era, or dispensation (thus the term *dispensationalism*), God dealt with mankind in different ways, and different spiritual principles were in effect. What God expected of man as a means of salvation varied in each dispensation. In this aspect dispensationalism began to experience serious difficulties.

Thus Darby inadvertently reduced the Old Testament to an historical book full of types, prophecies and interesting stories, but a book that had little to do with the believer's life. In fact, only the epistles were relevant to the present-day life of the Christian because according to

---

[*] In this sense Darby was the opposite of William Law (see chapter 21), who trusted that the corrupt churches, including his own Anglican denomination, could be reformed by the Spirit of God into the church of Christ.

[**] In premillennialism the second coming of Christ occurs before the thousand-year reign of Christ on earth. Thus the term *pre-* (or before) the millennium.

Darby, even the Gospels were not applicable for the current dispensation. With this extreme form of dividing Scripture many moral and ethical examples that the Bible provided became irrelevant to the modern Christian's life. Not since the time of the infamous Gnostic heretic Marcion (third century) had the Old Testament been so thoroughly devalued as an ethical guide.[2]

For Darby, as for Calvin before, healing and the spiritual gifts belonged to the dispensation of the apostolic times, and those spiritual powers ended with the death of the last apostle. Significantly, Darby witnessed an outburst of the gifts of the Holy Spirit, including healing, in the Irvingite movement, and judged them to be not of the Lord and not proper for the current age.[3]

The Irvingites, more formally known as the Catholic Apostolic Church, were a Pentecostal denomination founded in the 1830s. They exercised all forms of the gifts described in 1 Corinthians 12 and were promptly branded as enthusiasts and condemned as heretics by contemporary English Christians. In truth, like the French Huguenots of the Great Awakening period, the Irvingites had problems with nondiscerning of prophecy, though not as serious as the Huguenots.[4]

Theology as Paranoia

Although Darby was a man of integrity and simplicity of life, he grew increasingly authoritarian in his theology. He believed himself to be specially anointed by God to interpret Scripture. He formulated a conspiracy theory which claimed that the errors of the "ruined" (established) church were part of a conscious plot to perpetuate heresy and apostasy. Those who disagreed with him were part of the conspiracy and inspired by Satan.* Brethren historians are embarrassed to this day by the force and rancor with which he attacked in writing and sermon other Brethren and evangelical believers for conflicting with him on points of theological interpretation.[5] Thus, although he had a humble demeanor, he lacked the essential Christian virtue of meekness, which implies teachability — and openness — to the views of other Christians.**

---

* Compare Darby's personality with that of the authoritarian cult leaders described so well by Ronald M. Enroth in his *Churches That Abuse* (Grand Rapids, Mich.: Zondervan, 1992).

** See especially how the wise man of Proverbs is linked to acceptance of reproof by the brethren.

The Brethren became divided over the Lord's supper, which originated as a conscious symbol of unity. Increasingly more strict theological tests were placed on the Brethren to allow them into table fellowship. Darby's faction became known as the exclusive Brethren. Darby even excommunicated George Müller because Müller had received members whom Darby did not approve even though they had been examined by several other pastors.[6] Watchman Nee, another one of the Brethren's most famous converts, was excluded from fellowship with the English churches because he dared to break bread with a believer of unknown orthodoxy.[7]

Premillennialism

Darby's concentration on biblical prophecy and his premillennialism profoundly affected the main thrust of Brethren doctrine. Active concern for the poor and dispossessed, so important in early Brethren fellowship, ceased to be the center of Brethren life. Darby's gospel became synonymous with two items: preaching salvation and the nearness of end times. For Darby the end times were so near that evangelization was no longer the chief thing, but the only thing. There was no time for the church to concern itself with social issues or even to teach the disciplines of the Christian life. As one church historian put it, Darbyism became a "truncated gospel."[8]

Widespread evangelical acceptance of Darby's premillennialism had unintended, tragic consequences for the American church.[9] Darby's theology became popular in the 1870s as American evangelicals were undergoing the Modernist controversy. There was dissension between liberal and conservative, Darwin and anti-Darwin factions. Before the Civil War there was a united front of evangelical churches which agreed on the importance of both preaching the gospel and taking Christian social action. For example, the anti-slavery movement and the temperance movement were led by evangelical Christians who assumed that the church should set the goals of society.

Darby viewed that type of social action as futile. The real task of the Christian was evangelization of as many souls as possible before the collapse of society and rapture-tribulation. Because of the intense debate within the American evangelical church over Darwinism and higher biblical criticism, the united front that existed before the Civil War was dismembered. Conservative evangelicals tended to accept Darby's theology and drifted away from social issues. Liberal evangelicals rejected Darby's theology and concentrated on social issues. The liberals did the social action (often without wisdom and with entanglements with radical ideologies), while the conservatives did the evangelization. Few were the churches that did both.

In spite of these unattractive aspects of his theology, Darby's writings and theology became immensely, if not centrally, important in the formation of modern evangelical theology. His frequent trips to the United States made his views very well accepted in many American denominations. Ironically, he felt that his major failure in the United States was that his listeners failed to heed his call to separate from the mainline denominations and form a separate "true" church.

Scofield and Dispensationalism

Darby's system of biblical interpretation became normative to American evangelical circles through his own dynamic leadership and because several important evangelical figures adopted Darby's theology. Among these were Dwight L. Moody, the evangelist, and C. I. Scofield, the editor of the influential Scofield Reference Bible.[10]

Scofield placed Darby's theology in the notes to his famous reference Bible. To many devout Christians the Scofield notes became a sacred Talmud through which Scriptures were discerned. With the Scofield Bible the problems of dispensationalism became plainly manifest. With great logic and precision Scofield identified Jesus' Sermon on the Mount as an address intended to be the ethical guide for the restored-earth kingdom of Israel and implied that it was thus not relevant to the ethical demands of Christians in the present dispensation![11*]

The notes on the book of Ruth are instructive. Scofield calls it a "lovely story," but theologically it is principally a "foreview of the church (Ruth), as the Gentile Bride of Christ..."[12] The believer is *not* encouraged to see the eternal moral principles of Ruth, that Ruth's love for her mother-in-law and covenant with her were an eternal example of righteousness for Jew, Gentile or Christian.

Perhaps more unfortunate was the way in which dispensationalism reinforced the theology of cessationism. Scofield's notes on First Corinthians unfold the tragic story. In the introduction Scofield informs his readers that part of the problem with the Corinthian church was that it

---

*   Please note that the revised Scofield Bible published in 1967 is substantially different from the original published in 1909.

yielded "to a childish delight in the sign gifts, rather than to sober instruction." Further on in a three-part outline to 1 Corinthians 14, Scofield both misunderstands the true role of prophecy, believing it to be a form of preaching, and eliminates the gifts of the Spirit from the modern church.

> (1) The important gift is that of prophecy (v. 1). The N.T. prophet was not merely a preacher, but an inspired preacher, through whom, until the N.T. was written, new revelations suited to the new dispensation were given (1 Cor. 14. 29, 30). (2) Tongues and the sign gifts are to cease, and meantime must be used with restraint, and only if an interpreter be present (vs. 1-19, 27, 28). (3) In the primitive church there was liberty for the ministry of all the gifts which might be present, but for prophecy more especially (vs. 23-26, 31, 39).

Logically, after the formation of the New Testament the liberty to exercise the gifts was withdrawn.

Perhaps second only to liberal demythologizing, the radical dispensationalism of the Darby-Scofield tradition has been one of the most misguided forms of biblical interpretation of modern times. It created difficulties not only in regard to the healing ministry but in many other aspects of Christian life. The unfortunate minister who follows the Darby-Scofield dispensations cannot be sure that sermons from the Old Testament, or even the New Testament before Acts, will have any relevance for his flock. For example, some fundamentalist churches reject any form of instrumental music in church because the New Testament does not specifically authorize such music. The scriptural reproof that the Psalms were written with musical accompaniment was declared as invalid because the Psalms were for an earlier dispensation.

Scripture itself negates the Darby-Scofield form of interpretation, according to 2 Timothy 3:16: "All Scripture is inspired by God and profitable for teaching, for reproof, for correction, for training in righteousness; that the man of God may be adequate, equipped for every good work." Strangely, the reduced scriptural base of the Darby-Scofield theology produces not greater Christian freedom but a curious legalism that is not corrected by the whole counsel of Scripture.

In the next section our look at the working of the Holy Spirit moves into the nineteenth century. We will see how a healing revival flourished despite the damage done by Darby and Scofield's theology.

PART III

Pharisees and Healing
in Victorian America

NINE

Evangelical Healers
of the 1800s

Theological Setting

ALL THROUGH THE NINETEENTH CENTURY the Holy Spirit moved in powerful revivals, challenging the doctrine of cessationism at the very time it was reaching peak influence. Revivals broke out in England, South Africa, India and the United States and brought with them different gifts of the Holy Spirit for all to see. As Jesus promised, the Holy Spirit would "teach you all things, and bring to your remembrance all that I said to you" (John 14:26).

At the beginning of the nineteenth century revivals which demonstrated any of the gifts of the Spirit were labeled as heretical and enthusiastic, as the Irvingites in England were (see the previous chapter). Gradually, however, a theology of the gifts of the Spirit developed on the edges of the mainline denominations. Recent research has demonstrated that by the turn of the century several revival movements within Protestantism were manifesting one or more of the gifts of the Spirit. Writers within these movements developed both a theology of the gifts and an anticipation that they be fully manifest.[1]

One of these pre-Pentecostal revivals was the Holiness movement which had roots in the writings of John Wesley and early Methodism but developed as a general reform movement of American Protestantism. The Holiness movement sought a deeper commitment in the Christian life than was normal to the mainline churches. Another reform and revival movement was "perfectionism" which developed out of the teachings and ministry of evangelist Charles Finney (1792 – 1875). It too sought a deeper understanding and the higher standards of Christian life than those to which evangelicals had become accustomed.

Both movements believed in a second stage of spiritual experience beyond the salvation experience. Wesley called it the second blessing. Finney gave it its biblical term, the baptism of the Holy Spirit. Both movements went against the predominant cessationist theology of limited spiritual experiences, and both produced sporadic outbursts of the gifts of the Spirit. Out of the Perfectionist movement came the most sophisticated theology of the Holy Spirit and the gifts of the Spirit of the era. Specifically, Asa Mahan, friend of Finney and professor at Oberlin College, published a work in 1870 titled *The Baptism of the Holy Spirit*. The book shows that the gifts of the Spirit were already understood in terms of 1 Corinthians 12 and that they involved spiritual knowledge that was *not* dependent on the five senses.[2] This theology consciously opposed the mainline Christian materialism as described in the last chapter.

Phoebe Palmer (1807 – 1874)

But the most important development of Holiness theology came from the writings and ministry of Phoebe Palmer, a Methodist evangelist, writer and magazine editor. Her ministry spanned four decades, and she influenced ninteenth century American Christianity as no other woman did.[3]

Phoebe was born in Manhattan into a well-to-do Methodist household. Her father had been converted by John Wesley's preaching before he had emigrated to America. At age twenty Phoebe married Walter C. Palmer, a physician, whom she deeply loved. Dr. Palmer was also a devout Methodist and lay preacher. The couple began a family immediately.

Tragically, between 1828 and 1836 the Palmers' three children died as infants. The last to die was an angelic little girl who was burned to death when her crib veil was set ablaze by a nearby candle. With each tragic death Phoebe turned closer to the Lord. The death of her third child caused her to go into a period of extended prayer. She sought the Lord's wisdom and direction for the rest of her life. She discerned that the Lord had allowed these tragic events because she had placed her children above God in her heart. She vowed to place no one else above the Lord. On July 26, 1837, while at prayer, thanking the Lord for her beloved husband, Phoebe discerned the voice of the Spirit ask:

"Have you not professedly given up all for Christ? If he who now so truly absorbs your affections were required, would you not shrink from the demand?"

...My impression was, that the Lord was about to take my precious husband from me... And when I said, "Take him who is the supreme object of my earthly affections," I, from that moment felt that I was fully set apart for God, and began to say, "Every tie that has bound me to earth is severed...."[4]

She sensed the Tempter's voice:

"How do you know that God will receive you?" And here I paused, and pondered, *"How* may I know that the Lord *does* receive me?" To this, in gentle whispers, the Spirit replied, "It is written, *I will receive you*" [2 Cor. 6:17, italics added]. "Must I believe it, because it simply stands written, without any other *evidence* than the *Word of God?*" I exclaimed.

In answer to these questionings, the ever-blessed Spirit (given to guide us into all truth) suggested, "Suppose you should hear a voice, speaking in tones of thunder, from heaven, saying, *'I will receive you,'* would you not believe it then?" "I could not help believing it then, because I should have the 'evidence of my senses,'" was my reply.

In a moment I saw the inconsistency of my position, re-membering that I was taught by the Scripture most plainly, and had always known, that the blessing of entire sanctifica-tion was received by *faith,* inasmuch as it stands written, "Sanctify them through Thy truth, Thy *Word is truth*" [John 17:17, italics added].

...My faith was at once put to the test. I had expected that some wonderful manifestation would at once follow as the reward of my faith. But I was shut up to faith — *naked faith in a naked promise.*

Said the adversary tauntingly, "Where now is the great joy that you anticipated? Why do you not, from constraining in-fluences, praise the Lord, as many others do who receive the blessing of a clean heart?"...I began to reason with myself thus: "Do I wait to thank a friend who does me a great favor, till I feel an *impelling* influence to do it? Do I not do it because it is a duty?"[5]

What was most important about her experience was that it modeled a three-part process for sanctification that was to become the core of Holiness theology and practice (termed aptly, "altar theology"). Sanctification, which was defined as victory over all conscious sin, was possible to every Christian regardless of his or her call in life. It did not come through years of discipline and effort. Rather, it came through God's grace appropriated by the following three steps: 1) entire consecration to God (Rom. 12:1-2), 2) acceptance of the promises of sanctification in the Word by faith (2 Cor. 6:17 – 7:1) and 3) confession of the blessing received (Rom. 10:9-10). Critical to the altar theology was Phoebe's understanding that in the spiritual realm, the physical senses and emotions are to be subordinated to God's promises in the Word.

After her prayer experience Phoebe found herself filled with tremendous energy for God's kingdom and even increased love for her husband. What God had required of her, as He did Abraham, was a *willingness* to sacrifice her beloved, not his actual life. She and her husband were to minister together for decades to come, bringing her altar theology to many churches throughout North America and England.

In the Holiness tradition, the Holy Spirit was important in their ministry. A typical Palmer service in the 1860s would begin with a hymn about Pentecost, followed by Dr. Palmer reading Acts 2 and commenting on it. Then Phoebe would urge the congregation to receive by faith the Spirit's "baptism of pure fire" for empowerment in holiness. This was followed by an altar invitation for additional personal prayer and dedication. Last, an opportunity was given for personal witness (confession) by the participants.[6]

Phoebe Palmer's ministry was multifaceted. She wrote many influential books including *The Way of Holiness* (1843), which was reprinted more than fifty times during her lifetime.[7] Her Tuesday night home group became a model for hundreds of others and a focal point for the leadership of the Methodist church in America. She was a leader of the American prayer revival of 1857 – 1859, and of the abolitionist movement. She also helped raise support for the first Methodist missionaries to China.

Holiness influence, including Palmer's altar theology, spread far beyond Methodism to practically every denomination in America. National Holiness conventions drew Christians from almost every denomination in America. William Boardman took Holiness theology, gave it new vocabulary and spread it among a wide range of the evangelical public. The expanded movement was called "Higher Life," and in England, where it influenced the evangelical Anglicans, it was called the "Keswick movement." The new and influential denomination, the Christian and Missionary Alliance, became a center of Holiness teachings.

By the turn of the century the idea of the Christian's victory over sin through the power of the Holy Spirit was not a marginal idea of radical Methodists but a respected evangelical opinion. Ironically, as the theology of Holiness became generally accepted by evangelicals, Holiness advocates found themselves increasingly unwelcome within Methodism. The two decades before the end of the century found Holiness advocates separating, or being ejected, from Methodist churches and founding various Holiness denominations. These churches ultimately became the springboards for the Pentecostal revival in the new century.[8]

Historian Charles White said of Palmer's theological works: "When the Pentecostal and Charismatic movement rose out of the Holiness tradition, they took Phoebe Palmer's theology and added tongues to it."[9] That may be somewhat of an overstatement, because the theology of healing, which we will turn to next had not yet been developed. But her understanding that the promises of God superseded immediate sense evidence was a major step in understanding the dynamics of faith.

Precursors of the Faith-Cure Movement

The first sustained healing revival of modern Christendom occurred in the latter years of the nineteenth century among American evangelicals who were influenced by and interacted with the Holiness, Higher Life and Perfectionist movements. This healing revival had various names, such as the divine healing movement or the evangelical healing movement, but it was known at the time principally as the Faith-Cure movement. I will use this latter name. In this revival, healing was not merely an unexpected by-product of fervent prayer but the result of intended and direct prayer efforts. The leaders of the Faith-Cure movement held an anti-cessationist and biblically literal understanding of faith. They understood faith as the factor which allowed Christians to appropriate biblical promises to specific healing needs in their lives.

The first Christian healing evangelist in America was the uneducated itinerant Methodist (Holiness) minister Ethan O. Allen, who had an active healing ministry from 1846 to his death in the 1880s.[10] Allen's first healing prayer was for himself (around 1845). He had a serious liver ailment for years and felt led by the Lord to pray with two Christian brothers for healing.

> I had been thinking that day how Christ used to heal the sick, and I believed He could heal me if I could only exercise faith enough...I then laid my case of infirmity before the Lord, grasping hold of the Saviour as confidently as if He had been personally present. I told Him about the sickness in my side, and I believed He could help me *then*. I claimed the promise, and in a moment was blessed in a wonderful manner. I knew the Lord had heard my prayer; the evidence was very clear. I began to praise the Lord, exclaiming, "I am healed, I am healed!" But Satan was not far off, and soon attempted to defeat the work. As I started for home a sharp pain commenced in my side, even while I was declaring I was healed. I still held on in faith, declaring I was healed, pain or no pain...I exclaimed: "I have got the evidence, pain or no pain. Begone Satan! Begone pain! It is done! I believe it!" And here all pain and soreness left me, and I was as happy as I could be.[11]

One cannot help but notice how similar Allen's account of healing is to Phoebe Palmer's account of her "day of days." Allen probably had read her widely circulated *The Way of Holiness* and other of her many works. The stages of Allen's healing closely match the stage's of Palmer's insight into sanctification: Allen trusted that God would honor the promises of Scripture in the here and now (anti-cessationism); when his healing began, he gave thanks; when the symptoms of his illness returned, he assumed they were a form of spiritual warfare and rebuked them as such. He trusted the promises of Scripture over what he could immediately physically sense. Had Allen acted with the consensus orthodoxy of his day, he would have accepted the returning symptoms as the *final* reality and perhaps died shortly thereafter.

Allen went on to minister with and encourage others in the Faith-Cure movement, including Dr. Charles Cullis, with whom he formed an enduring friendship.

Dr. Cullis and the Faith Cure Movement

It was Dr. Cullis, a homeopathic physician from Boston, who was the true father of the Faith-Cure movement. He had the administrative ability and commanded the professional respect needed to bring the new Christian healing movement to national attention.

As a homeopathic physician, Dr. Cullis practiced a form of herbal medicine popular in the nineteenth century. Unlike standard doctors and surgeons, the homeopath attempted to assist the natural healing forces of the body with minute doses of highly potent herbs and compounds. Homeopathy began to lose favor in official circles toward the last decades of that century. It is now making a comeback in some states as part of the natural foods movement.[12]

Charles Cullis was born, raised and confirmed an Episcopalian. When he married he was looking forward to a normal life as a prosperous physician. However, his young wife died, and this triggered a spiritual crisis in which he dedicated his entire life and income to the Lord.

His specific ministry unfolded several years later when a sick beggar came to his door seeking help. As was the practice of the day, the beggar had been turned out of the local hospital as incurably ill with tuberculosis, a commonly fatal disease of the nineteenth century. Dr. Cullis felt the Lord's calling to do something about this problem. He had read of the ministry of George Müller who founded the Bristol orphanages on the prayer of faith. Müller raised all the money necessary for the purchase and upkeep of his orphanages totally dependent on prayer and without public solicitation.

Determined to follow the Müller pattern, Dr. Cullis opened a TB refuge in 1864 staffed by two full-time volunteer nurses. The patients were all poor and medically incurable. Cullis visited his patients daily and prescribed medications and treatment. A share of the income from his private practice went to maintain the home. But most of the funds needed came from donors who became aware of his ministry through word of mouth, newspaper coverage or, later, from a yearly financial statement (again, a Müller idea).

The emphasis at the TB refuge was not on healing. Rather the patients were treated medically, given a Christian setting in which to die, and gently evangelized. Many who entered accepted the Lord. But in spite of the emphasis on evangelism and not healing, from the beginning there was a steady stream of inexplicable recoveries. This happened even though healing prayers were not part of the program.

By 1871 Cullis's work had been blessed and had expanded to four TB refuges, a dispensary, an orphanage, a deaconness house (for the nurses), a local church, a publishing house (which published Holiness and Higher Life literature), an evening Bible college and a library. All of these projects were faith works following the Müller pattern, dependent on donations from Christians not only in the Boston area but throughout the United States.

Dr. Cullis's Healing Ministry

By 1870 Dr. Cullis was wrestling with the healing passages of James 5:14-16 and the issue of specific healing prayer. Providentially, he chanced to read a biography of the European healer Dorothea Trudel. This saintly and uneducated woman had established a healing institute in Mannedorf, Switzerland, where patients from all over Europe came for healing prayer. After reading of Trudel's work he dared to offer his first specific healing prayers, done in conjunction with anointing with oil.[13] Within a short time he had witnessed major healings through his prayers, including cancer, TB and other diseases.

In 1873 he visited Mannedorf. Although Trudel had died in 1862 the healing institute was functioning as strongly as ever. Dr. Cullis witnessed the physical healings and the exorcisms of the insane and came back determined to establish a similar healing ministry.

After 1873, prayers for the recovery from illness became a routine part of his TB refuges, and the numbers of healings greatly increased. As his fame as healer grew, persons with different types of diseases came to Dr. Cullis from all over the country.

His normal method was to interview patients, treat them medically and probe the status of their faith. He sometimes directed patients to meditate on James 5:14-16. When he felt the patient had sufficient faith to receive God's healing grace, he would pray for them, at times with oil, or simply with the laying on of hands.[14]

Interestingly, his venture into an open healing ministry cost him much support among his following. His supporters had heard of the Müller work at Bristol and were willing to accept the faith work of refuges, orphanages and the like as a legitimate Christian practice. But many were so influenced by cessationism that they considered this new turn in his ministry as cultic. Although the secular press lauded his work, he began to receive serious opposition from clerical sources.[15] In 1874 Dr. Cullis's friend, W. E. Boardman, published a book about the

TB refuges, picturing Dr. Cullis as another Müller, but prudently left out any mention of healing prayer.[16]

In spite of the opposition Dr. Cullis proceeded with the healing ministry. In 1879 he published a book titled *Faith Cures: or, Answers to Prayer in the Healing of the Sick,* which was issued by the Willard Tract Repository, his own publishing house. The Willard Tract Society published hundreds of thousands of evangelical tracts and dozens of books from the Holiness and Perfectionist traditions. After 1879 the Willard Tract Repository published many of the early books on Christian healing in America and reprinted European books on the subject.

Dr. Cullis's pioneer *Faith Cures* contained a brief commentary on the major healing Scripture verses from the Old and New Testaments, a description of how he entered the healing ministry and a series of testimonial letters of the healing of patients at his refuges. Significantly, Dr. Cullis stated clearly that there was no conflict between faith healing and medical practice and that he constantly used both in his ministry.[17]

This "mixed" view of the efficacy of medication *and* prayer was unusual for its time. He arrived at this position mainly from his own experience as a physician. But another factor was that as a dedicated Episcopalian he was familiar with those extra books of the Old Testament that Catholics hold as inspired but are disregarded by Protestants as apocryphal. The Episcopal view has been that those books are to be honored but not held as Scripture. In two of the books, Ecclesiasticus and especially the Wisdom of Solomon, there are verses which praise doctors and medication as a gift from God:

> Hold the physician in honor, for he is essential to you, and God it was who established his profession...God makes the earth yield healing herbs which the prudent man should not neglect...[God] endows men with the knowledge to glory in his mighty works, through which the doctor eases pain and the druggist prepares his medicines...Then give the doctor his place lest he leave; for you need him too. There are times that give him an advantage, and he too beseeches God that his diagnosis may be correct and his treatment bring about a cure. He who is a sinner toward his Maker will be defiant toward the doctor (Ecclesiasticus 38:1-15, NAB).

These verses have been critically important wherever the healing ministry has taken hold in Anglo-Episcopal or Catholic churches because they short-circuit that false conflict between medicine and faith that has often plagued evangelical Christians.

By 1881 Dr. Cullis was holding weekly healing sessions for the general public. A year later the first general healing home for all illnesses was opened. In the mid-1880s Dr. Cullis began sponsoring summer faith conventions in Framingham, Massachusetts (later at Old Orchard Beach, Maine). These were patterned after Holiness tent meetings and taught healing prayer to thousands. Christian healers from all over the United States and Europe came as guest speakers and participants. The conventions attracted much newspaper coverage, some of it surprisingly favorable. The conventions would end with a general healing service led by Dr. Cullis, who anointed and prayed over hundreds in what is now known as a healing line.

Untimely Death

In 1892 Dr. Cullis died at the age of fifty-nine from overwork, a common fate of many of the pioneers in the healing ministry. In addition to consolidating his healing homes into a large healing institution at Beacon Hill, Boston, he had established a Bible college to teach the prayer of faith and healing to new ministers. Unfortunately, the institution as he founded it did not last many years. It was converted into a general hospital at the beginning of this century.

Dr. Cullis taught many about healing and influenced practically every Christian healer of the next generation. Among those he introduced to the healing ministry were the South African evangelist Andrew Murray and William Boardman, who established an important healing ministry in England.[18] Dr. Cullis's American disciples included Miss Carrie Judd (Montgomery), A. B. Simpson and A. J. Gordon, all of whom were to have distinguished healing ministries.

Dr. Cullis's writings on healing were not prolific but were biblically sound and theologically mature. He knew that the healing ministry was filled with ambiguities, such as the persistence of non-healing among some with the deepest faith. His writings were secondary to his healing ministry and work of administration. Ultimately, his disciples labored to create a more complete theology of healing.

A. J. Gordon: Theologian of Healing

Perhaps the ablest theologian of the Faith-Cure movement was a

Baptist pastor, Adoniram Judson Gordon (1836 – 1895). He is remembered today for his work in missions and as founder of the Boston Missionary Training Institute, known today as Gordon College.[19] Gordon was ordained as a Northern Baptist and spent his life pastoring in the Boston area. He was both an intellectual and an evangelical, taking special delight in reading the literature of the church fathers. His writings on the activity of the Holy Spirit in the church are considered classics and are still in print.[20]

Gordon had been called to the prestigious Clarendon Street Baptist Church and managed to transform this stuffy, sophisticated, upper-class church into one of the most dynamic, evangelical and socially active churches in the nation. At the same time he effectively battled the Unitarianism that was so prevalent in New England. He also brought a major revival to Boston in collaboration with the famous evangelist Dwight L. Moody.

In 1878 a Chinese convert in his congregation introduced Gordon to the healing ministry.[21] Gordon's wide readings of early church literature had already made him open to the possibility of a present-day healing ministry. He then studied at the hand of Dr. Cullis and went on to develop a powerful healing ministry.

Gordon had been influenced by the then-new Brethren theology, especially the Darby views on biblical prophecy and the second coming. Although Gordon accepted the *idea* of dispensations, he did not copy Darby's rigid dispensations nor his cessationism. Gordon also differed from Darby in that he believed that social action, such as feeding and clothing the poor, was as necessary to the church as preaching the good news.

Gordon developed his own dispensational system of five ages: the Adamic, the Jewish, the age of the church (from the New Testament to the present), the future millennium and the final eternal age. This scheme fortunately permitted a healing ministry in the present time, as Darby's dispensational plan did not.[22] Had the healing revival survived to become a major influence on mainline denominations, Gordon's dispensational system might have allowed the Protestants to ease out of cessationism and radical dispensationalism.[23]

By the time Gordon entered the healing ministry in 1880, Mary Baker Eddy and her Christian Science movement were well established in the Boston area and expanding worldwide. Gordon's previous experience as a defender of biblical Christianity against Unitarianism was excellent preparation for his apologetic of Christian healing. Unitarianism resembled biblical Christianity in its externals yet was a serious heresy at its core. Likewise, Christian Science had similarities to the authentic Christian healing yet was a serious (Gnostic) heresy that fell outside biblical Christianity.[24]

Thus Gordon waged a two-front war of apologetic reasoning when he wrote his masterpiece on Christian healing, *The Ministry of Healing: Miracles of Cure in All Ages*.[25] On the one hand he had to counter the consensus orthodoxy of radical cessationism. On the other hand he had to make clear to his readers that Christian healing was not Christian Science.

He accomplished his aim in a forceful display of apologetic reasoning. In the first chapter he outlined the controversy. The key question was whether healing could be for the present age, or whether it was merely of the apostolic past (radical cessationism). In the next two chapters he laid that question to rest by a series of skillful exegeses on the principal verses pertaining to healing. Building on the work of others in the healing movement, he showed how healing and the eternal salvation of the soul were both part of the biblical meaning of salvation. Central to Gordon's argument was the fact that healing was included in Mark 16:15-20 the Great Commission to all believers.

Unfortunately, as Gordon was still working out an accommodation of Darby's dispensationalism, he attempted to separate the gift of healing from the other spiritual gifts mentioned in 1 Corinthians 12. He was uncertain that all the gifts of the Spirit belonged to the present church age. Furthermore, he felt sure that the nature miracles, such as changing water to wine or stilling storms, belonged only to our Lord.

Gordon held to the deep anti-Catholicism common to evangelicals of his day (and present in Dr. Cullis in spite of the similarities between the Episcopal and Roman churches). Because of this he was in a quandary as to what to do with the testimony of Roman Catholic miracles. His solution was to divide the dispensation of the age of the church into different stages. Up to the point where the church was officially sanctioned by the Roman emperor Constantine (A.D. 313), the church was reasonably pure and could perform miracles. Past that point the church descended into the superstitions of the Catholic era, and legitimate miracles ceased. Gordon attributed the healing miracles of the Catholic saints to satanic sources, similar to the spiritualist healing of his day.[26]

For positive evidence of healing Gordon jumped ahead a thousand years to the Reformation and related the healing miracles during intense revivals within certain Protestant denominations such as the Moravians and the Huguenots. He then described the ministries of the modern heroes of the European healing movement, Dorothea Trudel, Johann Blumhardt and Otto Stockmayer. Again, when it came to citing theological opinion, he cited only Protestant theologians, starting with Luther's healing prayer for his friend Philip Melanchthon and going on to the most prominent American Protestant theologian of the nineteenth century, Horace Bushnell, who bravely bucked the radical cessationism of his era in his book *Nature and the Supernatural* (1858).[27]

Gordon's *Ministry of Healing* ended with prophetic insight. Gordon argued that if the healing revival was ignored, the liberal theologians would continue to gain ascendancy and evangelical Christianity would be placed in severe jeopardy. Gordon understood that the long-standing separation between the Bible and experience brought on by radical cessationism was on the verge of overwhelming the mainline denominations as it had in the old Congregationalist church which produced Unitarianism.[28]

Carrie Judd Montgomery

Another important leader in the Faith-Cure movement was Carrie Judd Montgomery (1858 – 1946), a woman whose life and influence spanned three important Christian movements.[29] As a young lady Montgomery wrote a classic on prayer and healing, the *Prayer of Faith,* which served as the main inspirational healing work of the Faith-Cure movement.[30] As a mature woman she helped found and direct the Christian and Missionary Alliance, an important non-cessationist denomination. Later, as a trusted spiritual elder she helped guide the Pentecostal movement through its early, difficult years. Throughout all those years she edited a monthly magazine, *Triumphs of Faith,* which featured Holiness, Higher Life and the Faith-Cure leaders. After 1908, the magazine served to blend the new Pentecostal perspective with the earlier movements.[31] With her husband, George, Montgomery also assisted the Salvation Army in its home missionary efforts and established an orphanage and missionary rest home in Oakland, California, which exists to this day.

Montgomery was born into a faithful Episcopal family in Buffalo, New York. Like her father, she quickly displayed a love for education and talents in writing and poetry. By age fifteen *The Buffalo Courier* was publishing her work. Unfortunately, while attending school for a teaching degree she fell and received a severe blow that injured her nervous system and left her a complete invalid. In the ensuing months all medical efforts failed, and her health declined to the point where the doctors gave up hope for her life.

At this point her father noticed a newspaper article about Mrs. Edward Mix, an African-American Faith-Cure healer who herself had been healed of a fatal illness by Ethan O. Allen, the itinerant Methodist healer. The family wrote for her to come and minister to their daughter, but Mrs. Mix could not come in person. Instead, as was the practice among this first generation of Christian healers, she wrote a letter with detailed instructions explaining that the following week at a given hour she would pray "in faith" for Montgomery's healing. The letter directed Montgomery, her family and prayer group to pray also at the exact same time.

> I want you to pray for yourself, and pray believing and then *act* faith. It makes no difference how you feel, but get right out of bed and begin to walk by faith. Strength will come, disease will depart and you will be made whole. We read in the Gospel, "Thy faith hath made thee whole."[32]

Miraculously Montgomery got up as instructed, though earlier she had been unable even to lift her head. In the following weeks she made a total recovery (February 1879). The doctors were astounded, and her healing became a major news item in the *Buffalo Commercial Advertiser* (20 October 1880).

Montgomery was asked to witness to her healing at local churches, and in spite of her shyness she did so. She also began praying for others with great success. Her witness developed into her classic book, *The Prayer of Faith*. She had for sources her personal experiences, the writings of Holiness teachers on prayer and holiness (including Phoebe Palmer) and the insights of Dr. Cullis's *Faith Cures*. *The Prayer of Faith* was so lucid, encouraging and biblically sound that it immediately propelled her into the leadership of the Faith-Cure movement. In the following decade the book was reprinted many times and translated into several languages. It found wide circulation within Higher Life and other evangelical circles throughout the Protestant world.

The Prayer of Faith

The Prayer of Faith, like so many early healing books, had to establish its position by first arguing against cessationism, which the young author did with vigor and clarity.[33] The bulk of the work was on faith and effective prayer. Chapter 3, "The Nature of Faith," centered on a discussion of Hebrews 11:1, 8-12. She described trusting God beyond the immediate evidence and relying on His promises in the manner of Abraham. She wrote:

> Having faith in God is believing His word without looking at probabilities or possibilities, as humanly viewed; without regarding natural circumstances; without considering any apparent obstacles in the way of His keeping His promises...It is not faith simply to believe when we can see all the workings of Providence; it is faith not to be staggered at any complication of adverse circumstances.[34]

Montgomery believed that the highest demands of faith for the Christian came when physical evidence, such as the ravages of illness, contradicted a promise in Scripture, such as in Jesus' provision for healing.

> I was talking to an invalid about this, not long ago, and she saw instantly how Satan had been deceiving her. "I see!" she exclaimed; "I did not wait for my feelings to believe that Jesus saved me from my *sins,* but I *have* been waiting for my feelings before I would believe that He answered my prayers, and was curing me of *sickness.* When people have asked how I was, I would tell them I was no better, and so I have been making God a liar. I thank Him for this light!"
> We are not, of course, to say that we *feel* better, unless we do, but we may state the fact that we *are* being made whole, on the authority of God's word.[35]

Montgomery's experience with contemporary medical practice was not positive. Two of her sisters died of tuberculosis, and her own painful illness went unhelped in spite of the best medical care available. Her position on medication was that taking it was no sin, but it could *weaken* the faith of the believer. "If I really have faith to accept the promise of healing in James 5:14-15, I shall consider medicine superfluous (to say the least) and my giving it up will be evidence of my faith."[36]

We have not the space to detail the life of this immensely energetic and creative woman. Her marriage to George Montgomery, a successful

California businessman, allowed her to minister in many areas, pay her way around the world to encourage missionaries and continue editing *Triumphs of Faith* without concern about finances.[37] When she died in 1946 she left a legacy of writings and bridgebuilding among denominations that is only now coming into proper perspective.

Antimedical Extremism[38]

In comparison to Gordon, Montgomery and Cullis, many other leaders of the Faith-Cure movement were inferior in theological understanding and maturity. This was often expressed in a radical position which excluded doctors and medication from *any* role in Christian healing. Many of these radical leaders had deep ties with Holiness theology which understood that the baptism of the Holy Spirit took place in an instant, much like a conversion experience. They therefore reasoned that healing prayer was also instantaneous and complete, and any acceptance of medication or medical attention was a failure of faith.

Ethan O. Allen, the pioneer Christian healing evangelist, had taken this position. His influential autobiography and personal witness at healing camps widely spread his opinion of having to make a choice between faith in God's provision for healing and medication.[39]

In 1881 A. B. Simpson, a Presbyterian minister from New York City, was converted to the healing ministry at one of Dr. Cullis's summer conventions at Old Orchard Beach, Maine. When he returned to New York he established a healing home and a weekly healing service. Eventually he became second only to Dr. Cullis as spokesman and leader of the Faith-Cure movement. He made important contributions to the theology of healing, being one of the first to point out the relationship between Christ's atoning act and physical healing. According to Simpson, the healing work of the Messiah had been prophesied in Isaiah 53:4-5 and quoted in the New Testament in Matthew 8:16-17. Simpson wrote:

> Redemption finds its center in the Cross of our Lord Jesus Christ, and there we must look for the fundamental principle of Divine Healing, which rests on the atoning Sacrifice. This necessarily follows from the first principle we have stated. If sickness be the result of the Fall, it must be included in the atonement of Christ which reaches as "far as the curse is found."[40]

Unfortunately he also disparaged medication. In his *Gospel of Healing* he states of healing prayer:

> If that be God's way of healing, then other methods must be man's ways, and there must be some risk in deliberately repudiating the former for the latter...for the trusting and obedient child of God there is the more excellent way which His Word has clearly presented....[41]

John Alexander Dowie

The most extreme of the healers was John Alexander Dowie (1847 – 1907). Dowie was born in Scotland, raised in Australia and received a year of medical education in England. At medical school he was shocked to discover the uncertain and pretentious level of the so-called scientific medicine and was determined to have no part of it. While in England he came under the influence of Edward Irving's church (the Irvingites), the Catholic Apostolic Church, the Pentecostal denomination which taught the present-day reality of the gifts of the Spirit.

Dowie returned to Australia in the midst of a severe epidemic and out of desperation turned to healing prayer. He was greatly successful in this and soon after established a major healing ministry in Australia. He moved to the United States, first to California, then in 1890 to the outskirts of Chicago where he established Zion City. This utopian Christian community mixed radical theology (universal salvation) and populist politics with an antimedical healing ministry. Quite naturally Dowie drew bitter criticism from both clergy and politicians. They tried to close his healing homes and disrupt the progress of Zion City. In spite of this, Zion City prospered. In addition, by 1898 Dowie had established two hundred local congregations all over the United States.

Dowie's personal experience with medicine had been the direct opposite of Dr. Cullis's. For Dowie, doctors and medication were nothing more than licensed quackery. Dowie was not entirely wrong in this opinion.

Nineteenth-Century Medicine

Well past the mid-nineteenth century most "normal" physicians were indeed little more than quacks who used leeching, bloodletting, blistering agents and strong purgatives as medication. Blistering agents such as mustard plasters left scars and were extremely painful. Yet doctors claimed they "drove out fevers." This was termed "heroic medicine," perhaps because of the attitude expected of the patients.

We now understand those remedies as worthless. They had never been scientifically tested but merely passed on as authoritatively correct and given pretentious and mythical justifications at medical schools. A recent medical historian has concluded that until mid-nineteenth century medical textbooks were more destructive than helpful for the patient.[42] Dowie correctly saw the error and hypocrisy in all of this in his medical education. Knowing these facts about the practice of medicine in the nineteenth century helps clarify why many of the otherwise reasonable Christian healers of the era took the antimedication and antiphysician position.

Homeopathic medicine, which Dr. Cullis practiced, was based on herbal medications and, though possibly ineffective, was certainly less destructive than heroic medicine.[43] After mid-century, however, real improvements occurred in medical practice. Quinine was discovered as effective against malaria, and with the discovery of anesthetics improvements in surgery came quickly. After the 1870s, physicians gradually accepted the germ theory of disease, and new truly effective medications were formulated, tested and marketed.

While the Faith-Cure movement flourished, and then declined, most of America's doctors were still practicing heroic medicine. Old practices do not disappear as soon as new theories are publicized.[44] As late as 1890 bloodletting was still widely practiced, especially as a treatment against pneumonia. The doctors in Rochester, New York, who treated Carrie Judd Montgomery had no idea what was causing her neurological problems. They tried several useless medications. In this perspective, the Faith-Cure antimedication stand may have been a valid spiritual *discernment* which later became a *dogma* just at the point when normal medicine was becoming effective.

In any case, Dowie's attack on all doctors enraged the medical establishment and short-circuited any mature understanding of the role of medicine in the healing ministry.

Results of the Antimedical Position

Unlike Dr. Cullis, who attempted to avoid arguments with his critics, Dowie was a caustic and brilliant debater. This made him the target of further attack and continued the cycle of attacks on opposing beliefs. He and Dr. Cullis did share one characteristic: an inability to delegate authority. Dowie's church, the Christian Catholic Church, disintegrated after his death. However, he influenced many of the future leaders of the Pentecostal revival, particularly the theology and ministry of Charles F. Parham, whose Topeka, Kansas, Bible school was to initiate the modern Pentecostal revival.

Reports began reaching the public that missionaries who had accepted the theology of healing were dying in Africa and Asia for not taking normal medications. In 1885 Robert Stanton, a prominent Presbyterian clergyman and noted healing minister and advocate, died of malaria because he refused to take medication. In fact, he died on his way to the first international Christian healing convention held at London, England. Critics of the Christian healing movement made much of this. It seemed that Christian healers were committing the same errors as Christian Scientists.

Unfortunately, after 1892 and the death of Dr. Cullis, the Faith-Cure movement drifted into a consistent antimedical position and was showing other signs of immaturity. It needed reproof and correction in order to become a normal part of mainline evangelical practice.

The Early Debate on the Christian Healing Ministry

Dr. Cullis's faith conventions caught the public eye in 1882 when several important periodicals printed news stories about them. Most of the initial reports were positive. This sparked a four-year debate in the secular and religious press about the pros and cons of the healing ministry.

The debate reached a high point during the years 1883 to 1884 in the pages of the *Presbyterian Review*. The Rev. Robert L. Stanton defended the healing ministry, while the Rev. Marvin R. Vincent took the negative position. It was actually a gentlemanly debate, worthy of the best traditions of the Victorian Age. Stanton presented A. J. Gordon's theology of healing. Vincent's response and critique of the Faith-Cure movement was not an absolute condemnation. Rather he probed and debated the then-new theology with questions that could today be asked of any healing ministry. Vincent strongly disputed the appropriation of the atonement of Christ for physical healing and denied that Matthew 8:16-17 gave any such warrant. He was wary of Gordon's assertion that it was God's will for universal physical healing or that the passage in James 5 was really a command for a general healing ministry.

> Our real quarrel [with Faith-Cure theology] arises on the
> claim that the miraculous energy which accompanied the per-
> sonal ministry of Christ and attached to the Apostolic
> Church, must be a *standing feature* of the Church of the pre-
> sent day.[45]

Vincent pointed out that much healing was due to the power of suggestion that had nothing to do with God's grace. Yet he conceded that
some genuine healing miracles do happen, thus implying that the doctrine of cessationism could be shaken.

Jonathan Edwards would have relished this movement. The healing
ministry had been debated with discernment and had been cautiously
accepted by many. What was needed was a person with the theological
genius and stature of Jonathan Edwards himself to bring the discussion
to a more positive conclusion. Unfortunately, this person did not appear.
After 1884 the argument went increasingly against any form of healing
prayer. Instead of another Jonathan Edwards there appeared on the
scene a person with all of the biting satire, intelligence and prestige of
Charles Chauncy. This man's crushing opposition to the Faith-Cure
movement will be discussed in the following chapter.

TEN

The Healing Revival Destroyed by Victorian Pharisees

Buckley Leads the Attack[1]

WHAT HAPPENED TO THE FAITH-CURE movement after 1885 was another tragic case study in how Christian Pharisaism is able to quench the Spirit. The swing against the Faith-Cure movement was led by James Monroe Buckley (1836 – 1920), the editor of the preeminent Methodist journal *The Christian Advocate*.

At the turn of the century Methodism was the largest Protestant denomination in America. It was considered by all to have a particularly devout membership known for their camp meetings and evangelical work. Ironically, Methodism rose to prominence among American Protestantism by virtue of the very institution that Charles Chauncy so detested, the itinerant preacher. Methodist circuit riders were often little more than partially trained lay evangelists. They followed the westward frontier on horseback to preach the gospel in every settlement and campsite they could reach. None of the other mainline denominations made such determined efforts to reach the often paganized pioneers, and they ultimately paid for their laxity with declining numbers and influence.

James Buckley is now forgotten by all but church historians. In his day he was one of the most influential and honored clerics of American

Protestantism. As a child he suffered from poor health, and by the time he had reached his twenties he had almost died from tuberculosis. The doctors had given up hope of his recovery when he decided to become his own physician. By a regime of deep breathing and long walks he completely recovered from that fatal disease. In spite of observing his doctors' pessimism Buckley held the medical profession in great esteem. In his last years he even initiated the building of the first Methodist hospital in America.

Buckley had ambitions to become a lawyer but instead turned to the ministry. After ordination he pastored several churches in Connecticut and Brooklyn, New York. Becoming a minister did not end his interest in law for he became an expert in church law and a formidable parliamentarian at Methodist conventions and assemblies. He was a gifted debater with a measure of lawyer's reasoning always at work. Buckley also wrote a two-volume history of Methodism which accented the development of its legal and ecclesiastical institutions and all but ignored Methodism's beginnings as a denomination of religious experiences.[2]

From his youth he had been fascinated by the problem of moral evil and mental disorders. As a hobby, he studied what would now be called abnormal psychology and the various cults. His own words give significant insight into the associations he drew from these studies, such as equating spiritualism with effective prayer:

> The abnormalities that interest me are not those of wickedness, but such conditions in general as are "out of fix." Those which I have studied more than any other division of knowledge are such as these: idiocy, imbecility from birth, mental derangements, delusions, hallucinations of the sane, trances, mental or physical epidemics, panics of any kind, and the effects of drugs, drinks, and vegetables in the mind and emotion. To these I add certain diseases and habits which produce abnormalities; also Spiritualism so called, Christian Science so called, Faith Healers so called; in brief, all alleged methods of curing diseases which throw away surgery and medicine entirely, declaring that the "spirits" or the answer to prayer will do.[3]

At thirteen he saw his first hypnotic session, and somewhat later he saw a séance. He saw the Seventh-Day Adventists in their period of prophetic expectancy of the second coming and even witnessed a group of

Millerites attempt to raise a dead person through prayer.[4] The Millerites were the precursors of the Adventists, and some of them experimented with the healing ministry. From these experiences Buckley drew the conclusion that any deviation from normative theology was equivalent to cultism.

In 1880 he was called to be the editor of one of the most influential Christian publications of his day, the Methodist *The Christian Advocate*. He retained that editorial position for thirty-two years until his retirement in 1912. These were critical years for American Methodism because the Faith-Cure movement and the Pentecostal revival broke out at that time. Buckley vigorously opposed both. He played a key role in turning the Methodist denomination away from healing and Pentecostalism at a time when Methodism was a hair's breadth away from being the first mainline denomination to embrace both. Many Methodists were participants in the Holiness revival, and in the decades from the 1880s to 1910 many of these persons joined the Faith-Cure movement or later became Pentecostal. Sadly, they could not move the whole denomination to that persuasion, though not for lack of trying.*

Among the things Buckley opposed was the recovery of the ministry of exorcism, which was being rediscovered by Protestant missionaries and given wide, if fleeting, publicity with the publication of John Nevius's *Demon Possession and Allied Themes*.[6] The Rev. Nevius was an outstanding Christian missionary who had experience with the ministry of exorcism. Buckley, not unlike a humanistic psychologist of today, asserted that Nevius had paid insufficient attention to medical and psychological dimensions of the possession phenomenon and that he therefore had drawn false conclusions.[7] All in all, Buckley wanted to steer the Methodists away from experience-oriented Wesleyan theology and toward Calvinist cessationism.

Buckley's Attack on the Faith-Cure Movement

Throughout his life Buckley maintained an uncomplicated and consistent theological orientation. He was an unyielding conservative in both politics and theology. He strongly opposed giving women the right to vote or any role in church ministry.** He was a convinced cessationist

---

* What the history of American Christianity would have been like if Methodism had become a Pentecostal denomination in the 1890s can only be imagined.[5]

** One of Buckley's admirers wrote, "He was a conservative in his theological

and materialist, essentially reworking Calvin's radical cessationism in terms of nineteenth-century materialism. He believed that valid spiritual experiences took place only in Bible times and that phenomena such as dreams or visions had naturalistic explanations.[9]

Buckley battled the healing revival all through the 1880s with his personally written lead articles in *The Christian Advocate*. In 1886 his writings on the subject were brought together, combined with his articles on the cults and published as *Faith-Healing, Christian Science and Kindred Phenomena*. A brief look at the table of contents reveals his assumptions. All spiritual phenomena (ironically including many of the experiences of John Wesley) were lumped together as deviant and dangerous to the Christian's life. Faith-Cure was ranked with astrology and divination; visions were equated with witchcraft. Although he considered some classes of phenomena as natural, such as dreaming, even these could be dangerous for the Christian if taken as spiritually significant.

The major portion of this book was dedicated to the issue of non-medical healing: Christian Scientist, evangelical, spiritualist and so forth. He saw Christian Science as a charlatan religion that had the capacity of raising expectations with little else. His analysis of the Faith-Cure movement was more circumspect. He began his argument by granting that the healers occasionally did in fact heal people. He insisted, however, that most of the healings produced were psychosomatic in nature, that is, the product of suggestion rather than grace. He also suggested that doctors often misdiagnose toward the more serious, confusing a minor ailment for a more serious one. Thus, many healings are relatively minor or merely the product of the body's natural ability to become well again (as in his experience with tuberculosis).

In another work Buckley granted the possibility that some healings are indeed beyond the psychosomatic and involve true healing miracles.[10] This seems generous to the healing movement, but his admission is mixed with an argument that made it of negative value for the Protestant reader. He claimed evangelical healers had the same rate of true, nonpsychosomatic healing as the Christian Scientists or the famous Catholic healing shrine in Lourdes, France. Thus the healing done by the evangelical healers would not have been singularly Christian nor necessarily due to God's power.

This led Buckley to the heart of his argument against Christian healing

------

position,...and he was conservative in resisting innovation."[8]

and his reaffirmation of cessationism. Buckley believed he detected major differences between contemporary Christian healers and the ministry of Jesus or His apostles. Specifically, the evangelicals could not match Jesus' ministry in regard to raising the dead or restoring amputated limbs. Further, Buckley claimed that Jesus healed *all* who came to him, not just a few. This last point was flatly in error, as Jesus' ministry in Nazarath failed because of the "unbelief" of that town's populace (Matt. 13:58).

On this issue A. J. Gordon had earlier noted that the general faith level of Americans was insufficient for miracles of limb restoration or resuscitation, but Buckley seemed to have the better of the argument. Modern observations, though, verify Gordon's hypothesis. The greatest miracles of healing routinely take place in the Third World where charismatic evangelists such as Reinhard Bonnke can minister apostolic miracles at camp meetings of hundreds of thousands of persons.[11]

Buckley added a moral argument against the Christian healing ministry. He believed that turning to healing prayer would produce an effeminate Christian, that is, one who was morally weakened by a refusal to accept pain and suffering.[12] Ironically, this is nothing more than a reformulation of the old Roman Catholic position of redemptive suffering which he claimed to disdain.

Buckley skillfully focused his criticism of the evangelical healers on the radical, antimedicine wing of the movement. The careful reader notes he did not cite Dr. Cullis, father of the movement, on the practice of a ministry of combined prayer and medicine. Rather he repeatedly called attention to the cases of Christians dying for lack of proper medical care. In this regard, much of his literary output was spent on assaulting Dowie and his Zion City ministry.[13]

Buckley concluded that there was no distinction between one healer and another — evangelical, ancient pagan or modern Christian Scientist. They all worked through mental suggestion to heal (mostly) psychosomatic disorders. Buckley refused to deal with the obvious question of how nonpsychosomatic healings took place.

Buckley's writings on the healing issue were like lawyers' briefs; that is, he presented his conservative theology like a client's rights. Unlike Vincent's debate with Stanton, the truth or strong points of the opposition were ignored, and its faults were stressed. This makes for an excellent courtroom presentation, but it is a poor vehicle for achieving truth.

Although it is not immediately obvious, Buckley's method of argumentation had a deeper, tragic failure. Buckley, who was also an historian of

American revivals, was well informed on, agreed with and even wrote articles on Jonathan Edwards's view of evaluating revivals.[14] But what Buckley did in his writings on healing is precisely what Edwards warned against — he judged the entire movement by its extremes and avoided looking at its overall effect.

The Holy Spirit Quenched

Buckley's books and articles proved most effective in turning the tide against the Faith-Cure movement. From our perspective we can see that his arguments were deeply flawed, but given the theological assumptions of the nineteenth century they were impressive. Any minister who was suspicious of the healing movement could cite Buckley and rehearse his arguments to the curious Christian in his congregation. Even the careful reader who noticed that Buckley admitted occasional valid healing would dismiss the whole issue as capricious and dangerous to sound theology.

Mostly because of the assaults from Buckley and his colleagues, the Faith-Cure movement fell apart and scattered by the mid-1890s. The best leaders had passed away. There was no trained theologian of the stature of Jonathan Edwards to interpret the revival to the public. A few of the leaders, like Carrie Judd Montgomery, went on with their own healing ministries. In time they melded into the Pentecostal revival that was to come at the turn of the century. She and several others passed on to the Pentecostals beliefs that were most original to the Faith-Cure theology, such as Christ's atonement including the healing of the body, and the importance of the prayer of faith.[15]

Unfortunately, the antimedical theology also crossed over into Pentecostalism. One of the leaders of the Faith-Cure movement, Rev. R. Kelso Carter, offered an intriguing critique of the movement twenty years after its inception. In 1897 he published a book titled *"Faith Healing" Reviewed After Twenty Years.*[16] By then the Faith-Cure movement had been marginalized, and the coming Pentecostal revival was a decade away. Carter had been healed by Dr. Cullis in 1879 and had been associated with the Faith-Cure movement from that time. Although holding to the reality of healing prayer and citing many examples, he criticized many of the leaders of the movement for holding extremist views. He disagreed with associating healing directly with the atonement and was especially critical towards Dowie.

In a disarmingly honest account, he related how he had tried to overcome a bothersome illness with faith alone. It persisted for years until he took medication.[17] This caused him to reconsider the faith-versus-medication issue and to affirm both prayer *and* medication. It was the turn of the century, and the old medical quackery was undergoing its rapid transformation into modern medicine. From our perspective we can appreciate the prophetic nature of Carter's book. But the remnant Faith-Cure movement did not fully understand it, and the orthodox Protestant establishment had already written off the Faith-Cure movement as cultic.

Some of the writings of the Faith-Cure healers remained as underground classics, ignored by the theological establishment but read when Christians sought information about the healing ministry. This is especially true of A. J. Gordon's *The Ministry of Healing*. Even secondary writers of the revival such as T. J. McCrossan, whose writings were discovered by Kenneth Hagin and passed on to the present generation, had lasting if indirect influence.[18] Others from the healing revival retreated into orthodoxy, accepting fellowship and conventionality rather than risk being labeled as cultish.

Perhaps the greatest tragedy of the demise of the Faith-Cure movement was that it prepared the way for the rejection of the Pentecostal revival of the 1900s. The theological arguments that Buckley and others had honed against the gift of healing were easily modified to attack the gift of tongues and the other gifts of the Spirit that manifested in the Pentecostal revival.[19]

Benjamin B. Warfield's *Counterfeit Miracles*

How the arguments which defeated the Faith-Cure movement were repeated and expanded against the Pentecostals of the 1900s can best be seen in the crowning work of cessationism, *Counterfeit Miracles*, written by Benjamin B. Warfield (1851 – 1921).[20] Warfield stands as one of the preeminent theologians of the nineteenth century. He had the distinction of being the last advocate of the Calvinist Princeton theology which extended back to the foundations of Princeton University.

The Princeton theologians developed the doctrine of biblical inerrancy as a response to the myth interpretation of European theology. Unlike the later fundamentalists, the Princeton theologians encouraged scientific investigation and felt that true science would never be in conflict with biblical truth.[21]

Warfield taught more than twenty-seven hundred ministry students in his long career at Princeton and was editor of the prestigious *Princeton Theological Review*. More so than Buckley, his opinions were viewed by most evangelicals as the authoritative word from orthodoxy. In an age when liberal theology was sweeping the mainline seminaries, he was proud to declare that his theological base was rooted both in Calvin and the seventeenth-century Calvinist theologians.

Counterfeit Miracles became the definitive statement of cessationism, cited to this day by fundamentalists.[22] In that work Warfield unconditionally reasserted that healings, exorcisms and the gifts of the Spirit ceased after the death of the last apostle. Flying in the face of evidence, he affirmed that the documents from the early church did not prove that miracles continued for the first three centuries. He dismissed the evidence for that as an incorrect theory of the English church which he disdained (that is, the scholars such as F. W. Puller, Percy Dearmer and others of the Anglican church who pioneered an orthodox sacramental theology of healing at the turn of the century).[23]

In contrast, he presented the rather strange theory that only after the fourth century, with the formation of the Roman Catholic church, did miracles and the miraculous again become important in church life. Warfield believed that the Catholic miracles of the Middle Ages had their roots in the pagan wonder-tales of antiquity and were either myths or healings that resulted from the power of suggestion.[24]

He was especially critical of Augustine's description of the healing miracles in the *City of God* and took an entire chapter to ridicule the healing ministry of the Catholic church.[25] Taking Calvin's suspicion about exorcism to the extreme point reached by seventeenth-century Calvinist theologians, Warfield asserted that, with the establishment of the church, demons were banished from the earth, and therefore demonic possession was impossible. Thus the Catholic rite of exorcism was nothing but a regression to paganism. Significantly, to buttress this position he quoted the extreme liberal theologian Alfred von Harnack.

> Accordingly, as Harnack points out, "from Justin downwards, Christian literature is crowded with allusions of exorcisms, and every large church, at any rate, had exorcists" (p. 162). But this is no proof that miracles were wrought, except the great miracle, that in its struggle against the deeply rooted and absolutely pervasive superstition "the whole world and the circumbient atmosphere," says Harnack (p. 161), were filled with devils; not merely idolatry...Christianity

won, and expelled the demons not only from the tortured individuals whose imagination was held captive by them, but
from the life of the people, and from the world.[26]

After discrediting the Catholic tradition of healing and exorcism,
Warfield turned his attention to the Protestant faith healers. He began
with a lengthy, negative description of the Rev. Edward Irving's Catholic Apostolic Church, a Pentecostal church in England in the 1830s.[27]
Warfield described in detail the emotional outbursts that often took
place at that church as the people worshipped with the gifts of the Spirit.
His Victorian readership needed little persuasion to believe that such
emotionalism had nothing to do with the Holy Spirit. Indeed he stated
that the claimed manifestations of the gifts of the Spirit were nothing
more than hysteria and suggestion.[28] In discrediting the Irvingites, Warfield also had in mind the contemporary Pentecostals, who were already
being called holy rollers by mainline Christians.

Warfield dedicated chapter 5 of *Counterfeit Miracles* to a specific
critique of the Faith-Cure movement.[29] He began by describing the
then-growing movement of "healing homes" that had spread from
Europe to England and the United States (as in Dr. Cullis's tuberculosis refuges). Like Buckley, Warfield took the materialist-realist interpretation and credited whatever healing took place in these homes
to the body's natural ability to recover, and to the superior care, rest
and good food that the patients received at the establishments. According to Warfield healing prayer had nothing to do with their recovery
other than adding an element of mental suggestion![30]

Warfield went on to critique the healing theology of A. J. Gordon. In this
he was a better scholar than Buckley, who had focused on the radical writers of the healing revival. Warfield criticized Gordon for making too much
of James 5:14, where believers are told to anoint the sick with oil and pray
for healing. Warfield suggested that this verse was intended merely as a
general command for the church to pray and to use normal means of healing (medicine) within the fellowship of Christians. Certainly it was not a
specific command to use oil or lay on hands for healing!

What James requires of us is merely that we should be Christians in our sickness as in our health, and that our dependence
then, too, shall be on the Lord...The resources of civilization
are ours, and we use them to the utmost...It is God, however,
the real physician, who gives the chief medicine; who makes

drugs, operations, kindness, nursing to have true healing power....[31]

Further, Warfield reasoned that at the resurrection all Christians will be given perfect, glorified bodies which will be healed in an absolute way. However, to seek bodily healing for today was presumptuous.[32]

Warfield based his central argument against healing and the other gifts of the Holy Spirit on a reaffirmation of cessationism. (The gifts of the Spirit were a public issue due to the Pentecostal revival.) He attempted to prove that the gifts were always and only transmitted by the apostles by citing the events in Acts 8:4-24, where Philip evangelized Samaria. In that incident the converts did not receive the gifts of the Holy Spirit when baptized by Philip. Only after the apostles came up from Jerusalem and laid hands on them did they receive the gifts. Warfield concluded that the imparting of the gifts could only be done by an apostle. He cited Calvin to buttress this interpretation.[33]

From our perspective, a better interpretation of the passage would be that Philip did not understand the full process of baptism, as in using the name of Jesus only and not the full trinitarian formula for baptism (Acts 8:12). Thus he also did not know he should lay hands on the new converts. This was the church's first missionary expedition after Pentecost, and mistakes were likely. Ironically, Calvin saw this very point.[34]

Warfield's interpretation showed the weakness of the hermeneutics of consensus orthodoxy. He believed himself to be the defender of biblical truth but in fact merely asserted a specific tradition (Talmud). The only verification Warfield saw as worthwhile for his interpretation was comparing his view to Calvinist theology. Warfield did not test his interpretation by comparing it with the documentary evidence of the early church (which he had already ruled as irrelevant). Nor would he consider the experiences of the living believers, no matter how much good they produced in terms of increased devotion, faith, love and so on. It was a circular entrapment, much like Charles Chauncy's, in which the assumptions of consensus orthodoxy validated his present theology.[35]

Healing as Heresy

By the time Buckley and Warfield had finished their critiques of the Faith-Cure movement, healing had been declared a heresy and an illusion. Those who strongly held to healing prayer were heretics, and the religious communities to which they belonged were not really part of the Christian church at all but cults. Therefore they were not to be studied or valued as part of the kingdom of God. Rather any attention given to them would be of the curiosity nature, as in sociology professor's examining the ritual of snake handling.

Thus the Pentecostal and the surviving Christian healing movements, such as the CFOs (the Camps Farthest Out, a summer retreat begun in the 1930s), were written off the sweep of American Christian history and relegated to the category of cult and curiosity.[36] This is demonstrated in the work of two prominent Christian scholars, William Warren Sweet and Elmer T. Clark.

Sweet became dean at the divinity school of the University of Chicago and attracted an excellent faculty of church historians who wrote volumes of what became the accepted version of American Protestant history.

Sweet published the first edition of his influential *The Story of Religion in America* in 1930, which continued to be reissued and reedited for thirty years. In Sweet's vision, mainline Protestant Christianity was the Christianity of America. He paid attention to the fundamentalist-versus-liberal debates, church expansion and missionary activities of the Protestant churches. But neither the American Lutherans nor the Roman Catholics received much coverage in spite of their large numbers. The Pentecostals received no notice, and, similarly, the Faith-Cure movement was not mentioned.

Paul Chappell, who wrote a dissertation on the Faith-Cure movement, or, as he termed it, the divine healing movement, noted in 1983:

> Divine healing has been one of the most fascinating, yet controversial themes to develop in the modern history and theology of the American Church. It has also been one of the few significant developments in the American Church which has remained almost completely unexamined by Church historians.[37]

The other side of the coin is shown in the classic work by Elmer T. Clark, *The Small Sects in America*, which served for decades as the standard study of the cults in America.[38] There among the Jehovah's Witnesses, the Mormons and other true cults were the Pentecostals. In Clark's view the gifts of the Spirit and healing were "of a nervous or emotional character."[39] So the judgment remained until well into the 1960s for most mainline Christians.

The general outline of the Faith-Cure movement remained unknown to many church history professors until the 1980s. It was only through a pioneer article in *Church History* by Catholic historian Raymond Cunningham that the movement was rediscovered in the 1970s.[40] Subsequently several dissertations and articles have expanded our knowledge of this revival. A book on the history of the Faith-Cure movement has yet to be written.

The story of the Faith-Cure movement has many tragedies. There was the tragedy of the mainline churches choosing consensus theology (Talmud) over Scripture (Torah) and tradition over the way of the Holy Spirit. The spirit of Pharisaism won. There was tragedy for the churchmen involved in opposing this movement. Both Buckley and Warfield were fine churchmen who sincerely wished the best for the church. Yet they dramatically missed the mark in what the Holy Spirit was attempting to accomplish through the revivalists, and they descended into Pharisaism.

The greatest tragedy of all was that of missed opportunities for American Christendom, which could have reaped a great harvest of healing, renewed Pentecost and power in prayer. Instead a hailstorm of cessationism and materialist-realism destroyed the crop just as it was ripening. Only gleanings were left for others to pick up.

SUMMARY OF CONTENTS THUS FAR

IN PART 3 WE SAW HOW a great healing revival came to the American church, flowered and was destroyed. The revival produced the pioneer literature of healing prayer and ministered healing to thousands. However, there were areas of extremism and immaturity in its theology. Yet from the perspective of a hundred years removed one can unequivocally say God moved powerfully in spite of the revivals' rough edges.

Had theologians of the consensus theology (Talmud) followed the insights of Jonathan Edwards and attended to the plain understanding of Scripture (Torah), the healing movement might have been reproved, then might have survived and begun a general revival of American Christendom. Instead, a spirit of Pharisaism triumphed. Healing was declared to be heretical and cultish, and the accomplishments of the revival hidden for a century.

By rejecting the Faith-Cure movement the mainline churches cut themselves off from the analogous evidence that could verify the biblical witness. As A. J. Gordon had prophesied, the mainline churches slid into deeper levels of apostasy in the form of liberalism and demythologizing (discrediting the miracles of Jesus and the apostles).

As we look at Christianity in the Victorian era we can see that its theology resembled a gilded cave (to modify Plato's famous story). Plato told a parable in his *Republic* about a race of men who spent all their lives in deep caves. Their only light was from fire, though they had heard but not believed the rumor of the sun. Similarly most Victorian Christians lived all their lives without experiencing the touch of healing prayer or the gifts of the Spirit. They only had rumors of the former miracle power. Many disbelieved the rumors. Certainly individual Christians often lived in great holiness and prayed effectively. Such heroes as Hudson Taylor of the China Inland Mission achieved magnificent things for the kingdom. Those achievements were not accomplished with the help of consensus theology but in spite of it.

Thankfully both the Catholics and the evangelical Protestants held on to the orthodox Christology that had been painfully established in the church's first centuries. But from a biblical perspective even the best of Protestant and Catholic thought was "wounded theology." It had little or nothing to say to the ordinary believer about the prayer of faith, healing prayer or the gifts of the Spirit. These shortcomings severely limited what the Christian could accomplish individually or what the church could do corporately. Significantly, Europe slid into nominal Christianity and then into the post-Christian era as it lost its heart and soul to anti-Christian philosophies.

Christendom's wounded theology came from centuries of mistaken theology and philosophy. The Catholic church had entertained cessationism, rejected it but then developed a prayer theology of indirect petition to the saints that bore no resemblance to biblical models. Protestantism rejected the whole system of indirect petitions but elevated cessationism to a central doctrine. As a result, few Protestants prayed for healing or anything that demanded a miracle to accomplish.

With John Darby and the Scofield Bible, cessationism was elaborated into the popular doctrine of dispensationalism. Dispensationalism focused the believers' faith toward the millennium and away from the everyday ministries of intercessory prayer and actions for the healing of society or the individual. Among the mainline churches, such as the Presbyterians and Methodists, dispensationalism did not make major inroads. But in those denominations the theology of cessationism continued to hold sway and often took the demythologizing twist.

In Western Christendom, both Protestant and Catholic, the consensus orthodoxies were undergirded by various forms of materialist and realist philosophies. The groups differed in the degree to which they were aware of their philosophical underpinnings. They varied from the meticulously refined theology of Thomas Aquinas, which continued in Catholic universities until the 1960s, to the theology of John Darby, who was relatively unaware of his philosophical assumptions. In between were the mainline denominations where Scottish realism became the normative philosophy and an integral part of consensus orthodoxy.

The destruction of the evangelical Faith-Cure movement indicated that the philosophical-theological assumptions of consensus orthodoxy had indeed become a gilded cave immune to all biblical evidence, personal witness or logical reasoning. The leaders of the revival, Dr. Cullis and A. J. Gordon, were true prophets of their age, but their message went unheeded.

Yet the Holy Spirit would not be stopped in His task of reminding the church of the words of Jesus. If the church would not listen to its prophets, it would have to suffer the humiliation of learning from heretics and heathen. To that we will turn in part 4. Chapters 11 and 12 focus on scientific discovery — an excellent example of revelation coming through heathen. Specifically, principles discovered through quantum physics would break down the realist-materialist view of the universe that denied the power of prayer. Chapters 13 and 14 discuss the metaphysical cults used in reviving the church's interest in healing prayer. The last four chapters of part 4 explore the origins of prosperity teaching, spiritual laws, visualization and faith-idealism.

PART IV

From Quantum Physics to Faith

ELEVEN

Materialism Versus the Real World

Introduction

PART 3 SHOWED HOW MAINLINE theologians, burdened with the theology of cessationism and the philosophy of Christian materialism, discredited the Faith-Cure movement. Christian materialism and cessationism had merged in the Reformation and were enthroned as the consensus orthodoxy of Protestantism. The realist element of Christian materialism was reinforced by Scottish realism to the extent that mainline Protestant theologians assumed that any deviation from a realist perspective was tantamount to heresy.

This section will suggest that, contrary to the consensus assumptions of mainline theology, some form of moderate Christian idealism is a better way of understanding the world than is radical materialism. By Christian idealism we mean a viewpoint which understands that thoughts and words influence the natural world to some degree. At the same time it is understood that the universe and the material order are God-created and stable. With Christian idealism the believer is freed to exercise his faith in imitation of the biblical patterns of faith and prayer without regard to the restrictions of cessationism. Further, the hermeneutic of Christian idealism opens the biblical text to a greater depth of understanding.

The argument for moderate Christian idealism is not merely utilitarian.

Rather it has become increasingly clear from discoveries in modern science that the universe was created and continues to operate as some form of idealist system. That is, matter at its most fundamental level does not act according to realist-materialist assumptions. Unlike in other ages, when the idealist-realist controversy was purely an argument of philosophical preference, in our age the weight of science is now heavily shifted toward idealism.

Understanding the implication of modern science will place us in a position to appreciate the role of heresy in the nineteenth-century cults. These cults, especially Christian Science and New Thought, were essentially idealist cults with an exaggerated notion of the power of mind over matter. In interaction with these idealist cults, graced individuals such as E. W. Kenyon and Agnes Sanford were able to create a moderate Christian idealism which understood the biblical pattern of faith and the gifts of the Spirit yet avoided the exaggerations and Gnostic doctrines of the cults.

In this chapter we will first outline how and why science came to an idealist appreciation of the universe (quantum physics), then show how mainline Christian theologians have recently begun to appropriate these discoveries into theology. In the next chapter we will discuss three key biblical miracles in terms of Christian idealism.

The Discovery of the Idealist Universe[1]

Ironically, just when secular and Christian realism and materialism were most influential (in the nineteenth century), the very foundations of philosophical realism were being undermined. This was not done by academic theologians or biblical scholars, but by scientists and mathematicians. The emerging discipline of subatomic physics (quantum physics) was at the center of this revolution. Discoveries in this field made realism and materialism obsolete as descriptions of the physical universe.

The quantum physics revolution began as a result of attempts to study the nature of light. Experiments early in the nineteenth century had demonstrated that light was a wave. Later, however, other experiments demonstrated that light also behaved like a particle. It soon became apparent that light could be proven to be either a wave or a particle, depending on the experiment that was run. This concept, that the same matter can manifest in radically different ways, was called complementarity and became a fundamental concept of the new quantum physics.

The investigation on the nature of light led to the simple but significant two-hole experiment. This demonstrated that a beam of light projected against a photographic plate would appear on the plate as a wave if passed through two holes at the same time but would show as a group of particles if passed through one hole.

Through further experiments several astounding discoveries were made. If any person observed the beam during the two-hole experiment, the wave manifestation collapsed, and the light became a particle merely by being observed. The presence of the observer changed the results of the experiment! Without observation the beam of light existed in a ghost-like state, with potential for either a particle or wave but settling in neither. (It would eventually manifest as a wave if it remained unobserved.)[2] This all but shattered the fundamental assumption of materialist-realist science (and Christian materialism) that nature operated independently of the mind (the observer).

Mathematical and experimental work done by Max Planck, one of the pioneers of quantum physics, discovered that the power of the mind to influence matter by observation had a mathematical expression in the central equation of quantum physics: $E = \hbar f$. The most important value for this discussion is $\hbar$, the energy value of mind-observation that breaks the wave manifestation of light into a particle. The $\hbar$ is also called Planck's constant, and its value is one of those infinitely small numbers only mathematicians understand.

Later it was realized that the universe could not exist as we know it with much variation in $\hbar$. If $\hbar$ were a smaller value, the wave function would not break, and this would, among other things, make vision impossible. On the other hand, if $\hbar$ were slightly higher, then every thought would dramatically and dangerously alter matter. That nature is so delicately balanced for our good is now called the anthropic principle. It seems that from the very instant of the Big Bang (the moment of creation assumed by some scientists) many things went exactly right to allow for intelligent life on earth.[3]

Another blow to the materialist view of nature came when it was discovered that radioactive decay, the release of particles from the interior of elements such as uranium, was totally a random, unpredictable event. This was given mathematical definition in Heisenberg's principle of uncertainty and was discovered to be as fundamental an element of the universe as complementarity. This too shattered the materialist dream that the course of the natural world could be determined precisely, as Newton had determined the course of the planets.

By the 1920s there was a great debate among informed scientists as to what the discoveries in quantum physics meant. The mathematical equations which demonstrated these findings were producing startling advances in electronics and physics. In fact, the electronics industry would not have come about without quantum theory. However, many of the scientists who were at the forefront of these discoveries were disturbed by the philosophical implications. They had been educated as materialists and realists, yet everything in quantum physics suggested that at the atomic level the universe operated by idealist principles — and the mind could have influence on the behavior of matter.

Erwin Schrodinger, one of the great scientists and mathematicians of the era, explained the idealist conclusions of quantum physics with a teaching parable which came to be known as "the paradox of Schrodinger's cat." In this theoretical model a cat would be placed in a sealed box with a vial of poison gas, with the gas having exactly a 50 percent chance of being released and the cat being killed. Schrodinger postulated that before the box was opened the cat was in a ghost-like state, neither dead nor alive. The event of opening the box and observing the cat created the definite dead or live cat, just as the observer triggered the light wave to become particles in the two-hole experiment.

Albert Einstein disliked the implications of quantum physics, Schrodinger's cat and all, though he participated in many of the initial experiments and discoveries of the era. He particularly disliked the principle of uncertainty. His famous rejoinder to it was "God doesn't play dice!"

Looking at the equations developed in quantum physics, Einstein found that one of the implications was that particles generated from a single atomic source, such as two photons (light particles) coming out of the same atom, would be united in a special way regardless of their distance from each other. Any change on one particle would be instantly duplicated upon its twin. This would occur faster than the speed of light. This peculiar property of quantum physics was called nonlocality.

To demonstrate nonlocality let us imagine a quantum billiards table. On it are balls of different colors, but only two are red. These are balls from a single source. If I take a cue stick and hit one red ball, the other, for no apparent reason, will move in an identical manner with the first, as if an unseen force had duplicated my shot.

Einstein's own theory of relativity, which was also yielding excellent results, stated that no event in the universe could take place faster than the speed of light. The prediction from quantum physics that particles could interact instantly was thus in conflict with relativity. This conflict was called the EPR paradox. With the instruments available at the time, Einstein's objections could not be tested.

Idealism and the Copenhagen Interpretation

In 1927 the scientific debates about quantum physics reached a climax at the conference in Niels Bohr's institute in Copenhagen, Denmark. All the chief physicists and scientists of the era met and discussed the meaning of the new physics. Bohr was an enthusiastic supporter of the idealist implications, regardless of how little "sense" the discoveries made in terms of traditional Western realism. Bohr's view, called the Copenhagen interpretation, steadily won the arguments among scientists by virtue of its mathematical and experimental triumphs.

Modern scientists now side with the Copenhagen interpretation and accept, to one degree or another, the idealist view of matter as somehow interactive with the mind. Fresh experimental evidence continues to be found, verifying the importance of observation-measurement as a factor that influences matter.[4]

Interestingly, the EPR paradox was finally tested, and nonlocality was supported. This was done in the 1980s by a team of French scientists who bombarded calcium atoms with a laser, releasing twin photons from the target atoms. Measurements on the escaping photons done with extremely accurate instruments did in fact show exact duplication of movement for the pair of photons as nonlocality predicted. Bohr's Copenhagen interpretation won over its final objection.[5]

Secular Objections

Many scientists are wary of attempts to expand the discoveries of quantum mechanics from the world of atomic and subatomic interactions to the ordinary world. The argument from these scientists is that there is no direct evidence that ordinary matter can operate with the laws of subatomic particles. Similarly they claim that expanding quantum rules to the realm of psychic or spiritual events is not legitimate.[6] This line of reasoning is mostly advocated by those scientists of the materialist tradition who are still disturbed by any evidence that calls into question the assumptions of a mechanical and God-empty universe.

On the contrary, the evidence is mounting that under some circumstances ordinary matter operates with the mystical properties of quantum physics. (For instance, scientists have designed certain electronic devices of up to a half centimeter long to operate as a single atomic entity.[7])

Quantum Physics as Natural Theology

The theological implications of quantum physics are finally appearing in mainline Christian literature, as witnessed by a summary of recent trends that appeared in the February 1, 1985, edition of *Christianity Today*.[8] This came, unfortunately, half a century after the main discoveries of quantum physics were clarified in the Copenhagen interpretation.

Far worse, the mainline Christian writings have been produced after non-Christian writers launched several popular explanations of quantum physics based on Eastern mysticism. The most important of these was Fritjof Capra's best-selling work, *The Tao of Physics*, published in 1976. This book drew explicit parallels between quantum physics and doctrines of Eastern mysticism.[9] This book, though filled with many useful insights, gave the impression that quantum physics is a branch of Eastern occultism. Several other books in this vein have followed.[10]

Even secular critics have observed that this crop of quantum-physics-as-Eastern-mysticism has been little more than propaganda. What has really been accomplished in the quantum revolution has been the destruction of the traditional naive realism of science.[11] These Eastern interpretations should be viewed as temporary hypotheses that to fill in the vacuum in spiritual understanding created by Western materialism.

The importance of the observer has produced some wildly speculative theories. Some researchers now claim that the universe is only possible because we observe it, and even its creation was due to our present observation of it![12] Another example of speculative idealist interpretations is the "many universes" theory. In this view every time a person makes a decision, as in opening the door to Schrodinger's box, the universe splits into both possibilities, one with a dead cat, another with a live one. This happens in infinite repetition as each human being creates new universes every time he makes a decision.[13]

The Eastern mystical interpretations given by Capra and others are plausible because the spiritual implications of quantum physics are of a general nature. They can be interpreted in terms of many religious systems and belong to a category that the Christian tradition calls natural theology.[14]* By its very nature, natural theology is incomplete and subject to misguided interpretations. For example, Paul pointed out that creation points to a creator (Rom. 1:20). Yet creation gives only a natural theology of God, not the specifics of God as a loving father. This comes from revelation. Natural theology without the specific correction of Scripture can drift into incorrect conclusions or dangerous models, as in the Greek father-god Zeus who lusted after and fought with lesser gods.

In the next chapter we will look at the implications that the natural theology of quantum physics has for Christian theology. In other words, what happens when one applies the insights of quantum idealism to biblical revelation?

---

* As I mentioned earlier, natural theology refers to those things that man knows about God and morality by reason and conscience only.

TWELVE

The Spiritual Side
of Quantum Physics

Quantum Laws and Biblical Spirituality

MAINLINE THEOLOGIANS ARE FINALLY DEALING with the theological implications of quantum physics. As a result, new areas of understanding and appreciation of the Scriptures have opened. However, to claim that quantum physics validates a particular doctrine of the Bible is to err in the same way that the Eastern mystical school of quantum writers has erred. What follows must be understood to be analogies based on the natural theology of quantum physics that have been extended and corrected through confidence in biblical revelation. Analogies suggest but never give proof.

The theories of quantum physics simply show that the philosophy of radical materialism, which has been used to support cessationist theology, is inadequate to explain all the occurrences of reality. However, to view miracles simply in terms of quantum physics misses the point. Miracles are works of God which change the natural course of our present (fallen) universe. In some way God's will and power cooperate with man's mind through the biblically named "faculty" of faith. Some miracles, as in the original creation, are purely the sovereign work of God.

151

Complementarity, Nonlocality and Christian Doctrine

Complementarity was the first quantum principle discovered, and it serves well as the first point of analogy to the spiritual life. Recall that complementarity deals with a reality that can have more than one manifestation, as light being both a wave and a particle. Because complementarity is so alien to ordinary logic, it is almost impossible for the human intellect to understand complementarities. A complementarity is not so much *understood* as true as it is *accepted* as true.

In biblical revelation there are many such fundamental complementarities, traditionally called mysteries. For example, Jesus is both man and God,[1] or man is free to choose his spiritual destiny, but God has predestined those who enter into the kingdom.[2] These mysteries might be understood as complementarities.

It is also easy to see that nonlocality has analogies in the spiritual world (when a change in one particle is duplicated in its twin from the same source). I have seen so many examples in Christian literature that choosing which ones to highlight is difficult. By coincidence, as I was working on this section, I read Charles Farah's *From the Pinnacle of the Temple*, which has a chapter called "Marty's Death." There Farah recounts how his local church prayed through the cancer of their pastor's wife, Marty. In Marty's case there was no physical healing in spite of an heroic prayer campaign. However, in a dramatic manifestation of spiritual nonlocality, many of the prayer intercessors acquired the pains of the cancer victim and consequently relieved Marty of her horrible terminal pains.[3]

Something very similar happened when C. S. Lewis's wife, Joy, was dying of cancer. As with Marty, some of Joy's agony was relieved when Lewis prayed that he could receive some of her sufferings. The materialists may still choose to disregard such accounts, but they no longer can claim that such phenomena are alien to the laws of nature.

Paul's description of the sacrament of the Lord's supper also demonstrates principles of nonlocality.

> Is not the cup of blessing which we bless a sharing in the blood of Christ? Is not the bread which we break a sharing in the body of Christ? Since there is one bread, we who are many are one body; for we all partake of the one bread (1 Cor. 10:16-17).

The ability of a sacrament to create nonlocality among the members of the body has been noticed by the English scientist-theologian John C. Polkinghorne in his book *One World: the Interaction of Science and Theology*.[4] Polkinghorne was for many years professor of particle physics at Cambridge University but in 1979 resigned to become a priest in the Church of England. He is now a master Christian apologist to the scientific community in Great Britain.

God as the Prime Observer

We had noted earlier how the equations of quantum physics suggest that observation is necessary for creation to take place and to be completed. This had led to fantastic speculations about the role of man in creation. While the natural theology of quantum physics suggests that mind-observance is necessary for the world to exist, revelation tells us who that mind is. No less than seven times in the first chapter of Genesis a conjunction is made between God creating the universe and affirming it by observation. Genesis 1:31 is clearest on this: "And God saw all that He had made, and behold, it was very good." With this we can see that the ultimate source of stability and continuity in the universe is God, not man (thank goodness).[5]

The critical question in quantum theology is this: Why does ordinary matter not manifest the mystical properties of nonlocality and responsiveness to the mind more easily? Paul addressed this problem nineteen hundred years before the scientific issue could even be defined. He saw that God masked the spiritual behavior of the ordinary world for the purposes of His overall plan. But in the fullness of time, ordinary matter will be bestowed with its true spiritual functions.

> For the anxious longing of the creation waits eagerly for the revealing of the sons of God. For the creation was subjected to futility, not of its own will, but because of Him who subjected it, in hope that the creation itself also will be set free from its slavery to corruption into the freedom of the glory of the children of God. For we know that the whole creation groans and suffers the pains of childbirth together until now (Rom. 8:19-23).

In quantum terms this passage means that God created the universe with a low $\hbar$ (see previous chapter) for our safety. He knew that before mankind came into the full conformity of His Son a higher $\hbar$ would lead to the chaos and mind wars of battling magicians. As the elect become "in Christ" and have the "mind of Christ," such dangers cease to exist.

Lost Opportunities

The implications of quantum physics for Christian theology were ignored by mainline theologians for more than fifty years. The fine work done from the late 1970s by Christian scientist-theologians might well have been done in the 1930s. The reality of the spiritual world and the miraculous might have been proclaimed with renewed force to a generation of European and American intellectuals seeking answers from fascism and Marxism.

Instead mainline Christian theology from 1920 to 1980 went through its most apostate and heretical period. The mainline seminaries in the United States followed European fashions and adopted what is called higher criticism of the Bible (the myth hermeneutic), combined with various forms of Nietzschean or Marxian philosophy. These theologies assumed a materialist worldview and proclaimed that modern man could not believe in miracles because miracles were incompatible with modern science. Thus for half a century after it was scientifically obsolete, mainline Christian theology taught the materialist doctrine that miracles were scientifically impossible and words or thoughts could not influence the natural world.

In the 1950s Don H. Gross, an Episcopal priest, documented how mainline theologians stubbornly resisted the good news that quantum physics gives analogous validation of the biblical worldview.[6] *The Case for Spiritual Healing* contained a pioneer section on the relationship between quantum physics and healing, though it was too far ahead of its time for the general public to appreciate.[7]

Gross received a graduate degree in physics just after World War II. He then received a call to the Episcopal priesthood and was ordained in 1949. His interest in healing was flamed in 1949 by a lecture given by Alfred Price, a pioneer of the healing ministry among Episcopalians. Subsequently Gross investigated several of Katherine Kuhlman's rallies and witnessed several healings.

Gross noticed that when he presented his seminary professors with evidence for spiritual healing, they would not pursue an investigation, no matter how well-documented the evidence, nor would they modify their cessationist theories and Christian materialism. No data contrary to their theology was accepted. While his professors listened politely to his enthusiastic presentation of why the miraculous was possible in terms of quantum physics, it made no impression on their beliefs. In spiritual terms, the deist theology and its associated realist-materialist philosophy formed a mental stronghold over the minds of the professors.[8]

The Miracles and Christian Faith-Idealism

Let us turn to several of the miracles of the Bible to see how helpful the analogies of quantum physics and its idealist implications are in hermeneutics. The first miracle we will note is an example of faith unsustained, Peter's aborted water-walk (Matt. 14:28-31). In this incident Peter initiates the miracle by asking Jesus to call him. Jesus calls, and Peter does walk on the water, "But seeing the wind, he became afraid, and beginning to sink, he cried out...." After Jesus saved Peter, He rebuked him with the words, "O you of little faith, why did you doubt?"

This incident is especially instructive because it is fatal to the sovereignty-only theory of Christian materialism. Although God's sovereignty and power (through Jesus) were the basis of Peter's water-walk, it was Peter's mind and spirit acting in faith, then fear, which determined the outcome. If the only important factor in the miracle was that God sovereignly decided that Peter could walk on water, it should not have mattered that Peter feared, nor would Jesus' rebuke make sense.[9] Similar conclusions must be drawn from Jesus' failed ministry in His hometown of Nazareth (Matt. 13:54-58; Mark 6:1-6; Luke 4:16-30). Matthew summarized: "And He did not do many miracles there because of their unbelief." Again the sovereignty-only theory fails.

Faith and the Resuscitation of Schrodinger's Cat

Quantum physics suggests that observation finalizes the structure of matter. The Bible demonstrates that faith, or anticipated observation, not only finalizes but changes the course of events. Note the central New Testament definition of faith (Heb. 11:1): "Now faith is the assurance of things hoped for, the conviction of things not seen." Two resuscitations, one in the Old Testament and another in the new, demonstrate this quite clearly.

The first one is the resuscitation of the Shunammite woman's son (2 Kin. 4:8-37). Elisha and his servant Gehazi passed this woman's house

155

often, and she discerned that Elisha was a prophet. She had a guest room built especially for him. Elisha reciprocated her kindness by praying for her to become pregnant, since she was childless and her husband old.

Within a year she gave birth to a son. Later, as a young boy, he became feverish and died on her lap. Her immediate actions are most revealing. The woman told no one, quickly laid the boy on Elisha's guest cot, closed the door to the room and rushed to get the prophet. Her husband asked why she was leaving, and she replied, "It will be well," an equivalent to the American "it's OK" (v. 23).

Before she arrived at Elisha's residence, the prophet sensed that something was wrong and that she was in distress. He sent Gehazi to inquire. When Gehazi asked as to her family, she replied, "It is well" (v. 26). At the feet of the prophet she did not blurt out, "The boy is dead!" but in circumspection reminded the prophet that his prayers had been responsible for the lad's birth.

Elisha understood at once but did not speak out the problem. He sent Gehazi ahead of him to place his own staff on the boy's body, and Elisha himself followed with the mother. Before Elisha and the woman arrived, Gehazi returned with the news that the staff had not helped yet and that "the lad has not awakened" (v. 31). When Elisha got to his guest room he closed the door behind him, prayed to the Lord and twice stretched himself out on the boy. The boy came to life and was restored to his mother.

From the perspective of Christian materialism the actions and dialogue of the incident are incomprehensible. The Shunammite woman was deluded; things were not "well." But with an idealist understanding of the spiritual power of anticipated observation to change events, both the dialogue and the actions make perfect sense.

No one in the incident ever proclaimed the death of the boy. The actions of the woman certainly took it into account, but she did not say it in spite of her anguish. On the contrary, she affirmed that things were OK. Similarly, neither Elisha nor Gehazi used the words *death* or *dead* in the incident. When Gehazi had to report that his master's staff had not resuscitated the boy, he used the phrase "not awakened." He was reporting that the *dunamis* of God in the staff was not enough to accomplish the miracle. Elisha continued, and the miracle was completed by his prayers (the one element of the whole incident understandable in Christian materialism) and by stretching out on the boy so that even more of the *dunamis* of God would flow from him into the lad. By revelation from the Scriptures (not by the natural theology of quantum physics), we can understand that speaking in faith is an extremely powerful form of observation.

A similar sequence of events took place in Jesus' ministry in the resuscitation of Jairus's daughter (Matt. 9:18-26; Mark 5:21-43; Luke 8:40-56). Matthew, Mark and Luke give varying details about the incident, but the sequence is quite clear. Jairus meets Jesus and requests that He come to the bedside of his dying daughter. Jesus starts on the way, heals the woman with the issue of blood, and continues. News then comes that the girl has died. Jesus reassures Jairus: "Do not be afraid any longer; only believe, and she will be made well" (Luke 8:50).

At Jairus's house Jesus tells the crowd, "Stop weeping, for she has not died, but is asleep" (v. 52). They howl in derision, but He puts them out and enters the girl's room with His disciples and the parents. Jesus then takes the girl's hand and commands her to arise. Luke writes: "And her spirit returned, and she rose immediately" (Luke 8:55).

The sequence of events and statements is again unintelligible and contradictory from the perspective of Christian materialism. Jesus said the girl was sleeping. This could be interpreted to mean that with divine wisdom Jesus knew the girl was only in a coma. Also the crowd could have been mistaken because of the limited medical knowledge of the times. However, Luke makes it clear she was really dead — "her spirit returned." Thus in the realist hermeneutic Jesus was either mistaken or lying.

Obviously this was not the intention or understanding of any of the evangelists. The crowd and messenger were right: the girl was observed as dead. By saying she was asleep, Jesus was affirming that the initial observation of death could be overruled by the power of God mobilized through faith, just as the Shunammite woman believed that the power of God would overrule the death of her boy. Jesus was not misjudging the issue or lying, nor was the crowd mistaken. Rather Jesus used His words as part and parcel of the miracle event.[10]

One can note the vast difference between our hermeneutic (Christian faith-idealism) which is buttressed with the analogies of quantum physics and the hermeneutics of Christian materialism based on the science of the eighteenth century. Whereas the understanding of materialist science forced a radical discontinuity between spiritual activities and the material order, those discontinuities have now evaporated. The spiritual order can now be understood to operate in harmony, not in contradiction, with fundamental laws of the universe. The analogies between quantum physics and the spiritual life reveal a continuity of intention in the mind of the Creator. God intended the universe to be spiritual — from subatomic particles to archangels. His laws for subatomic particles are the first level of a universe created for spiritual ends.

It should also be made clear that we are not implying that Christian spiritual life is a mechanical execution of the laws of quantum physics. Rather what we have done is create a faith-idealist hermeneutic which is useful in describing biblical spirituality. At the core of the Christian's life is the relationship of creature to Creator, of dependent child to loving Father, which is intensely personal, not mechanical. Being a Christian involves the directing of the human mind and spirit to worship, repentance, praise and love, all of which are activities of the will which have nothing to do with mechanical applications of laws or principles.

In the hermeneutics we presented we used the vocabulary and imagery of modern physics, but the critical element is its Christian faith-idealism. This form of moderate idealism is vastly different from the Christian realism of consensus orthodoxy. It is derived from the Christian faith-idealism of Phoebe Palmer, the Faith-Cure pioneers, E. W. Kenyon and others such as Agnes Sanford who were all unaware of the philosophical issues of quantum physics. We will examine Kenyon's pioneer contributions to Christian faith-idealism in chapter 18.

Christian Faith-Idealism as the Natural Hermeneutic of the Bible

Similar forms of biblical interpretation and active faith have recurred in the lives of the pioneer Christian healers and men of faith. Most often they simply called their noncessationist understanding of Scripture the plain or literal interpretation of the Bible. But both their hermeneutics and their ministry displayed a natural understanding of Christian faith-idealism.

We saw this in the Holiness theology of Phoebe Palmer. A skeletal faith-idealism theology could be found in the sayings of Smith Wigglesworth (1859 – 1947). Wigglesworth, who reportedly never read any book except the Bible, was noted for his strong faith and miraculous answers to prayer. His most often quoted saying was, "I am not moved by what I see or hear; I am moved by what I believe" (that is, the promises of Scripture).[11] It is significant that he arrived at this position of faith-idealism because he certainly did not read it from New Thought sources.

In the same way that it is unexpected to find principles of healing through quantum physics, it is also surprising to find spiritual truth within non-Christian philosophies. Yet in the following chapter we will discuss how this occurred in the Metaphysical movement.

THIRTEEN

What Does a Heretic Know About Truth?

Revelation and the Heathen

THE PHARISEES HAD GREAT TROUBLE understanding both the process and the nature of God's revelation. They missed the revelation that was undergoing its climax right in their midst by missing the very Messiah to whom Scripture had pointed (Heb. 1:2). As we have shown, their failure was mostly due to their own assumptions. They believed that further revelation from God, further clarification of Scripture and, of course, the Messiah Himself would come out of their rabbinical schools or at the very least be in harmony with them.

Yet even the Scriptures available to them would undermine the two basic assumptions the Pharisees held concerning the Messiah: that He would have the proper origin and pedigree and that He would confirm their current consensus orthodoxy (Talmud). For instance, the true prophets of the Old Testament were not part of the religious establishment and were most often opposed to the consensus religious opinions of their day. In fact, official prophets who were part of the king's court fared especially poorly in the biblical record (1 Kin. 22).

At the root of the court prophets' failure lies the singular fact of God's sovereignty. God uses whomever He wishes and whatever group He wishes to achieve His ends. The Old Testament shows through repeated examples that God uses the most unusual and unexpected persons to give His message or do His will. The properly religious are most embarrassed by the biblical instances where revelation is given through those with questionable origins and even through the heathen. The revelation is usually rejected by the elect for that reason.

159

Perhaps one of the most dramatic incidents demonstrating this is found in the account of the death of King Josiah (2 Chr. 35; 2 Kin. 23). Josiah, king of Judah, drove out the mediums, ended every form of idolatrous worship in his kingdom and repaired the temple. Scripture says:

> And before him there was no king like him who turned to the Lord with all his heart and with all his soul and with all his might, according to all the law of Moses; nor did any like him arise after him (2 Kin. 23:25).

However, his reign ended before its time because he did not discern the voice of the Lord. Neco, pharaoh of Egypt (and an idolater), was at war with Babylon and requested safe passage for his army through Judah. Josiah, without consulting the Lord, challenged Neco's intrusion. Neco assured Josiah that God had sent him to fight the Babylonians, not the Jews. But Josiah did not "listen to the words of Neco from the mouth of God, but came to make war on the plain of Megiddo" (2 Chr. 35:22). As a result, he lost his life in battle, and the crown of Judah passed on to an ungodly king, who returned to idolatry.

Balaam

Another example of the Spirit of God speaking both a revelation and a blessing through the heathen is found in the prophecy-prayers of Balaam (Num. 22-23). The Israelites had begun conquering the promised land and had come to the borders of Moab. Balak, king of Moab, sent for a local shaman, Balaam, to conjure a curse against the Israelites (Num. 22:7).[1]

As a shaman Balaam served other spirits but also recognized the voice of the Lord. Like many shamans before and after him, Balaam had a form of natural theology that recognized a supreme god (Rom. 1:18-23). If modern reports are a valid guide, he probably experienced the shaman's dilemma, that of having to appease the lesser spirits while hating them. As a heathen he lacked the specific good news to separate himself from the lesser spirits' powers and to serve the high God only.[2]

Three times Balaam was bribed to do Balak's bidding and conjure a curse against the Israelites. Each time he discerned that the high God, the Lord, had directed him to do the opposite. He would find himself prophesying and blessing the Israelites rather than cursing them. Thus, in spite of being a shaman, he was used to deliver an authentic prophecy of the Lord.

The New Testament and the Irony of Revelation

The New Testament repeats the Old Testament assertion that God sovereignly reveals His will through whom He pleases. It also gives specific light on the revelatory function of the Holy Spirit. Within the Godhead it is the function of the Holy Spirit to teach the church "all the truth" (John 16:13) and remind it of the words of Jesus (John 14:26).

The New Testament accentuates the irony of revelation that was hinted at in the history of Josiah and Neco. Those who were waiting for the Messiah should have received Jesus (the greatest revelation of all), but they did not. Gentiles, whose minds were on other matters, received Him. Throughout the Gospels it was often the heathen, such as the Roman centurion or the Canaanite woman, who had the strongest faith in Jesus, while most of the Jewish religious leaders remained skeptical.

God's delight in the ironic and the unexpected is a central theme in the theology of Paul. The letter of Romans reveals the great mystery of the church (Rom. 11) in the metaphor of wild and cultivated olive trees. The Jews were God's cultivated olive trees, and the Gentiles were the wild. Paul reveals that from the foundations of the earth God had ordained that the Jews, His chosen people, would at first reject their Messiah so the Gentiles could accept Him. In the formation of the church there would be a mysterious engrafting of wild and cultivated branches to make a new whole.

Similarly, New Testament writers were not reluctant to affirm the truth of God when it was discovered in heathen sources.[3] Paul began his speech to the Gentile crowds in Athens by quoting their own playwright Aratus, from his play *Phenomena*, about the fatherhood of God (Acts 17:22-28). In this case Paul understood that the Greeks' natural theology could be a starting point for the gospel. A quotation in the letter to Titus (1:12) comes from the *Oracles* of Memander. In these cases Paul was not concerned about the "unclean" origins of the sayings; rather he used whatever truth there was in them and incorporated them into Scripture. The key was to discern the grain of truth in what the heathen had to say.

161

Revelation and Heresy in the Church Era

Christians are generally comfortable with the idea that God still speaks to the church through an occasional prophet. Most Christians would agree, for example, that Martin Luther was a prophet to the church of his day. For many Martin Luther King Jr. was a prophet for our day. From our perspective today these individuals were correct in fundamental doctrine, though their shortsighted contemporaries often ridiculed them as deviant and heretical. Indeed, what marks a prophet is the sound (orthodox) doctrine he derives from both the spirit and the letter of biblical revelation. In contrast the majority of churchgoers hold a more superficial view of what is orthodox, believing it to be equivalent to their current denominational understanding (consensus orthodoxy).

More difficult to understand within the structure of God's ongoing revelation and activity is the role of the heretic. Common sense says that heretics go against the teachings of the church and thus must have nothing truthful to say. The basis of this is the assumption that current orthodoxy is the high point of God's ultimate revelation. We have shown how this was the position of the Pharisees in regard to Jesus and His disciples (see chapter 1). Yet the heretic in the church era can play a similar role to the heathen in biblical times. Heretics can be used by God whenever the elect (the church) are too stubborn to hear the voice of the Lord directly or pay attention to its prophets.

Harold O. J. Brown has shown in his book *Heresies* just how extensively heretics have forced the church into the discovery of its deepest truths.[4] Specifically, most of the great doctrines of the church were forged as responses to initial heresies, often incorporating fragments of truth first brought to light in the original heresy.

For instance, as Brown pointed out, in the first century A.D. the person of Jesus was subject to all sorts of explanations. Among the most damaging and erroneous was the explanation of the Docetists. This was the heresy that Jesus did not incarnate in the flesh but appeared on earth as a ghost. First John 4 alludes to this heresy and challenges it directly. Other theories about Jesus occupied the attention of the church for the first three centuries. Some claimed that Jesus was God but not man or, inversely, man but not God. In any case these heretical views forced the church to think about the person of Jesus and to come to its orthodox (scripturally sound) understanding of Jesus as God-man. Similarly, the shifting beliefs, tentative hypotheses and sometimes absurd theories about the relationship between Father, Son and Spirit stimulated the church to come to its orthodox doctrine of the trinity.*

Even the development of the Bible was stimulated by the early heretics. Marcion, the great Gnostic heretic of the second century, was among the first to identify Paul's writings as divinely inspired, though he interpreted them in a heretical manner. This sparked a general debate in the church about Paul's letters which eventually led to their full acceptance in the fourth century.[6]

Whether the heathen or heretic stumbles upon an occasional truth or whether it is an instance of divine inspiration (as with King Neco) only God can know. The fact that throughout church history heretical groups have at times introduced truth is often unrecognized. In the early years of the Reformation the Anabaptists developed as an independent movement. Most were pacifists, but some became anarchistic and established communes where both property and wives were held in common. Luther and Calvin opposed the Anabaptists and encouraged their persecution.

Though their theology contained some unacceptable tenets, the Anabaptists were also among the first to preach the separation of church and state. They saw that in the New Testament the church had nothing to do with the state and believed that to be the divine model for the church. The Reformers and Catholics held to the more traditional view, that the model for the church was found in the Mosaic law where there is no distinction between church and state. Catholics and Protestants alike agreed that the state must support the church to suppress heresy. Yet it has become increasingly clear that the Anabaptists were right on this issue.[7]

Brown also draws an important distinction between heresy and heretics. Although the heretics did the church a service in stimulating the debates that led to orthodoxy, this is not the same as saying that they or their heresies were good.[8] Heresy must be opposed and its spiritual destructiveness exposed. In spite of the chaos, confusion and damage that the great heretics did to the body in their day, the Spirit of God sovereignly used them for His long-range goals, bringing good out of what Satan meant for evil.

Brown also noticed a tragic element in the history of the church's struggle against heresy. The pioneer Christian theologians who battled most

---

* Brown's insight, that heresy forces orthodoxy into action, has been known to Christian scholars and was studied by the Catholic monk-theologian Dom Odo Casel.[5] Casel calls the relationship between heresy and truth "shadow truth."

fiercely and effectively against heresy were often unjustly criticized and judged by later generations.[9] For example, Origen (185 – 255) and Tertullian (150 – 225), both of whom played critical roles in combatting heresy, were condemned as heretics for not agreeing with the *consensus* orthodoxy of *later* centuries! Origen, the most important of the two, sketched out the first Christian systematic theology, including the theology of trinity.[10] In fact, both Tertullian and Origen remained well within the bounds of biblical revelation.

FOURTEEN

A Critique of New Thought and New Age

Truth and Heresy in the Idealist Cults

HOW A PORTION OF THE church came to overthrow the theology of cessationism and break the hold of its realist-materialist philosophy forms one of the most interesting chapters of church history. In short, while the mainline church rejected the Faith-Cure movement, the Victorian idealist cults, known more commonly as the Metaphysical movement, rose to play a role in God's revelation to the church.[1]

The Metaphysical movement went through several stages, the first of which was the Mind-Cure period. This was roughly contemporary with the Faith-Cure movement (discussed in chapters 9 and 10). Mind-Cure was based on radical idealism and included Gnostic and spiritualist influences. As the name implied, Mind-Cure centered on using the powers of the mind for healing. Mary Baker Eddy's Christian Science cult was the most successful and best known of the Mind-Cure sects.

The second stage, starting in the 1880s, was that of New Thought. Here the accent shifted from purely healing to general prosperity and well-being. Many in New Thought turned away from radical idealism and toward more moderate forms of idealism.

The first instinct of the Christian reader is to dismiss the possibility that the Holy Spirit could work with the unsavory witches' brew that made up the Metaphysical movement. Recall, however, in the previous chapter that the Spirit seems to delight in taking improbable characters, many times those who are out to destroy the church, and using them to achieve God's purposes. It should not astonish us to realize that Gnostic and heretical individuals were used by the Holy Spirit to break finally the theology of cessationism and the stranglehold of realism-material-ism on the church.

Only rarely have evangelical scholars and cult watchers demon-strated appreciation of the limited truth that existed within the heretical metaphysical groups. Walter Martin, among the most learned of the cult-watchers, expressed in his classic work *The Kingdom of the Cults*:

> Within the theological structure of the cults there is con-siderable truth, all of which, it might be added, is drawn from Biblical sources, but so diluted with human error as to be more deadly than complete falsehood. The cults have also emphasized the things which the Church has forgotten, such as divine healing (Christian Science, Unity, New Thought), prophecy (Jehovah's Witness and Mormonism), and a great many other things which in the course of our study we will have opportunity to observe.[2]

The revelation of the Spirit in response to the heresy within the Meta-physical movement took more than a hundred years, from the mid-nineteenth century to the mid-twentieth century. These developments paved the way for healing miracle ministries in the twentieth century and the emergence of the charismatic renewal. As we have indicated, the controversies surrounding the theological and philosophical changes are still with us. Fortunately, at the beginning of the process America was still very much a Christian nation in which children prayed in public schools and practically everyone read and knew the Bible well.

Thus the Bible was always a standard which the various idealist (metaphysical) groups had to compare to their doctrines. This produced, in current terminology, an environment of spiritual warfare within the Metaphysical movement. On one side were the demonic elements of Gnosticism and spiritualism, and on the other were the Bible and Amer-ica's Christian heritage. Those individuals who chose to affirm the Bi-ble above all other writings separated from the Gnosticism and spiritualism of the movement to one degree or another. Significantly, they derived new and valid insights on the Bible and spiritual life through their idealist perspective.

166

On the other hand, those groups and leaders within the Metaphysical movement who gave the Bible less importance, usually by thinking it was only of equal value to the scriptures of other religions, quickly entrenched themselves in the deepest levels of heresy and delusion. For example, they interpreted the Bible allegorically. That is, they said its literal meaning was unimportant and pointed to something else at a deeper level. Christian Science used the allegorical hermeneutic extensively and thus remained a true cult and heresy.[3]

The Idealist Roots of the Metaphysical Movement

Historically, the Metaphysical movement originated as a rebellion against the arid realist theology of nineteenth-century Protestantism and its cessationism. Warren Felt Evans, the educated spokesman of Mind-Cure was particularly conscious of this:

> May an age of living faith and spiritual power succeed the present reign of materialism and religious impotency, so that the so-called miracles of history may be reproduced as the common facts of our age.[4]

The philosophical inspiration for Evans and others in the movement was the writings of Ralph Waldo Emerson (1803 – 1882). Emerson is remembered mostly for his essays and as the founding father of Transcendentalism. Deeply dissatisfied with the Calvinist orthodoxy of his New England, he became an ordained Unitarian minister. Emerson came to his idealist philosophy through several sources which included the idealist philosophers of classical philosophy (Plato and the neo-Platonists) but also readings from Eastern religions. His lifelong quest was to make idealist philosophy the basis of spiritual renewal, and this was adopted as the goal of the Metaphysical movement. From our perspective we can see that both Emerson and Evans correctly understood the debilitating effects of realism and materialism on the spiritual life of their age. Yet their heretical inclinations and propensity for Eastern philosophy could never bring spiritual renewal to their society.

Idealism as a Healing Cult

Philosophical idealism was not the only, or even main, component of the Metaphysical movement. Rather, from its very beginnings in the

1860s, the movement became infiltrated by a Gnostic spirit. Perhaps this occurred because the healing aspect of the movement was pioneered by Phineas P. Quimby (1802 – 1866), a person who had a raging hatred for the church and Christianity. Quimby was an uneducated clock repairman who spent much of his life in poor health. He was healed by a traveling French hypnotist and then took up therapeutic hypnotism himself. He hypnotized his patients and gave them healing suggestions and affirmations after which many became well.

Because hypnotism often opens the mind to demonic delusions and influences, it is rejected by most Christians. However, hypnosis can immobilize a person's fear, which makes hypnotism effective in eliminating many psychosomatic illnesses, though as experience has indicated, at considerable spiritual cost.[5]

Quimby developed a loose system of ideas which he put in manuscript form but was not published until after his death. He adopted the Gnostic belief that sin, disease and all evil were caused by mental error. Thus by knowing what was right and by positive thinking all evil could be avoided. Quimby's system turned the Metaphysical movement toward healing and ushered in the Mind-Cure era. He was most influential through his disciples, especially Mary Baker Eddy, founder of Christian Science, who used his writings as the basis of her own works.

Gnosticism: The Other Perennial Heresy[6]

Because Gnosticism was such a major element in the Metaphysical movement, it is important to understand something about Gnostic beliefs. Gnosticism, like Pharisaism, is a perennial heresy that has plagued the church since its very foundations. It emerged in the New Testament church; it persisted as a strong movement for the first four centuries of the church era; it recurred as an underground movement in the Middle Ages; and it reappeared within the Metaphysical movement.[7]

One of the most prominent scholars of Gnosticism, R. M. Grant, has identified three interlocking assumptions which are common to all its forms.[8] The first is that *salvation comes through knowledge*. This is where the word *Gnostic* originates since it means "one who knows." The second is *an attitude that is self-centered*, as contrasted with most religions which are God-centered. Third, Gnosticism is *subjective*; it relies on personal revelations and continuous spiritual experiences with little or no concern for tradition or discernment.

Gnosticism is fatal to the human spirit principally because it obstructs a faith-trust relationship with God. The person believes himself spiritually self-dependent and a god. This is why meditation instead of prayer (worship) is the central spiritual activity of any Gnostic sect. By trivializing and universalizing the word *Christ* to mean one who is enlightened, Gnosticism cuts the worship relationship with Jesus Christ. By its interlocking beliefs of self-centeredness, nondiscernment and nonworship, the person is led to a total moral and ethical breakdown where knowledge of salvation by the true Christ is virtually impossible.

Christian Science

The most Gnostic, most radically idealist and most influential Mind-Cure sect is Christian Science. Founded by the disciple of Quimby, Mary Baker Eddy (1821 – 1910), the cult grew to possess a worldwide following which survives to the present day. Christian Science healing methodology replaced Quimby's hypnotism with repeated suggestions to the patient that illness was unreal and that only the good was real. Mrs. Eddy coupled this with exhortations not to fear. The Christian Scientist healer ("practitioner") also had to perform several mental exercises. He had to name the disease, convince himself of its unreality and maintain a mental picture of the patient as perfectly well.[9] Naturally medicine of any kind was unnecessary and counterproductive because it was a futile case of the unreal (matter) attempting to cause a change on mere illusion (illness).

Like other Gnostics, Mrs. Eddy taught that the resurrection of the dead was a crude and untrue doctrine because true spirit does not need a body (*Science and Health* 73:19). All healing, spiritual growth and even salvation come to the seeker through knowledge of Christian Science doctrines and principles.

Naturally such a system made gibberish of biblical revelation. Jesus' blood sacrifice was irrelevant to man's sin situation since blood is material and therefore had no spiritual meaning. Mrs. Eddy finessed the meaning of Jesus' blood atonement into triviality:

> The efficacy of Jesus' spiritual offering is infinitely greater
> than can be expressed by our sense of human blood. The ma-
> terial blood of Jesus was no more efficacious to cleanse from
> sin when it was shed upon "the accursed tree," than when it
> was flowing in his veins as he went daily about his Father's

business. His true flesh and blood were his Life, and they truly eat his flesh and drink his blood, who partake of that divine Life (*Science and Health* 25:3-9).

Christian Science influenced many millions of Christians who did not accept all its doctrines or formally separate from the orthodox churches.[10] For the most part such persons believed the exciting news that healing was possible in the present age and ignored its more extreme doctrines. In this matter Mrs. Eddy's obscure and convoluted writing style protected many sincere Christian readers from its heresy. Merely proclaiming that healing was possible was enough for many a Christian to turn to the Bible and individually to reject the doctrine of cessationism.[11]

New Thought[12]

In the 1880s the name New Thought was coined for the followers of the Metaphysical movement. Although healing was still a main concern, new interest had grown around the ideas of prosperity and personal success. New Thought authors became the motivational writers of Victorian America.[13] Many of the New Thought leaders were refugees from Christian Science who could not tolerate the authoritarian structure or doctrines of Mrs. Eddy's "mother church."[14]

In 1914 many New Thought groups joined an umbrella organization called the International New Thought Alliance (INTA). Many in New Thought dropped every pretense of being Christian and affirmed Gnostic universalism and higher consciousness. Others, however, believed that they were the true Christians of the age and continued to affirm their belief in biblical revelation. Several important New Thought leaders continued the process of developing truth from heresy that started in the Mind-Cure movement. The Unity School of Christianity, founded by Charles Fillmore, was one link in this process.

Charles Fillmore (1854 – 1948) and the Unity School of Christianity[15]

Charles Fillmore was a frontier baby. He was educated by his mother and a neighbor who sparked his interest in the Transcendentalists, especially Emerson. He married Myrtle, a highly intelligent and devout woman who had graduated from Oberlin, the famous Christian college.

After they married, it was discovered that Myrtle had tuberculosis and was dying. In 1886 both Charles and Myrtle attended a New Thought lecture on healing. Myrtle immediately began practicing its methods. She spoke healing to her lungs and affirmed, "I am a beloved child of God." She quickly became well.

This made a strong impression on Charles, and he delved into metaphysical studies. He investigated a range of Christian Science, theosophy, New Thought and Eastern religions. He also studied under Emma Curtis Hopkins, a prominent New Thought writer and exile from Christian Science. Charles attempted to meditate his way into clarifying the contradictions he found among these systems and developed a theological mix that included some biblical elements.

Charles and Myrtle founded a series of prayer groups called Silent Unity. The Fillmores' original intent was to educate and influence the whole of Christendom without becoming a separate denomination. Although Unity did and still does make special attempts to reach all Christians with its message, it became an organized denomination with its own church buildings, seminary and impressive headquarters. Today it remains the largest surviving New Thought denomination.

Unity's core teaching centers around idealist positive thinking, affirming the positive and negating evil by mental and spoken assertions. Unfortunately, reincarnation also became a major doctrine of Unity with Charles believing that he had once been the apostle Paul.[16] In common with Christian Science, sexuality was seen as a necessary evil, and married couples were urged to abstain as much as possible.

In spite of these and other cultic ideas, Fillmore resisted flirtation with spiritualism and mediumship though other New Thought groups were delving into both. The Fillmores held the Bible to be the definitive Word of God and understood the reality of sin as moral failure that needed forgiveness, a core biblical concept suppressed in most metaphysical circles. The Fillmores became increasingly wary of other New Thought groups which turned non-Christian and toward Eastern religions. Their dissatisfaction was such that they pulled Unity out of the INTA as a protest.

This is not to say that Unity ever reached biblical orthodoxy. The Gnostic spiritual fortress within Unity was never broken. The Bible, when held as the Word of God, has inherent power to rectify heresy. Had Fillmore not followed Mrs. Eddy's allegorical hermeneutic, Unity might have made a full transition to orthodoxy, as, for instance, the Seventh-Day Adventists did in spite of their cultic beginnings.

The Metaphysical Movement as New Age

Here we want to clarify the distinction between turn-of-the-century New Thought and the current New Age movement. Both New Age and New Thought originated with a Gnostic-demonic component. However, New Thought began in an age when the Bible and Christian doctrine influenced everything in the culture. This factor is missing in today's society where the New Age movement flowers. The Gnostic-demonic powers that rule over the New Age movement have no restraining hand and can proclaim witchcraft, paganism and anti-Christian beliefs openly. No faction within the New Age movement clings to biblical revelation and the lordship of Jesus. The New Age movement is steeped in witchcraft, spiritualism, divination and occultic practices to a degree that was true of only the most extreme New Thought groups.

Here an historical analogy is in order. The European Enlightenment (1688 – 1789) was a deeply anti-Christian and secularizing movement. The great Enlightenment thinkers were either nominally Christian like Immanuel Kant or anti-Christian like Hume and Voltaire. From the Enlightenment the philosophies of Marxism and secular humanism developed which have done so much to cripple our moral and spiritual heritage.

Yet the Enlightenment was birthed in the humanism of the 1500s. At that time humanists such as Sir Thomas More and Erasmus of Rotterdam attempted to *revive* Christian civilization with a dose of rationality and beauty modeled after classical civilization. Christian historians today view that stage of humanism as a necessary and positive element for Christianity. Although it contained some anti-Christian elements, it countered the excessively ascetical and antiworldly attitudes of medieval Catholicism. However, the Enlightenment, which came out of humanism, developed only the secular and pagan elements of humanism and became completely anti-Christian.[17]

Similarly, the Metaphysical movement had pagan and demonic elements from the beginning. However, they were accompanied by elements of philosophical idealism and healing, areas in which the materialist/cessationist church needed adjustment. After the 1950s, what Christian influence existed within New Thought dwindled away, and what was left in the Metaphysical movement was the spiritualist, Gnostic and pagan elements which would become the New Age movement of today.

Evaluating the Metaphysical Movement

In spite of their Gnostic-demonic elements, certain New Thought groups and individuals, such as Unity Christianity and Emmet Fox, salvaged elements of biblical truth from the Metaphysical movement. They rejected cessationism and materialist-realist theology and probed for a biblical understanding that was idealist. More than any orthodox Christian group, these groups recognized the influence of mind to body, what today would be termed the psychosomatic factor of disease.[18]

The influence of New Thought was also enhanced by the fact that it flourished outside the church. The theologians of consensus orthodoxy had used their authority and influence to discredit the Faith-Cure movement within a few years of Dr. Cullis's death. The same theologians, such as Buckley, denounced the metaphysical sects as heresy (which they were). However, the persons who were attracted to Mind-Cure and New Thought were not under the discipline of the mainline denominations and could not be frightened into renouncing their ideas. Thus, more effectively, and on a longer range than the orthodox Faith-Cure movement, the heretical metaphysical sects forced the church to face the issue of healing and cessationism.

An Evangelical Difficulty

Evangelicals have a difficult time facing the issue of the power of words and thoughts to influence the natural world. For Calvin and subsequent Reformers the powers of the mind not related to the five senses were the source problem of Catholic mysticism and therefore evil. This theology of total depravity of the soul has been updated by the influential Chinese theologian Watchman Nee, who died in 1972. In his works, especially *The Latent Power of the Soul*, he elaborated on Calvin's suspicions and concluded that the fall caused the powers of the soul to become tools for demonic use only. Thus, words and thoughts have no legitimate power over natural circumstances.[19]

There seem to be biblical and practical exceptions to this theory. In the Bible both believers and heathen are shown to have quite legitimate and God-directed "soul" experiences. Pharaoh's prophetic dream of coming abundance and famine, and the dream of Pilate's wife that Jesus was a just man are but a few examples. It may be true that the soulish powers of man were damaged at the fall, but there is no evidence that this damage was so total that God does not speak to man through them

173

or that their use is *only* for witchcraft.[20]

Here the traditional Catholic understanding of preternatural powers is probably closer to the biblical truth than the evangelical. Catholic theology states that the soulish powers are natural and neutral. They can be used and enhanced by either demonic forces or God.[21] As pointed out, quantum physics has conclusively shown that the mind inherently has some tiny power, enough to cause light to act like a particle. The real question is how much more power the mind has naturally.

The evangelical researcher is handicapped in exploring this issue because the concept of the power of thoughts and words goes counter to both his materialist-realist philosophy and Calvinist doctrine of total depravity. Here Gary Collins's book *Your Magnificent Mind* is a wonderful exception. As does Catholic theology, he credits the mind with certain natural powers. He frankly admits those powers are difficult to define, especially when one takes into account the problem of demonic interference and enhancement of the powers as happens in true witchcraft.[22]

Certainly words and thoughts have more legitimate power than Calvin-Nee (materialist-realist) theology understands. Scientific research has proven, for instance, that the mind can be trained to stimulate the body's immune system and help in the healing process.[23] Yet it is also obvious that the beliefs of the idealist cults, that powers of mind were god-like and needed only cultivation, were a gross exaggeration. A sign of this is the fact that the public, after buying millions of copies of New Thought works, got tired of it. America was not transformed by positive thinking into a paradise on earth. Somewhere between Planck's constant (a tiny influence) and the exaggerated metaphysical presumptions lies the truth.

Yet the biblical promises that Jesus made in regard to faith and its ability to move mountains (Matt. 21:21) and uproot mulberry trees (Luke 17:6) by verbal command are even more incredible than any New Thought claims of business success. Herein lies the core issue. If the power of the mind (through thoughts and word confessions) is only very limited by itself, then the real power of the mind comes through making the choice of faith. By faith the mind acts in the power of God and can move mountains.

Thus we should be cautious in judging the Metaphysical movement's techniques of positive thinking, visualization and affirmation (see chapter 17). Certainly all those activities are capable of demonization and witchcraft, but they are not, as the Calvin-Nee theology holds, *necessarily* witchcraft. They all may have a legitimate place in the uses of thoughts and words as God originally intended. The key in these areas is the cultivation of biblical discernment.

From Heresy to Faith

In *Walter Martin's Cult Reference Bible* we find this interesting and perceptive comment about Unity literature:

> The positive faith in God's provision which Unity encourages would be commendable were they [Unity writers] born-again Christians. However, not having believed in the atoning power of the blood of Christ, they have not entered into God's new covenant (Heb. 9:13-15)...Unity interprets Scriptures that are specifically addressed to the redeemed as though they were meant for everyone.[24]

This comment hits at the core of the Gnostic presumption of all the metaphysical cults, but it also points to the potential redemption of some of their theology. What if indeed the Gnostic assumptions of universality are dropped, and the laws, promises and assertions of Unity and the other Bible-affirming New Thought writers are rewritten to be applied restrictively to the Christian believer? The answer is that much of the literature becomes a valid description of the spiritual authority of the believer and the power of Christian faith loosed from cessationism.

Some individuals who began with the discoveries of New Thought were led by a spirit of discernment to reject its Gnostic and unbiblical beliefs. These persons, best identified as Bible-affirming New Thought, directly influenced the Pentecostal and charismatic movements.

Four persons were especially important in this biblical filtration of New Thought theology and its introduction into the mainstream of Christendom: 1) Glenn Clark, founder of the national summer retreat program, the Camps Farthest Out, which served as the schoolhouse for the leadership of the charismatic renewal during the 1950s and 1960s;[25] 2) Rufus Moseley, who circulated among CFO camps and other church groups in the 1950s and brought many people to the baptism and gifts of the Spirit;[26] and 3) Mrs. Agnes Sanford, who served as the apostle of healing to the mainline churches;[27] and perhaps the most influential of all, 4) E. W. Kenyon, a pioneer radio evangelist of the 1940s. Unfortunately the limitations of space permit us to examine the life and work of only E. W. Kenyon (see chapter 18). Our detailed examination of the others must await a later volume.[28]

The chapters immediately following comprise a series of topical discussions of some of the ideas that were sparked by the Metaphysical movement. The series begins with a look at the revival of prosperity teaching that had been lost, along with the Puritan work ethic, by the nineteenth century.

FIFTEEN

The Revival of Prosperity Teaching

N EW THOUGHT WAS DISTINGUISHED FROM the earlier Metaphysical movement by an emphasis on prosperity and success. New Thought writers applied idealist principles to these issues and in the process became one of the most widely read movements of popular literature. One New Thought writer alone, Orison Swett Marden (1850 – 1924) wrote dozens of books on success in business and society which sold almost twenty million copies.[1]

As in its healing literature, part of the success of New Thought was due to a deficit in mainline Christian literature. This deficit was both tragic and unnecessary. Unlike the absolute gap in Protestant healing theology that started with the Reformation, there was a great legacy of Christian motivational and prosperity literature until the Victorian era. From the 1600s Puritan writers had written many books on work, success and their relation to the Christian life. These formed the foundation of the American and European work ethic.

Inexplicably the Puritan works were not updated and consequently were no longer part of mainline Victorian Protestantism. Perhaps the clergy yielded to the ongoing temptation among church leaders to devalue the spiritual dimensions of the secular professions. This error has persisted throughout church history in spite of the biblical injunctions for normal work as part of the demands of righteousness. Paul's writings in particular stress the importance of work as part of a person's righteousness (1 and 2 Thess.).

Starting with the first-century Christian church, this chapter gives an overview of the literature that discussed the spiritual dimensions of prosperity. The chapter ends by describing the prosperity teaching in the Bible-affirming wing of New Thought.

Early Church and Lay Direction

Early Christian writers said little about secular life and work. Perhaps they felt the Old Testament already gave obvious guidelines. Or perhaps they were distracted by the major demands to establish the foundations of a dogmatic theology. An exception is one of the gems of Christian spirituality, *Christ the Educator*, written about 190 by Clement of Alexandria.[2]

Clement attempted to guide the new converts in how to live amidst the pagan world. He gave attention to such problems as modesty in the public baths and behavior at festivals. Unlike some of the later writers who denounced bathing, all entertainment and the like, Clement tried to find a Christian middle ground for those things not forbidden in Scripture or not plainly immoral. For instance, he believed it was all right to go to the public baths but encouraged care and modesty. On the issue of wealth Clement suggested that it was proper for the Christian to be rich but urged, "We should possess wealth in a becoming manner, sharing it generously, but not mechanically nor with affectation."[3]

Monastic Christianity and the (Missing) Literature of Lay Spirituality

In the third century the church entered into a period of severe persecution where the topic of the Christian's graceful accommodation into the Roman world did not have much relevance. After the persecutions, Christian monasticism became the predominant heroic model for the church. Much of the church's theology was henceforth written for or by monks.

The monastic tradition stressed a rhythm of work and prayer, but the pattern was unrealistic for laymen. No working farmer or tradesman could wake up in the middle of the night to chant the holy office. The economic model of the monastery was also inappropriate for the lay Christian. The first monks of the Egyptian desert worked on simple projects, such as weaving baskets out of reeds, to be traded for flour, writing and study materials. With some modification, Western monasticism followed this pattern. Work provided the minimum necessities. The biblical concept of prosperity was no longer discussed.

The practical economic advice and encouragement that the Old Testament directed to the believer (especially in the book of Proverbs) was subordinated to Jesus' warning against the deceit of riches. Catholicism came to understand Jesus' command to the rich young ruler (Luke 18:18-25) as absolute. A cult of poverty arose, exemplified by Francis of Assisi who lauded "Lady Poverty" and the life-style of absolute impoverishment.

Economic Consequences

Because of the predominance of monastic theology the medieval church offered little direction for the layman in regard to economic activity. Christian civilization, as it arose out of the ruins of the Roman empire, developed into a feudal pattern with classes sharply divided into social and economic functions. In feudalism the landed gentry supervised the peasants and administered local justice, but they did no manual or commercial work. If a local gentleman felt the call of God in his life the church invited him to monastic perfection. No one suggested that imaginative enterprise or commercial activity would be a way of Christian stewardship. Jesus' parable of the talents, which relates to these very matters, was interpreted spiritually to mean anything but economic enterprise (Matt. 25:14-30).

The classic of Spanish literature, *Don Quixote*, gives the picture of a civilization which attempted to be Christian without a sound lay theology of work. Don Quixote was an *hidalgo*, a landed gentleman. He was also on the edge of poverty; yet, without the slightest twinge of guilt, he did no work. No priest or monk appeared in the novel to counsel him to become an honest poultry farmer or merchant. Instead Don Quixote believed he could do good and please God by reinstituting knighthood and administering justice by force of arms. It makes a good story, but it also reflects the deficit of traditional Catholic theology.[4]

For the past sixty years various revolutionary groups in (Catholic) Latin America have tried, like Don Quixote, to bring social justice and prosperity by swift, heroic actions. In Cuba, where the Marxist revolutionaries won power, they succeeded in demonstrating that one cannot produce prosperity with a work ethic that glorifies manual labor but disdains mercantile occupations. Just as in the rest of the communist world, the attempt to mobilize and motivate society by focused hatred on the merchant class (the bourgeois) leads to impoverishment, self-deception and ruin.

Reformation and the Biblical Work Ethic

Thankfully, the Anglo-American world rejected the false Marxist solution. The Reformers accomplished this indirectly by overthrowing monasticism as the ideal for Christian perfection. Sadly, the change was accompanied by some tragic excesses. For instance, the dissolution of the monasteries in England led to the wholesale destruction of much of the art and literature that the monasteries had housed. However, the break from the tradition of the monasteries and desert monks sparked a search for a new pattern of holiness that could be fulfilled by laypersons. To be a dedicated Christian no longer implied celibacy, poverty and monastic obedience. Patterns of spirituality derived from the Bible, not the Desert Fathers, could be established.

Calvin made major contributions in this new area of theology. The model community he established in Geneva had faults, but it was a success in an area he did not imagine. Its lay theology of work established the pattern for the coming prosperous Europe. Men could pursue the devout life and labor in any lawful business at the same time without guilt that they had missed the "way of perfection," that is, monastery life (see the following discussion on Max Weber).

Legacy of Puritan Literature[5]

Literature of Christian laymen flowered in all the countries influenced by Reformed theology but more so in England and especially within the Puritan branch of the Church of England. An example is the work of the merchant John Browne, who specialized in trade with Spain. In 1591 he published a textbook for aspiring merchants. It included practical advice on dealing with foreign merchants, rates of exchange and the like, all interspersed with a biblical perspective:

> The Godly and diligent man shall have prosperitie in all his wayes: but he that followeth pleasure and voluptuousnesse, shall have much sorrow before he die....
>
> If thou wilt prosper well pray: if thou wilt have blessings, restore what thou hast evil gotten: if thou wilt have joy of thy labors,

be single in thy tongue and eye, use no lying, nor deceit....[6]

What is noticeable of Browne is that he took the book of Proverbs literally and seriously. He had rediscovered the literal meaning of the biblical precepts and advised their use as principles of successful business. Browne's guide for merchants was one of many that combined biblical piety with practical living. John Norden, another lay writer, wrote *A Pensive Man's Practice*, which was a prayer book filled with model prayers for such occasions as safe voyage and competent living. It was reprinted forty times between 1584 and 1640.[7] Significantly, opposition to the new layman's prayer books and manuals came from the clergy who believed these works were too worldly and not sufficiently concerned with theological matters.[8]

Thankfully, several Puritan clergymen within the Church of England saw the benefits of such lay piety and wrote more sophisticated works on the issue. Among them was William Perkins, a Puritan pastor and the most influential and widely read of Elizabethan theologians. He wrote an essay which clearly demonstrated the change in attitude that the Reformation brought to the idea of poverty and prosperity. In his work *A Treatise of the Vocation or Calling of Men*, written about 1600, there could be no Christian *hidalgos*, such as Don Quixote, who did good but did not work. Honest labor was essential to righteousness, and idleness was a sin:

> Sloth and negligence in the duties of our callings are a disorder against the comely order which God hath set in the societies of mankind, both in church and commonwealth. And, indeed idleness and sloth are the causes of many damnable sins. The idle body and the idle brain is [*sic*] the shop of the devil.[9]

Unlike the Catholic tradition which saw a hierarchy of vocations with the celibate religious life as the highest calling, Perkins proclaimed that man could please God perfectly by living in faith in whatever honest occupation he was called.

> And the action of the shepherd in keeping sheep, performed as I said in his kind, is as good a work before God, as is the action of a judge in giving sentence, or a magistrate in ruling, or a minister in preaching.[10]

The works of William Perkins were among the most often imported for the personal and pastoral libraries of the colonies. His and other works like it established the theology of work for the American colonies (an exception being the South, where slavery distorted the work ethic back to a hierarchical pattern with the slaves at the bottom). Cotton Mather, a Puritan pastor and contemporary of Jonathan Edwards, re-worked Perkins's themes a century later in *Two Brief Discourses, One Directing a Christian in His General Calling; Another Directing Him in His Personal Calling.*

Mather reworked Perkins's idea that every Christian has a general calling on his life to worship and serve the Lord, but, in addition, the person has a calling from God for a specific, useful livelihood. He compared a Christian using both callings to a rower using both oars.

> If he mind but one of his *Callings*, be it which it will, he pulls the *oar* but on one side of the Boat, and will make but a poor dispatch to the Shoar of Eternal Blessedness.[11]

Mather believed it was the individual's duty to seek God for specific direction as to which business, trade or profession to follow. Once the Christian has discerned the heavenly directive he could trust in God's promises to give him success, provided that daily he commend his work to the Lord in prayer.

> Would a man *Rise* by his Business? I say, then let him *Rise* to his *Business*. It was foretold. Prov. 22.29, *Seest thou a man Diligint in his Business? He shall stand before Kings*; He shall come to preferment.[12]

Secular Temptations: Ben Franklin

In his famous *Autobiography* Ben Franklin described how another of Mather's books, *Essays to Do Good*, influenced him. Franklin accepted the ethical teachings of Puritanism while rejecting, like other Enlightenment intellectuals, the core doctrines of Christianity. Franklin became a deist but labored like a Puritan, a pattern that became common in the United States. Franklin's *Autobiography* at times reads like the journal of Jonathan Edwards because both had long lists of things to do for self-improvement. The critical distinction was that Edwards always closed his lists by saying "with God's help." Franklin trusted in his own willpower.

182

In the nations influenced by Reformation theology an era of innovation and scientific progress developed that was to be called the industrial revolution. The German sociologist Max Weber was the first to understand that this economic revolution was indeed sparked by Reformation theology. Weber's masterwork, *The Protestant Ethic and the Spirit of Capitalism*, also showed that other aspects of Catholic theology, aside from its inadequate work ethic, had delayed Europe's economic expansion.[13]

As Franklin's life showed, the danger with the Protestant ethic is that it can become pure materialism when the biblical underpinnings are taken away. A successful man or woman can acquire the admiration of his or her colleagues, and this can fulfill the basic human need for self-esteem. It also acts as a counterfeit religion. Instead of working to please God, the person works to please society. The flower-children period of the 1960s marked a drastic breakdown in the American work ethic and its associated moral restraints. It simply demonstrated that Franklin's secularized Puritanism could not last indefinitely when separated from its biblical roots.

Gaps in Christian Motivational Literature

Mainline Protestant theology became more sophisticated in the nineteenth century and lost interest in the issue of work and spirituality. It seems the constant temptation of the clergy and academic theologians is to focus on fashionable theological issues as the only ones worthy of serious consideration. The layman's issues of work ethic and motivation are dismissed as lacking interest. But to be fair, we must note that nineteenth century theologians were occupied with many serious issues: slavery, abolition and the Civil War followed by the modernist controversy which pitted the theory of evolution against Genesis.

In the past thirty years most academic theologians have been influenced by Liberation Theology which has a destructive anti-business (Marxist) bias. It has been the Mormon, Stephen Covey, who has given us the contemporary definition of godly motivation in the workplace in his masterpiece, *The Seven Habits of Highly Effective People.*[14]

In the Victorian era, only devotional writers continued with the prosperity themes of Puritanism. For example, the original McGuffey readers contained the Puritan assumption that hard work and honesty would be rewarded by prosperity. Popular Christian novels often centered their plots around the biblical promise that ethical acts have worldly consequences. These novels have not been recognized in standard histories of American literature because they did not conform to the coming pattern of agnosticism and non-Christian values that would become a hallmark of modern secular literature.[15]

New Thought Prosperity Literature

Even though some New Thought writers abandoned key tenets of Christianity, they continued the Puritan tradition of writing about work and prosperity. One of the historians of Puritanism noted the surprising continuity between Puritanism and New Thought:

> Theologically they were poles apart, but in one fundamental they were alike. The law of prosperity was a cardinal statute upon the books of New Thought as it had been in the teachings of the Puritans.[16]

The thinkers behind the Metaphysical movement, such as Ralph Waldo Emerson and other Transcendentalists, advocated self-culture (self-improvement, self-education, self-affirmation, self-discipline). This was essentially Ben Franklin's self-improvement with updated vocabulary and philosophical assumptions. As noted earlier, New Thought was roughly divided into a secular, mind-power wing which was non-Christian or deist and a wing which attempted to maintain a Christian and biblical base. The New Thought literature on prosperity was divided the same way. The deist wing believed that the key to prosperity and success lay in applying mind-power to the individual situations. They also included attention to (Swedenborgian) spiritual laws (see next chapter). The Bible-affirming wing often accepted these elements but maintained the scriptural base that was the legacy of the earlier Puritan writings.

The most important New Thought deist to concentrate on the success issue was Orison Swett Marden (1850 – 1924). Marden's books were a staple for Victorian businessmen and aspiring businessmen. Marden came to New Thought via the philosophical route. He had read Emerson's *Representative Men*, which suggested that the great men of history, such as Napoleon and Lincoln, had embodied spiritual laws in their lives. Marden elaborated this idea in his early and highly successful books, as in his 1894 *Pushing to the Front: Or, Success Under Difficulties.*[17] Gradually he shifted to writing about the other motifs of New

Thought, idealism and mind-power. The title of one of his later works says it all: *Every Man a King: Or, Might in Mind-Mastery.*[18]

New Thought Prosperity: The Biblical Echo

The best known writer of the Bible-affirming wing of New Thought was Ralph Waldo Trine (1866 – 1958). Born in a small town in Illinois, he received an excellent education both at the University of Wisconsin and Johns Hopkins. *In Tune With the Infinite*, his most famous book, became an international best-seller which sold one and a half million copies in its English version and was translated into twenty languages.[19] It is often read to this day.

Trine believed that the major spiritual task for the person seeking enlightenment was to come into alignment with spiritual laws:

> If one holds himself in the thought of poverty, he will be poor, and the chances are that he will remain in poverty. If he holds himself, whatever present conditions may be, continually in the thought of prosperity, he sets into operation forces that will sooner or later bring him into prosperous conditions. The law of attraction works unceasingly throughout the universe, and the one great and never changing fact in connection with it is, as we have found, that like attracts like.[20]

As a practical technique Trine advised the reader:

> See yourself in a prosperous condition. Affirm that you will before long be in a prosperous condition. Affirm it calmly and quietly, but strongly and confidently. Believe it, believe it absolutely. Expect it, — keep it constantly watered with expectation.[21]

But Trine also echoed the Puritan tradition of faith in God's provision:

> God holds all things in His hands. His constant word is, My child, acknowledge Me in all your ways, and in the degree that you do this, in the degree that you live this, then what is Mine is yours. Jehovah-jireh, — the Lord will provide.[22]

Trine's views were idealist but not magical. He followed the biblical pattern of understanding that faith has an ethical demand, as well as the practical one:

> All the time be faithful, *absolutely* faithful to the situation in which you are placed. If you are *not* faithful to it the chances are that it will not be the stepping-stone to something better, but to something poorer...Don't fold your hands and expect to see things drop into your lap, but set into operation the higher forces and then take hold of the first thing that offers itself. Do what your hands find to do, *and do it well.*[23]

Though mixed with Gnostic assumptions Trine's theology of prosperity echoed the Puritan literature of earlier centuries. He saw that the promises of the Old Testament in regard to material blessing were valid in this day. Trine understood that one of the main revelations of God in the Old Testament was God as Jehovah Jireh, the provider. Trine encouraged the reader to seek a "medium" of prosperity, a concept derived from Swedenborg (see next chapter). In this case it was in full harmony with biblical revelation (Prov. 30:7-9).

Charles Fillmore

Unity's Charles Fillmore wrote perhaps the definitive discussion of prosperity in New Thought titled simply *Prosperity*. Like Trine's work it is a mix of New Thought idealism and the old Puritan heritage. The first chapters are heavily metaphysical and contain several fanciful theories such as the idea that believers could tap the power and energies of God through the ether, the rarefied element once believed to fill the upper regions of space.[24] In spite of these and other flights of fancy (and Gnosticism) the book contained much that was in harmony with Scripture and with the Puritan heritage. Fillmore's fundamental understanding of prosperity was balanced.

> There is a kingdom of abundance of all things and it may be found by those who seek it and are willing to comply with its laws. Jesus said that it is hard for the rich man to enter into the kingdom of heaven. This does not mean that it is hard because of his wealth, for the poor man gets in no faster and no easier. It is not money but the ideas men hold about

money, its source, its ownership, and its use, that keep them out of the kingdom.[25]

Like other leaders of Bible-affirming New Thought, Fillmore understood tithing as more than an Old Testament command. He and others had discerned in tithing the operation of a spiritual law. In this matter Fillmore was completely orthodox and laid aside his more fanciful theories. He quoted Malachi 3 and said:

It sets forth clearly a law of prosperity for all classes of people; for those who need protection for their crops from frosts, droughts, floods; for those who would escape the plagues, pestilences, and manifold things that would destroy their supply and support. It is a simple law but so effective; simply give a tithe or tenth of the "first-fruits" or their equivalent to the Lord. God should not be expected to meet all of man's requirements in the matter of giving this protection and increase unless man fulfills the requirements of God.[26]

This last statement indicates both the continuity and difference that Fillmore and other Bible-affirming New Thought leaders had with the Puritan heritage. Whereas Puritans would talk of the promises of God as the guiding principle for action, New Thought spoke of laws. That distinction would be a source of great controversy, and we will return to it in later chapters.

Summary

Even though Paul exhorted his churches to labor honestly in the world, the Catholic tradition elevated the separated life of the monk as the ideal for Christian perfection. Thus the relationship between work and prosperity was ignored for centuries. After the Reformation, laypersons again began to seek holiness through honest work, resulting in several centuries of prosperity in Europe. The Puritans carried this work ethic with them to America, yet prosperity literature had faded from the Christian scene by the nineteenth century. Bible-affirming New Thought writers filled in the gap left by the church, gleaning spiritual laws of prosperity from the Scriptures.

The following chapter continues this discussion by looking into the revival of spiritual law that started with the Metaphysical movement.

SIXTEEN

The Resurrection of Spiritual Laws

Swedenborgism: The Background Heresy of Spiritual Law

OF ALL THE ELEMENTS THAT made up the Metaphysical movement, the one that demonstrated most clearly that some truth is often found in heresy was the discovery of spiritual law. A clear, biblical understanding of spiritual law has come only in recent decades, although concepts similar to it formed the foundations of Christian theology from New Testament times. Simply defined, spiritual laws are those biblical principles which govern the interaction between man's ethical acts and their consequences, especially consequences in this world.

For background we need to examine an eighteenth-century cult, Swedenborgism. This was the first Western spiritualist cult. Although the Swedenborgian churches never were important numerically, Swedenborg's doctrines were influential on many of the religious leaders of the eighteenth and nineteenth centuries. Swedenborgism became the base theology of many of the metaphysical cults.

Emanuel Swedenborg (1688 – 1772) was a Swedish engineer and scientist who experienced a long series of visions in which he supposedly held conversations with angels and persons long dead, including Jesus. Out of these experiences he produced volumes of a new revelation about the nature of the spiritual and physical worlds.

188

In reality the basis of his new revelation was the ancient Gnosticism. Just as in the teachings of the Corinthian Gnostics or the Gnostics of the third century, Swedenborg's Jesus was a highly evolved being, but not God or Savior. Swedenborg claimed that it was Paul who exaggerated the role of Jesus. Central to Swedenborg's system was the repeated assertion that entrance into the kingdom of God in the universe, including the other planets of our solar system, was through ethical actions (not repentance and salvation through Jesus). For instance, the beings on Mars, the most perfect in the solar system, knew that the kingdom was achieved by good works, clean living and vegetarianism.[1]

The scientific revelations included such information as the nature of the men on the moon and other planets. According to Swedenborg, the moon men were the size of children and had thunderous voices and mouths in their stomachs.[2] Such scientific nonsense could not be exposed with the instrumentation of his day but was plausible to his contemporaries.

Spiritual Laws

At a time when Enlightenment elites were discarding faith in Christianity and the Bible and ridiculing natural law, Swedenborg's revelations offered a system that claimed to wed spirituality and science. Like every great heresy and demonic system, part of the attraction of Swedenborgism was based on the weak points in consensus orthodoxy. Specifically, Swedenborgism reasserted that moral acts have earthly consequences (a biblical truth discussed below). A particular pattern of acts and consequences was called a spiritual law.

Swedenborg's spiritual law became one of the cornerstones of the Metaphysical movement and continued through its Gnostic descendants to today's New Age movement. This law supposedly governs both the spirit and the earthly realms. The law includes such universals as the law of attraction (like attracts like) and the law of correspondence, by which a person's physical appearance reflects his inward, spiritual state.

To many the Swedenborgian laws sound innocent enough, if somewhat trite, but every one is deadly to the authentic spiritual life. From the law of correspondence one can discern the true demonic intention: interior repentance, prayer and the grace of God were not important to one's spiritual state — you can just judge it from the person's outward appearance. The law of attraction (like attracts like) is equally deadly. I observed in many New Age groups that "like attracts like" served as an antidiscernment affirmation. Since all in the group are seekers of spiritual truth, then, by this law, nothing evil would be attracted to the group. They assumed they did not have to be concerned with discerning of spirits in the phenomena they experienced or in the doctrines they accepted. "Like attracts like" is a lie that flatters the ego and shuts down discernment.

The Bible and the This-Worldly Moral Order

Actually, the Bible clearly asserts that moral actions have worldly consequences. However, traditional Christian theology has concentrated on the afterlife rewards and punishments of moral acts to the exclusion of the this-worldly consequences. This theological gap provided an opening for bogus spiritual laws. The same gap in traditional theology can be observed in the way Christian leaders react to AIDS. Few are willing to accept that in many cases disease is a manifestation of the wrath of God against sin, as is indicated in Romans 1:21-27:[*]

> For although they knew God, they neither glorified him as God nor gave thanks to him, but their thinking became futile and their foolish hearts darkened...Therefore God gave them over in the sinful desires of their hearts to sexual impurity for the degrading of their bodies with one another. They exchanged the truth of God for a lie, and worshiped and served created things rather than the Creator...Because of this, God gave them over to shameful lusts. Even their women exchanged natural relations for unnatural ones. In the same way the men also abandoned natural relations with women and were inflamed with lust for one another. Men committed indecent acts with other men, and received in themselves the due penalty for their perversion (NIV).

Notice the sequence of moral acts and consequences: an ethical act of ignoring God (idolatry) leads to a darkening of the intellect and delusion, which leads to sexual perversion, which leads to a penalty "in themselves," that is, disease. This is an earthly cycle, not an afterlife

---

[*]   I am *not* saying that all cases of AIDS are punishment for individual sin. Many times exposure to the virus is accidental. People in this category are not being punished for their personal sin, yet they suffer from the results of others' sins.

threat, although certainly breaking the law of God also has afterlife consequences.

The earthly moral orderliness and lawfulness are central to biblical revelation. The book of Proverbs is practically a handbook of the relationships between moral acts and their worldly consequences. For example, Proverbs 10:27 declares the relationship between righteousness and length of earth life:

> The fear of the Lord prolongs life, but the years of the wicked will be shortened.

Many of Solomon's proverbs proclaim a relationship between morality and wealth, for example:

> Poor is he who works with a negligent hand, but the hand of the diligent makes rich (10:4).

> The generous man will be prosperous, and he who waters will himself be watered (11:25).

Treachery and evil acts would also come back to the perpetrator:

> He who digs a pit will fall into it, and he who rolls a stone, it will come back on him (26:27).

Rabbinical commentaries from before the time of Christ to modern times have stressed the principle in Proverbs of moral, this-worldly reciprocity. This principle was understood to be "the greatest of the principles which underlie or govern the divine rule."[3] It was called plainly the "tit-for-tat" and often served as a hermeneutical tool. For instance, a medieval commentary on the story of Joseph and his brothers explains:

> When Joseph's brethren were arrested and accused of stealing his cup, "they rent their garments" (Gen. XLIV, 13). God said to them, "Because you caused your father to rend his garments for a lie, so do you now rend your own garments for a lie!" (To locate this teaching in the Jewish Talmud, see Tanh. B., Mikkez, 99b.)[4]

The Scripture scholar Gerhard Von Rad calls these biblical associations the act-consequence relationship, a somewhat more dignified term than tit-for-tat.[5] The same this-worldly reciprocity is affirmed in the New Testament, though given a greater degree of ambiguity. For example, Jesus confirmed the Old Testament revelation that some sickness was due to sin (Mark 2:1-12 and John 5:2-15). However, Paul's "thorn in the flesh," probably an unsightly eye disease, was given to him to preserve his humility, not because of sin (2 Cor. 12:7).

Biblical Law Versus Karma

Some may believe that the biblical act-consequence relationship (tit-for-tat) is the same as the Eastern concept of karma. Though similar, there are critical differences between them. Karma is a mechanical law of moral actions and consequences that takes place without regard to grace or God's mercy. In fact, in Buddhism, karma operates without any concept of a personal god. The Eastern concept of karma declares that whatever moral acts one performs in one lifetime will be reaped in another life. Thus karma is intimately linked with the idea of reincarnation. On the other hand, the biblical act-consequence relationship usually reveals an immediate, this-world consequence of moral acts. However, this-world consequences also include a concept of generational blessing or curse that passes through the family line (Ex. 20:5).

Early in the formation of the Bible the Holy Spirit prevented the revelation of the act-consequence relation from degenerating into karma. The book of Job, perhaps the earliest book of the Bible, can be seen as an antikarma tract. The major lesson is that Job's tragedies were not due to karmic fault, as his advisors attempted to establish, but were the result of his testing at the hand of Satan.

Thus the Bible presents a mosaic of revelation in which the moral order of the universe is lawful but modified by mercy, grace and other factors such as the role of hardship in holiness formation. Man's rewards and punishments are distributed between earth life and the afterlife. That compound revelation is difficult to preach, and the temptation is to stress the consequences in the afterlife. This has the advantage of avoiding the problem of ambiguity (that is, some good men are poor; some evil men are rich).

Christian Theology Ignores the Tit-for-Tat

Early Christian theologians, especially those influenced by Desert Christianity's asceticism, were simply uninterested in the fact that many of the act-consequences of Scripture promised worldly blessings of prosperity and contentment. Just as Desert Christianity had ignored the healing power of Scripture, it also disdained the earthy tit-for-tat as unworthy of Christianity.

The values of Desert Christianity were combined with the tendency to spiritualize the interpretation of Scripture. Scripture was interpreted by the allegorical method developed by other theologians (especially Origen). Therefore, any time the Scriptures were too "earthy" they were given spiritual meaning; that is, Song of Solomon was not about romantic love but only a type of Christ's love for His church.[6] In this interpretive tradition the positive blessing of economic well-being in Proverbs was understood spiritually to mean rewards in heaven. By the time of Augustine, the allegorical-ascetical hermeneutic had become almost universal. It became part of the consensus orthodoxy of the Catholic church and was not seriously challenged until the Reformation.

All of this means that the biblical revelations that obedience or disobedience to God's laws had earthly consequences had long been finessed out of Christian theology as crude and unspiritual. Catholic theology asserted that man's obedience or violation of God's laws was accountable only in the afterlife (heaven, hell or purgatory). This was challenged by the Reformers mainly on the issue of purgatory. Calvin also began to see that some of the biblical promises were related to economic activities (see chapter 15). Yet he did not understand the act-consequence relationship in regard to other aspects of life.

The philosophy of Hegel, Swedenborgism and the Metaphysical movement that followed all fed upon the sense of moral vacuum and devaluation of earth life common in Christian theology. These attitudes were accentuated when belief in natural law and natural theology was abandoned (see chapter 7). Unlike Hegel, Swedenborg did not offer salvation and significance through political action. Rather he offered a system of personal salvation through good works and spiritual laws. Earth life and the things of the earth were again directly related to man's spiritual and eternal existence.

As destructive as Swedenborg's spiritual laws were, they brought forth the suppressed truth that moral acts on earth have direct earthly consequences. Satan took a chance in the Swedenborgian revelations of creating an attractive system by revealing some truth. Satan is always forced to do that; every heresy is in fact based on some hidden truth, for the human spirit can only be attracted by truth. The demonic payoff is that the truth revealed can be so demonized as to be morally and spiritually destructive.

The Swedenborg system released into religious conversations the new phrase "spiritual law." This is a very powerful expression, for with it a person can interrogate the Bible to see if there are indeed patterns of moral lawfulness and further ask if these patterns have much to say about earthly consequences.

In fact, metaphysical writers took up the concept of spiritual law with great gusto. Practically every author had his own ideas as to what these laws were and when they applied. Most followed Swedenborg, while introducing a measure of biblical accountability to the concept. As we saw in the previous chapter, New Thought writers often mixed valid biblical precepts with Swedenborgian spiritual laws. This muddled mix of the authentic and the bogus remained a characteristic of New Thought writing and was not fully resolved until recent times. A major landmark along the way toward biblical purity was the fine book by Dr. Loring T. Swaim, *Arthritis, Medicine and Spiritual Laws*. In this work, Dr. Swaim showed that a major cause of arthritis was unresolved anger (see Prov. 12:4 and 14:30).[7] The final biblical filtration which eliminated the last vestiges of Swedenborgism from the concept of spiritual law was done through the counseling and writing ministry of a husband and wife team, John and Paula Sandford.

John Sandford: Spiritual Law Clarified[8]

Both John and Paula Sandford were born in depression times, their characters forged by the difficulties faced by that generation. John's mother had been raised in the old exuberant tradition of Methodism which believed in the Bible and affirmed the absolute reality of its moral law. However, they defined their Christianity in the tradition of liberal Protestantism. Paula's household, on the other hand, was richly and devoutly evangelical Christian.[9]

At age seventeen John felt a call to the ministry. He attended Drury College in Springfield, Missouri, where he met Paula. Both felt that the Lord had placed them together for His service. John earned a scholarship to the renowned (and liberal) Chicago Theological Seminary, where he received his master of divinity degree while pastoring a small

194

church in Streator, Illinois (one hundred miles southwest of Chicago). All during his seminary years he resisted the deadening teachings of liberal theology but had no access to an intelligent alternate system. He ended his seminary years as a reluctant liberal and might have become a normal, socially active, semi-believing, liberal minister.

Within a few months of his ordination in July 1958 he made a conscious and radical decision to reject his liberal theological heritage and accept the gospel as true and literal. In October of that year the Lord blessed that decision in a prayer experience where John received the baptism of the Holy Spirit.

A few months later in 1959 John attended Agnes Sanford's (no relation) School of Pastoral Care, held in Springfield, Missouri. John was suffering from severe back pain, and Agnes laid hands on him for healing. His pain disappeared.[10] She sensed John's deep thirst for the things of the Lord and his keen intellect, and a close friendship began between the two. After his experiences at the School of Pastoral Care he rapidly read through the Agnes Sanford books and the charismatic books which were beginning to appear. In a few months John was being used by Agnes as her assistant at healing missions and speaking engagements. From 1959 to 1970, when Agnes retired from her active speaking ministry, John was one of Agnes's assistants and prayer partners as she traveled the country in her teaching circuit (others included Tommy Tyson and Francis MacNutt).

His academic training and pastoral experience made him superbly qualified to assist in the Schools of Pastoral Care. From 1961 to 1970 he served as Agnes's lead minister at the schools. More important, it was during these years with Agnes that John was forced to examine the biblical basis of their theology. They were consistently challenged by participants on the issues of inner healing and spiritual law. This forced John to "search the Scriptures" diligently.

He and Paula began ministering together, putting into practice what they had learned from Agnes Sanford and being attentive to the Lord's direction. They continued to read the literature of the charismatic renewal and were particularly influenced by Derek Prince and by the writings of Watchman Nee.

Spiritual Law: The Tit-for-Tat Among Nations and Marriage Partners

Central to the Sandfords' theology is the concept of spiritual law. In their writings we see its cleansing and refinement by way of alignment with biblical revelation. The Sandfords have been meticulous in separating the biblical concept of spiritual law from its occult cousin, the concept of karma. Although they might have used the word *karma* with a modified, biblically defined meaning, they chose instead to use the more awkward but soundly biblical phrase "the law of sowing and reaping." (They apparently had no knowledge of the rabbinical tit-for-tat, discussed in chapter 15 and little known among Christians.)

In *The Elijah Task*, the Sandfords took special care to define the meaning of spiritual law. They saw much of the work of the prophet as that of understanding the workings of spiritual laws. Just as the prophets of the Old Testament saw that the act of idolatry would bring about disastrous political and military consequences, so too the contemporary prophet must be attentive to the working of spiritual laws in his community. The modern prophet (and spiritual counselor) must also be able to see the ethical actions and attitudes of his brethren or counselees in relation to the ultimate consequences. With this knowledge he may warn others, pray in intercession for others, proclaim the good news of forgiveness or perhaps bring people to repentance before the disastrous working out of the law takes place in the life of the individual. In a few pages in *The Elijah Task* the Sandfords summarize the meaning of spiritual law and its relationship to Jesus' sacrifice on the cross.

> Law has its source in the nature of God. It is principle and order, the very structure and discipline of the entire universe...The ten commandments, indeed all of the moral law given to man, are what God has chosen to reveal of His whole scheme of order which is far beyond our ability to comprehend....
>
> That law is relentless, for nothing changes it. Even God himself does not break His own principles. If He did, His name would be Chaos rather than Father. What seems miracle and mystery to us is in truth operation of principles beyond the principles we know.
>
> "Whatsoever a man soweth, that shall he also reap" (Gal. 6:7). That is the will of God. He has built the universe to operate upon principles of balance and retribution. "For every action there is an equal and opposite reaction." All of our science and technology are based upon the certainty of God's principles. If His laws were not immutable, no architect

would dare to build a skyscraper, no astronaut would venture beyond earth, no electrician could wire a house.

We have somehow lost hold of the basic principles of life, the good will of God revealed in the Bible. Men who have better sense than to violate business or engineering principles, somehow think they can hop into bed with any man or woman with impunity....

Now perhaps we are prepared to understand the efficacy of the cross. In countless hymns we have sung that He paid the price for us. Did we understand the weight of what we sing? Every time any man in all the universe has sinned, he has set in motion forces which must come to resolution. This is impartial inescapable law. Full and exact payment has been made for everything. God, knowing all the horrible things men unconsciously had set in motion, let alone what was due for conscious sin, gave, and constantly continues to give unmerited deliverance. In Jesus, on the cross, the law was not abolished; it was fulfilled (Matt. 5:17).

Nevertheless, that mercy is not automatic. It waits upon confession. If we live outside the cross, we must reap accordingly. The moment we repent and confess, the Lord takes the due results of our sins to the cross.[11]

The Tit-for-Tat of the Mind

The Sandfords discovered that one of the most important manifestations of spiritual law was in the area of self-inflicted mental sins. These are those attitudes we hold and judgments we make, often without any manifest behavior, but which nonetheless violate the law of God. These mental sins set in motion destructive forces which will rebound upon a person unless the original attitude or judgment is brought to the cross. The New Testament gives clear warning that attitudes are as important as acts, as is Jesus' warning that anger or lust makes a person just as subject to judgment as murder and adultery (Matt. 5:21-28).

In the Sandfords' writings the most common mental sin is unforgiveness, which can take many forms. Most of the text of *The Transformation of the Inner Man* is dedicated to identifying the varied and subtle manifestations of unforgiveness and discussing how a counselor can help an individual bring these patterns of unforgiveness to the cross. Two forms of unforgiveness, bitter-root judgments and inner vows, are

197

the special concern of the counselor as they occur in most individuals. They are both manifestations of spiritual laws.

An inner vow is a statement of intent which is most commonly expressed in the negative, such as: "I'll never beat my kids the way Dad beats us!" At times inner vows are subconscious and are never clearly or consciously articulated. The Sandfords gave an example of an inner vow in a woman in her thirties who came to them for ministry. She still had baby fat on her face and had no breast development, nor had she started menstruation. She was born as an unwanted child in war-torn Czechoslovakia. The parents wanted no child but wished for a boy after the pregnancy was discovered. Subsequently she had never been affirmed as female. As a result of all this the girl had unconsciously vowed that she would not grow up to be a woman.

The Sandfords prayed for the inner healing and affirmation of the little girl within her and led the woman through prayers of forgiveness and repentance. They counseled that she pray affirmative prayers ("Thank You, Lord, for life...") as part of her daily prayers. Within two years she lost her baby fat, developed breasts, began menstruating and developed into a beautiful woman.[12] The Sandfords believe that inner vows cannot be broken by confession alone. They must be destroyed by the church's power to "bind and loose" (Matt. 18:18). Specifically, the counselor must speak the words of authority, such as "In Jesus' name I break this vow of...."[13]

Bitter-root judgments are very similar to inner vows. They also tend to be generated in childhood as a response to negative family situations. Like inner vows, bitter-root judgments bring to pass the very circumstances which the person most hated. A common example of this is in alcoholism. A child may say, "I'll never be like my mom! I'll never touch a drop of liquor as long as I live!" The fact that the mother was an alcoholic and therefore guilty of sin is both true and unfortunate. However, children are forbidden by the sixth commandment from dishonoring (judging) parents. Thus what is a natural judgment and anguished cry nonetheless sets in motion spiritual forces which will manifest in later life.

The son or daughter who judged the parent for alcoholism is often destined to attract a mate who will either become an alcoholic or behave like an alcoholic (as in a workaholic). This spiritual law operates so consistently in alcoholic families that many in the medical profession believe that alcoholism is a genetic disease. It is really a chain of bitter-root judgments that continues *spiritually* from generation to generation until broken by the blood of Jesus.

Bitter-root judgments can affect every area of life, not just choice of spouse. The Sandfords relate the problems of a businessman who came to them for counseling. It seems he had a recurring problem of having his closest business associates cheat and betray him. The bitter-root judgment was traced to his judgment of his father as dishonest. Only when his judgment was confessed and forgiven was he able to prosper without recurring ruin.[14]

The Superficial Quality of American Christianity

Through years of pastoral counseling the Sandfords identified the shallowness of Christian life as perhaps the most severe problem for the American church. This shallowness is nurtured by popular evangelical theology which has two serious flaws in its theology.

The major contributing factor to the tragic superficiality of many American Christians is abandonment of the concept of law and its role among born-again believers. While American Protestantism has accepted the Reformers' central understanding of salvation by grace, they have for the most part abandoned the Reformers' insistence that law (moral and civil) still holds an important part in the role of the believer.

American Christians accepted the Enlightenment judgment that moral law was a myth. On the contrary, to be born-again saves a Christian from his sins, but it does not place him above the moral or spiritual law. The Reformers understood that law was indispensable in channeling the love of the believer to effective and godly social action. Luther and Calvin believed that the law of God was indispensable for the regenerated Christian in directing and structuring his good works. Love provides the motivation for the Christian, but biblical law gives that love orientation.[15]

The second problem is that modern Christians (and ministers) do not understand the biblical term *heart*. Thus when they read Paul's definition of conversion, "If you confess with your mouth Jesus as Lord, and believe in your heart that God raised Him from the dead, you shall be saved" (Rom. 10:9), they interpret it to mean "believe in your intellect." This is the legacy of faculties psychology that stuck to evangelical theology from its Calvinist roots. On the contrary, the biblical heart means *all areas* of the mind, including the deepest areas.

The confusion has profound implications. Many Christians make an altar call and/or a born-again commitment but do not follow up with persistent seeking after holiness. They have only presented the intellect to the Lord and not brought under conversion the deeper levels of the mind (heart). It is these unconverted areas of the mind, areas of memory, ambition, sexual desires, unhealed emotions and so on, that prevent the Christian from moving to greater areas of sanctification. This confusion between intellect and heart has tragic consequences and produces much scandal among nonbelievers. Specifically, nonbelievers scorn the countless persons in America who claim to be born again but who do not live like Christians.

Some time ago my wife and I viewed the movie *Murphy's Romance*. Sally Field played a divorcée trying to make a living for herself and her child. Her ex-husband comes home and, as before their divorce, continues to steal, cheat and live licentiously. He wants to rejoin the family; he announces that he is a "born-again Christian" and had responded to an altar call. The movie audience gave a loud, derisive laugh, perhaps to say, "Yes, we've met many like him." The author of the screenplay, regardless of his theological understanding, caught an important defect in American Christianity.

The Sandfords' definition of spiritual law may be a way of returning to a biblical appreciation of law which was lost in the Enlightenment (chapter 7). In one of their newsletters the Sandfords warn that no true revival can come to America until Christians understand and accept the concept of spiritual (and moral) law and repent before God for lawless acts. Any coming revival must be one in which Christians return to holiness as well as lawfulness.[16]

We now turn our discussion to another controversial development in the church today — the use of visualization in prayer. This current uproar can be traced all the way back to the tension between the Reformers and Catholicism.

SEVENTEEN

Visualization and the Christian[1]

The Controversy

IN 1985 DAVE HUNT'S BOMBSHELL *The Seduction of Christianity* appeared in Christian bookstores and began its climb as the best-selling and most influential Christian book of the 1980s. Using cessationist arguments, Hunt accused the charismatic movement of unintended sorcery because of its use of visualization. We will deal more specifically with this and other aspects of Hunt's theology in later chapters. Now it is only important to note that *The Seduction of Christianity* produced much soul-searching and analysis about the proper role, if any, of visualization among Christians.

The use of visualization is overlaid with historical problems, theological issues and a biblical silence that could be interpreted in many ways. In this chapter we will review the fundamental issues at stake. To do this we need to examine briefly the issues of idolatry and human imagination as they may relate to visualization. We will trace how traditional Catholicism fell into a cult of statues and, in response, Reformers attempted to "fence" (prevent sin by being overly restrictive) the second commandment by forbidding all mental imagery. They attempted to prevent sin by going further than Scripture demanded (1 Cor. 4:6). After all of this, and with the help of several evangelical sources, we will bring the problems and the potential of Christian visualization into focus.

The Bible Versus Idolatry

The revelation of one God, Yahweh, came within a setting where many gods were represented and worshipped through idols. It was not until the Ten Commandments were given during the exodus that idolatry was revealed as a major sin. The commandment against idols is repeated several times in Scripture, and for our purpose the most significant variant is given in Exodus 20:4-5:

> You shall not make for yourself an idol, or any likeness of what is in heaven above or on the earth beneath or in the water under the earth. You shall not worship them or serve them; for I, the Lord your God, am a jealous God....

This variant makes clear that the injunction is not merely against graven images (that is, sculpture or relief) but against other forms of idolatrous representations. The prohibition is against artifacts that are the objects of worship, not against sculptures or painting in general. This exception is verified by the fact that God commanded the ark of the covenant to be decorated by sculptures, the gold cherubim (Ex. 25:18). Similarly, the bronze pillars of Solomon's temple were topped by graven bronze pomegranates, and sculptured oxen supported the temple water basin (1 Kin. 7:13-45). This allowance of sculpture and art for decoration has not always been understood.

Christianity came into a Greco-Roman world that assumed idolatry was the normal and pious form of religious expression (Acts 17:16). In this context the early church took the Mosaic injunction against idols with utmost seriousness. The absolute refusal to use religious idols made early Christians quite distinct in the pagan world. Many died because they would not burn a pinch of incense in front of the emperor's bust.[2]

However, by the fourth century Christian laymen began to produce popular art, as in decorated oil lamps or vases. Some of these had symbolic representations of Christ, as in a shepherd holding a stray sheep. These early examples were within biblical bounds of decorative art and were not intended as icons for the focus of worship.

The Church and Statues

Serious problems developed when Christians began imitating pagan sculpture. Statues began to be made of the saints. This was often accomplished by the crude process of changing the name of a statue from a pagan god to a Christian saint. Soon the statues were honored with flowers and even dressed in expensive clothing. By the sixth century many sections of the church were into unintentional, but real, idolatrous practices.

In the eighth century several Byzantine emperors attempted a reform of Christendom by suppressing the growing cult of statues and limiting the power and influence of the monasteries. They had temporary success, but with later emperors the antistatue (iconoclast) party lost to the popular clamor for the restoration of statues and icons. In fact, the iconoclasts succeeded only in stimulating theological justifications for the use of icons. The theory was brought forth that by meditation on an icon, the worship of the believer would ascend through it and to God. This was an importation from paganism. Any good pagan theologian would have said precisely the same of his idols.

On the other hand, the pro-icon theologians were dealing with an aspect of New Testament revelation that truly modified the absolute prohibition against representations of Yahweh, that is, the incarnation. Jesus, the God-man, was the perfect representation of God (Heb. 1:3). Jesus appeared in the flesh, and those seeing Him obviously did not break the second commandment. Further, the testimony of both Scripture and the continuous life of the church was that Jesus continued to appear to persons as a sovereign act of grace. The New Testament reports showed that Jesus appeared both in His fully glorified state, as in Paul's Damascus road experience or the transfiguration scene with Moses and Elijah, and His more recognizable human manifestation (Acts 9:3-7; Matt. 17:1-8; Luke 24:38-39; Acts 23:11).[3]

With the triumph of the pro-icon party in the Byzantine East, the Christian West became totally permissive in its attitude toward statues and icons. By the time of Thomas Aquinas, Catholic theology allowed the veneration of saints through statues because it was "not really" worship. It sounded clear in Latin. God was given worship (*latria*), the saints were honored (*dulia*), and Mary was given *hyperdulia*. Statues of Christ, Mary and the saints were dressed, flowered, paraded and given all matter of obeisance.

The cult of statues and icons was one of the most grievous failures in the theologies of both the Eastern Orthodox and the Roman Catholic churches. The church had fallen into a tragic pattern of allowing popular devotion to establish practice and define theology.[4]

203

The Reformation as Iconoclasm

The Reformation was in great part a new iconoclastic movement. Many in Catholic Europe were easily convinced by the Reformers' arguments that the cult of statues was idolatry.* Some of Calvin's best writings critiqued Catholic statues and icons. With precise scholarship and crisp logic he demolished this flawed theological edifice of the medieval church, exposing it as contrary to the plain understanding of Scripture and the early practice of the church. He warned:

> Therefore, when you prostrate yourself in veneration, representing to yourself in an image either of God or a creature, you are already ensnared in some superstition. For this reason, the Lord forbade not only the erection of statues constructed to represent himself but also the consecration of any inscriptions and stones that would invite adoration.[6]

Calvin correctly saw that an act of homage, commonly termed *to bow down* in the Bible, is indistinguishable from worship, regardless of mental reservations which distinguished worship from honor (Lev. 26:1; Is. 44:12-17).

Fencing the Second Commandment

Although Calvin permitted paintings of historical and biblical scenes, he never really understood the need for religious art. This is indicated by his nervousness about the cherubim on the ark of the covenant, calling them "paltry little images."[7] Later Reformed theologians went further and for all practical purposes closed down serious religious art within the Protestant nations, abandoning the fine arts to secular hands. Again this had unintended tragic consequences. Western art began a separation from its spiritual roots, which eventually led to art without meaning and ultimately to the godless fashions of modern art.[8]

Shutting down Protestant religious art was one way of fencing idolatry so that the Catholic abuses would never recur. Reformed theology also rejected the Catholic insights that the incarnation had modified the prohibition of representing God through Jesus. Thus, for rigorous

---

* In many pro-Reformation towns and cities the populace moved before the authorities in removing statues from churches.[5]

204

Calvinists, not even a painting of Jesus in the setting of a Gospel incident was legitimate.[9]

Yet another way to extend the biblical injunctions against idols was to prohibit images *in the imagination.* That step was hinted at in Calvin's writings but completed after him. Calvin had a low opinion of the imagination from the faculties psychology he inherited through medieval theology.[10] He also declared that the mind "is the perpetual factory of idols."[11]

By the time the theologians of the famous Westminster catechism had written their proclamation of Protestant doctrine, the explicit step had been taken to extend the biblical prohibition against idols from sculpture and paintings to images in the mind. Question 109 of the larger catechism explains the sins against the second commandment as "the making of any representation of God, of all or any of the three persons either inwardly in our mind, or outwardly in any kind of image...."

This was simply and purely a pharisaical fence. The pious Protestant was thus prohibited from imagining Jesus during prayer. Of course, the prevalent cessationism gave no consideration to the problem of Jesus' appearing to a Christian because in the post-biblical era that would simply not happen.

Yet the Calvinists and later Puritan theologians were not unreasonable. They understood that the imagination, which was created by God, had to have some positive functions. Thus the dilemma: How could the mental images of prayer, which often gravitated to Jesus, be idolatry? One of the favorite Puritan devotional books was *Looking Unto Jesus...or, The Soul's Eyeing of Jesus* by Isaac Andrews, first published in the middle of the seventeenth century and continuously reprinted until the nineteenth. In spite of its Calvinist theology this book contained the following passage:

> O but my Jesus was crowned with thorns, and sceptred with a reed, and that reed was taken out of his hands to beat the crown of thorns into his head; and, besides, my Jesus was whipped with cords, and rods, *and little chains of iron*; that from his shoulders to the soles of his feet, there was no part free, and being now this plight, thou art called on to "Behold the man:" *Dost thou see him? Is thy imagination strong?* Canst thou consider him at present, as if thou hadst a view of this very man![12]

205

Jonathan Edwards on Mental Images

Into this dilemma of attempting to avoid mental idolatry yet affirming the positive function of the imagination in the Christian's life came Jonathan Edwards, the theologian of the Great Awakening. As we have shown in part 1, he was aware of the role of imagination in authentic revival and purposely stimulated the imagination of his audience to sow fear and prepare for the grace of conviction. His early experience in the Northampton revival had given him pastoral experiences with the phenomenon of visions and their relation to the imagination. When the Great Awakening came he explained the relationship between visions and the imagination to the Yale graduation class in his famous *Distinguishing Marks of a Work of the Spirit of God*:

> Such is our nature, that we cannot think of things invisible, without a degree of imagination. I dare appeal to any man, of the greatest powers of mind, whether he is able to fix his thoughts on God, or Christ, or the things of another world, without imaginary ideas attending his meditations....
>
> As God has given us such a faculty as the imagination and so made us that we cannot think of things spiritual and invisible, without some exercise of this faculty; so, it appears to me, that such is our state and nature, that this faculty is really subservient and helpful to the other faculties of the mind, when proper use is made of it...It appears to me manifest, in many instances with which I have been acquainted, that God has really made use of this faculty to truly divine purposes....
>
> Some are ready to interpret such things wrong, and to lay too much weight on them, as prophetical visions, divine revelations, and sometimes significations from heaven of what shall come to pass; which the issue, in some instances I have known, has shown to be otherwise. But yet it appears to me that such things are evidently sometimes from the Spirit of God, though indirectly; that is, their extraordinary frame of mind, and that strong and lively sense of divine things which is the occasion of them, is from his Spirit...though the imaginations that attend it are but accidental, and therefore there is commonly something or other in them that is confused, improper, and false.[13]

Edwards was saying something complex and important. In regard to mental images, visions and spiritual experiences (such as a vision of Jesus), the details may vary according to the personality of the visionary, but this does not mean that the visions are merely fantasies. Rather they are personal images empowered by the Holy Spirit and thus valid in their broadest meaning. Note also that Edwards was presenting his discernment of this issue in the older faculties vocabulary with which the Yale graduates (and the educated public of the time) were familiar. He used faculties vocabulary to affirm the importance of mental imagery, whereas that traditional view had disvalued all such phenomena.

Edwards's *Distinguishing Marks* triggered a pamphlet war among Scottish Reformed clergymen. Scotland had been having its own revival during the years of the Great Awakening, and colonial developments were watched carefully. The issue of images and visions of Jesus took central attention in Scotland, more so than in the colonies. The Scottish opponents of the revival echoed many of Charles Chauncy's views (see chapter 3). In the heat of argument the antirevivalist side even went to the extreme of saying that Jesus' physical appearance on earth presented an impediment to true faith because of the danger it posed of idolatry![14]

This obscure but heated Puritan debate points to several important issues. The attempt of Reformed theologians to fence the real sin of idolatry with the imaginary sin of mental idolatry was doomed to futility and confusion. The debate also resurfaced the original medieval position that the incarnation modified the prohibition against representing God. It was a real issue that cessationist theology could not adequately deal with, especially in a time of revival when spiritual phenomena were more common.

Catholic Tradition of Pious Visualization

Visualization is mental imagery that is purposely induced or suggested. This distinguishes it from images or visions that may arise in the mind without effort. The fire-and-brimstone sermons from Jonathan Edwards, and most revivalists after him, purposely stimulated the imaginations of their audiences. Thus, in the broadest sense, they encouraged personal visualizations as part of the conversion process. This is not to say that Jonathan Edwards or Isaac Andrews or any other Puritan was the first to introduce visualization into Christian practice. The Catholics had beaten them to it by hundreds of years.

In fact, the systematic use of visualization has quite a long history in

Christianity. As early as the thirteenth century, a popular book, attributed to St. Bonaventura but written by some unknown monk, urged visualization as a form of prayer and Bible learning. The author of *Meditations on the Life of Christ* encouraged his brothers to read sections of the Bible, especially the Gospels, and then creatively enter into the scene with their imaginations. For example, he urged his readers to become one of the shepherds that visited the newborn Jesus in Bethlehem:

> Kiss the beautiful little feet of the infant Jesus who lies in the manger and beg his mother to offer to let you hold Him awhile. Pick Him up and hold Him in your arms. Gaze on His face with devotion and reverently kiss Him and delight in Him. You may freely do this, because He came to sinners to deliver them, and for their salvation humbly conversed with them and even left himself as food for them.[15]

This form of Bible meditation became a common form of prayer for many Catholics. Those who practice it, and many still do, have always found it spiritually refreshing. It brings the good fruit of a deeper love of Jesus and a better ability to remember the incidents in the Gospels. In the Middle Ages, before the printing press, Scripture memory was important since few had personal Bibles. Unfortunately, this form of prayer was lost to Protestantism in the heat of the Reformation.

Another form of Catholic visualization exercises was developed during the height of the Reformation-versus-Counter Reformation years by St. Ignatius of Loyola (1491 – 1556), founder of the Jesuits.[16] The training exercises he developed for his priests (part of a month-long retreat) were aimed at strengthening their determination and resolve to lead a sanctified Christian life. Later the exercises were modified for use among the general Catholic public.

At the heart of the exercises was a series of individual visualizations wherein the person was given a general theme and encouraged to allow his own imagination to create the specific details. In one, the retreat master would suggest meditating on hell and suggest imagining all the screams, smells and sensations of the tormented souls. In the subsequent session the participant would then spend time imagining the joys of heaven. The trained retreat master would inquire as to the specific images developed by each participant and use that information for the purposes of spiritual direction.

Visualization and Healing

Prior to the nineteenth century there is no evidence of the use of visualization for healing. Certainly the Protestants would have thought it impossible because the healing ministry was not for the current age. Catholics were used to the intercession-through-saints pattern of healing and would have thought it a presumption.

No one knows for certain when visualization was first used in connection with healing. Evidence indicates that it may have been an innovation of Ethan O. Allen, the pioneer of the Faith-Cure movement. Allen's book on the first years of his healing ministry shows a pattern familiar to today's faith movement but gives no indication of healing visualizations. Paul Chappell, one of the historians of the Faith-Cure movement, cited a biography which showed Allen as using healing visualization.[17] When the movement was destroyed by the Pharisees of the 1890s (see chapter 10), Allen's innovation may have been passed on to the nonorthodox Mind-Cure and metaphysical groups that continued to practice healing. (For example, in the 1870s Christian Science practitioners offered healing prayer by employing visualization in conjunction with affirmations of perfect health.) At this point no more definitive statements can be made.

The Metaphysical Movement and Visualization

While the beginnings of the use of visualization for healing prayer are unclear, it is certain that visualization had many other roles in the Metaphysical movement. Those in the Bible-affirming wing of New Thought were cautious with the use of visualization. It became a way to affirm that what was hoped for would come to pass. Bible-affirming New Thought leaders taught that visualization was to be used in cases of need or to help others rather than simply for personal pleasure.

For those in the deist wing of the movement, visualization unfortunately functioned as a substitute for prayer. Those who desired money, a trip or a fine house were told to imagine themselves in possession of it so that it would be theirs. The power of visualization was described as independent of the constraints of God's will.

The lesson from the visualization practices of the Metaphysical movement is this: If visualization is a form of mind power unconnected to God's will, then it is not prayer and becomes either wishful thinking or a doorway to Gnostic vanities and possibly occult involvements.

An Evangelical Discernment

The issue of visualization has recently been examined in a masterful article by Brooks Alexander, founder of the prestigious evangelical anticult institute, the Spiritual Counterfeits Project. The SCP, as it is known for short, was founded in Berkeley, California, during the 1970s at the height of the occult revival. Alexander and others got together to provide an informed, evangelical perspective on the cults and the occult. Their publications, especially the *SCP Journal*, have reached the highest standards of evangelical apologetics and discernment.[18]

In 1990 an entire issue of the *SCP Journal* was dedicated to visualization. Alexander provided the central article.[19] He carefully demonstrated the occult uses of visualization and cited various sociological works that show that visualization is the central practice of shamanism. Alexander cites evidence that visualization was used by highest levels of Hitler's Nazi party to plan world conquest. More common in present-day America is the use of visualization in New Age circles as spiritualism to contact spirit guides.

Alexander traces visualization's introduction into the mainline Christian church through the ministry of Agnes Sanford and her New Thought theology. He is particularly critical of the popular Christian writer Richard Foster and faults him for suggesting visualization that could lead to unintended spiritualism.

The article could have closed there and claimed, as have other evangelical authors who have followed the Hunt lead, that visualization is always evil and only an occult practice. But Alexander is a scholar, and his article takes a turn worthy of Jonathan Edwards. As Edwards did, he sees the imagination as God-created; therefore, visualization has its good and proper functions. Alexander repeatedly compared the imagination and its capacity for visualization to man's sexual function: it can easily be misused, but it is a wonderful gift from God.[20] Surprising for a convinced evangelical, Alexander credits the Catholic practice of Bible story visualizations as a legitimate practice and even admires the Ignatius exercises. His summary is worth quoting at length:

> There is nothing wrong with inner imagery *per se*. Our imagination is a gift of God, and it was given to be used. But there is a simple rule of thumb for exercising that gift in religious and spiritual life.
>
> Use images in prayer as a means of communication *to*

God. Do not use your own created images as a source of communication *from* God. Use images as you use words — to express your worship and your petition. Do not use images as instruments of control, having power in themselves because of their nature.

And remember who you are praying to. God almighty, the creator of heaven and earth, knows the heart of the atom and the heart of man. He certainly knows what you want before you ask for it. And He knows what you need better than you do. Visual detail is no more important to God's hearing of prayer than is verbal detail. What *is* important is the inclination of your heart — your real reasons for wanting this moment alone with God.

When we use our imagination to speak *to* God, or to make biblical history vivid, we are doing what is natural and intended — we are walking in the light. When we use our fallen imagination to hear *from* God, or to manipulate reality, we are treading in the shadows between shamanism and superstition.[21]

Visualization was not invented by the Metaphysical movement, although it became universal in its literature either as a form of prayer or an expression of mind power. On the contrary, visualization has a long and honorable history in Christianity. Visualization is also a technique of the occult world. Thus, as Alexander has so clearly shown, visualization is a double-edged sword that can be used for either good or evil.

EIGHTEEN

E. W. Kenyon and His Faith Theology

THE PIONEER THEOLOGIAN AND TRUE father of the contemporary Word-Faith movement was E. W. Kenyon. Because of that, he was also a major influence on the charismatic movement. Through him the first modern, sustained and scripturally orthodox idealist hermeneutic of the Bible was developed. Its inspiration was largely from the Holiness and Higher Life literature and the Faith-Cure movement, which were reaching their climax during his young adulthood.[1] He was also influenced in his theological development through his contact with the New Thought literature and personalities. All of this was wedded to a traditional evangelical appreciation of Scripture and a passion for saving the lost. Kenyon's synthesis was a creative original theology that challenged not just cessationism, but the whole realist-materialist assumptions of consensus orthodoxy.

A prolific writer, Kenyon self-published his works, and they circulated among a restricted public, mostly Pentecostals. After the 1960s his theology was widely broadcast through the ministry of Kenneth Hagin (usually without credit). Until the recent controversies about Kenyon's theology, he was practically unknown outside of his followers. He did not write an autobiography, and no biography was written of him. Thankfully, several investigators have recently tackled the Kenyon materials (including new recovered early sources) with systematic thoroughness. The Christian public will shortly have several biographies of

Kenyon which will give a more complete picture of his position within Christian theology.[2]

E. W. Kenyon (1867 – 1948)

Essek William Kenyon was born in Saratoga County, New York, in 1867. He was the fourth child of a family of ten. In his early teens his family moved to Amsterdam, New York. His was a working class household: his father was a logger, and his mother was a rural school teacher and a devout Methodist. At fifteen Essek went to work at a carpet mill although he had not yet begun his secondary education. He attended a local revival and felt the Lord's call on his life. He later described the first reaction from his family.

> The third night when I came home from the service my mother asked me where I had been, and I told her. My brother, older than I, a witty fellow, said, "Mother, that fool will be preaching next." I ran upstairs to get away from him, for I dreaded his wit, but I said as I went, "Eddie, you are right; I am going to have an education, and I am going to preach." Eternal Life had come into my spirit, and my old life dropped away from me. At once I became a student.[3]

He joined the Methodist church and by age nineteen was ordained as an "exhorter" and preached his first sermon. His early years as a Christian were filled with enthusiasm and evangelical effectiveness as he brought many to the Lord.

He supported himself with several jobs, including one as a piano salesman, where he learned the spiritual principle that success in any job comes by seeking to serve the public rather than aiming for commissions. Decades later he summarized his experiences in sales ethics in a pamphlet, *Sign Posts on the Road to Success*.[4]

However, Kenyon noticed that many in the church were hypocrites, and he began to grow cynical. He recalled: "I lost it, and went back to sin; I dropped back deeper and deeper until I went back into agnosticism."[5] It was during this "backsliding" period that Kenyon developed the ambition to become an actor. To fulfill that desire he enrolled at Boston's Emerson School of Oratory (1892). Boston was the center for both the Faith-Cure movement and Christian Science, where Mary Baker Eddy had her headquarters.

Emerson School of Oratory

At the time this college, named after its founder, Charles Wesley Emerson, was considered one of the best schools for oratory and acting in America. Many ministerial candidates attended for the purpose of improving their preaching skills. It was also a place where Metaphysical and New Thought influences were in ascendance. The teachings of Plato (the classic idealist philosopher), Ralph Waldo Emerson (the transcendentalist who favored Eastern religious doctrines) and early New Thought writers formed much of the curriculum. In the years after Kenyon left Emerson School of Oratory it became a center of New Thought teaching.

Kenyon stayed only a year and did not get a degree from Emerson. But during his stay there, Ralph Waldo Trine, later famous as the leader of the Bible-affirming wing of New Thought, was both a student and an instructor at Emerson. Kenyon's modern critic, Dan McConnell, claims that Kenyon thoroughly imbibed New Thought teachings while at Emerson. That is a reasonable assumption, although as with many Christians of the era, he may have read Christian Science literature even before he came to Emerson.[6]

Yet by the time he published his first theological work, *The Father and His Family* (1916), he had discerned and rejected the Gnostic core of Metaphysical philosophy. His writings consistently show that he considered himself strongly opposed to the whole Metaphysical movement, either in its most extreme form, as in Christian Science, or its milder variety, as in Unity. Kenyon understood the movement as a spiritually dead religion which distorted the nature of man, the ministry of Jesus and the character of God the Father. Kenyon wrote:

> Christian Science, Unity, and the other Metaphysical and philosophical teachers of today do not believe that God is a person.
>
> They will tell you that He is perfect mind, but He has no location.
>
> It is just a great universal mind which finds its home in every individual. He has no headquarters...
>
> They do not believe in sin as Paul taught it in the Revelation given to him.
>
> They do not believe that Jesus died for our sins, but that He died as a martyr.
>
> They do not believe He had a literal Resurrection, a physical

Resurrection, but puts it as, "a metaphysical resurrection" (whatever that means).

If God is not a person and Jesus did not put sin away, then who is Jesus and what is the value of our faith in Him?[7]

Such critical remarks of the metaphysical movement are common to Kenyon's writings. He seems to have taken pleasure in his confrontations with cult members, as when he prayed for healing for a lady who was dedicated to Unity, and then converted her.[8]

Rededication and Evangelical Ministry

While in Boston at Emerson Kenyon met a fellow student named Evva Spurling. They married in May 1893, when both were non-professing Christians. A month later they attended A. J. Gordon's Clarendon Street Baptist Church to hear Gordon preach. At the service Kenyon heard "the voice of God" calling him back to His service.[9] He repented for his sins and rededicated his life to the Lord. His wife followed suit shortly. Kenyon began reading Faith-Cure and Higher Life literature. Years later he described his reaction to reading Dr. Cullis's biography:

> I cannot describe to you the emotions that stirred in my heart as I began to read it. I went into it chapter after chapter until I came to some of the great battles. I lived with him in his fights; I knew what it meant. It was like a soldier, who having gone through a severe engagement, is reading the field notes of the other parts of the battle.[10]

Kenyon and his wife also encountered a preacher from a Free Will Baptist church and were convinced of the need of baptism by being fully submerged in the water. In spite of his upbringing, they both joined that denomination. By January 1894 Kenyon had been ordained a Free Will Baptist preacher and had accepted his first charge. Kenyon preached in several congregations in New England and Canada. He was especially anointed as an evangelist and had much success.[11] Even though he believed in divine healing, he avoided healing prayer in order to avoid controversy. While pastoring a Free Will Baptist church in Worcester, Massachusetts, he attempted to follow the George Müller faith pattern, trusting in God to provide for the church's needs. The deacons did not have as much faith and forced him to resign.[12]

He then started an independent church in Worcester, the Tabernacle Assembly. He continued his evangelistic ministry, and the Lord drew him into the healing ministry as people at his meetings requested healing prayer. He also developed a strong deliverance ministry. This itself is significant, for it shows that by accepting the reality of the demonic and the need for a deliverance he had truly rejected the naive New Thought assumption that exorcism was "negative" and unnecessary. His entrance into the deliverance ministry was not planned. Kenyon wrote:

> I was called to a neighboring town to pray for an insane man. When I went into the room where he was, his mother introduced me to him. He turned his back to me and would not speak. Like a flash, the truth dawned upon me. I was the Righteousness of God in Christ. I had the superiority over the forces of darkness. I stepped up to the man, and in the Name of Jesus, I demanded the demons to come out of him and never return.
>
> It wasn't a minute before he grasped my hand, and we had the sweetest fellowship the rest of the visit. How his mother rejoiced. In the Name of Jesus her son had been set free.[13]

Deliverance of the insane became a regular ministry for him.[14]

While pastor of Tabernacle Assembly, Kenyon began a Bible school for young people. In 1900 he received the donation of a large farm in nearby Spencer to house the school. Kenyon renamed the school Bethel Bible Institute and ran it on the Müller principle. No salary was paid to instructors, and no tuition was charged to students. Kenyon was president but left most of the teaching to others as he continued his itinerant evangelistic and teaching ministry. The profits from his evangelistic tours went to support Bethel Bible Institute.

Evva Kenyon died after a prolonged sickness in February 1914. Kenyon remarried in November of the same year to Alice Maud Whitney. They had two children: Essek Whitney (born 1916) and Ruth Alice (born 1919).

Bethel Bible Institute grew but not painlessly. Kenyon and the board of directors clashed. He wanted to maintain the faith policies of Müller; they wanted to pay the full-time staff and charge tuition to the students. Kenyon resigned and moved his family to California.[15] They settled first in Oakland and then moved to Los Angeles where he established an independent Baptist church.

It was in Los Angeles that he first produced several radio programs. He was gaining a reputation as a gifted speaker and anointed expositor of Scripture and was frequently invited to speak to Pentecostal audiences though he did not consider himself a Pentecostal. He was also invited to speak at Aimee Semple McPherson's famous Angelus Temple. In this period he also ministered with F. F. Bosworth, another noted Pentecostal healing evangelist of the prewar era. Bosworth's book on healing, *Christ the Healer,* was a major influence on the theology of Kenneth Hagin.[16] Bosworth's book showed substantial influence from and similarities to Kenyon's theology of faith-idealism.

In 1931, after a divorce from his wife, Kenyon relocated one last time and settled in Tacoma, Washington (near Seattle) where he established New Covenant Baptist Church. There he also pioneered Christian radio for that area with his daily program "Kenyon's Church of the Air." In Tacoma Kenyon began his influential newsletter *Herald of Life.*

After 1942 Kenyon resigned his pastorship to write and serve again as a traveling evangelist and teacher. Kenyon lived for only a few years after World War II, but these were his most influential and creative. He finished some of his most theologically advanced works and gathered notes and materials for many others. Perhaps most important he participated in the great Pentecostal healing revivals then underway. In this manner his works and ideas circulated among such Pentecostal evangelists as Oral Roberts, William Branham, T. L. Osborn and others of that generation.[17]

Shortly before his death in 1948 he told his daughter:

> Ruth, dear, I have a feeling I won't be with you much longer. This work must go on. It is up to you now. You have been looking after it all these years, and with the help of the Lord, I know you can carry on.[18]

Ruth Kenyon continued to work with her father's materials — the book notes, sermons, letters, radio messages and *Herald of Life* articles — to produce most of the Kenyon literature posthumously. She continued as president of Kenyon's Gospel Publishing Society, which markets his materials, until her death in December 1993.[19]

The Theology of Faith-Idealism[20]

In the early days of Kenyon's evangelical ministry, German higher criticism (liberal demythologizing) had become fashionable in many

American seminaries. It was deceitfully put forward under the slogan "Back to Jesus." This meant that Jesus saw Himself only as a very human prophet and a Messiah, but Paul exaggerated Jesus' person and mission to Godlike status.

Kenyon investigated this hypothesis with an exhaustive Scripture study and rejected it. In fact, he came to the conclusion that rather than being an imaginative creation, the Pauline epistles were the highest stage of biblical revelation.[21] Kenyon believed the epistles were superior to the Gospels because Paul's theology was based on direct revelations from Jesus, who gave Paul the ultimate secrets of the kingdom (Eph. 3:5). On the other hand the Gospels only reported the public events of Jesus' life. Kenyon's theology was Pauline theology; that was his ambition and intention.

Central to Kenyon's faith-idealism is the view that knowledge can be divided into two basic categories, sense knowledge and revelation knowledge. Sense knowledge comes through the five senses and gives information about the physical world but never gives the reason or intention *behind* the world. On the other hand revelation knowledge answers questions such as why or for what purpose. Revelation knowledge comes from God either by way of the Bible or by way of the Holy Spirit communicating with man's spirit, as in personal guidance or clarifying the meaning of Scripture.[22]

Kenyon's doctrine of the difference between sense knowledge and revelation knowledge is the key to his Christian idealism, but it also reflects Paul's division between the natural and spiritual (Christian) man:

> We have not received the spirit of the world but the Spirit who is from God, that we may understand what God has freely given us. This is what we speak, not in words taught us by human wisdom but in words taught by the Spirit, expressing spiritual truths in spiritual words. The man without the Spirit does not accept the things that come from the Spirit of God, for they are foolishness to him, and he cannot understand them, because they are spiritually discerned (1 Cor. 2:12-14, NIV).

Kenyon believed many of the problems of the modern world originated when man rejected revelation knowledge and attempted to answer the why questions through sense knowledge. Darwin's attempt to understand the animal kingdom is a case in point. Most of the failures of the

Metaphysical movement occurred, according to Kenyon, because of the rejection of revelation knowledge (the Bible). Their religious speculations were sense knowledge, but they masqueraded as revelation.[23]

Kenyon placed major emphasis on the Pauline doctrine of identification (Gal. 2:20; Eph. 2:6); that is, Paul's understanding that Christ became sin for us so that we could then be *in* Him with the righteousness of God (2 Cor. 5:21). This was a pure work of grace, and Kenyon emphasized its tremendous consequences. Through identification with Christ we can approach the throne of God perfectly guiltless with our prayer requests (Eph. 2:18). Further, because of that identification we have the same powers that Jesus had on earth. The incredible promises that Christ made about the believer's ability to heal, to cast out demons and to do greater works than He did, by faith and in His name, are all possible because of His gracious identification with us.[24]

Faith as Practical Reality

Kenyon anchored his understanding of faith on the biblical definition found in Hebrews 11:1:

> "Faith is giving substance to things hoped for." Faith is grasping the unrealities of hope and bringing them into the realm of reality.
> Faith grows out of the Word of God.
> It is the warranty deed that the thing for which you have fondly hoped is at last yours. It is the "evidence of things not seen." ...Real faith in the Word says, "If God says it is true, it is. If He says that 'By his stripes I am healed,' I am. If He says that God shall supply every need of mine, He will do it....
> So quietly I rest on His word, irrespective of evidences that would satisfy the Senses.[25]

For Kenyon biblical faith has several counterfeits in the realm of sense knowledge. Among these counterfeits are hope and mental assent, which is the faith of the cessationist Christians.

> Mental assent agrees that the Bible is Revelation, that it came from God, and that every Word is true, and yet when the crisis comes it does not work. It simply recognizes the truthfulness of that wonderful Book, but it does not act upon it.

Hope says, "I will get it sometime." Faith says, "I have it now." Mental Assent says, "It is beautiful. I know I should have it. For some reason I don't get it. I cannot understand it."[26]

Faith grows by both meditating on the Bible and acting on it:

> It must be fed continually upon the Word of God and upon our acting on that Word.
> Simply reading the Word, meditating on the Word, will not build faith. It will build a capacity for faith, but faith is only built when that Word becomes part of daily use, our daily conduct — a part of our daily speech.[27]

The importance of speaking out in affirmation had already been understood by those in both the Faith-Cure and Metaphysical movements. (Recall that Phoebe Palmer stressed the need for "confession of the blessing" of sanctification as early as the 1840s.) Like others in the Faith-Cure Movement, Kenyon was careful to clarify that positive speaking in faith must be based on the promises of the Word. Unlike Ralph Waldo Trine and other New Thought writers, Kenyon understood that the issue of affirmation was complicated by the demonic and had a dimension of spiritual warfare.

> I make the confession that "by his stripes I am healed;" the disease and its symptoms may not leave my body at once, but I hold fast to my confession.
> I know that what He said He is able to make good.
> I know that I am healed because He said I was healed, and it makes no difference what the symptoms may be in my body. I laugh at them, and in the Name of Jesus I command the author of disease to leave my body.
> He [Satan] is defeated, and I am the victor.
> I have learned this law, that when I boldly confess, then, and then only, do I possess.[28]

Further, Satan will empower negative faith in a manner analogous to God's empowering the faith and positive confession of the believer:

> Talk poverty and you will have plenty of it. Confess your want, your lack of money all of the time, and you will always

have a lack...these confessions of lack and of sickness shut the Father God out of your life and let Satan in, giving him the right-of-way.[29]

Corresponding Action

The most characteristically idealist practice of faith-idealism is *corresponding action*. This behavior affirms that a prayer offered in faith has been accomplished before there is physical evidence (sense knowledge) of its manifestation. Corresponding actions can be discerned in several of Jesus' miracles. Among the most obvious is the healing of the ten lepers described in Luke 17:

> And they raised their voices, saying, "Jesus, Master, have mercy on us!"
> And when He saw them, He said to them, "Go and show yourselves to the priests." And it came about that as they were going, they were cleansed (vv. 13-14).

Note that *before* they were healed they were on the way to show themselves to the priests as clean, as commanded by the Law of Moses (Lev. 14:1-3).

Corresponding action was part of the healing strategy of Christian Science, easily meshing with its radical idealism. The Faith-Cure and early Pentecostal healers also used corresponding action. One of the eyewitnesses of Smith Wigglesworth's healing services reported:

> He [Wigglesworth] had the whole assembly join with him in prayer, and then, addressing the [paralytic] man, he said, "Now, put down your sticks [crutches] and walk with me." The man fumbled for a time; then he let his sticks fall to the ground and began to shuffle along. "Walk, walk!" Brother Wigglesworth called, and the man stepped out. "Now run," he commanded, and the man did so to the amazement and great joy of all who were present.[30]

Kenyon often cited examples of corresponding action from his own healing ministry. Unfortunately, like many of the Faith-Cure ministers, Kenyon believed that taking medication after saying a prayer of faith for healing invalidated the prayer.[31] As the experience of the Faith-Cure movement showed, this practice is fraught with danger. This issue will be discussed when we examine the controversies surrounding the contemporary faith theology (see chapter 19).

Kenyon believed that a Christian who realized who he was in Christ (identification) and lived out the promises of the Bible by practicing faith would become a "Christian superman." Perhaps this was an unfortunate phrase. It was meant to contrast the believing, spiritually empowered Christian with the cessationist Christian. The superman Christian would heal the sick regularly and cast out demons without fear. He would hear the guidance of the Holy Spirit on a consistent basis and speak the words of God to his neighbors in power, love and healing. In other words Christ's life in him would reproduce the Jesus life on earth in reality, not just in theory.[32]

Kenyon and Pentecostals

In spite of his great stress on the Holy Spirit, Kenyon did not consider himself a Pentecostal. He gave little attention to the word-gifts of the Spirit, such as tongues and prophecy. His theology of the Holy Spirit may be called noncessationist evangelical. That is, he believed that as soon as the person was born again and realized his identity with Christ, he could begin a ministry of healing and deliverance and effective prayer. On the other hand Pentecostals, building on the tradition of the Holiness movement, believed that the gifts of the Spirit needed to be released by a second stage. Further, Pentecostals insisted that the second experience was inevitably manifested through the speaking with tongues.

Kenyon was suspicious of Pentecostals and their tongues theology. His writings show the scars of what must have been unpleasant encounters with them:

> In that wonderful movement called the Tongues Movement, immature believers who had received that startling demonstration, felt that they could no longer fellowship with anyone who didn't have the same experience.[33]

Later in his ministry, as he worked with and ministered among more mature Pentecostal leaders, he modified his theology. He came to accept the importance, if not the absolute necessity, of the laying on of hands for the release of the gifts of the Spirit.[34] To the end of his life he saw tongues as a minor gift, not worth the contentions that they often created among Pentecostal believers.

Evaluation and Influence

Kenyon's system of Christian faith-idealism was a major codification of the idealist elements already present in both the Faith-Cure and Metaphysical movements. Unlike Faith-Cure theologians and writers, it was unabashedly idealist. Unlike the metaphysical writers, it was grounded by biblical bounds and divested of Gnostic elements (see chapter 16). His theology has a tremendous exuberance about it. To Kenyon, Christians can move mountains by faith and have not done so because we have not taken the Bible at its face value. It was as if he had been the first Christian to read the book of Acts and the epistles and take every word literally.

The faith-idealism of Kenyon did not exaggerate principles beyond biblical evidence, an error common among some of the present faith teachers. Kenyon understood that the Bible was self-limiting, and one cannot ask in faith for those things which are not promised in Scripture. Success in life is a process of discerning God's gifts and then working hard in an area compatible with the gifts.[35] Further, the Christian must, like Paul, be content in both difficult circumstances and in abundance. The truly mature Christian is recognized by longsuffering and patience in adversity.[36] Even Kenyon's severest critic, D. R. McConnell, recognized his moderation.[37]

As creative and as original as Kenyon's faith-idealism was, it made little impact on the general Christian public until the 1960s when it was reintroduced through the ministry of Kenneth Hagin. Through Hagin, Kenyon's faith-idealism became one of the major theological sources for the charismatic renewal.

Now that we have discussed some of the people and movements that set the stage for the charismatic renewal, we turn in part 5 to those individuals who have tried to offer reproof for the fledgling movement. These include Charles Farah, a professor at Oral Roberts University; D.R. McConnell, one of Farah's students; Dave Hunt, author of the best-selling *The Seduction of Christianity;* John MacArthur Jr., author of *Charismatic Chaos;* and Hank Hanegraaff, president of the Christian Research Institute.

PART V

From Reproof to Pharisaism

NINETEEN

Reproof for the Charismatic Renewal: Charles Farah Jr.

Extremism in the Charismatic Renewal

WHILE THE CHARISMATIC RENEWAL WAS undergoing its greatest expansion, it was also sliding into extremism. The faith-idealism theology of Kenyon, which was qualified and bounded by the promises of the Word, was being simplified into a system of absolutes. The new faith-popularizers were presenting a form of Christianity which claimed that suffering and sacrifice were no longer part of the price of the kingdom because proper faith could overcome all adversity.

An example of this perspective can be found in the popular book titled *How to Live Like a King's Kid* by Harold Hill.[1] Hill, a NASA engineer, was converted and baptized in the Spirit, and his book described his successful, prosperous and protected life. Although the emphasis of the book was on trusting God in all situations, Hill also seemed to imply that a Spirit-baptized Christian will *never* be harmed by a serious accident or stricken by a fatal disease that cannot be prayed through. While Christians certainly have angelic protection, that kind of absolutism would be false.

Many within the charismatic renewal were disturbed by the absolute nature of such theology. But the person destined to bring a Jonathan Edwards-like reproof to the renewal was Charles Farah Jr. (born in 1926), retired professor at Oral Roberts University and former co-pastor of Tulsa's Christian Fellowship Church, a charismatic congregation.

Farah had grown up in a pious Christian and Missionary Alliance household. That denomination did not accept tongues, but they did believe in divine healing, and as a child Farah had seen his parents pray for the sick. He received one of the best Christian educations possible. He gained an undergraduate degree and a master's degree from Wheaton College (noted for its evangelical fervor), a bachelor of divinity degree from Fuller Theological Seminary and, finally, a Ph.D. from Edinburgh University in Scotland. Farah called Edinburgh the "Annapolis" of Protestant universities for its sparseness and rigor of academic program. In between his master's and doctorate degrees, Farah pastored several Presbyterian churches in upper New York. After earning his doctorate he went to work for the Navigators, an international evangelical organization.

At Edinburgh he encountered the healing power of the Holy Spirit. A fellow ministerial student described how he had been blessed with this gift of healing and how he exercised it in his church. Farah invited this minister to pray for his ailments, which were poor vision and a bad back. The friend prayed in faith for both. Farah's eyes were miraculously healed, but his back remained unhealed. This experience reaffirmed his childhood belief in healing and provided him with an opportunity to understand healing within a more mature theology. It also showed him an element of mystery and incompleteness in this ministry.[2]

On his return to America Farah listened to a tape by Dennis Bennett, the pioneer Episcopal charismatic leader, and through it experienced the baptism of the Holy Spirit. By his own admission, Farah became one of those enthusiastic, and sometimes imprudent, charismatics of the 1960s era. He read the literature of the new Faith movement, but due to his excellent education in Christian doctrine and history he became suspicious of its extreme claims.

By the Lord's providence Farah was allowed to test the faith theology and see it fail in a minor matter. Farah had an embarrassing case of dandruff. On previous occasions it had responded to medication. Now as a Spirit-filled believer he chose the "faith" way to healing and affirmed his cure by Jesus' stripes. However, his dandruff steadily became worse. He was ultimately forced to take medication and was healed in that manner.[3]

At the same time Farah developed a powerful prayer ministry. In one case, to his own utter amazement, he gave a bold prophetic word that the wife of a faculty member at Oral Roberts University would be healed of a heart obstruction. Then he and his wife prayed for her healing, and the obstruction was miraculously dissolved before the scheduled operation.[4]

But Farah noticed that although the faith theology was ministering healing to many, it was also producing tragedy and confusion. Farah had moved to Tulsa in 1967 to become a professor at Oral Roberts University. There he kept abreast of the ongoing charismatic renewal. He learned of a couple in Southern California who decided to stop providing insulin to their twelve-year-old son and instead to trust the Lord for his complete healing. The boy died three days later. Farah followed the case as the sincere and grieving parents were tried and convicted in court. The death of the boy moved Farah to a search for the theological roots of this tragedy.[5]

Faith Versus Presumption

Farah discerned that the core of the problems with the Faith movement was a sin of presumption. He did a Bible search of presumption and its relationship to faith. He found the dividing line between one and the other is not set. Rather "one man's faith is another man's presumption."[6] That is, a faith-filled person may be given direction to do a specific miraculous act by God. His obedience to God's direction is an act of faith. A follower of less spiritual maturity or faith or a person who is acting without God's direction may attempt the very same act and fail. The second person sinned by presumption.

Presumption is the sin with which Satan tempted Jesus at the beginning of His ministry (Matt. 4:1-11). Everything that Satan offered Jesus was legitimately His: bread, the protection of angels and even the kingdoms of the earth. But taking them from the hand of Satan and before God's timing (before the cross) would have been the sin of presumption, not an act of faith.[7]

Farah's insight clarifies what we have seen with the tragedies of the early Faith-Cure and Pentecostal movements. Men such as Ethan O. Allen or Smith Wigglesworth had spent years of faith-filled dedication to the Lord. As Kenyon would later describe, they had built up their faith by intense personal study of the Word and obedience to it. When they turned their attention to healing, they had the faith to move medical mountains or do corresponding actions safely.

This was not so with many Christians who came into the healing ministry later. Many were new Christians or Christians who had not exercised their faith before they jumped into the deepest waters of healing. The tragedy is that this type of presumption was inadvertently encouraged by those who had great faith themselves. Many of these leaders did not have the theological maturity or perspective to understand the need for faith development or discerning the faith level of their followers. As Farah learned from his theological studies, "Bad theology is a cruel taskmaster."[8]

Farah also discovered that the sin of presumption is closely related to an error of biblical interpretation that confuses the general with the specific, the *logos* with the *rhema*. The *logos* is God's universal word to mankind, as in the Ten Commandments. It applies to everyone in all circumstances. A *rhema* word is an instance when God speaks a specific word to a specific person. For example, Jesus called Peter to exercise his faith and walk on the water. Certainly, Christians have never understood Peter's water-walk as a command to avoid boats.

Tragic confusions occur when Christians appropriate specific promises in Scripture as applicable to themselves. Certainly the Holy Spirit speaks a *rhema* word to individuals, and it is often through Scripture, but here discernment must be used. Is it really the voice of God, or is it presumption? This discernment step is often avoided by the faith teachers and leads to presumption and personal hardship or disaster.

While at ORU, both Farah and his wife, Jo Ann, observed the ministry of Kenneth Hagin, the Tulsa-based healing evangelist and teacher. In the late 1960s he had risen to become the leading proponent of Kenyon's faith-idealism. The Farahs were disturbed by the authoritarian atmosphere of Rhema Bible Training Center, Hagin's newly established Bible school. In its first years students were not allowed to ask questions during class time (this has since changed). Farah felt that behind this was the presumption that Hagin had so much revelation knowledge that the answers to any questions would be solved by paying close attention. This was never explicitly stated, but dissenting inquiry was certainly not encouraged.[9]

Among many charismatics, at Rhema and elsewhere, Kenyon's understanding of revelation knowledge had gotten out of hand to become a presumptuous disdain of serious theological, or even biblical, study. This was evidenced in one student Farah met who claimed that even the Bible was a waste of time because God spoke to him directly.[10] Clearly revelation knowledge had become a form of Gnostic delusion.

The Farahs participated in one of Hagin's yearly camp-meeting revivals. Farah described his reaction to what one warm-up speaker said:

"Please pick up this brochure and turn to page 4. Look into those eyes. Don't look anywhere else. How many of you think that Kenneth Hagin is the greatest man alive?"...

Mr. Hagin, to his credit, redirected the glory to God, but my wife was horrified because she caught a frightened glimpse into the future. She had a living example of how easy it is to transfer glory from the Creator to the creature; from Son of God to a man....[11]

Reproving the Faith Movement

Farah presented his reflections and fears about the charismatic renewal and its faith theology in a brief paper presented to a group of charismatic Presbyterian pastors.[12] Jamie Buckingham, one of the leading figures of the renewal, suggested that his paper be expanded into a book.

A tragic event pushed Farah to begin writing. His pastor's wife, Marty Sanders, was suffering from terminal cancer. Farah and his wife and the entire congregation began a strenuous prayer campaign for her healing. In spite of these faith-filled prayers, Marty died. Everyone felt disappointed.

Farah and Buckingham met again about the book, and they prayed that the forthcoming work would bless the body and not further divide it. In 1979 that book appeared, *From the Pinnacle of the Temple*, published by Logos International, the banner publisher of the charismatic renewal. Subsequently the basic message was republished in several forms, as an article for *Logos Journal*[13] and later a more academic presentation in *Pneuma*, the journal of the Society for Pentecostal Studies.[14]

From the Pinnacle of the Temple and its derivative articles provided the early charismatic renewal with its most effective and important reproof. That is because the reproof came not from someone who was opposed to the renewal or did not understand the gifts of the Spirit but from one who cherished both the renewal and the gifts. Farah had no desire to give up the gains of the Faith movement and return to the cessationism of his seminary years.[15] Rather, like Jonathan Edwards, he was for the renewal but concerned by elements of immaturity, extremism and poor theology, and he wanted to bring the renewal to biblical accountability.

Elaborating his original insights about faith and presumption, about *rhema* and *logos*, Farah warned of the Faith movement's overemphasis on generalizations, as in "all must be healed." This did an injustice to the biblical record and denied the sovereignty of God. At a deeper level Farah charged that the Faith movement had become a form of human-

229

ism. It was becoming man-centered rather than God-centered. This old Gnostic error was now subtly infecting the new renewal.

The exaggerated doctrine of prosperity was an example of the new humanism. Some faith teachers were preaching that one could exercise one's faith for any material luxury, such as expensive houses and cars. In fact, the same Faith movement teachers were asserting that the Christian could avoid all suffering and adversity through properly exercised faith. Farah reproved this with the strongest language he had used:

> It is clear that this new Gospel has nothing to do with the New Testament Gospel. It is an "improvement." It is another Gospel. It is a crossless, costless, effortless Gospel that disdains the way of the cross in the name of the cross. It in effect rewrites large passages of the New Testament, such as Luke 9:23, to read, And he said to them all; if any man will come after me, let him ask: Cadillacs, diamonds and furs, and according to his faith, so be it unto him.[16]

In Farah's *Pneuma* article, "A Critical Analysis," he identifies E. W. Kenyon as the originator of the faith theology: "The faith teachers have simply fleshed out many of the teachings from Kenyon and have radicalized them for popular teaching."[17] Farah understood that Kenyon was a pioneer and credited him with moderation in most doctrines. However, Farah believed Kenyon created the initial confusion between the *rhema* and the *logos* promises of Scripture by claiming that the believer could personalize every promise in Scripture.[18]

While he made an excellent analysis of the Faith movement, Farah had not caught the importance of the philosophical shift that had occurred with Kenyon's faith-idealism. Given his theological training in the best realist-materialist theology of Christendom, this is understandable. We can catch a glimpse of his misunderstanding when he dismisses Kenyon's discovery of corresponding action, acting as healed before one is healed:

> Who left the presence of Jesus without physical evidence of his healing? Whoever crawled away from the presence of our Lord, saying, "I am healed! I am healed! Only I have these lying symptoms."[19]

Certainly the last two sentences reflect the extremism of some faith teachers, but Farah's conventional philosophical assumptions prevented him from seeing that, in some cases at least, Jesus did miracles with corresponding action; for example, the healing of the ten lepers.

Farah's solution for the crisis of charismatic theology and practice was typically Presbyterian. It was a renewed appreciation of the sovereignty of God. This would allow for both healing and the occurrence of non-healing. It would center faith back on God and away from man

Impact of Farah's Reproof

From the Pinnacle of the Temple did not become a stupendous best-seller, but it and Farah's other articles circulated where they did the most good, among the leadership of the renewal.[20] Unfortunately most of the faith teachers, including Hagin, did not discern its prophetic wisdom. In fact, some even forbade their students to read it.[21] Gradually, as Hagin and others in the Faith movement matured, they heeded much of what Farah had said. On the other hand, some paid no attention to Farah at all.

Although Hagin never specifically responded to Farah's criticisms (it is his policy never to defend himself), he began taking care in presenting and qualifying his faith-idealism. For instance, he published a book in 1982 titled *Must Christians Suffer?* in which he recognized the importance of suffering in the Christian life. Like Smith Wigglesworth did decades before, Hagin made the distinction between illness and Christian suffering. Christians must suffer from persecution or suffer in their ministry, as in martyrdom or reviling, but sickness is not redemptive suffering and can always be prayed through.[22] Regardless of the ultimate truth of that assertion, it shows that Hagin was returning to Kenyon's more moderate and biblically bounded faith-idealism.[*]

Recently Hagin publicly admitted that there was not enough teaching about the role of suffering in the Christian life in his or other Faith ministries' teachings. In an article that candidly described his early years of poverty and struggle as an itinerant faith minister, Hagin writes:

---

[*]   This has been confirmed by Charles Farah himself. Sometime around 1994 he reviewed current Rhema materials brought to his attention by a student and was surprised by their moderation and new stress on evangelization and missions.[23]

What's happened with the faith message is that we've told about the good things, but in telling only about the positive side, some people don't even realize that the suffering side exists. Certainly, we are to emphasize the positive aspects of walking in faith because there's victory in Jesus! But at one time or another, all of us suffer persecution, insults, and criticism that test and try us.[24]

Ultimately this permitted his ministry to continue to serve the body and influence millions of believers all through the world with the positive accomplishment of the faith-idealist perspective.[25]

The faith ministers who chose to disregard Farah's prophetic reproof drifted into further extremism. The decade of the mid-1980s to the mid-1990s was the era of judgment for them. Their ministries fell with public exposure of their unholy lifestyles and distorted porsperity teachings. Because even the more mature faith ministers never acknowledged Farah's prophetic reproof, they and the entire charismatic renewal became subject to a new wave of pharisaical assaults. It was a repetition of the pattern seen in earlier revivals. If the Jonathan Edwards are not heeded, the Charles Chauncys will be sure to arise with unbalanced accusations.

TWENTY

Mistaken Critique:
The Work of
D. R. McConnell

FARAH'S REPROOF WAS CAREFULLY BALANCED between criticism and affirmation. As Edwards did, he attempted to distinguish between a core truth and the extremism of a theological position. Unfortunately, that balanced approach has not always been followed by others who have launched attacks on the faith theology. Ironically, one of Farah's students at Oral Roberts University, D. R. McConnell, produced an influential but unbalanced critique of E. W. Kenyon and the faith theology. McConnell titled the book *A Different Gospel: A Historical and Biblical Analysis of the Modern Faith Movement* (1988).[1]

Daniel R. McConnell, born in 1957, was raised in a Disciples of Christ household in Houston. He had a conversion experience at seventeen and almost immediately became involved in the charismatic renewal, a dramatic shift from his liberal upbringing. He subsequently went to Oral Roberts University for undergraduate and graduate degrees. While at ORU McConnell worked with Youth With A Mission in urban church planting.

At ORU he studied under Charles Farah. As we have seen, it was Farah who identified Kenyon as the father of the faith theology and also suggested that the Faith movement was becoming Gnostic. McConnell started with Farah's insights but carries them further. McConnell believes that Kenyon's theology was merely an heretical mishmash of fundamentalism and metaphysical ideas (an example of syncretism).[2] With these ideas as the origin of the Faith movement, McConnell concludes that the tenets of the Faith movement are heretical and must be renounced by the evangelical and charismatic community. McConnell's central and repeated argument is the origins argument: "I believe that because of its cultic origins, the faith theology represents a serious threat to the theological orthodoxy and spiritual orthopraxy [practice] of the independent charismatic movement."[3]

McConnell structured his master's thesis in 1982 to prove this point.[4] The origins understanding of Kenyon and the information from the thesis became one of the principal sources for Dave Hunt's best-selling books *The Seduction of Christianity* (1985) and *Beyond Seduction* (1987), which we will examine in the next chapter.[5] McConnell's thesis was upgraded into *A Different Gospel*.

Theological Orientation

Perhaps the different conclusions in Farah's and McConnell's reproofs came from their fundamentally different spiritual experiences. Farah had spent his adult life in cessationist Presbyterianism before he discovered the charismatic renewal. He understood that theological change could be good in spite of the dangers. McConnell spent practically all of his Christian life among charismatics in the Tulsa area where the abuses of the faith theology were becoming more obvious. From that perspective it is easy to understand that for McConnell theological change meant danger and heresy. He wrote: "I must agree with a former professor of mine who said, 'All that is old is not gold, but if it is new it cannot be true!'"[6]

That certainly resonates with the yearning of many conservative Christians, Catholic or evangelical; but it is scriptural nonsense as well as being an opening to a spirit of Pharisaism. Jesus Himself foretold of the ability of "kingdom scribes" to bring forth new insights: "Therefore every scribe who has become a disciple of the kingdom of heaven is like a head of a household, who brings forth out of his treasure things new and old" (Matt. 13:52). Paul described in his letters a process of discernment to test such "things new" (see chapter 1).

As a charismatic and Pentecostal, it is absurd for McConnell to criticize the new faith theology just because it is an innovation over traditional theology. To be consistent he would have to say that the Pentecostals of the 1900s were heretical for their innovative insights beyond evangelicalism into the gifts of the Spirit, because "what is new cannot be true."

The flip side of McConnell's fear of new theological perspectives is the absolute base he established to judge the heresy or orthodoxy of a doctrine. Not surprisingly, he writes, "These standards are the Bible and historical orthodoxy."[7] This sounds fine, but as we have seen in our survey of both Catholic and Protestant theology, historical orthodoxy has been wounded by serious errors from the very beginning. The errors of Charles Chauncy in opposing the Great Awakening or of James Buckley in opposing the Faith-Cure movement were founded on the same principle of defending historical orthodoxy. It is becoming increasingly clear that *only* the Bible itself can be used to identify heresy; historical orthodoxy cannot be the measure of heresy. This biblical standard was what the Reformers originally attempted, although they quickly developed an historical orthodoxy themselves.

McConnell's Origins Argument

McConnell's critique of Kenyon is a lengthy elaboration of the Pharisees' origins argument. The specifics of his argument are as follows: Kenyon borrowed ideas and philosophical orientation from the Metaphysical movement. But the Metaphysical movement is a Gnostic heresy; therefore, Kenyon's syncretic theology, for all its well-meaning goal of saving Christianity from the threat of Christian Science, is still a form of heretical Gnosticism.[8]

McConnell's work does not seem to consider that the church in the past has discovered and affirmed theological truth in response to heretical movements containing half-truths. With his education at ORU one can be sure he knew about that process in early church history. But it remained something distant and not applicable in modern times. McConnell assumed that consensus theological interpretation needed to learn nothing new. Therefore, no truth could be extracted from the Metaphysical movement by putting its teaching through a biblical filter.

A more serious error in McConnell's work comes from the fact that he did not consider the Faith-Cure movement or its influence on Kenyon. As we have seen, most of Kenyon's theology can be traced to earlier pioneers of the Faith-Cure movement. Kenyon's theology may *seem* dependent on Christian Science and New Thought, but only because the Faith-Cure movement shared a general idealist perspective with the other non-Christian groups. Dale Simmons, who was a fellow student at ORU with McConnell and who similarly pursued postgraduate research on Kenyon (see chapter 18), informed McConnell of the Faith-Cure influence on Kenyon. Unfortunately McConnell rejected Simmons' findings and insisted that his interpretation of Kenyon's theology was the valid one.[9]

Kenyon as Gnostic Theologian

To prove his unclean-origins-to-present-heresy hypothesis, McConnell tries to show that Kenyon's theology is fundamentally Gnostic. This he attempts to prove in part 2 of his book (chapters 6–10). We do not have the luxury of rebutting every charge of Gnosticism, but we will focus on the most serious accusations.

McConnell accuses Kenyon of being a Gnostic on two principal counts: the doctrine of revelation knowledge and Kenyon's idea of the superman Christian. Both accusations seem to have merit, but as Richard M. Riss, the noted historian of modern revivals, has stated, Kenyon's theology has only a superficial resemblance to Gnosticism.[10]

McConnell also believes that the doctrine of revelation knowledge forced Kenyon into dualism as well as Gnosticism.[11] At first sight McConnell's thesis seems plausible. Many of Kenyon's books have seemingly dualist titles, such as *Two Kinds of Faith* or *Two Kinds of Knowledge*.

True dualism, as in various Gnostic or Eastern religions, asserts that the earth and matter, including man's body, is evil, while the spirit is good. The purpose of religion then is to allow the spirit of man to escape matter and the body and return to "pure" spirit again.

As discussed, Kenyon followed Paul's view which was not dualist but dialectical, meaning Paul compared opposing forces as a way to understand God's working on earth. Paul's dialectical theology is superficially similar to true dualism.[12] In Paul a tension exists between the flesh and the spirit, but this tension does not represent the ultimate forces of good and evil. Rather, matter was created as good, but after the fall it has been used as the vehicle for sin. Ultimately man's body will be glorified in the resurrected body. Only in the present era does the flesh war against the spirit.

> But I say, walk by the Spirit, and you will not carry out the desire of the flesh. For the flesh sets its desire against the Spirit, and the Spirit against the flesh; for these are in opposition to one another, so that you may not do the things that you please (Gal. 5:16-17).

With this perspective one can see that all of Kenyon's apparently dualistic titles and statements are really dialectical, as Paul's are. Kenyon believed in the resurrection and man's glorified body. For him neither the body nor the mind nor even sense knowledge is evil, but they are used by Satan and sin to war against the spirit.

Revelation Knowledge: Biblical or Gnostic

McConnell attempts to equate Kenyon's theology of revelation knowledge with the Gnostic doctrine of knowledge in Christian Science. He cites Mary Baker Eddy as saying that matter is unreal and that the Christian Scientist must deny sensory information. He then concludes that this is substantially the same as Kenyon's view of sense knowledge.[13]

As we have shown earlier, Kenyon had a Pauline understanding of sense knowledge. For Kenyon sense knowledge was important and real but gave no information about spiritual matters (see chapter 18). Kenyon's faith-idealism was an elaboration of Paul's faith — "for we walk by faith, not by sight" (2 Cor. 5:7) — or Smith Wigglesworth's — "I am not moved by what I see or hear; I am moved by what I believe."[14] Perhaps McConnell's commitment to historical orthodoxy (that is, materialism-realism), makes him reluctant to distinguish between denying the reality of matter (the Gnostic error) and recognizing matter as real but asserting that faith can change matter (the faith-idealism of Paul, Wigglesworth and Kenyon).

The other aspect of revelation knowledge that bothers both McConnell and others is the claim that the believer can have continuous communication with the Holy Spirit on theological matters. As we have seen with Farah's reproof of the Faith movement, this certainly *can* become a Gnostic position.

Kenyon and Luther

The way Kenyon used revelation knowledge was bounded by Scripture and, significantly, very similar to what Martin Luther originally proclaimed:

> Let me show you the right method for studying theology, the one that I have used. If you adopt it, you will become so learned that if it were necessary, you yourself would be qualified to produce books just as good as those of the Fathers and the church councils. Even as I dare to be so bold in God as to

pride myself, without arrogance or lying, as not being greatly behind some of the Fathers in the matter of making books; as to my life, I am far from being their equal. This method is the one which the pious king David teaches in the 119th Psalm and which, no doubt, was practiced by all the Patriarchs and Prophets. In the 119th Psalm you will find three rules which are abundantly expounded throughout the entire Psalm. They are called: *Oratio, Meditatio, Tentatio.*[15]

Luther used Latin terminology for words that have in some cases shifted in meaning. *Oratio* still means prayer, and by this Luther means that without a deep prayer life no theologian should dare write a word. *Meditatio* means the biblical form of meditation, study, concentration and reconsideration of the biblical text. Lastly, *Tentatio*, which is literally translated as "temptation," means, in Luther's use of the word, experiential involvement in spiritual life.

But behind the gap of language and time, what Luther was describing was very similar to Kenyon's theory of revelation knowledge. Luther believed that every Christian could be inspired by the Holy Spirit to the same level as the fathers of the church. A generation later, Reformed theologians claimed considerably less for the normal believer. The change came after the abuses of Reformation revelation knowledge by way of the peasants' revolt and the Anabaptist radicals who believed they had revelation knowledge about communism and wife swapping.

Biblically, Luther and Kenyon were correct in their reading of Paul. Every believer can be inspired by the Holy Spirit to some sort of revelation knowledge. The problem is that any theology of revelation knowledge must be accompanied by a Pauline theology of discernment. Because Christians live in a spiritual world of both the Holy Spirit and unholy spirits, ideas that seem to be revelation knowledge must not only be compared to the Bible but also tested and discerned by the body.

Here both Luther and Kenyon, living centuries apart, were remiss. Neither took care to complete their doctrines of revelation knowledge with a doctrine of spiritual discernment. McConnell, coming into the charismatic renewal amidst the wreckage of nondiscerning revelation knowledge, believed that Kenyon's error was just another sign of its Gnostic root, but the parallel with Luther indicates that the failure lies in discernment not Gnosticism.

McConnell sees another sign of Gnosticism in Kenyon's proclamation of the coming superman Christian.[16] True, the original Gnostics be-

238

lieved that the way to salvation was by knowledge and that their special knowledge gave them a superior status. The Gnostic "illuminated ones" and Kenyon's superman Christian do have superficial analogies. But as we have indicated earlier (chapter 18), Kenyon was merely contrasting a fully empowered Christian with the normal, cessationist Christian who neither did healings nor exorcism nor ever experienced miraculous answers to prayer.

Kenyon's superman Christian has a better analogy in Watchman Nee's "normal Christian." Nee, the famous Chinese Christian leader, was also disturbed by the powerlessness of cessationist theology. Like Kenyon, he believed that the normal Christian should heal and deliver the oppressed. He expressed his view by laconically pointing to the biblical normal Christian who did such things and comparing him with the normative, powerless Christian of mainline denominations.[17]

The Descent Into Hell

McConnell strongly criticizes Kenyon's theory of the atonement as destructive and heretical. Kenyon taught that after Jesus died on the cross He descended into hell, was tormented by the demons and "died" spiritually just before His resurrection by the Father.[18] Kenyon anchored his theory on a literal reading of Isaiah 53:9 which prophesies the Messiah's death.

> His grave was assigned with wicked men,
> Yet He was with a rich man in His death,
> Because He had done no violence,
> Nor was there any deceit in His mouth.

In the original Hebrew the word *death* is in a plural form. Kenyon took this at its most literal sense, that Jesus died twice, once in the body and once in the spirit. McConnell points out that in the Hebrew language a plural often is used for emphasis, so that the real meaning is that the Messiah will die a horrible death.[19]

McConnell goes on to suggest that Kenyon's "revelation knowledge" was an obvious failure and his whole theological system was untrustworthy. McConnell chose to take such a strong stand on this issue partly because Kenyon's theory of Christ in hell has been widely adopted by present-day Word-Faith teachers, including Kenneth Copeland. If McConnell could show Kenyon's theory to be heretical and destructive, that would mean a heresy is being repeated and preached today by Word-Faith ministers. Further on (in chapter 22) we will see how the influential anti-cult Bible teacher Hank Hanegraaff elaborates on McConnell's analysis in his book *Christianity in Crisis*. Hanegraaff makes Kenyon's theory, and McConnell's refutation of it, a main point of attack on the present day Word-Faith ministers.[20]

In this section we need to show two things. First, although Kenyon's theory was speculative and probably wrong, it does not deserve to be labeled as heresy. His interpretation was based on a biblically orthodox, although no longer popular, theory of the atonement. Second, Kenyon's interpretation of Christ in hell merely expands what was suggested by John Calvin, the father of Reformed orthodoxy. Thus McConnell (and Hanegraaff) have made a heretical mountain out of a doctrinal molehill.

Historical Theories of the Atonement

Kenyon started out with the ransom theory of the atonement. This is one of three general theories of the atonement which have been believed by orthodox Christians throughout the ages. None of these theories contradicts the others; rather each stresses different aspects (complimentarity). The ransom theory was the first theory elaborated by church theologians. In this theory Christ's suffering was the ransom *paid to Satan* to enable man to be freed from sin and damnation. It was based on Jesus' own words in Mark 10:45:

> For even the Son of Man did not come to be served, but to serve, and to give His life a ransom for many.

Paul echoes this in the first letter to Timothy:

> For there is one God and one mediator between God and men, the man Christ Jesus, who gave himself as a ransom for all men — the testimony given in its proper time (1 Tim. 2:5-6, NIV).

Later in church history other theories were elaborated to help understand the great mystery of the atonement.[21] Anselm of Canterbury (1033 – 1109) developed a new insight that stressed that the atonement was satisfaction paid by Christ *to God the Father* for sin's offense. Anselm's theory finds its basis in Romans 5:9-11:

> Since we have now been justified by his blood, how much more
> shall we be saved from God's wrath through him! For if, when
> we were God's enemies, we were reconciled to him through the
> death of his Son, how much more, having been reconciled, shall
> we be saved through his life! Not only is this so, but we also
> rejoice in God through our Lord Jesus Christ, through whom we
> have now received reconciliation (NIV).

In the Middle Ages Peter Abelard (1079 – 1142) developed the theory that the atonement reflected Christ's perfect obedience to the Father
and acted as a moral example to pull man out of his self-centeredness.[22]
Calvin followed the understanding of Anselm, as have most modern
evangelicals. Luther, on the other hand, followed the earlier ransom theory.

Kenyon attempted to explain Christ's descent into hell as part of the
ransom theory of the atonement. Unfortunately, like many of the Reformers, he did not understand that the first epistle of Peter was the key
to understanding this event.

> For Christ died for sins once for all, the righteous for the un-
> righteous, to bring you to God. He was put to death in the
> body but made alive by the Spirit, through whom also he
> went and preached to the spirits in prison who disobeyed
> long ago when God waited patiently in the days of Noah
> while the ark was being built (1 Pet. 3:18-20, NIV).
>
> For this is the reason the gospel was preached even to
> those who are now dead, so that they might be judged accord-
> ing to men in regard to the body, but live according to God in
> regard to the spirit (4:6, NIV).

The fathers of the early church understood 1 Peter 3 – 4 literally —
Christ descended to Sheol (*hell* is a poor translation) where He preached
to the dead. Further, many received Him and were led to heaven (Eph.
4:8). Early tradition elaborated these scriptures. For example, Clement
of Alexandria taught that after their deaths the twelve apostles each followed Jesus with a preaching tour in Sheol and rescued additional
souls.[23]

Serious confusion started in the Middle Ages when a false gospel circulated, the *Gospel of Nicodemus*. This forgery described Christ in hell, overpowering Satan, but releasing only the Old Testament patriarchs, certainly not the "disobedient spirits" of 1 Peter 3:20. It received wide acceptance among Catholic teachers, including Thomas Aquinas. It was ultimately accepted by many Protestant theologians.

John Calvin, in his great systematic theology, *The Institutes of Christian Religion*, wanted to affirm the ancient doctrine of the descent into hell without affirming the Catholic doctrine of purgatory. To his credit he was one of the first to reject the authenticity of the *Gospel of Nicodemus*, so that "easy" explanation was closed to him. Instead, he developed a theory of Jesus' spiritual descent into hell, which, although not completely consistent,[24] anticipated Kenyon's in many ways.

Calvin's doctrine, found in *The Institutes*[25] was repeated in his famous *Geneva Catechism.* He asserted that "if it [doctrine of descent into hell] is left out, much of the benefit of Christ's death will be lost."[26] Like Kenyon, Calvin believed that Christ experienced a form of second death through His extreme mental suffering on the cross.

> If Christ had died only a bodily death, it would have been ineffectual. No — it was expedient at the same time for him to undergo the severity of God's vengeance, to appease his wrath and satisfy his just judgment. For this reason, he must also grapple hand to hand with the armies of hell and the dread of everlasting death.[27]

Also like Kenyon, Calvin envisioned a certain dramatic battle between Christ and Satan in Sheol.

> Therefore, by his wrestling hand to hand with the devil's power, with the dread of death, with the pains of hell, he was victorious and triumphed over hem, that in death we may not now fear those things which our Prince has swallowed up.[28]

This theory overly spiritualized Scripture. In this theory, Christ suffers in hell, but the locale of hell is Christ's own mind. Calvin's suggestion reappeared among Reformed theologians from time to time, although it never became a central doctrine. John Darby taught a version of it that incorporated some of Luther's teaching on Christ being the object of God's full wrath. Henry C. Mabie, a national Baptist missions secretary at the turn of the century and well-known writer, wrote several books elaborating Calvin's theory.[29] Kenyon read his works and was influenced by them.[30]

Flawed but Not Heretical

All of this is to say that Kenyon's theory of Christ's suffering and death in hell is based on evangelical assumptions that date from the Reformation. Neither Kenyon nor the Reformers gave the scriptural account in 1 Peter 3 – 4 due attention. That is a critical flaw in all their theories, but neither McConnell nor Hanegraaff take note of that. To call Kenyon's theory heretical and dangerous is to say the same of Calvin's theory.

McConnell's main intention, to invalidate Kenyon's theory of revelation knowledge, misses the point. True, any theology of revelation knowledge needs a strong counter theory of reproof and accountability. But all great theologians have made mistakes.

For instance, Luther expected the Jews to convert to Christianity once the errors of Catholicism were exposed. When they didn't he turned against them in rage, and many call Luther the founder of modern anti-Semitism.[31] Eventually the Nazis used Luther's writings to justify their anti-Semitism. Yet Luther's errors in theology do not invalidate his valid biblical understanding of the Christian's ability to be inspired by the Holy Spirit. Rather it was a case of the Reformer not being reproved by fellow Reformers.

Kenyon and Hagin

We should note here some things McConnell pointed out about the relationship between Kenyon and Kenneth Hagin. Kenyon's theology has been most influential in the charismatic renewal through the writings and radio ministry of Kenneth Hagin. Unfortunately, the debt that Hagin owed to Kenyon was not properly acknowledged. McConnell has labeled Hagin's writings as pure and simple plagiarism. Certainly he showed that many of Hagin's books and pamphlets mirror earlier Kenyon texts word for word, or sentence for sentence.[32]

Other researchers had found further evidence of Hagin's widespread plagiarism.[33] Hagin steadfastly rejects the accusation of plagiarism. He suggests that perhaps God spoke the same revelation to both Kenyon and himself.[34] That is not possible. It seems like that if the Lord had given the same core revelation to both Kenyon and Hagin, He would not have done so in identical language and organization so as to embarrass Hagin with a plagiarism accusation. Both Simmons and Lie (Kenyon scholars, see chapter 18) maintain that Hagin's plagiarism was conscious and systematic.[35]

On the other hand, Hagin is a person of integrity. He has lived moderately and made many personal sacrifices in his ministry. It would be hard to believe that Hagin has lied about this issue. Hagin readily admits to reading the Kenyon literature during the 1950s. The Hagin literature was written starting in the 1960s and continuing on until today. That interval is enough to blur the source of a text. Hagin has an almost perfect photographic memory, but like others who have that gift, it is the text content and not necessarily the source that is retained in memory.[36]

Hagin has even cited Kenyon on several occasions. For instance, Hagin's preface to his own *The Name of Jesus* (1979) credits Kenyon's *The Wonderful Name of Jesus* as the inspiration for that work.[37] The problem is that Hagin's acknowledgments of Kenyon are not systematic enough to meet minimum requirements of publishing ethics or law. Rather, they reflect the informal "borrowing" that was normative for the ministers of his time and background. Hagin was raised in the Depression era in East Texas where ministers were credentialed without much formal education. His education ended with high school.

In a sense, on every Sunday in countless pulpits across the nation there occurs similar widespread plagiarism. Normally a pastor does not begin his sermon by saying, "This sermon, 'Serving Others,' is a patchwork put together after about thirty minutes prayer time and after consulting the following sources:

A) What I remember of Charles Swindoll's *Improve Your Serve,* which I read a couple of years ago, but didn't finish the middle chapters.

B) What I remember of my seminary professor's lecture on the letter of James (can't remember the teacher's name).

C) Observation on the life of my Uncle Fred, who had ruined his life by trying to avoid helping others at all cost."

Not mentioning sources is acceptable in a sermon, but not so in publication. However, with Hagin, many spoken sermons were transcribed and printed. In fact, Hagin's books and pamphlets are mostly transcribed radio or camp meeting sermons.[38] Therefore the lack of sourcing in sermons carried over into print.

Hagin may have developed his own theology of faith-idealism before he encountered Kenyon's writing. We have shown in earlier sections that both Smith Wigglesworth and Ethan O. Allen had developed unrefined systems of faith-idealism from their unlettered but intense study of Scripture and their personal experiences. Our contention in this book has been that faith-idealism is a more natural way of interpreting Scripture than the materialist-realist tradition of mainline idealogy. It's quite possible that Hagin developed the essential elements of faith-idealism from his desperate search for healing amidst a family environment which was piously cessationist.[39] Thus when Hagin encountered Kenyon's theology it must have seemed more like a clarification and affirmation than a brand-new theology.

McConnell also accuses Hagin of passing off his theology as pure "revelation knowledge" without any credits to human sources. As pointed out, Hagin *did* acknowledge some human sources, although he certainly should have done a better job in crediting his sources or encouraging further readings from other writers. Hagin has testified of several long visitations from our Lord, at which times he was given certain revelations to the nature and activities of demons and other matters.[40] He has written about these experiences, and much of his popularity has come from these revelations.

Hagin has never claimed that *all* of his writings are based on personal revelation, but his general silence about his sources may have given many that impression. Again, in his era there was an expectation among the fundamentalist preachers not to cite "book learning," but to preach "straight from the Word." Perhaps Hagin was too concerned about conforming to this tradition, or it tempted him to vanity not to reveal fully his sources.

It seems that Hagin's most serious moral flaw has been in not acknowledging his plagiarism and offering compensation to Kenyon's Gospel Publishing Society. Here lies the crux of the issue: Can a minister be a true servant of God and have a major moral flaw? The historical answer is a resounding yes. One can think immediately of Luther's vulgar anti-Semitism or John Knox's lack of charity to his fellow ministers. God uses persons not because they are fully conformed to His Son but because they are faithful to their calling. Hagin has faithfully served the church through his healing and teaching ministry, but it is clear that his character still has unsanctified areas, as do all of ours.

Summary[41]

It was McConnell's professor, Charles Farah, who produced a Jonathan Edwards-style reproof of the Word-Faith movement. However, McConnell asserts that Hagin and the modern Faith movement are Gnostic and heretical because Hagin derived his teachings from Kenyon, who in turn was associated with the Metaphysical movement. In fact new research has shown that most of Kenyon's theology was derived from Holiness, Higher Life and Faith-Cure sources, with only minor Metaphysical influence.

In logic, McConnell's reasoning would be condemned as a genetic fallacy, that is, rejecting an idea because of where it comes from rather than disproving the argument. In theology, it is called the pharisaical objection of origins. In the next chapter we turn to another writer who relied heavily on pharisaical arguments — Dave Hunt.

TWENTY-ONE

A Pharisee's Assault on the Charismatic Renewal: Dave Hunt

Mr. Hunt's Method

WHEN DAVE HUNT'S BOOK *The Seduction of Christianity* went on sale in Christian bookstores,[1] it not only became one of the biggest-selling Christian books of the 1980s but also one of the most influential books of recent decades.[2]

Before the sales of *Seduction* skyrocketed, Dave Hunt had been known for his excellent anticult writing. *The Seduction of Christianity* was Hunt's second book in a series aimed at forming a theology for what he deemed to be the very edge of the end times. The first was *Peace, Prosperity and the Coming Holocaust* which appeared in 1983.[3] It gave an upgraded vision of John Nelson Darby's view of the end times: There would be a large counterfeit church in alliance with the Antichrist and a smaller church of true Christians. Since then, other works by Hunt have appeared in rapid succession, perhaps the most important of which is a sequel to *The Seduction of Christianity* titled *Beyond Seduction*.[4]

Peace, Prosperity and the Coming Holocaust created little stir among the critics or the public. Not so with Hunt's other two books in the series which fired a storm of controversy, critical reviews and books to counter them.[5]

Hunt's Spiritual Heritage[6]

Dave Hunt was born into a pious Plymouth Brethren household where the doctrines and values of the Brethren were carefully observed. In his autobiography Hunt recalls that he was taught as a boy that the Pentecostals were "of the devil" and that their services were filled with orgies. The more official Brethren view was that the Pentecostal heresy of believing in the present-day gifts of the Spirit was a sign that the apostasy and deception of the church in the last days was at hand.[7]

In college Hunt majored in mathematics. During his Army service he took a correspondence course in accounting and after his discharge became a certified public accountant. Hunt married a woman who was also a Brethren Christian, and the Hunt home was used by his congregation for midweek prayers. At this stage of his life Hunt had ambitions to become a prosecuting attorney. He was on his way to a self-taught law degree when the press of his family and business commitments forced him to drop that goal.

Hunt became the accountant for a lumber and real estate firm which was in poor financial condition. At its most desperate moment he became its general manager. This led to a situation where as chief officer he could be prosecuted for the debts of the company. With a possible jail term facing him, he turned earnestly to the Lord. In a deep prayer experience he heard the voice of the Lord assure him that all would be well.[8] That began several years of living on the edge of a financial precipice, where one miracle after the other saved the business from folding.

It was a spiritually exciting time for Hunt as he learned to trust totally in the Lord's miraculous intervention in his daily life. When the business crisis was finally over, Hunt did not wish to go back to the dull cessationism of his Brethren upbringing:

> Would I be left with the emptiness of an orthodox "faith" that contents itself with beautiful prayers and songs about a God who hides far away in heaven and waits to free men after death, but who plays no real part in their here and now?[9]

At this point Hunt caught the flu and in solitary prayer asked for healing and received it. The sudden healing finally broke his confidence in cessationism and led him to a private Bible study on the work of the Holy Spirit. He became convinced that the powers of the Spirit were as valid today as in the days of the apostles.

Again in private prayer (1963) he received an infilling of the Holy Spirit and worshipped in tongues for hours. Significantly, he did not make praying in tongues an ongoing event in his prayer life, nor did he seek fellowship with other charismatic or Pentecostal Christians. He remained in his beloved Brethren congregation, sharing his experience only with his wife. She had noted a transformation in his personality, especially in his newfound control of his temper. He continued to teach Sunday school at his congregation but strained at the burden of keeping to Brethren doctrines.

Months later Hunt began attending a charismatic home group but committed the imprudence of bringing a Brethren college student with him. The elders of his Brethren church learned of this and began heresy and excommunication procedures against Hunt. Before he was excommunicated he followed the Lord's promptings and preached an anticessationist sermon at his Sunday school class.

Hunt's account of his trial and excommunication is a fascinating description of the mind-set of a cessationist congregation which would accept no evidence or even rational arguments. At that time Brethren doctrine allowed the gifts of the Spirit to be used by missionaries in foreign lands, but in the United States the same gifts were considered demonic. Dave Hunt deeply loved his congregation, and after his excommunication the Hunts still went to the Brethren Sunday worship. While his family and others in the church went to the communion rail for the Lord's supper, he remained seated in the back row, officially "shunned" by his friends.[10]

Unfortunately, the prayer group that had led to his shunning also had divisions and immaturities. He was particularly distressed at the tendency of charismatics to accept anyone into their ranks no matter how weak his or her commitment to the Lord. Specifically, there was a case of a young college lad who was an alcoholic and had been prayed over and had managed to mumble a few syllables. The young man was declared to have received the baptism of the Spirit. Hunt questioned him and discerned that his experience was not an encounter with the Lord. The young man did nothing to further his Christian commitment and continued to be an alcoholic. This contrasted vividly with Hunt's personal experience of deep seeking after the Lord.[11]

Like Darby a century earlier, Hunt became dissatisfied with *all* the denominations of Christendom for falling far short of the love and unity of the early church.[12] Hunt addressed an assembly of college Christians and scolded them for not being as dedicated to Christ as the campus radicals were to communism.

The cream of Christian youth sat before me. I pleaded,

scolded, derided their complacency. I told them they were tin soldiers if soldiers at all. Their country, their freedom, their faith would hang in the balance, and they would continue to play their religious games as usual; not the denial of self, not blazing zeal, not a passion for Christ's kingdom and surrender to his will, but Halloween parties, Thanksgiving ski trips, picnics at the beach....[13]

A close reading of the New Testament shows that the early church had its share of problems, disunity and lukewarmness. In his judgments of the charismatic prayer group and the evangelical college students, Hunt had fallen into the classic trap of judging the contemporary church by the standards of a mythically perfect first-century church. It seems the temptations of Pharisaism were beginning to cloud his spiritual vision.

Dave Hunt Attempts a Theological "Middle Way"

From the time of his initial deep prayer experience, Hunt read widely in the classics of Protestant literature. He encountered the writings of Andrew Murray (1828 – 1917), the South African evangelist. Murray sparked a major revival in South Africa with his pioneer Pentecostal teachings and preaching.[14] Murray had learned about the importance of the Holy Spirit from the writings of William Law and had put Law's insights into practice in his teachings and revivals. Murray's references to Law led Hunt to Law's original writings, and he became an expert in them. In 1971 Hunt edited and updated Andrew Murray's edition of Law's *An Humble, Earnest and Affectionate Address to the Clergy*. Murray had already retitled the work as *The Power of the Spirit*.[15]

The introduction that Hunt provides to his new edition of *The Power of the Spirit* is a landmark on Hunt's spiritual journey. In it he describes Law's theology as an ideal between the charismatic immaturity and evangelical cessationism:

He [Law] would rebuke the pride, lack of love, and inconsistencies in both camps, and would seemingly take sides with neither extreme. But he would unquestionably maintain a Scriptural basis of the present full display and vitality of New Testament Christianity. To the mainline

250

denominational adherent he would press home the necessity of the sovereignty and power of the Holy Spirit for today; and upon the Pentecostal he would impress the fact that the power of the Spirit is bestowed primarily to witness and to live a holy life.[16]

Return to Brethren Theology

Unfortunately, the middle ground Hunt attempted to define between evangelical and anticharismatic slid into a strange theological system that gave lip service to the gifts of the Spirit while essentially asserting cessationism and Brethren theology. His suspicions about the immaturity of his prayer group became generalized into an attack on the fundamental assumptions of the charismatic renewal. By the time he wrote *Beyond Seduction* Hunt had returned to cessationist beliefs, such as the claim that God speaks to His church exclusively through the reading of Scripture, *not* by the gifts of the Spirit such as prophecy or interpretation of tongues.[17]

Hunt had returned to his Brethren fundamentalism and its anti-Pentecostal and anti-charismatic heritage. He seemed to express pain over the success of the charismatic movement and the decline of evangelicalism as he wrote: "Some of the most sincere servants of the Lord are accepting ideas completely at odds with what evangelicals stood for only a few years ago," and fundamentalists are in "their increasingly isolated corner."[18]

Hunt's writings seem especially critical of the fact that Christian television in the United States is dominated by charismatic preachers. Two of the most popular programs of Christian television have been Pat Robertson's *The 700 Club* and Kenneth Copeland's *Believer's Voice of Victory*. These personalities have effectively put those who are anticharismatic on the defensive as they witness to the present-day reality of the miraculous and healing power of the church. Hunt laments:

> The Bible does not teach that the great need today is for a miracle ministry, as is so heavily emphasized on much Christian television. Rather, it warns us that we need discernment to know the difference between what is of God and what is of Satan.[19]

Implying an opposition between discernment and the gift of heal-

251

ing or miracles is a linguistic rabbit-in-the-hat illusion. The "great need" today, as in every age, is for the exercise of *all* the gifts of the Spirit. Hunt repeats the error of false conflicts in *Beyond Seduction* where he puts miracles in opposition to the virtue of self-surrender to Jesus.[20] Miracles, spiritual power and the like are not in opposition to humility, self-sacrifice and love, but they stand in a relationship of complementarity. The gifts of the Spirit, properly understood, empower the Christian for witnessing and ultimately help develop the fruits of the Spirit.

Hunt's theology resembles in many ways that of St. John of the Cross, the Spanish mystic who urged avoidance of the gifts of the Spirit because of their danger to humility (see chapter 4). Like all cessationists, Hunt does not consider, or simply overrides, Jesus' commission to do greater works than His through the power of the Holy Spirit: "Truly, truly, I say to you, he who believes in Me, the works that I do shall he do also; and greater *works* than these shall he do; because I go to the Father" (John 14:12).

Hunt Versus Power Evangelism

In the context of Hunt's renewed cessationism, his attack on John Wimber becomes understandable.[21] Wimber has been instrumental in turning Fuller Theological Seminary from its traditional cessationist views to an institution where gifts of the Spirit are respected and their role in evangelization recognized. Further, Wimber has been successful in drawing evangelical believers into the charismatic understanding of the gifts of the Spirit through his worldwide seminars.[22] The Wimber organization, Vineyard Ministries International, teaches both American and foreign missionaries that evangelization with the power of the gifts of the Spirit (1 Cor. 2:4) is more effective than the cessationist tradition of evangelization by the Word only. The term Wimber applies to the use of charismatic gifts in evangelization is *power evangelism.*

The latest evidence in support of Wimber's position is overwhelming. This is clear, especially in the Third World, where cessationist churches are growing at relatively slow rates, but churches which practice the gifts of the Spirit are expanding explosively.[23] Hunt criticizes Wimber's notion of power evangelism and nostalgically pleads for a return to traditional principles in evangelization (that is, no gifts of the Spirit).

The idea that "power evangelism" requires miracles has not been the understanding or the emphasis of the church in the past. Paul declared that "the power" is in preaching of the cross. Even in the book of Acts there were instances of powerful gospel preaching with many pagans converted (Paul "*so spoke* that a great multitude...believed" — Acts 14:1) without any miracles being performed.[24]

This is perfect cessationist logic, but the biblical interpretation is so weak that it verges on dishonesty. Hunt cites Acts 14:1 as the authority for his "word only" position. The verse describes the mission of Paul and Barnabas in the city of Iconium. Yet to see the complete picture, one must continue to verse 3 which reads: "Paul and Barnabas spent considerable time there, speaking boldly for the Lord, who confirmed the message of his grace by enabling them to do miraculous signs and wonders" (NIV). This verse clearly describes power evangelism.

As an evangelical it seems incredible that Hunt cannot have great joy at the millions who have been brought into the kingdom of God through power evangelism, as in the ministry of Reinhard Bonnke. His criticism makes sense only in terms of Darby's assumption that the resulting large charismatic churches are not "real" Christian churches because the true church of Jesus Christ must be small, insignificant and powerless.

Dave Hunt: Fruitless Theology

Hunt's reaffirmation of cessationist Brethren theology meant that he abandoned the fruit criterion of discernment and sought discernment through doctrine and tradition. A sign of this is the way Hunt repeatedly quotes Jesus' warning about end-times prophets[25]:

> For false Christs and false prophets will arise and will show great signs and wonders, so as to mislead, if possible, even the elect. Behold, I have told you in advance (Matt. 24:24-25).

He should have also cited Jesus' test for discerning false prophets:

> Beware of the false prophets, who come to you in sheep's clothing, but inwardly are ravenous wolves. You will know them by their fruits. Grapes are not gathered from thorn

bushes, nor figs from thistles, are they? (Matt. 7:15).

Discerning spiritual phenomena by their fruits is more demanding than the pseudo-discernment of reference to consensus orthodoxy. We should remember that Jonathan Edwards faced this very same problem. He understood that a revival would bring confusing phenomena but that it should be judged by its overall fruits (see chapter 2).

Discernment from fruits can be especially difficult in situations where spiritualism is involved. Here we can have sympathy for Hunt, who was deeply involved in anticult activities and witnessed demonic miracles. Yet even in judging the cults the biblical fruit criterion is still valid. Demonic fruits, such as healings and exorcisms, are superficial and often temporary, leaving the patient in spiritual bondage to demonic entities. Spiritualist miracles *never* give glory to Jesus or God, while Christian miracles always do. The fruit of Christian miracles leaves the person with a new, deeper experience of freedom and ability to develop the fruit of the Spirit such as joy, peace and longsuffering (Gal. 5:23).

By rejecting the fruit criterion Hunt placed himself in the spiritual inheritance of Charles Chauncy, who could not see the good fruit of the Great Awakening, or of James Buckley, who could not discern the difference between the Faith-Cure movement and Christian Science or spiritualism.

Assault on the Faith Movement

Now faith is the assurance of things hoped for, the conviction of things not seen (Heb. 11:1).

I felt the necessity to write to you appealing that you contend earnestly for the faith which was once for all delivered to the saints (Jude 3b).

Unlike Farah's reproof of faith theology, which recognized its achievements as well as its faults, Hunt's reproof of the faith teachers turns into total condemnation. It is a Darby-like assault based on the Pharisees' origins argument and a narrow understanding of biblically defined faith. In *The Seduction of Christianity*, Jude 3 (faith-doctrine) is cited several times as the full measure of faith, once as a chapter lead.[26] Hunt's own definition of faith is also unfolded for us in *Beyond Seduction*. Hunt puts it together from the writings of the turn-of-the-century cessationist theologian, W. H. Griffith Thomas: "Faith can be analyzed as including (1) renunciation of self; (2) reliance on God. These two aspects sum up its meaning."[27]

This fails to do justice to the biblical concept of faith-expectancy since it does not come to grips with Hebrews 11:1. Hunt's discussion of Hebrews 11:1 is found in *Beyond Seduction*, but it is purely a negative statement, warning the reader that this Scripture verse cannot be used to justify visualization. Most significant, in *The Seduction of Christianity*, Jude 3 functions as the *total* definition of faith by which Hunt judges the biblical validity of the faith teachers. It is simply impossible and irrelevant to judge the faith-expectancy of the faith teachers from the perspective of Jude 3, as it would be impossible to judge the faith-doctrine of any minister from the perspective of Hebrews 11:1.

In this matter Hunt most clearly repeats the pattern of Pharisaism. The Pharisees viewed Jesus' ministry as insulting to their concerns with the purity of faith-doctrine. Examples include their disputes about Sabbath-keeping and their discomfort with Jesus' emphasis on faith-expectancy (see chapter 1). Christian faith needs both faith-expectancy and faith-doctrine, which would be confession of our reliance on His promises and affirmation of the truth of the gospel. These elements of faith need to be held in a relationship of complementarity, not conflict.

Hunt's attack on the faith ministers is based on D. R. McConnell's master's thesis, "The Kenyon Connection" (discussed in chapter 20) and repeats the origins critique of Kenyon, Hagin and the faith theology.[28] Hunt never stops to consider whether what Kenyon said was biblically valid and, therefore, a positive and useful influence on Kenneth Hagin. He only reveals that Kenyon was a New Thought writer so whatever Kenyon said *must* be heretical.

Hunt's tendency for inaccurate footnotes (a much-noted failure of his writings) worked against Hagin as early as 1983. In *Peace, Prosperity and the Coming Holocaust* Hunt claimed that Hagin taught his followers that one could have effective prayer power without any faith in God. In other words, one could have power through magic. As proof he cited the article "Having Faith in Your Faith" in Kenneth Hagin's monthly magazine.[29] The title of the article seemed to substantiate Hunt's assertion. However, someone who reads the article himself would notice it was addressed to born-again believers, and their faith in God was assumed and encouraged. The subject matter of the article was *perseverance* of faith-expectancy in the face of personal tribulation, specifically, not to despair if healing does not manifest immediately after prayer.[30]

In *The Seduction of Christianity* Hunt suggests by innuendo that Hagin, in common with all faith ministers, believes one can *command* God to act in response to one's need.[31] This is a distortion and a basic misunderstanding of Hagin's position. In fact Hagin believes, as did Kenyon, that the Christian has authority of command over demons and command over sickness through the name of Jesus.

In his relationship with God, the believer has the right of *negotiation*. That is, the Christian can plead with God in the same manner in which Moses pleaded for the survival of the Israelites after they had made the golden calf; Abraham pleaded for Sodom; or Paul pleaded for the removal of his "thorn in the flesh" (Ex. 33:12-17; Gen. 18:22-32; 2 Cor. 12:7). Hagin, again following Kenyon, affirms this form of bargaining-pleading for the ordinary believer.[32] Biblical revelation shows that the Lord desires that we learn to intercede and plead with Him, even though sometimes our requests will be denied.

The Christian's right of "pestering intercession" (Luke 18:2-8) is part of the primary revelation in the New Testament of God's being "Daddy" to us. Hunt's confusion in evaluating the Kenyon-Hagin theology possibly comes from Hunt's full acceptance of Calvin's image of God's unalterable will and sovereignty which gives little room for intercession.

The Origins Critique of Spiritual Laws

Hunt has also found any concept of spiritual law unacceptable to Christians for several reasons,[33] primarily because the concept of spiritual laws came into acceptance by way of unorthodox sources, especially New Thought writers. Therefore the concept is occult and cannot be valid. This is the Pharisees' origins argument, that valid theological development can only come from orthodox circles.

Another Hunt argument against spiritual laws is that they violate God's sovereignty. Hunt presents a false either-or situation. One either accepts the sovereignty of God or accepts spiritual laws which exclude a personal God, as in the Hindu concept of karma and reincarnation. This is an example of the nonlogical argument by exaggeration. True, the Hindu concept of spiritual law (karma) leaves little room for a personal God. But spiritual law as defined in the Bible no more excludes a personal God than do mathematical laws. God sovereignly instituted a lawful universe at the moment of creation. That is not a violation of His sovereignty, but rather an expression of His loving creativity. He foreordained a universe that is filled with regularity so that His creatures can observe and conform to its regularities. It is the only way science or mathematics is possible.

This is another case of complementarity; what God revealed in the Bible is *both* personal and lawful. Hunt's view of God, much like Calvin's, is closer to the concept of God depicted in the Koran — all sovereign yet ruling the universe capriciously — than God revealed in the Bible.[34]

Hunt finalizes his argument against spiritual laws with an unintentional logical contradiction. He claims that although God's sovereign character forbids the existence of spiritual law, "we can rely upon God's *promises* because of His integrity and love — not because He is bound by 'scientific law.'"[35]

The understanding of the reliability of God's promises is an element of evangelical theology of long standing. We agree with it completely. But notice, if God's promises are reliable because of His character, they will always be executed when humans meet their conditions. If this is the case, then there is only a semantic difference between God's promises and spiritual laws. In fact one might be defined in terms of the other: The key element is that God's character is so righteous, and His power so awesome, that *His promises behave as laws.*

In fact, Hunt's argument that spiritual law violates the sovereignty of God can be used against his own concept of promises. If God cannot tolerate the bounds of law as an insult to His sovereignty, then the reliability of His promises is equally intolerable to His sovereignty. He should be sovereign even over His promises.

Visualization: Prayer or Sorcery?

In *The Seduction of Christianity* Hunt asserts that *any* use of prayer visualization by Christians is sorcery.[36] In classic legal style, Hunt brings to bear against visualization a whole array of primary and secondary arguments. Following the old Scottish Calvinists (see chapter 17), Hunt believes that persons who form an image of Jesus in prayer are committing an act of idolatry and sorcery, possibly opening themselves to a demonic "spirit guide."[37] Hunt's arguments are principally concerned with inner healing but pertain to any form of visualization.

Hunt's central argumentation declares guilt by association and proves nothing, but it gives the illusion of logic. It is as follows: The technique of visualization is not specifically found in the Bible, nor is it found in Christian literature before its introduction by Agnes Sanford. Further, visualization is often found in occult literature as a technique of magic. Therefore visualization is always and essentially an act of sorcery.

In fact Hunt is partially correct about the role of Agnes Sanford. She was the person who took the tradition of prayer visualization from the Bible-affirming wing of New Thought and introduced it to mainline Christian literature. We will reserve our comments on Mrs. Sanford's ministry for a future volume.[38]

The assertion that visualization is not in the Bible and therefore cannot be Christian reflects the Pharisees' way of thinking, which is to evaluate something by its specific biblical reference (or lack of it) rather than also testing its fruit as both Jesus and Paul asserted. Using the same criterion one would come to the amazing conclusion that neither Sunday school nor church steeples are biblical. By the same logic some have concluded that musical instruments should be forbidden because they are not mentioned in the New Testament. Christians tend to forget that this form of argument was made one hundred years ago when Sunday schools were introduced into America. In fact, one could repeat the Hunt argumentation by saying Sunday schools are not described in the Bible, but schools of occult knowledge have existed in pagan religions since earliest times; therefore, Sunday schools are occult.

It must be stressed that visualization is not condemned in Scripture or even specifically mentioned. Hunt's arguments against visualization are all from analogy and result in fencing, making overly restrictive rules to avoid the possibility of sinning. Paul specifically warned against this type of argumentation because he realized how quickly this would become a legalistic entrapment of the type he had known as a Pharisee.

Hunt is greatly disturbed by the use of visualization by David Yonggi Cho, pastor of the world's largest church in Seoul, Korea.[39] Cho prayed for his church's growth by actively imagining it to be bigger than it was. When he began his Christian ministry he had a very small, impoverished congregation, but in his imagination he saw himself preaching in a church that had three thousand members. His congregation in fact grew to his visualized size and subsequently has become the largest single church in Christendom.[40] According to Hunt, what Cho did was an act of sorcery.[41]

In the case of Cho, Brooks Alexander (discussed in chapter 17) sides with Hunt and considers Cho's use of visualization dangerous. Alexander believes that Cho uses visualization too often in his prayer life and may have learned his technique from Korea's shamanistic environment.[42] It seems, however, that here Alexander is violating his own criteria. Cho's prayer style (perhaps 80 percent visualization, 20 percent oral and mental) may be culturally defined, but this does not make it shamanism. If one prayer-visualization is godly, repeating it ten times does not make it sorcery. Rather, Cho is conforming to Jesus' injunction of persevering prayer with his faculty of imagination instead of his voice (Luke 18:1-8). The critical factor for determining whether visualization is godly or sorcerous is the attitude and belief behind it. If it is offered to the throne of God, it is certainly a form of prayer; if it is believed that the visualization itself is the source of power, it is an attempt at magic.[43]

Hunt's Reversal

A sure sign of the unworkableness of Hunt's absolute condemnation of visualization is his difficulty with imagination in the arts. Hunt recognized, for example, that when an architect plans a new building he needs to imagine it complete. Similarly, an artist often imagines the finished work at the start of a task. For Hunt this was the proper role of the imagination and not visualization. But an unsolvable legalism arises with this exception. Is the demarcation between imagination and visualization a function of time or intensity? For example, if the architect vaguely imagines his new building for five minutes, is that good? But if he vividly sees his building for ten minutes, is that then sorcery?

These problems came to a head in *Beyond Seduction* in a section that should have begun — rather than ended — a mature discussion of the problem of discerning visualization. Hunt admits that the imagination can be used in certain circumstances in prayer. As an example of an acceptable use of imagination in prayer, Hunt gives an evangelical instance which we need to quote in full:

> It is not wrong if a pastor on his knees, because this is the passion of his heart, sees in his mind his church filled to overflowing and people going forward to repent, and cries out to God in prayer for this to become a reality. It is wrong,

259

however, if he thinks that by concentrating on this imaginary scene until it becomes vivid in his mind he will thereby help it to occur, and he then practices this technique in order to make what he visualizes come to pass. Mental imagery is a normal function of the human mind, and the use of mental pictures can be helpful in such areas as memorization, planning, recalling, gaining insight, or helping to explain a complex concept. But to attempt to visualize God or Jesus, or to change or create reality by visualization, is to step into the occult.[44]

Aside from the evangelical word changes, this is precisely what Cho did in praying for his church. Hunt feels Cho's visualizations were sorcery, but the pastor in Hunt's example has offered an acceptable prayer. Hunt stumbles for a clarifying distinction between sorcery-visualization and acceptable imagination in prayer. In the last sentence he asserts that the mark of sorcery-visualization is the attempt to change or create reality. This is not a strong argument. Most prayer is an attempt to change reality through God's power.[45] If my wife is ill (a reality), I pray for her healing (a change in what is real).

If some form of visualization can be legitimate, it should be openly discussed, as in Brooks Alexander's article. Yet Hunt continues to claim that *all* visualization is sorcery and does not acknowledge what Alexander has discovered.[46] Hunt has again used an illogical argument. He affirmed a universal principle (all visualization is bad) and condemned those who disobeyed it. Then he made an exception to the universal without reflection or apology by saying it is good to visualize people getting saved. This form of illogical argumentation might best be termed an affectatious universal. It was used by many of the antiwar protesters of the 1970s who claimed to be pacifists ("make love not war!") but who often supported Marxist wars of their liking, as in the Sandinista (communist) guerillas of Nicaragua.

Hunt and Darby

Hunt's writings contain most of the theological assumptions and much of the style of John Darby. Darby saw the origins of the church's apostasy as a conspiracy by theological liberals. Because Darby believed his theological opponents were under satanic influence, there was no point in making a sincere effort to understand their positions or to summarize their writings fairly. It was all demonic anyway. The important thing for Darby was to expose heresy and error and save a remnant of the church.

Hunt has these same tendencies. For him the origins of the satanic attack and deception on Christians is the New Age movement and its allied occult and quasi-occult organizations. His broad generalizations, as in his caricature of Christian psychology and his summaries of his opponents' thoughts, are more in the nature of caricature than the understanding that forms the basis of useful reproof. Hunt probably never intended to be unfair to his opponents in these ways. He did much of his theological study on Darby and Calvin, who also used zealous styles of argumentation, and perhaps he assumed that these techniques of argumentation are *normal.*

Another way of describing Hunt's theology would be to say that he could not separate himself from the archetype of Pharisaism that resides in his home denomination, the Plymouth Brethren. Here we are not using the term *archetype* in the Jungian sense but in the sense developed by the great evangelical theologian Francis Schaeffer. Unlike Jung's quasi-spiritualist system of archetypes, Schaeffer believed that there were indeed archetypes, but they were forces carried by *language;* that is, the way a group expresses itself and uses words has powerful influences on the thinking of every individual within that group.[47] Thus Hunt, in his rejection of the charismatic renewal, fell back into the language archetypes within the Brethren. This doomed his subsequent work to a similar exaggeration, lack of meekness, condemnation and paranoia that was present in Darby's original theology.[48]

The Last Irony: Hunt, William Law and Jakob Böhme

Hunt knows well the heresy-to-orthodoxy process we have described in this book, by which the Holy Spirit brings truth to the church through mixed movements or heretical persons and writings. When he studied the writings of William Law earlier in his career, Hunt found that Law had been inspired by the writings of the German mystic and semi-occultist Jakob Böhme (1575-1626). At that time Hunt intended to point out how valuable Law's writings were, and he did not consider the origins argumentation as important.

Böhme was both one of the strangest and most influential of the Christian mystics. He was born into a German Lutheran community in an age when Protestantism was already suspicious of any form of mysticism and had lost the traditions of discerning visions. Because of this, he did not get proper spiritual direction at the critical period of his life.

Böhme was a family man and shoemaker by trade but received intense visions and revelations which he wrote down. His writings contain a mix of revelations and insights that came from both the Holy Spirit and other, unholy spirits. His central message was that the Holy Spirit wished to inform and inspire his church constantly and that everyone had the capacity to listen to the Holy Spirit. This concept was outlandish at the time. This idea inspired William Law to consider the role of the Spirit and also inspired Andrew Murray.

But Böhme also had revelations which clearly contradicted Scripture. For example, Böhme taught that Adam was created androgynous and was separated into male (Adam) and female (Eve) after the fall. He also claimed that Christ ascended into heaven in his heavenly body but that his earthly body remained on earth. This is clearly a Gnostic idea.[49]

In spite of these biblical lapses, William Law structured his theological understanding around Böhme's system. Law was intimate with Scripture and intense in his prayer life so that he could filter out most of Böhme's heretical revelations while adopting his valid insights. However, Law's biblical filter, like E. W. Kenyon's two centuries later, was not perfectly applied. Law's *On the Love of God* accepted Böhme's idea that the wrath of God does not exist. In any case, out of an originally mixed and contaminated revelation came a (generally) sound and insight-filled theology of the Holy Spirit that was two centuries ahead of its time.

In both the introduction to his edition of Law's *The Power of the Spirit* and in a recent article on Law, Hunt clearly identifies Böhme's influence on Law.[50] Hunt does not, however, use the origins argumentation to discredit the writings of Law. On the contrary, Hunt uses a common sense approach to Law's writings. He evaluates and appreciates them not on their theological origins but on their overall biblical compatibility, their contribution to our understanding of Scripture and their ability to inspire Christians to holiness. Strangely enough, Hunt does not mention even one of Böhme's heretical ideas, nor even that Law often referred to Böhme as "blessed Böhme."

Had Hunt used the same origins methodology that he applied to E. W. Kenyon and the Faith movement, his argumentation would have run something like this: Böhme was a mystic and heretic. His writings were riddled with demon-inspired Gnostic beliefs. William Law was an important Christian writer who was influenced by Böhme's Gnostic writings. Therefore, the writings of Law (**and** Andrew Murray) are heretical and will seduce the average Christian **reader** into Gnostic heresy.[51]

We have just seen how a devoted Christian and fine anticult writer, David Hunt, delved into a spirit of pharisaism. We will now examine how certain Christian institutions function in a similar pharisaical way.

TWENTY-TWO

The Tragedy of Hank Hanegraaff and the CRI

FOUR NATIONALLY KNOWN CHRISTIAN MINISTRIES have been attacked with excessive and unchristian zeal by anticult organizations. In each case the persecuted ministers needed some correction and reproof. These attacks are examined in a recent study by James Spencer, titled *Heresy Hunters: Character Assassination in the Church*.[1] Spencer is a respected anticult minister himself. A long time member of the Mormon church, he was released from that bondage by the grace of God and in turn has established a highly successful ministry to the Mormons.[2]

What bothered Spencer (and the other anticult ministers he consulted) was that such attacks passed well beyond biblical reproof and entered into the realm of character assassination. The goal seemed to be to *destroy* a ministry, not to *correct* it.[3]

This is not altogether surprising, as the anticult ministries are in a literal sense extra-biblical. In other words, they are not described in Scripture nor are they disallowed. These ministries have arisen in response to the tragic situation in the mainline churches where the office of bishop (overseer) has been weakened to ineffectiveness.[4] In the epistles we see the bishop as one who both encourages and corrects the churches under his charge. Paul's ministry to his churches serves as a perfect example. He rejoiced and encouraged his churches when they exercised their faith or generosity (Phil. 1:3-7, for example), yet when they transgressed the moral law or were disorderly in worship they were rebuked (1 Cor.). Further, when false doctrine arose Paul swiftly corrected it (Gal. 1 and 1 Cor.). This is the biblical pattern of the bishop: encouragement and correction.

This pattern continued in the early church. The most distinguished antiheresy work of the early church was *Against Heresies* by Irenaeus (130 – 200), bishop of Lyons. Irenaeus, like Paul, supervised and encouraged his deacons. Besides his classic work on heresy, he wrote apologetical works to evangelize the pagans. Irenaeus had the advantage of living in an era of persecution, when he had no church properties to worry about, no extensive paperwork and legal structure, no retirement funds to manage. He concentrated on the spiritual aspects of his ministry: prayer, building the body and defending it.[5]

In contrast, modern bishops are forced to be both bureaucrats who oversee the church's assets and politicians who mediate among the various factions within the church. More tragically, liberal theology has so captivated the mainline seminaries that many bishops now are as likely to *encourage heresy* as to fight against it.[6] In the Episcopal church, for example, Bishop John Spong of Newark has acquired an infamous reputation for defending every sort of heresy and unbiblical practice in the name of openness. Spong may be a vocal extremist, but his heretical theology reflects what has been taught in many mainline seminaries for decades.[7]

Into this spiritual vacuum have stepped the anticult ministries. They now do the reproof and apologetic ministry that modern bishops and overseers have abandoned. It is not the biblical pattern that these functions should be separated from the authority of the bishop. Rather, it is tragic necessity.

The 1960s was the critical decade; America went into cultural upheaval, and a popular counterculture arose that glorified non-Christian values and sometimes bizarre forms of spirituality. Persons like Walter Martin *Bible Answer Man* and Tal Brooke of Spiritual Counterfeits Project were called by God to respond to the double threats of cultism outside of the church and unreproved heresy within the church. Many of the persons called to this ministry had to educate themselves in the essentials of Christian orthodoxy.[8] Usually this has meant going back to the founders of classical Protestantism, especially nineteenth century evangelical theology, which was pre-liberal and unfortunately cessationist.

This has meant that often anticult specialists, especially those from the smaller ministries, have little awareness of the multiple forms of Christian orthodoxy and faith-filled communities that have flowered across Christian history. A recent notable exception is Robert Bowman, formerly with the Christian Research Institute, whose superb work, *Orthodoxy and Heresy,* provides an excellent, readable overview of trans-denominational orthodoxy.[9]

Unfortunately many anticult writers fall far short of the education and sophistication of Bowman. Some self-educated anticult ministers come into their ministry with a mythical view of the Reformation and evangelical Protestantism. It is a view derived from Sunday school history and reading only the Reformers' best writings. The myth pictures the Reformers as morally and spiritually perfect. In fact, the Protestant Reformation, like every move of God upon His church, was "messy." Reformers debated each other with less than perfect civility and even persecuted one another. Radical sects arose which spread heresy. Several major Reformers had serious moral flaws. For instance, St. Jerome, who translated the Scriptures in Latin (the Vulgate), was uncharitable in his writings. Luther mixed theology with obscenities, and John Knox may have engaged in ongoing incest.[10] Few of the church's major reformers reached the sanctification level of St. Francis or of John and Charles Wesley.

The issue at stake is that God has often used less than perfect persons for His kingdom's business. Anticult writers often compare contemporary ministers to their myth of flawless Reformers. Naturally the contemporary minister falls short, and thus must be counterfeit, heretical and dangerous.

The record of the post-World War II anticult ministries has been mixed. Many have done excellent work in bringing heresy to account. Several have created outstanding research libraries and attracted sound scholarly staff. Others have remained at a primitive level, where anything that is not familiar to their evangelical tradition is labeled heresy.

Some of the ministries had problems in the 1970s accepting that the Pentecostal-charismatic perspective was not cultic or deviant. Others were able to make the transition without difficulty. Walter Martin's acceptance of Pentecostalism and the perpetuity of the gifts of the Spirit, after years as an evangelical cessationist, was a critical positive model for other anticult ministries. However, even the best of them are subject to the temptation inherent to their intrinsically unbalanced ministry — an unceasing critical perspective. Here one of James Spencer's observations about the anticult ministries is pertinent. Many have, without intending, adopted the world's (fallen) stance of investigative journalism, where exposure to the point of ridicule and destruction is considered fair.[11]

The Christian Research Institute

Perhaps the preeminent anticult ministry is the Christian Research Institute (CRI), founded by Walter Martin, one of the best educated of the anticult investigators.[12] When Martin died of cancer in 1989, Hank Hanegraaff took over as CRI's director. Hanegraaff identifies himself as a charismatic and, in his earlier years, he assisted the staff of a fine charismatic congregation in Atlanta. Now he distances himself from many facets of the charismatic movement. In addition, Hanegraaff does not have the same educational credentials as Martin did, but he describes his most important mentors as Charles Spurgeon (nineteenth-century evangelist), Jonathan Edwards and C. S. Lewis.[13]

Under Hanegraaff's leadership the CRI has continued to do much excellent work. *Christian Research Journal* has been expanded and publishes outstanding articles that not only expose cults but educate and help bring to maturity its own evangelical audience. Many who listen to the daily radio program, *The Bible Answer Man*, and subscribe to the *Christian Research Journal* are evangelical fundamentalists. As such, many have deep suspicions of all things academic.[14] Hanegraaff could have pandered to their prejudices, but he has chosen not to. For instance, the *Christian Research Journal* did an excellent five-part series on Roman Catholicism in which it refused to label Catholicism as heretical or cultic.[15] This offended many of its more conservative readers.

Similarly, the Winter 1995 issue of *Christian Research Journal* had the first of a three-part study on the role of psychology in Christian counseling. Again, the CRI could have easily written off all secular psychology as hopeless paganism. In fact, the articles, written by Bob and Gretchen Passantino, took a middle ground which recognized the valuable contributions that psychology can make to the church but warned of its excessive use.[16]

Hanegraaff, as talk show host of the *Bible Answer Man* spent three programs interviewing John White, the author of *The King James Only Controversy*.[17] This book exposed the harmful myth, held by many fundamentalists, that the King James Version of the Bible is the only reliable and inspired modern version. Several irate fundamentalist listeners called in to battle with Hanegraaff and White on behalf of the King James Bible. All of this means that Hanegraaff has carried on Martin's tradition of bringing sound evangelical scholarship to the public's attention, regardless of popular fundamentalist prejudices.

Further, Hanegraaff has played a major role in bringing the Worldwide Church of God (Herbert W. Armstrong) back into biblical orthodoxy through his patient years-long dialogue with its leadership. This exciting story in itself is enough to make Hanegraaff an important figure in twentiety-century Christianity.[18]

Tragically, on certain major issues Hanegraaff has had poor discernment and has slipped into modes of destructive heresy hunting (Pharisaism). In each case his lack of a broad Christian historical perspective seems to have contributed to his misjudgments.

As noted earlier (chapter 19), Farah's reproof of the Word-Faith movement went unheeded by many of the faith ministers. Some, like Kenneth Hagin, grew in maturity and moderation, but little or no progress has been made to define limits on "revelation knowledge." Thus even some of the more mature ministers continue to mistake every meditative thought and idea as a revelation from God.[19] New Word-Faith ministries have grown and continue to preach excesses in healing and prosperity.

However, it is disappointing the Hanegraaff took the "total error" view of Hunt and MacArthur (see chapters 21 and 24) rather than the approach of Farah. It is also understandable how this happened. Walter Martin, the revered founder of CRI, felt the Word-Faith ministries were indeed a serious threat to authentic Christianity. One of the last pieces he wrote was a critique of the "little gods" theology of some faith ministers.[20]

Hanegraaff continued (and exaggerated) Martin's critique with the release in 1993 of *Christianity in Crisis*.[21] It has been an astounding best-seller, helped by his authority and prestige as head of CRI. He cites his book often as a resource on the *Bible Answer Man*. Like Hunt's *Seduction of Christianity*, Hanegraaff's book appears to be a work of great scholarship with its massive notes and frequent quotations. Unlike Hunt, Hanegraaff took great care to assure that the footnotes were correct, and his work has few if any technical errors. The average Christian reader invariably concludes it is a truthful assessment of the Word-Faith movement.

The Deception of Selective Collections

However, behind its numerous citations and quotations lies a profound methodological error — the assumption that listing the worst errors of a movement is a truthful representation of that movement. This was Chauncy's error in *Seasonable Thoughts,* and Buckley's in *Christian Science and Other Superstitions* (see my analyses in chapters 3 and 10). It is an error easily made, but it results in caricature, not analysis, and results in destructiveness, not biblical reproof.

Let me demonstrate this with an imaginary example. Suppose I returned to my adolescent years when I was a fervent and intolerant Catholic.[22] Suppose also that I wished to expose the origins of Protestantism by showing that Martin Luther, the first Reformer, was a boorish, prejudiced lout, and therefore could not have led a movement of God. This could be easily accomplished by going to his collected writings (over fifty volumes) and selecting his most imprudent writings. I would select all of his violent, anti-Semitic sermons and pamphlets. I would select his address during the Peasants' Revolt, when he called on the knights to slaughter the rebel peasants without mercy. Lastly, I would add certain sermons and "table talk" where Luther expressed theological concepts with foul ("earthy") language. Also, I would *avoid* any of Luther's better writings, such as his classic *Commentary on Romans,* which has enlightened generation upon generation of Christians. My anthology would be completely true, and, presuming that I took care, all the footnotes and quotes would be correct.[23] But on a deeper level it would be untrue and unfair.

The key is recognizing the difference between "collections" and history; between assembling a scrapbook of errors and writing a fair description of another's theology. A good historian attempts to take a whole measure of a person and his writings and place him within his times. For instance, Luther's anti-Semitism was common to practically all Christians in Luther's time.

The methodology of evaluating "messy" religious movements was of course first sketched out by Jonathan Edwards. However it was elaborated a century and a half later by William James, the famous philosopher and psychologist.[24] In his classic work, *Varieties of Religious Experience,*[25] James showed (as Edwards) that no religious movement or class of experiences should be judged only by its extreme manifestations.

A clear demonstration of James' methodology is found in his analysis of the Christian practice of celibacy. James showed the bizarre and destructive manifestations of celibacy that are scattered in Catholic tradition, dating back to the Desert Fathers of the third century. In this extreme form celibacy was mistaken as the supreme Christian virtue, to be protected by fleeing from all contact with women. James, with his knack for words, terms this behavior "theopathic." At this point, James could have agreed with the materialist and secular viewpoint of his peers that all forms of celibacy are neurotic. He probably would have gotten some Protestants to agree with him. But James went further. He examined Christian saints who lived in normal society but surrendered their sexual life to allow for deeper service to the Lord, and who succeeded in ways that were graceful and effective.[26] James, as psychologist and philosopher, did not cite Scripture to affirm his argument. He could have cited Paul (1 Cor. 7:32-35) to show that indeed some are called to lead especially focused, celibate lives for the kingdom.

Hanegraaff's attack on the Word-Faith ministers and theology violates the historian's mandate of fair representation and James' (and Edwards') understanding that religious movements generate both the extreme and the moderate examples. Just as I did with my fictitious anthology of Luther, *Christianity in Crisis* chooses only Word-Faith's most extreme statements as representative of the whole movement. Reproof is lost in caricature. In fact, Hanegraaff begins *Christianity in Crisis* with a rendition of the Word-Faith theology in the form of a child's fairy tale. Here are presented all of the extremes of this theology, from believing that Jesus and the apostles were rich men to the speculations of Jesus' suffering in hell. All are made most ridiculous.

Several items in Hanegraaff's anthology of the ridiculous are especially unfair.

We have shown earlier that McConnell's scandal at Kenyon's theology of Christ in hell was misplaced. In fact Kenyon elaborated on a long-standing evangelical tradition that only came out of fashion in the last half-century (chapter 20). In his book, in a major section called, "Atonement Atrocities," Hanegraaff elevates McConnell's objections into an elaborate pummeling of the related Christ-in-hell theories.[27] At the foundation of Hanegraaff's polemic is his misinformed view that the ransom theory of the atonement, held by Kenyon and many Word-Faith teachers, is heretical. In a review of Benny Hinn's book, *The Anointing,* Hanegraaff wrote:

Hinn displays his ignorance of atonement theology by

confusing justification (Eph. 2:8-10) with sanctification (Rom. 8:26-30)(14 – 15) and by repeating the heretical "ransom" theory of the atonement — that Jesus had to "buy back" an innocent humanity from the wicked Satan (133) — refuted by Romans 5:9-21.[28]

By labeling the ransom theory as heretical, Hanegraaff is doing a serious injustice to many orthodox believers and expressing a form of evangelical provincialism (see chapter 20). Similarly, when, on an absolute basis, he claims that Jesus never "descended into hell" (Sheol), and asserts that believing that He did is heresy, Hanegraaff is refusing to recognize a broader orthodoxy than his own tradition.[29] Such claims demonstrate a tendency to avoid scriptures not conducive to his own specific theology (especially 1 Pet. 3 – 4).

The exalted state to which Adam is often elevated is another doctrine of the Word-Faith movement that Hanegraaff finds intolerably heretical. Hanegraaff quotes Benny Hinn as teaching that before the Fall Adam was such a perfect and empowered being that he could even fly. Hinn cites Adam's God-given dominion over the birds in Genesis 1:26 as proof text. Hinn even believed that Adam could have gone to the moon if he wished.[30]

Although this far-fetched theory of Adam's powers is worthy of reproof (and a laugh), it is not a serious heresy as Hanegraaff would have one believe. The exaltation of Adam was a venerable tradition dating back to the religious teachers (proto-rabbis) of the Jewish exiles in Babylon. By New Testament times many rabbis taught similarly fantastic doctrines of Adam. For instance, some believed he was enormous, and even after the Fall measured a hundred yards. Others taught that Adam's face and body gave off light brighter than the sun.[31] Paul was greatly influenced by this literature and took his doctrine of Christ the "second Adam" from the assumptions of these rabbis (Rom. 5:15-18; 1 Cor. 15:20-23). Certainly, had Paul not considered Adam super-human, then the comparison of Adam with Christ that Paul advocates would have been demeaning to Christ. Hanegraaff is again making a heretical mountain out of a speculative molehill.

Unfortunately in *Christianity in Crisis* Hanegraaff allows his abhorrence of the Word-Faith movement to take him where no Christian should go — to plain distortion. This distortion is illustrated by his assessment of Kenneth Copeland as "the worst of the false teachers."[32] Hanegraaff attempts to prove that Copeland does not even believe in the deity of Christ, quoting one of Copeland's taped sermons about the atonement as proof:

> What [why] does God have to pay the price for this thing [The price of sin]? He has to have a man that is like that first one. It's got to be all man. He's got to be all man. He cannot be a God and come storming in here with the attributes and dignities that are not common to man.[33]

Copeland's statement sounds conclusive; he is indeed a heretic! However, by giving attention to the rest of the taped sermon it becomes clear that in the quoted segment Copeland was stressing Christ's *human* nature. He very quickly dicusses Jesus' *divine* nature by saying:

> There had to be a man, but it also had to be man as pure as that first one [Adam], and there wasn't anybody left like that but God. Now somehow or another there's got to be an incarnation, there's got to be a man filled with God — there's got to be a God-man come into the earth.[34]

In the context of his sermon, Copeland was completely orthodox on this issue.

In summary, the reality of current Word-Faith teaching bears scant relationship with Hanegraaff caricature.[35] For example, my monitoring of Hagin's *Word of Faith* magazine during the last seven years has shown me a surprising moderation of tone and substance. (Hagin seems to have accepted many of Farah's criticisms, although as a matter of policy he never responded to them.) Certainly some Word-Faith teachers have come out with overimaginative speculations, and their prosperity and healing doctrines often need reproof. But Hanegraaff's rendition of their theology is simply false by its exaggeration of emphasis. The reader is challenged to listen to Hagin, Copeland or Marilyn Hickey for several weeks and see what the Word-Faith teachers are saying now.

Hanegraaff Versus Holy Laughter (the Toronto Blessing)

In 1993, a new revival of the church broke out in North America. Emotional and spiritual healings and a new sense of joy have been its most evident effects. By 1994 the revival was widespread. John Wimber, founder and overseer of the Vineyard churches, where the revival has had the most impact, prefers to label this work of God a "refreshment" of the church. In his opinion, this current move is mostly among those who are already Christians. By contrast, traditional revival is marked by the addition of large numbers of nonbelievers into the church. However, in recent months it is increasingly clear that nonbelievers are indeed being attracted and converted by this movement.[36]

Like other moves of God, this current move has had a gestation period and many outbreaks. It is called the "Toronto Blessing" because its most publicized focal point has been the occurrences at the Toronto Airport Christian Fellowship (formerly known as the Toronto Airport Vineyard) church pastored by John Arnott.[37] Ironically, Arnott received an anointing for revival in 1993 in Argentina, at the hands of evangelist Claudio Freidzon. Arnott and his wife had gone to that nation to witness the revival taking place there. Sustained laughter which often spread throughout an entire crowd was the peculiar manifestation of the revival in Argentina; thus, this current move of God is also referred to as the "Laughing Revival." It is unfortunate that this name focuses on the revival's most popularized *manifestation* ("exercise"). It would be far better to call it the "Joyful Revival" after its predominant fruit or the "New Wine Revival" after a phrase often heard at its meetings.

In North America the revival has been closely associated with South African evangelist Rodney Howard-Browne. Howard-Browne came to the United States in 1987 as an itinerant preacher. Two years later, while ministering in New York state, manifestations broke out at his meetings which included fallings and laughter. From then on his ministry mushroomed. His most important engagements were at the Carpenter's Home Church in Lakeland, Florida, and at Rhema Bible School and at Oral Roberts University in Tulsa (1993).

At Rhema, Randy Clark, a Vineyard pastor from St. Louis, returned to the blessing line four times to receive consecutive laying on of hands from Howard-Browne. When Clark returned to St. Louis, revival broke out in his church. Soon after that, Pastor John Arnott invited Clark to speak at the then Toronto Vineyard for a four-night engagement in January 1994. Clark stayed for several weeks as God's special presence fell on the Toronto church. Soon visitors, including clergy, from all over the world began making their way to this "warehouse" church.[38]

This visitation of God has now spread worldwide, affecting almost every continent. It is even reviving the church in Europe which had been particularly resistant to revival during this century. The situation is especially impressive in the United Kingdom where over fifty-five hundred churches have seen dramatic increases in attendance and in the godly devotion of their congregations.[39] An English pastor describes renewal in his own congregation:

> When we pray [for people], they laugh or weep. In the following days they talk of a sense of God's presence, of their marriages being different, and of ethical changes in their lives. [Our church has] discovered a new lease on life; our prayer meetings have quadrupled.[40]

The Anglican revival stems from the close relationship between John Wimber and his Vineyard staff and several influential Anglican clergymen. The Toronto Airport Christian Fellowship, because of its former association with the Vineyard, has attracted, perhaps as no American church could, Anglican clergy from both Canada and the United Kingdom. The relationship between the Vineyard and the Anglican Church is truly a divine "odd couple." The Vineyard is the most "American" and least liturgical of modern denominations (jeans and sweaters are their priestly attire, pop bands their choirs). Yet their leaders can often be found teaching and encouraging the people in ancient churches and beautiful cathedrals throughout the United Kingdom.

Although the present revival has produced numerous reports of physical healings, it is most noted for the large numbers of spiritual and emotional healings. A Canadian Baptist pastor reports his experience at the Toronto church:

> As I stood to receive prayer, I was determined not to fall down as some did, wanting to worship Jesus and invite his presence in my own way. But then my legs completely melted, and I fell backwards to the carpet for several minutes. My mind was still alert, wondering, until convulsions started in my stomach, and I began having sobs from the pit of my being.
>
> A sense of peace followed my crying in which I knew I was deeply known, forgiven, and loved in the presence of God.[41]

Hanegraaff on the Laughing Revival

In the face of such positive witness and of the revolutionary evangelical

274

impact the revival is having in England and elsewhere, Hank Hanegraaff still believes that the Laughing Revival is not a move of God. Rather he labels it a delusion, empowered by psychological manipulation or worse.[42] He calls it a "Counterfeit Revival."[43] Hanegraaff and the CRI staff have consistently attacked the Laughing Revival and its leadership in their publications, and often several times a week on the *Bible Answer Man* since about August 1994.[44]

Hanegraaff's objections to the Laughing Revival are neither surprising nor especially original. They are remarkably similar to Charles Chauncy's complaints about the Great Awakening. As early as September 1994 Hanegraaff claimed that the revival did not meet the biblical criteria established by Paul for "decent order."[45] He summarizes his point by saying that "God does not manifest himself in out-of-control behavior."[46] He cites 1 Corinthians 14:29-33 in which Paul describes the discipline and order he expected of a Christian church service:

> Two or three prophets should speak, and the others should weigh carefully what is said. And if a revelation comes to someone who is sitting down, the first speaker should stop. For you can all prophesy in turn so that everyone may be instructed and encouraged. The spirits of prophets are subject to the control of prophets. For God is not a God of disorder but of peace (NIV).

This scripture was intended to regulate *normal* church services, not to apply to the special circumstance of revival. Our problem is that we often use the word *revival* to include normal evangelical activity such as a Billy Graham crusade. Crusades are very good and necessary, but they are planned *evangelism*. By looking at Scripture one can see that a true revival is a sovereign *intrusion* of God's presence and energies into His people, and the results are neither orderly nor controlled by man.

The Old Testament gives a hint of this, but *only* a hint, because the Spirit was fully poured out only after Christ's ascension. The dedication service of Solomon's temple described in 2 Chronicles 5:13-14 contains this interesting passage:

> When they lifted up their voice accompanied by trumpets and cymbals and instruments of music, and when they praised the Lord saying, "He indeed is good for his lovingkindness is everlasting," then the house, the house of the Lord, was filled

> with a cloud, so that the priests could not stand to minister because of the cloud, for the glory of the Lord filled the house of God (NAS).

Note that the normal order of worship was disrupted by the power of God. The result was neither planned nor orderly.

The New Testament description of the original Pentecost (Acts 2) shows a similar though much more powerful "God intrusion" into a prayer gathering:

> When the day of Pentecost came, they were all together in one place. Suddenly a sound like the blowing of a violent wind came from heaven and filled the whole house where they were sitting. They saw what seemed to be tongues of fire that separated and came to rest on each of them. All of them were filled with the Holy Spirit and began to speak in other tongues as the Spirit enabled them (vv. 1-4, NIV).
>
> Amazed and perplexed, they [the gathered crowd] asked one another, "What does this mean?"
>
> Some, however, made fun of them and said, "They have had too much wine."
>
> Then Peter stood up with the Eleven, raised his voice and addressed the crowd: "Fellow Jews and all of you who live in Jerusalem, let me explain this to you; listen carefully to what I say. These men are not drunk, as you suppose. It's only nine in the morning!" (vv. 12-15, NIV).

Note again the pattern: It began as a normal prayer meeting, which was interrupted by a godly intrusion, which resulted in unusual manifestations and led to activity not related to traditional order.

Supporters of the Laughing Revival believe verse 15 indicates that one manifestation of the original Pentecost was a drunklike demeanor among some of the disciples. They cite their own experience with drunklike states after receiving ministry as analogous evidence for this.[47] Hanegraaff derides this interpretation, saying that Peter was attempting to defend speaking in tongues as the phenomenon in question, not the drunklike demeanor, and that Peter, for one, showed no signs of inebriation.[48]

In the post-Apostolic age revivals have had varied intrusive and "disorderly" manifestations: fallings, jerks, groaning and laughter. This happened during Edwards's, Whitefield's and Wesley's revivals, as well as during many other revivals and renewals throughout the ages.[49] Hanegraaff has felt scandalized by Arnott's claim that the type of meeting common at the Toronto church will become normative. On his *Bible Answer Man* program he often plays a sound bite which was taped at the Toronto Airport Christian Fellowship on which one can hear the background noise of people laughing while John Arnott is saying, "We can never go back to church the way it used to be."[50]

Perhaps they are both wrong. As much as some modern revivalists would like to institutionalize the excitement of the present "exercises," the historic pattern for revival shows that after a time God's special presence and grace lifts. The congregation then falls into a more normal pattern of worship, but one that is livelier than what was normal before the revival.

Hanegraaff's and other anticult ministries' critiques of the Laughing Revival are hampered by the fact that much of their foundational theology contains imbedded cessationism. For example, Hanegraaff strongly criticizes current revivalists for holding "cultic" and mistaken views of the Holy Spirit as an energy field. Hanegraaff cites as evidence Arnott's observation that God's power can jump from one person to another, as in a healing line when the power of God may jump past a supplicant to the "catcher" behind the supplicant. Also, Hanegraaff finds highly objectionable Howard-Browne's anointing lines, where the evangelist moves quickly to touch hundreds while saying, "Fill, fill!" as they fall. Hanegraaff sees this as blasphemy; to him it is saying that the Holy Spirit is a "force," and even a "misguided missile."[51] The fault is not in Arnott's thinking or Howard-Browne's practice but in Western theology as a whole which says little about the *energies* of God — the real point at issue (see chapter 5).[52]

There are several passages in Scripture which show that God's *energies* (not His *person*) do in fact act in mechanical and not wholly controlled ways. The prophet Ezekiel wrote about the priests in the future restored temple:

> And it shall be that when they enter at the gates of the inner court, they shall be clothed with linen garments; and wool shall not be on them while they are ministering in the gates of the inner court and in the house. Linen turbans shall be on their heads, and linen undergarments shall be on their loins; they shall not gird themselves with anything which makes

them sweat. And when they go out into the outer court, into the outer court to the people, they shall put off their garments in which they have been ministering and lay them in the holy chambers; then they shall put on other garments that they may not transmit holiness to the people with their garments (Ezek. 44:17-19).

And a woman who had a hemorrhage for twelve years, and could not be healed by anyone, came up behind Him, and touched the fringe of His cloak; and immediately her hemorrhage stopped...Jesus said, "Someone did touch Me, for I was aware that power had gone out of Me" (Luke 8:43-44,46).

And God was performing extraordinary miracles by the hands of Paul, so that handkerchiefs or aprons were even carried from his body to the sick, and the diseases left them and the evil spirits went out (Acts 19:11-12).

Hanegraaff and others at CRI have misunderstood the claims of the revivalists. They believe that Arnott and others consider laughing as the "fruit" of this revival,[53] arguing that it is easy to prove that laughing itself is not a fruit of the Spirit. Hanegraaff has pointed out that Eastern Yogis can impart laughter on their disciples much like Howard-Browne does in his anointing lines. In fact Arnott and others in the revival have consistently understood that laughter, fallings, drunken demeanor and the occasional roaring are responses of the human body to interaction with God's Spirit — manifestations, not fruit. Jonathan Edwards called these "exercises." The fruit — changes that occur within the person — comes *after* the manifestations. Fruit that has been a result of this revival includes physical and emotional healings, renewed spiritual fervor, closeness to God and new awareness of His love.[54]

This confusion was demonstrated recently when a young woman called the *Bible Answer Man* radio program and spoke to Elliot Miller (editor of the *Christian Research Journal* and host that day). She first thanked Miller for the help the program had given her with her Christian walk. Then she related an incident that happened a few days earlier. She had attended a local Vineyard church where she was slain in the Spirit and began to laugh uncontrollably. The following day she discovered that she was completely healed of long-standing depression.

Miller advised her that manifestations can be suggestive or demonic and Christians must be careful of them. He avoided dealing with the *fruit* — her healing of depression — and lectured her on the dangers of spiritual experiences. The young woman, who obviously respected her host, asked Miller earnestly about her healing, saying, "But, this was not cool?"

Miller did not answer her question.[55]

Two Views of the Laughing Revival:
CRI and *Christianity Today*:

Hanegraaff and his staff at the CRI have attacked the Laughing Revival unceasingly at every possible point and for every possible reason. Some of the issues they have raised are serious and needed to be addressed, such as the problem of prophetic excess; but others are trivial On one program Hanegraaff criticized Arnott for manipulating his audience by using background music during an altar call (ironically, a standard evangelical technique since the turn of the century). On another occasion, a sound bite of Arnott speaking in tongues from the pulpit was broadcast on the *Bible Answer Man*. Arnott was ridiculed as irrational (*anyone* speaking in tongues sounds irrational).[56] Thus the CRI's methodology has become, like Dave Hunt's, that of a prosecuting attorney: throw every possible argument; find every fault; claim that nothing is *good* about the revival and its leadership has never done anything well. This is courtroom methodology, not true Christian apologetics.

This unremitting assault on the Laughing Revival is in sharp contrast to the view of another great evangelical publication, *Christianity Today* (which includes several sister magazines, including *Christian History*).[57] The staff and editors of *Christianity Today* cover current events of the Christian world from an evangelical viewpoint. They blend both reproof and affirmation in their publication, more often praising a ministry than criticizing it. Although their focus is on the present, current events and issues are discussed within the context of Christian history.

As the Laughing Revival spread, the editors of *Christian History* produced a splendid issue, "Camp Meetings and Circuit Riders," which highlighted Cane Ridge and the Second Great Awakening.[58] The articles showed the positive effect of the Second Great Awakening as well as the extremist dangers of that revival, including the drift toward Shakerism. It was a balanced approach that affirmed both the presence of God in the Second Great Awakening and its wonderful fruit in American Christianity but did not slight the troublesome issues. The issue quickly sold out at the newstands which carried it. One caller to the *Bible Answer Man*, again obviously a supporter of the CRI, questioned Hanegraaff about the *Christian History* issue, asking if the Toronto manifestations might be of the same kind. Hanegraaff did not answer the question but immediately denounced the dangers of manifestations and experiences.[59]

Thankfully *Christianity Today* recently tackled the Toronto Blessing directly, doing a cover story on it which included two feature articles and two sidebars. As usual they called on the best evangelical scholars for their articles.

The first feature article was by Dr. James Beverley, an evangelical scholar from the Reformed tradition and a longtime student of the Vineyard churches. He had just completed a book-length analysis of the Laughing Revival titled *Holy Laughter and the Toronto Blessing*.[60] Beverley's article summarized the findings in his book, and both do justice to the tradition of Jonathan Edwards. Beverley takes to task both the many uncritical apologists of the revival and its harsh critics. Beverley notes, "True discernment demands thoughtful probing of the authentic blessings and the real dangers that accompany any divine work involving human beings."[61]

Beverley finds clear indicators that what is happening at the Toronto Airport Christian Fellowship is from God. These include: a proven record of true spiritual renewal and refreshment for thousands; a social and evangelistic impulse; joyful worship and celebration; and maintenance of orthodox beliefs.[62] He states, "If laughter is the best medicine, there is something disturbing in any rush to prove that holy laughter is simply fraudulent."[63]

On the negative side, Beverley notices that the church leadership is often unresponsive and defensive to criticism, unaccountable for its prophetic utterances and manipulative in the way it gives aggressive warning of God's wrath to its critics. Beverley believes tne Toronto Blessing movement as a whole often manifests weak preaching and an anti-intellectual bias. Last, he indicates that some leaders have slipped into an elitist view, purporting that the Holy Spirit today is moving strongly only in the Toronto Blessing circles.[64]

A second major article, "The Surprising Works of God," was written by Dr. Richard Lovelace, professor of church history at Gordon-Conwell Theological Seminary.[65] (His seminal work on the worldwide nature of revivals was cited in chapter 2.) Lovelace tackles the difficult and interesting question of how Jonathan Edwards would respond to current revival. He believes that Edwards would be little disturbed by the fall-ings or the laughter, both of which occurred in his times. However, since nothing in the recorded history of the Great Awakening parallells the "prophetic roaring" found at Toronto, Lovelace asserts that Edwards may have shown concern about this. Edwards, Lovelace purports, would more probably be concerned by the temptation of spiritual pride and elitism in the leadership of the revival.

In spite of these reproofs, neither Beverley nor Lovelace suggest that the Toronto Blessing is counterfeit. Both affirm its authenticity as a genuine move of God (due to its manifest fruit). Lovelace ends his arti-cle with a wise observation:

> In any case, Edwards would find many parts of modern evan-gelicalism much stranger than the Vineyard, full of theologi-cal weakness, cultural conformity and the disfiguring effects of spiritual pride...His own final approach to the Great Awak-ening was to subject it to the most rigorous critique, on the one hand, and to solicit extraordinary prayer for its advance-ment, on the other. These are strategies we need to follow today.[66]

TWENTY-THREE

The Renewals of the Spirit as "Messy" Revivals

Jonathan Edwards and the Charismatic Renewal

T HE EXPOSÉ OF CHARISMATIC TELEVISION evangelists, aired on *Prime Time Live* (21 November 1991) dealt yet another blow to the confidence of the charismatic community.[1] Coming three years after the major television scandals of the Bakkers and Jimmy Swaggart, it demonstrated to the church community that more accountability needs to be developed among charismatic ministries. Many Spirit-filled Christians felt they had reached new depths of humiliation and confusion. Most recently, there has been much publicity in both the secular and religious media on the strange phenomena of the Toronto Blessing and the Vineyard revivals.

The present situation resembles the confusion of 1741 when the Great Awakening experienced a crisis of confidence brought about by a few irresponsible and deluded itinerants. Jonathan Edwards's analysis of the Awakening had led him to divide the multifaceted phenomena of revival into two categories. He considered some elements to be ambiguous and unreliable signs of whether a revival was from God or not, but other signs were sure indicators of God's presence. Under the heading of ambiguous signs he grouped most of the exterior and attention-attracting phenomena: the emotionalism of the crowds, and the physical faintings and visions. Certainly God had the sovereign right to use these new means to revive His church since none of these was forbidden in Scripture. Yet Satan or the people themselves could counterfeit these manifestations.

Further, Edwards admitted that some of the leaders within the Awakening were "guilty of great imprudences and irregularities in their conduct," and others "fall away into gross errors or scandalous practices."[2] These too were ambiguous indicators. They did not verify, as the Awakening critics claimed, that the revival was *not* of God. Edwards pointed out that failed leadership was true not only of Paul's rowdy Corinthian congregation, but also of Peter, the pillar of the Jerusalem Christian community. This apostle attempted to please the Jewish Christians of Jerusalem by refusing table fellowship with the Gentile brethren at Antioch, and he had to be reproved by Paul (Gal. 2:11-13). The task of the Holy Spirit is to make men Christlike, but that is a process, not an instant achievement. Thus any renewal movement, like the early church itself, will have an imperfect leadership capable of sinning.

Rather, Edwards stressed that the manifestations of certain "sure, distinguishing, scripture evidences" marked a renewal as being truly from God.[3] Satan does not, and cannot, counterfeit these indicators. Their presence in the Awakening marked that revival as truly Spirit-inspired. The following review of the charismatic renewal from Edwards's "evidences" will show clearly that the present renewal, though flawed, is indeed from the Holy Spirit.

1. A true revival raises the esteem of Jesus in the community, proclaiming Him as Scripture depicts Him, Son of God and Savior.[4]

In the Great Awakening this meant that the revived communities rejected deism and its tendencies to view Jesus as merely an inspired teacher. In our own age the equivalent is the error of demythologizing, denying that the miracles in the Bible actually occurred. In this respect, there is a particularly great contrast between the charismatics' Jesus-proclaiming spirituality and the theological fence-riding of the liberal mainline denominations. Edwards would rejoice in the way Jesus is unabashedly praised and worshipped within the charismatic community.*

2. A true revival works against the kingdom of Satan, which encourages sin and worldly lusts.[6]

Here the record of the current renewals is dramatically positive in

---

* Significantly, none of the critics of either the charismatic renewal (or its Faith movement component) has seriously objected to the present Christology of the renewal.[5]

several regards but ambiguous in another. On the positive side, it was first through the Pentecostal revival, and especially the charismatic renewal, that the church as a whole has recovered its ministry of exorcism and deliverance. This has certainly dealt a major blow to the kingdom of Satan. On this issue a comparison with either the liberal or evangelical wing of Christendom is especially telling. The mainline liberals continue to resist the deliverance ministry and misinterpret demonic manifestations to be simply manifestations of abnormal psychology.[7] Many evangelicals, though now generally open to the need for some exorcism, originally resisted that ministry as stubbornly as they resisted healing.[8]

Certainly the charismatics' deliverance ministry had a period of immaturity and exaggeration in the 1960s and early 1970s when many spiritual problems were attributed to demons. Thankfully this subsided, and now the charismatic community has a well-balanced and sophisticated body of literature about exorcism as well as many experienced ministers of exorcism and deliverance.[9]

In regard to the other facet of Edwards's criterion, the issue of worldly lusts, the charismatic renewal has a less positive record. The temptations of an unbalanced prosperity doctrine have, in fact, been the Achilles' heel of the charismatic renewal. Only in the last few years have major charismatic authors addressed this failure forcefully.[10] Richard Foster, who was deeply influenced by Agnes Sanford, has attempted to find a balanced solution in his celebrated book *Money, Sex and Power*, which guides the Christian in the biblical approach to these "this-worldly" concerns.[11] The other approach from a distinctly faith corner is to affirm the prosperity doctrine but to stress the *purpose* of prosperity. Here Kenneth Copeland, who is often criticized as an extremist of the Faith movement, has focused again on the biblical evidence. By pointing to Deuteronomy 8:18 and Ephesians 4:28 Copeland has shown that the biblical intention of prosperity has a communal goal, although it may be extended to the individual too. Prosperity's purpose is to enable the establishment of God's covenant on earth and to supply provisions for the needy.[12]

3. A true revival will stimulate "a greater regard to the Holy Scriptures, and establishes them more in their truth and divinity...."[13]

This one of the "sure, distinguishing, scripture evidences" is especially clear in the present renewal. Again, in comparison with mainline denominations which have been weakened in their belief of Scripture by demythologizing, the charismatic record is especially good. Try telling a charismatic that miracles are impossible and that the stories of

Jesus were exaggerated tales. He will most likely respond with a personal story of miraculous healing. While the mainline churches and theologians have scrapped the biblical standard in sexual morality, the charismatics and evangelicals have held to the scriptural standards.

Less obvious, the charismatic renewal (by way of its New Thought influences) has given the Christian community a renewed Hebraic perspective with which to view Scripture. This view is that God gave mankind the earth and all that is in it as a good gift to be enjoyed. For Israel, Yahweh was the God of the here and now, as well as hereafter. Prayer concerned itself (as evidenced in the Psalms) mostly with "this-worldly" problems, desires and needs. This was obscured in the church by theological traditions which stressed the "other-worldly" goals of the Christian life. For instance, the Catholic fathers strived for perfection in prayer and asceticism, ending in union with God. Evangelical spiritual-ity focused on the salvation of the soul. These goals are "other-worldly," and some are critically important, but they do not reflect the wholeness of life that is characteristic of biblical spirituality.

In recent decades many Christian scholars have come to suspect that the early church too readily surrendered its Jewish roots in exchange for Greek philosophy and Roman culture. They have suggested that there was something intrinsically valuable and spiritual in the original Hebraic view.[14] The issues here are complex. The church has always debated how much of the Old Testament is applicable to the Christian. Certainly Paul stressed the futility of gaining salvation through the Mosaic law and the new freedom from it. Yet Christians have always understood that at least some parts of the Mosaic law pertain to Christians, if only the moral law. On this issue spiritual law is a major theological discovery because it revives the Jewish understanding of moral law. One can now understand the joy of the author of Psalm 119 as he praises the Law. His enthusiasm was not necessarily over the prohibition against pork or camel meat. Rather he celebrated what a joy life can be when one can navigate its shoals with an understanding of God's moral law and its covenant promises.

At the same time many congregations are discovering the blessings of the Old Testament rites and sacraments, such as having a Jewish Seder meal on Good Friday. These do not bring salvation, but they give a noticeable blessing.[15] All of this indicates that the Holy Spirit is encouraging the church as a whole to return to its Hebraic roots. From this perspective, the "this-worldly" view of Bible-affirming New Thought and the charismatic renewal is truly prophetic.

4. A true revival is marked by a spirit of truth.[16]

Edwards felt that under the impact of true revival the Christian community turned away from heretical or erroneous views and returned to biblical truths (this point is similar to the previous evidence). Here the charismatic record is both positive and consistent, especially compared with the unrenewed mainline churches. The Pentecostals always resisted liberal theologies. In current decades the Pentecostal and charismatic churches have resisted liberation theology, an attempt to integrate Marxism and Christianity. With the fall of communism the absurdity of Liberation Theology is becoming increasingly clear, even to its supporters. Had the Marxist guerrillas and their Christian collaborators won in El Salvador and the rest of Latin America, the peoples there would have been doomed to the impoverishment of a command economy and the terror of one-party states for decades to come.

5. An authentic revival will manifest a renewed love of God and of man.[17]

If love of God is measured by public worship, then certainly the charismatic renewal has an unrivaled record. If love of man is defined as social action, the record is much less clear. Mainline denominations initially criticized the charismatics as being so obsessed with worship that little time was left for social concerns. Certainly both the Pentecostal and charismatic renewals began as outbursts of worship. Although both movements had a component of social action and concern, the social element did not become central in either movement.

In the view of the noted evangelical scholar Richard Lovelace, a revival *begins* as a sovereign move of God but *continues* only if its initial piety and worship components are supplemented by specific social actions.[18] Some may claim the charismatic renewal stopped its dramatic rate of growth in the United States after 1980 because of a lack of social action. However, this issue is extremely difficult to judge. Often the critics who have faulted the charismatic renewal on its social commitment have had a specific left-wing agenda in mind, as in supporting Liberation Theology.

Similarly, when charismatic churches do perform social actions they are often ignored by the media because many of these churches do not follow the liberal agenda. For example, the secular media give little recognition to the major efforts of Pat Robertson's ongoing Operation Blessing, which responds with food and other supplies to local disasters and emergency situations. In fact many charismatic congregations are making major contributions to the social and spiritual transformation of their communities.[19] Within the charismatic renewal, the kingdom-now theology, articulated by Earl Paulk's church in Atlanta, Georgia, lays special emphasis on Christian social action that is Spirit-inspired.[20]

The Charismatic Renewal as a Biblical Middle Way

Thus, except for a few areas of weakness, the charismatic renewal generously matches the sure evidences of revival articulated by Edwards. Beyond these evidences, Spirit-filled Christians need to be affirmed that their basic theological position is within the biblical center and is not an extremism. In contrast, the theologies which claim that the gifts of the Spirit are inoperative, or that God rarely, if ever, acts miraculously in the present age, are biblically extreme and unbalanced.

In addition, the Pentecostal/charismatic tradition occupies the biblical middle ground between Pharisaism and Gnosticism. Pharisees recognize the role of doctrine and tradition in religion but disdain spiritual experiences and power as dangerous to "sound doctrine." Gnostics revel in experiences but disdain traditions and believe that current experiences or revelations can override Scripture. Spirit-filled Christians accept spiritual experiences bounded by discernment and Scripture yet also revere the theological heritage of the church. This charismatic middle ground has been little recognized because consensus orthodoxy has long leaned toward Pharisaism. Like Charles Chauncy of Boston, many mainline ministers have had a long memory for spiritual abuses and little interest in chancing the spiritual gifts.

Spirit-filled Christians should also understand that the faith-idealism inherent in their hermeneutics, theology and practice is not an extremism, but biblically normative. The extremism is the mix of radical realism and Christian theology.

The Merging of Power and Holiness

In spite of the achievements of the Pentecostal and charismatic theologians in creating a new theology that counters cessationism and reflects the Hebraic perspective, the system is by no means perfect. As strange as it may seem to say, Dave Hunt's original attempt to create a middle way between charismatic and evangelical has much to commend it. If the failure of traditional Catholic and Protestant (including evangelical) theologies was that they emphasized piety without sustaining spiritual power, then the problem of much charismatic theology is that it rediscovered spiritual power but minimized piety. Biblical Christianity subordinates neither one. Holiness, which is the fruit of the Spirit, and spiritual power, which is the gift of the Spirit, are complementarities. Just as light can manifest as a wave or particle, so the Christian should be both holy and spiritually empowered.

The last few years have not only brought a maturation of the prosperity and healing doctrines but also a renewed appreciation of holiness.[21] With attentiveness to holiness, imbalance in any aspect of life is easily reproved. The renewed appreciation of holiness should end the current dispute between evangelicals and charismatics.

When Christians agree that the goal of life is Christlike holiness, then other things fall into proper perspective. This proper perspective is developed as a spirit of appreciation comes to the fore. Specifically charismatics and Pentecostals will appreciate the evangelicals' traditional concern for holiness and appropriate their rich devotional literature. The great heroes of evangelical missionary efforts, such as Hudson Taylor of the China Inland Mission, become celebrated models of holiness. (One almost wishes the Protestants had a rite of canonization, like the Catholics, to recognize outstanding holiness.) Conversely, if the evangelicals also focused on Christlike holiness, they would appreciate the recovery of the gifts of the Spirit because gifts that are used properly empower holiness and facilitate missionary work and evangelization.

The fact that the charismatic renewal came to the mainline churches has been a blessing to the whole of Christendom. But it had a negative element: The new charismatics had no historical memory or appreciation of the Holiness and Higher Life literature and personalities who molded the older Pentecostalism. In doing the revision for this book I was brought to study the writings of Phoebe Palmer and leaf through years of Carrie Judd Montgomery's magazine, *Triumphs of Faith*. It was both a shock and inspiration to see how passionately that generation sought after holiness and Christlike character. Contemporary Christians pale in comparison. Recovery and recirculation of their writings should be a priority of the current charismatic leadership.

Spiritual Warfare Brings Maturity

In a sense, evangelicals and Pentecostals/charismatics are beginning to merge their strengths under the umbrella of spiritual warfare. An example is their unprecedented union in citywide prayer crusades. The Pentecostals/charismatics mature as they focus on a form of prayer that has no direct material benefit for the prayer warrior but is an act of kingdom power and love. The evangelicals also experience a gentle, nonobtrusive use of the gifts of the Spirit that does not offend even the most traditional among them. Books such as John Dawson's *Taking Our Cities for God* and George Otis's *The Last of the Giants* have been written by charismatic leaders but have been read and taken as prayer models by evangelical and Pentecostal/charismatic believers.[22]

The alliance that evangelicals and Pentecostals/charismatics have forged to pray for our nation and revival points to an end to the friction between evangelicals and charismatics. One example is the 1992 crusade by Billy Graham in New York City. The crusade was supported by a wide spectrum of pastors and churches from mainstream evangelical and Pentecostal/charismatic backgrounds. In a place as spiritually desperate as New York there was no time for theological debating. There was only time for earnest prayer — in dramatic terms that described the need of the church throughout America today.

TWENTY-FOUR

An Evaluation of
Modern Pharisaism

The Perennial Nature of Pharisaism

IN THIS BOOK WE HAVE examined carefully just a few pharisaical episodes of the American church. In these cases we have focused on leading Pharisees of each age. This does not imply that the heresy of Pharisaism occurs only in rare moments and in a few individuals. Rather our technique has been one of identifying what sociologists refer to as ideal types. This simplifies the characteristics of any given movement. For example, scores of lesser clerics condemned the Great Awakening as "of the devil." Yet they were not as public or as influential as Charles Chauncy. Hundreds of ministers and laymen of the Victorian era denounced the Faith-Cure movement as a cult, calling it demonic or simply delusional. Again, Buckley was the most public and influential of the group. Similarly, we do not see Dave Hunt as either the most extreme or only Pharisee of the last decade. He was, however, one of the most influential.

Witch Hunt, by Bob and Gretchen Passantino, has examined the problem of the Christian cult-watchers' attacks and slander against other Christians.[1] I cannot express my appreciation for this book in adequate terms. I recommend it to every Christian leader as an indispensable aid to the discernment issues of today.

Like James Spencer (chapter 22), the Passantinos themselves are evangelical cult-watchers. They studied under the hand of Walter Martin, and Martin's foreword to *Witch Hunt* was one of the last things he wrote before he died. The Passantinos were grieved at how Dave Hunt and others were indiscriminately attacking other Christians for failing to observe "sound doctrine" (consensus orthodoxy). Although Hunt was cited as a clear example of a witch-hunter, he was by no means the only one or the most extreme of the group. For instance, the anticult writer Constance Cumbey is far more intemperate and paranoid in her writings than Hunt. She once accused Pat Robertson (of *The 700 Club*) of being in league with the New Age and even claimed (irony of ironies) that Dave Hunt had a spirit guide and was a "stooge of the New Age."[2]

The Passantinos did not use the words *Pharisee* or *Pharisaism*, but their description of witch-hunting makes it clear they were dealing with a specialized aspect of Pharisaism. Interestingly, in our study we found that both Buckley and Hunt were specialists in the cults. Although the same cannot precisely be said of Charles Chauncy, he was exceptionally well-informed on the history of Christian enthusiasts. Though cult-watching is a necessary function within the body of Christ, but it calls for a grace of discernment and mercy and not just evangelical zeal.[3]

John MacArthur Jr. and the New Hyper-Cessationism

Just as *Quenching the Spirit* was in the final stages of editing, a new attack on the charismatic renewal appeared in bookstores — *Charismatic Chaos*. The book was authored by John F. MacArthur Jr., a long-time critic of the renewal.[4] *Charismatic Chaos* is an expanded and updated version of his earlier book, *The Charismatics: A Doctrinal Perspective* (1978).[5] In both books MacArthur asserts that the Pentecostal/charismatic movement has done little but create chaos and confusion among the Christian churches and that it is based on delusions and wrong theology.

MacArthur is pastor and Bible teacher at Grace Community Church in Sun Valley, California, where his fundamentalist preaching attracts more than ten thousand people for Sunday services. His many books include several which have great insight. However, MacArthur is known among evangelicals not only for his challenges against charismatic theology but also for his intemperate attacks against fellow evangelicals. He was at the forefront of a theological dispute with fellow dispensationalists on the relationship between salvation and discipleship.

MacArthur believes that a *valid* salvation experience must lead to a process of discipleship. He opposes those who hold the more traditional view that the salvation experience is sufficient to guarantee eternal life. Impartial evangelical scholars have lamented how the dispute, which should be a rational exchange of views (James 3:17), has become a verbal donnybrook (free-for-all), each side accusing the other of "heresy." Others have commented that MacArthur usually misrepresents or exaggerates his opponent's position before attacking it.[6]

One evangelical critic, Millard Erickson, former dean of Bethel Theological Seminary (St. Paul, Minnesota), has faulted MacArthur's theology for not understanding what it means for the Christian to be "in Christ."[7] This is especially pertinent to MacArthur's critique of Pentecostal/charismatic theology since it is precisely Paul's doctrine of being "in Christ" that defines the Spirit-filled life and confidence in use of the gifts of the Spirit.[*]

Hyper-Cessationism: The Theology of *Charismatic Chaos*

As for most fundamentalists, the assumptions of Scottish realism underlie (and undermine) MacArthur's spiritual understanding. This can be seen in his definition of mysticism which carries for him only negative connotations and which he equates with charismatic belief:

> Mysticism is a system of belief that attempts to perceive spiritual reality apart from objective, verifiable facts. It seeks truth through feelings, intuition, and other internal senses. Objective data is usually discounted, so mysticism derives its authority from within.[8]

In contrast to mysticism, MacArthur allows the Christian to have "authentic spiritual experiences." These specific experiences include the emotions of the salvation process, as in repentance, anxiety, joy and such pious emotions as compassion for the lost.[9] All else, according to MacArthur, is mystic-charismatic and equivalent to pagan mysticism.[10]

As to be expected, MacArthur believes the basis of objective truth to be the Bible *and* Reformed theology: "Objective historic theology is Reformation theology. It is historical evangelicalism. It is historical orthodoxy."[11] MacArthur's logic is simple: Pentecostal/charismatic theology does not fully comply with Reformed theology, thus it is in error.

---

[*]   See our discussion of E. W. Kenyon's seminal theology in chapter 18.

MacArthur's assault on the charismatic renewal begins with the cessationist understanding of the gifts of the Spirit. He cites as his main authority B. B. Warfield (discussed in chapter 10).[12] But he goes beyond Warfield or James Buckley (also in chapter 10) to an extreme form of cessationism seldom seen since seventeenth-century Calvinism. According to MacArthur, biblical history only had three periods when miracles or the gifts of the Spirit were operating: the time of the Exodus, the period of Elijah-Elisha, and the years of Jesus' ministry and the New Testament church.[13]

At the other times of biblical history no miracles took place, though God did (and does now) act sovereignly to answer prayers. The distinction is that there is no present-day *ministry* of healing or exorcism or of the gifts of the Spirit, though with fervent prayer some people may be healed. Thus, saying the words of deliverance, as in the command, "Be gone in the name of Jesus!" is, in MacArthur's view, a vain exercise.

As "proof" for this theory MacArthur writes that he investigated the healing claims of several major evangelists and found no evidence for true, nonpsychosomatic healings.[14] The outlandish assertion that no real healing happens in the church today reveals the shallow nature of his investigations. A century earlier James Buckley, who wanted to come to the same conclusion about the Faith-Cure movement and studied that healing revival with considerable care, was forced to admit that true healing for real disease was an actual, if rare, occurrence.[15] Buckley admitted the facts but refused to modify his theology.

The problem lies not in the lack of evidence of healing miracles but in having a *will to disbelieve*. Medical verification of miraculous healing is found throughout the literature of Christian healing, but no evidence will satisfy a person determined to negate it. An early example of the meticulous documentation of miraculous healing is Dorothy Kern's 1914 classic, *The Living Touch*.[16] A recent book which carefully documents the healings of a Wimber conference in England is David Lewis's *Healing: Fiction, Fantasy or Fact?* (1989).[17] The Christian Broadcasting Network, also keeps extensive documentation of the healings it dramatizes on its shows (such as *The 700 Club*).

Arguing as Buckley did against the Faith-Cure movement, MacArthur attempts to prove that the modern healing ministry is harmful by pointing to its extremes. Buckley had cited and ridiculed the extremist theology of John Alexander Dowie as representative of Christian healing. Similarly, MacArthur cites the healing cult of Hobert Freeman, who urged a radical antimedication position, as an example of charismatic healing.[18] Other gifts of the Spirit, such as prophecy and tongues, are likewise judged as having no authentic manifestation in the present day.

Like Dave Hunt, MacArthur justifies the theology of cessationism and spiritual powerlessness by implying that Paul preached the Word but disdained the miraculous and the "mystical." As proof MacArthur cites how little the miraculous is mentioned in Paul's letters.[19] He concludes that not even Paul was a "charismatic." It seems to me if Paul's epistles do not show him performing miracles, it is because they are his theology, not his biography. In the book of Acts we see Paul's ministry of the Word often authenticated by miraculous works such as healings, resuscitation and so on. Even within the epistles Paul reminds the readers that his gospel was not mere empty words, as the false teachers, but verified with works of power (1 Thess. 1:5). Paul also informs the reader: "I thank God, I speak in tongues more than you all" (1 Cor. 14:18).

Attack on John Wimber

Also like Hunt, MacArthur spent considerable effort in critiquing the ministry of John Wimber. Wimber's ministry attracted thousands of evangelicals to the charismatic viewpoint even before it experienced the new wave of revival in the 1990s. Furthermore, Jack Deere, one of MacArthur's longtime friends and a noted cessationist scholar from Dallas Theological Seminary, defected to the charismatic viewpoint and joined the Wimber staff.[20] MacArthur's description of Wimber's church services are reminiscent of Charles Chauncy's disdainful and distorted descriptions of the Great Awakening:

> Some men from our church staff recently visited Wimber's Vineyard in Anaheim. The evening they were there, they witnessed virtual pandemonium. Wimber tried to get everyone speaking in tongues at once. Women were convulsing on the floor; one man lay on his back in a catatonic state; and all around, hundreds of people were dancing, running, shouting, and standing on chairs.[21]

Not surprisingly, Charles Chauncy did not recognize the phenomenon of "resting in the Spirit" because the Protestant theology of 250 years ago had no notion of it. It is difficult to understand how MacArthur could be so unaware of the phenomenon as to use such derogatory psychological jargon.

Just as MacArthur presents somewhat unbalanced summaries of the ideas of fellow evangelicals, he sets up a straw-man caricature of Wimber's theology. MacArthur says that Wimber disregards the basic gospel of the cross and presents "signs and wonders" for their own sake.[22] In fact Wimber carefully keeps the cross at the center of his ministry to the unsaved, though he teaches other evangelicals (who are already saved) the importance of reinforcing the gospel with manifestations of the Spirit.[23] Wimber stresses that the goal of power evangelism is to have people encounter God's touch, as in healing or prophecy, so that they are encouraged to move on to discipleship. In theory, this should be attractive to MacArthur, who is also concerned with discipleship. Unfortunately his theological blocks do not allow him to acknowledge this positive aspect of power evangelism.

MacArthur's Faculties Psychology

One time MacArthur was confronted by a young seminary student who was suffering from a deep depression. Perhaps this young man needed deliverance prayer. Within the framework of his theology, MacArthur and his church did everything they could to help him recover, providing counseling at the church and with professional psychotherapists. The young man was counseled that his thoughts were sinful and that he should stop thinking them.[24]

Unfortunately MacArthur's approach to the problem was based on the faculties psychology that originated in the Middle Ages and was used by Calvin. By its logic, the will has the highest faculty of the mind, and it has the power to rule over the lesser emotions and thoughts (see chapter 2). Therefore the student simply needed to *will* himself to stop thinking depressing thoughts. The case eventually ended in tragedy. The young man committed suicide after several months, and the church staff was confronted with the nation's first clergy malpractice suit (it was eventually dismissed).[25]

Theology of Arrogance

In reading MacArthur's *Charismatic Chaos* one is struck by how little he refers to the writings of the universal church. It seems that little useful information came from the church fathers or any tradition of Christendom other than classical Reformed theology. The evidence presented by A. J. Gordon, for example, on healing in the early church in

Protestant ministries is ignored (see chapter 9). For MacArthur, nothing except Reformed theology matters. His teachings seem to treat the church as if it disappeared after A.D. 90 and reappeared fifteen hundred years later during the Reformation.

Perhaps the most tragic element in MacArthur's theology is the way he defines and dismisses the problem of opposing the Holy Spirit and the sin against the Spirit. For MacArthur, sinning against the Holy Spirit was rejecting the Spirit's evidence for Jesus' divinity *when He was present on earth*. This sin is, therefore, not possible for Christians today.[26] This surprising theological development is yet another example of the danger of rigorous dispensationalism. It separates the Bible reader from the convicting grace of the Holy Spirit by declaring sins against the Holy Spirit no longer possible. If the "still, small voice" begins to alert a person to an imminent danger of opposing the Holy Spirit's work, the intellect can easily override the voice as being contrary to sound doctrine (consensus orthodoxy).

In this sense MacArthur's theology becomes the perfect Pharisees' theology: *my* denominational theology is perfect, and anything that is unusual or new cannot be of God. If a fellow Christian disagrees with me, he is flirting with heresy. A vision or dream that challenges my theology cannot be from God because God no longer talks to men directly in this dispensation.

Thus a cessationist following the tradition of the Pharisees will not accept theological reproof either from man or God.[27]

Significantly, Dave Hunt holds to a similarly self-deceiving and destructive view with his definition of Pharisaism. Hunt defines Pharisees as those "who use Scripture for their own purposes and disregard the truth." In other words they misinterpret Scripture.[28] This, of course, is marginally true, but it serves to insulate the Christian from considering the core sin of Pharisaism, which is opposing the work of the Spirit.

Pharisaism as a Failure of Discernment

Though Pharisaism has a clear historical pattern, it is difficult to identify it at any given moment. Thankfully, there are several ways to identify Pharisaism and to separate it from the true Christian mandate to reprove error and not to be subject to every new wind of doctrine (Eph. 4:14).

First, persons influenced by a spirit of Pharisaism will center their reproofs on consensus orthodoxy, and they will seldom check the biblical evidence to see whether the issue under discussion reflects a weak point of their own theological tradition.

Another major characteristic of Pharisaism is its reluctance to wrestle with the fruit criterion. None of the persons we have identified as contributing to Pharisaism within Christianity — Chauncy, Buckley, Hanegraaff, MacArthur or Hunt — gave serious attention to the overall spiritual fruit of the movements they attacked. Here Jonathan Edwards was the great clarifier. He saw that a revival would have "mixed fruit" insofar as the edges of the movement would produce extremism and confusion, yet the movement itself must be judged by its overall effect. Rather than discerning good and bad fruit within a movement, the Pharisees we have examined made up their minds about the movements and then sought for evidence from the extremes to prove their points.

The Pharisees' arguments and American legalism share interesting similarities. We American Christians must be especially alert to the fallacy of court procedures and legalism in argumentation. For decades our television heroes have been defense lawyers or prosecuting attorneys. The characteristic method of legal presentation is to accentuate the fault of the opposition and hide one's own weaknesses. Such style may be useful in court, but it is destructive of spiritual truth. It fails to admit that the person or group under discussion may have some element of truth. To attack Christian ministries or individuals by lining up their faults and not recognizing their insights and strong points infects the argument with a spirit of Pharisaism.

We should note the difference between authentic Christian reproof and Pharisaism. The former has a quality of sadness and mercy, while the latter is filled with righteous glee and a spirit of "I told you so!" Farah's classic *From the Pinnacle of the Temple* has those qualities of sadness and moderation which show that the author disliked the task. Additionally, there was no sequel to his book.[29] On the other hand numerous teachers seem to have made professions of criticizing their fellow Christians. The Christian community needs to be especially wary of such persons. Genuine Christian reproof hopes for repentance, correction and restoration. It also gladly recognizes the positive elements of those movements or persons criticized. Pharisees do none of these things, and their only interests are in pointing out the errors and winning the cases.

Pharisaism as a Christian Tragedy

All Pharisaism contains a tragic element of missed opportunities. Chauncy, had he not taken personal offense at Gilbert Tennent's challenge, could have been an effective reprover of the Awakening and not its executioner. Perhaps George Whitefield's tour of 1744 would have resulted in an even greater move of the Spirit.

Had James Buckley incorporated the insights of Jonathan Edwards, which he knew so well, into his analysis of the Faith-Cure movement, perhaps it would have survived the death of its best leaders and led directly into a Pentecostal renewal of the mainline churches.

Hunt's ministry also represents a tremendous tragedy. In both *The Seduction of Christianity* and *Beyond Seduction* he raised important issues that the church needed to address. We can see from his spiritual journey that he wanted to call the body of Christ back to an ideal of holiness and separation from compromises with secular culture, much in the same way that William Law had called English Christendom into account.[30] Significantly, Hunt also cites A. W. Tozer as his model modern theologian. An evangelical pastor, Tozer eventually accepted the Pentecostal position concerning the gifts of the Spirit. Tozer also had reservations about the theological shallowness of the charismatic renewal and attempted to forge a middle ground incorporating his evangelical heritage into the Pentecostal experience.[31]

However, Hunt based his attempt at a middle ground on continued cessationism and the sectarian spirit of Darbyism. In contrast, Law and Tozer had deep respect and love for Christian theological traditions not their own.[32] This ecumenical spirit marks those who have a successful prophetic ministry of reproof because reproof degenerates into sectarian argumentation without it. Hunt's writings seem intolerant of opinions and traditions outside of the Reformed churches. Thus Hunt seems to measure other ministries against Calvinist and Brethren theology rather than Scripture.

The immediate task of the church is to pray that the harm from this latest wave of Pharisaism be dissipated quickly. With God's providential intervention, the confusion, division, fear and paranoia that have been loosed by the current Pharisees and witch-hunters could be turned to good. If the church can collectively learn that Pharisaism is indeed a perennial heresy of the church and recognize it as it manifests, then the current crisis will have served as a painful but necessary landmark along the road to a higher level of discernment and spiritual maturity.

NOTES

*See the bibliography for full publication
information on abbreviated citations.*

Introduction

1. Sharon E. Mumper, "Where in the World Is the Church Growing?" *Christianity Today*, 11 July 1986, 17-21.
2. See D. B. Barrett, "Statistics, Global," in *Dictionary of Pentecostal and Charismatic Movements*, ed. Stanley M. Burgess and Gary B. McGee (Grand Rapids, Mich.: Zondervan, 1988).

Chapter 1
The Longevity of the Pharisees

1. For the best discussion of heresy see Harold O. J. Brown, *Heresies: The Image of Christ in the Mirror of Heresy and Orthodoxy From the Apostles to the Present* (Garden City, N.Y.: Doubleday & Co., 1984).
2. See the seminal scholarship on the presence of Gnosticism in the New Testament churches by Walter Schmithals, *Gnosticism in Corinth: An Investigation of the Letters to the Corinthians*, trans. John E. Steely (Nashville: Abingdon Press, 1971) and his *Paul and the Gnostics*, trans. John E. Steely (Nashville: Abingdon Press, 1972).
3. For a discussion of the literature on Pharisaism, see William L. DeArteaga, "Pharisaism: A Pneumatological Perspective" (paper presented at the Twenty-first Annual Meeting of the Society for Pentecostal Studies, Lakeland, Fla., 1991). It is available from the society by writing to the executive secretary, P.O. Box 2671, Gaithersburg, MD. 20886.
4. William Coleman, *Those Pharisees* (New York: Hawthorn Books, 1977), 66.
5. On this critical issue see John Bowker, *Jesus and the Pharisees* (Cambridge, England: Cambridge University Press, 1973), 43.
6. See also Jude 11.
7. They are described in Eusebius *Ecclesiastical History*, b. 3, chap. 270.

Chapter 2
Stirrings of the Spirit in the Great Awakening

1. Johnson to George Berkeley, 3 October 1741, *The Great Awakening at Yale College*, ed. Stephen Nissenbaum (Belmont, Calif.: Wadsworth Publishing Co., 1972), 57-58.
2. David S. Lovejoy, "The Great Awakening as Subversion and Conspiracy," chap. 10 in *Religious Enthusiasm in the New World: Heresy to Revolution* (Cambridge, Mass.: Harvard University Press, 1985).

3. Richard F. Lovelace, "Jonathan Edwards and the Jesus Movement," chap. 1 in *Dynamics of Spiritual Life: An Evangelical Theology of Renewal* (Downers Grove, Ill.: InterVarsity Press, 1979). See also William Reginald Ward, *The Protestant Evangelical Awakening* (Cambridge, England: Cambridge University Press, 1992).

4. Arnold A. Dallimore, *George Whitefield* (Wheaton, Ill.: Crossway Books, 1990), 99-100.

5. The literature on Jonathan Edwards is vast and growing — thanks mainly to the pioneer work of Perry Miller, which is still sound today. His books, dating from the 1930s, rekindled Edwards's reputation as a profound philosopher and theologian. My analysis of Edwards is based largely on Miller's, but I am also indebted to the fine new biography of Edwards by the evangelical scholar Iain H. Murray, *Jonathan Edwards: A New Biography* (Edinburgh, Scotland: The Banner of Truth Trust, 1987).

6. The following section was clarified by Perry Miller's essay, "The Rhetoric of Sensation," in *Errand into the Wilderness* (New York: Harper & Row, 1964); James Hoopes, "Jonathan Edwards' Religious Psychology," *The Journal of American History* 69 (March 1983): 849-865; and Wayne Proudfoot, "From Theology to a Science of Religions: Jonathan Edwards and William James on Religious Affections," *Harvard Theological Review* 82 (April 1989): 149-168.

7. Samuel Hopkins, *The Life and Character of the Late Reverend Mr. Jonathan Edwards* in *Jonathan Edwards: A Profile*, ed. David Levin (New York: Hill & Wang, 1969), 6.

8. For a survey of this confusing issue see *New Catholic Encyclopedia* (New York: McGraw-Hill, 1967), s.v. "faculties of the soul" by J. Bobik.

9. Jonathan Edwards, "Personal Narrative, I, 13," cited in Murray, *Jonathan Edwards: A New Biography*, 36-37. Used by permission.

10. Jonathan Edwards, "The Terror of the Law," in David S. Lovejoy, *Religious Enthusiasm and the Great Awakening* (Englewood Cliffs, N.J.: Prentice-Hall, 1969), 41. Used by permission.

11. E. Brooks Holifield, *A History of Pastoral Care in America: From Salvation to Self-Realization* (Nashville: Abingdon Press, 1983), chap. 2.

12. Jonathan Edwards, Faithful Narrative, in *The Great Awakening*, ed. C. C. Goen (New Haven, Conn.: Yale University Press, 1972), 194. Used by permission.

13. Francis MacNutt, "Resting in the Spirit," chap. 15 in *The Power to Heal* (Notre Dame, Ind.: Ave Maria Press, 1977). Limp states were commonly described in the literature of Catholic contemplative prayer. Francis MacNutt has also commented on the issue in *Overcome by the Spirit* (Old Tappan, N.J.: Fleming H. Revell, 1990).

14. Edwards, *Faithful Narrative,* 207. Used by permission.

15. Lovejoy, "Benjamin Franklin Describes George Whitefield," in *Religious Enthusiasm*, 35. Used by permission.

16. Edwards to Rev. Thomas Prince of Boston, *The Great Awakening*, ed. Goen, 546. Used by permission.

17. Ibid., 550. Used by permission.

18. George Whitefield, "The Grand Itinerant," in Lovejoy, *Religious Enthusiasm and the Great Awakening*, 26.

19. The best discussion of this is in a taped message given by Howard Ervin, *Lesson on Prayer*. It is tape 5nyc6b, available from the Full Gospel Business Men's Fellowship International in Costa Mesa, California, date unknown. Ervin is a former professor at Oral Roberts University and among the best theologians of the charismatic renewal.

301

20. Jonathan Edwards, *The Distinguishing Marks,* in *The Great Awakening*, ed Goen, 249ff.

21. Ibid., 250.

22. Ibid., 253.

23. Ibid., 254.

24. Ibid., 253.

25. Ibid., 275-276. Used by permission.

Chapter 3
The Great Awakening Quenched

1. A modern biography of Chauncy has been done by Edward M. Griffin, *"Old Brick": Charles Chauncy of Boston, 1705 –1787* (Minneapolis: University of Minnesota Press, 1980). An incisive biographical sketch is given by David Harlan in his *The Clergy and the Great Awakening* (Ann Arbor, Mich.: UMI Research Press, 1980), 53-58.

2. Harlan, *The Clergy and the Great Awakening*, 54.

3. Ibid.

4. Lovejoy, *Religious Enthusiasm in the New World,* 168ff.

5. Lovejoy, *Religious Enthusiasm and the Great Awakening*, 62-63. Used by permission.

6. Ibid., 65. Used by permission.

7. Cited in Griffin, *"Old Brick,"* 68. Used by permission.

8. Charles Chauncy, *The Heat and Fervour of Their Passions,* in Lovejoy, *Religious Enthusiasm and the Great Awakening*, 76. Used by permission.

9. See Murray's comment on *Seasonable Thoughts* in his *Jonathan Edwards: A New Biography*, 207-208.

10. Ibid., 208, n. 1.

11. See, for example, Amy Schrager Lang, "A Flood of Errors: Chauncy and Edwards in the Great Awakening," in *Jonathan Edwards and the American Experience,* ed. Nathan O. Hatch (New York: Oxford University Press, 1988).

12. Jonathan Edwards, "Some Thoughts," in *The Great Awakening*, ed. Goen, 324. Used by permission.

13. Paul Conkin, *Cane Ridge: America's Pentecost* (Madison, Wi.: University of Wisconsin Press, 1990), 20. In this superb book Conkin notes the "eerie resemblance" between the two revivals.

14. The background and history of this revival are examined in Arthur Fawcett's *The Cambuslang Revival: The Scottish Evangelical Revival of the Eighteenth Century* (London: Banner of Truth, 1971).

15. Cited in Dallimore, *George Whitefield*, 116.

16. Fawcett, *The Cambuslang Revival,* chap. 10.

17. Conkin, *Cane Ridge,* 94. See also Catherine C. Cleveland, "Phenomenon of Revival," chap. 4 in *The Great Revival in the West, 1797 – 1805* (Chicago: University of Chicago Press, 1916). The exuberant "exercises" at Cane Ridge have particular relevance to those who are following the current Laughing Revival.

18. A wonderful and balanced account of Cane Ridge and its influence on American Christian can be found in *Christian History* 45, no. 1 (1995). Reprints are readily available.

19. Jonathan Edwards, *Religious Affections*, ed. John E. Smith (New Haven, Conn.: Yale University Press, 1959), editor's introduction and section 4, "Learned Background: Edwards' Readings."

20. See Lovelace, *Dynamics of Spiritual Life.*

Chapter 4
Spiritual Gifts in the Early Church

1. Documentary data for the continuity of the healing ministry is provided in several of the classics of the literature of Christian healing: A. J. Gordon, *The Ministry of Healing: Miracles of Cure in All Ages* (Boston: H. Gannett, 1882; reprint, Harrisburg, Pa.: Christian Publications, 1961); Frederick William Puller, *The Anointing of the Sick: Scripture and Tradition* (London: Society for Promoting Christian Knowledge, 1904); Percy Dearmer, *Body and Soul* (New York: E.P. Dutton, 1908); and Evelyn Frost, *Christian Healing* (London: Bradford & Dickens, 1940).

2. Irenaeus, *Against Heresies*, in Frost, *Christian Healing*, 104.

3. John Wimber and Kevin N. Springer, *Power Evangelism* (San Francisco: Harper & Row, 1986) and the earlier work by Edwin B. Stube, *According to the Pattern...* (Baltimore: The Holy Way, 1982).

4. Justin Martyr, "Dialogue With Trypho," sect. 39 in Ronald Kydd, *Charismatic Gifts in the Early Church* (Peabody, Mass.: Hendrickson, 1984), 26.

5. James L. Ash Jr., "The Decline of Ecstatic Prophecy in the Early Church," *Theological Studies* 37 (June 1976): 227-252.

6. Puller, *The Anointing of the Sick.* These findings verify the insights of the great Catholic lay theologian Friedrich von Hugel. Von Hugel showed that every period of church history has tensions between three distinct elements within the church: the mystic (or in today's terms, charismatic), the ecclesiastical and the intellectual. When any of these elements predominated to the point of suppressing the others, difficulties resulted. A church without the charismatic becomes legalistic; without the intellectual, irrelevant to the world; without the ecclesiastical, disordered and heretical. Rapid expansion in the early church made the ecclesiastical element predominant. See Friedrich von Hugel, "The Three Elements of Religion," chap. 3 in *The Mystical Element of Religion: As Studied in Saint Catherine of Genoa and Her Friends* (London: J. M. Kent, 1908).

7. For a balanced view of the Montanists see R. A. Knox, *Enthusiasm: A Chapter in the History of Religion* (New York: Oxford University Press, 1950), chap. 3.

8. Alasdair I. C. Heron, *The Holy Spirit* (Philadelphia: Westminster Press, 1983). An exception may be found in the theology of Gregory of Nyssa (335 – 395), who was more influential in the East than in the West. See his "On the Christian Mode of Life" in *Ascetical Works*, trans. Virginia Woods Callahan (Washington, D.C.: Catholic University of America Press, 1967).

9. For a scholarly history of Desert Christianity see Derwas J. Chitty, *The Desert a City* (Crestwood, N.Y.: St. Vladimer's Seminary Press, 1977), and for a sample of Desert Christianity theology and life see Thomas Merton, *The Wisdom of the Desert* (New York: New Directions, 1970). On the negative effects that this tradition had on the Christian ministry of healing see Morton T. Kelsey, *Healing and Christianity* (New York: Harper & Row, 1976), pp. 159ff.

10. Palladius, *Lausiac History*, trans. Robert T. Meyer (Westminister, Md.: The Newman Press, 1965), sect. 12.

11. Frost, *Christian Healing*, 189.

12. Athanasius, *Life of St. Anthony the Great* (n.d.; reprint, Willits, Calif.: Eastern Orthodox Press, n.d.), chap. 47. There is a paperback edition currently in print.

13. Ibid., sect. 71. Compare St. Anthony's ministry with Matt. 15:21-28.

14. Ibid., sect. 38.

15. Cited in Kelsey, *Healing*, 195.

16. See especially *Ascent of Mount Carmel* written by St. John of the Cross.

17. See Kelsey's discussion of the relationship between the exaltation of humility and the decline of healing in medieval spirituality in his *Healing*, 195ff. Frost was the first modern scholar to document the harm their extreme asceticism did to the ministry of healing. See her *Christian Healing*, 188ff.

18. A balanced critique of the extremes of Catholic ascetical spirituality is found in the classic work of William James, *The Varieties of Religious Experience* (London: Longmans, Green, 1903). James called the extreme Catholic ascetics "theopaths," a brilliant coinage of language. He also recognized that in each of the ascetic disciplines — celibacy, poverty and the like — there was, in its moderate form, a profound spiritual and ethical usefulness (*Varieties*, lectures 14 and 15, "The Value of Saintliness"). What James was hinting at, but did not come to because he was not a believer, was the concept of *biblical accountability*.

19. Judith Tydings, *Gathering a People: Catholic Saints in Charismatic Perspective* (Plainfield, N.J.: Logos International, 1977). The best description of the gifts of the Spirit operating in the context of traditional Catholic spiritual life was presented by Fr. A. Poulain, S. J., in his *The Graces of Interior Prayer: A Treatise on Mystical Theology*, trans. L. L. Yorke-Smith (St. Louis, Mo.: B. Herder Book Co., 1950).

20. Vinson Synan, "The Role of the Holy Spirit and the Gifts of the Spirit in the Mystical Tradition," *One in Christ* 10, no. 2 (1974), pp. 193-202. Dr. Synan is the Dean of the School of Divinity, Regent University and the chairman of NARSC (North American Renewal Services Committee). He has also authored many books on the Pentecostal and charismatic renewals.

21. Vinson Synan, *The Holiness-Pentecostal Movement in the United States* (Grand Rapids, Mich.: William B. Eerdmans, 1971).

Chapter 5
Truth and Error in the Catholic Ministry of Healing

1. Augustine *The Lord's Sermon on the Mount* 1.4.

2. See Kelsey's excellent study of Augustine's theology of healing in his "Healing in the Victorious Church," chap. 8 in *Healing*.

3. Augustine *On the True Religion* 25.47.

4. Augustine, *The Advantage of Believing the Fathers of the Church*, trans. Luanne Meagher (New York: Cima Publishing, 1947), 438.

5. Frederick E. Greenspahn, "Why Prophecy Ceased," *Journal of Biblical Literature* 108, no. 1 (1989): 37-49.

6. Kelsey, *Healing*, 186-187.

7. Augustine, *The Retractions*, trans. Sister Mary Inez in *The Fathers of the Church*, vol. 60 (Washington, D.C.: Catholic University of America Press, 1968), book I, sect. 11.7.

8. Augustine, *The City of God*, trans. Gerald G. Walsh in *The Fathers of the Church*, vol. 24 (Washington, D.C.: Catholic University of America Press, 1960), b. 22, sect. 8.

9. For example, Jim McManus, *The Healing Power of the Sacraments* (Chawtaon, England: Redemptorist Publications, 1984).

10. Paul Tillich, *My Search for Absolutes* (New York: Simon and Schuster, 1967), 132-133. The use of the word *demonization* also admits the possibility of direct demonic influence over persons and institutions.

11. This insight into the basic problem of classical Greek philosophy is derived from Karl R. Popper, *The Spell of Plato*, vol. 1 of *The Open Society and Its Enemies* (New York: Harper & Row, 1963).

12. *New Catholic Encyclopedia*, s.v. "relics."

13. Roland Zimany, "The Divine Energies in Orthodox Theology," *Diakonia* 11, no. 3 (1976): 281-285, and George Maloney, *Uncreated Energy* (Amity, N.Y.: Amity House, 1987). Unfortunately this literature, like the beliefs of the Desert Fathers, assumed that the experience of God's energies was a rare event limited to the spiritually "advanced."

14. This history is detailed in a pioneer classic of the literature of Christian healing by Puller, *The Anointing of the Sick*.

15. See John Calvin's fine insight into this in his *Institutes*, b. 1, chap. 7, sect. 1-2.

16. The relationship between the philosophy of Aristotle and Thomas Aquinas and the resulting difficulties in forming an adequate understanding of the spiritual life have been studied by the Episcopal scholar Morton T. Kelsey. Two of his works have been especially useful in this section: *Tongue Speaking: An Experiment in Spiritual Experience* (London: Hodder and Stoughton, 1968) and *Healing*.

17. On this issue see James E. Bradley, "Miracles and Martyrdom in the Early Church: Some Theological and Ethical Implications," *Pneuma* 13, no. 1 (spring 1991): 65-81.

18. See Francis A. Schaeffer, *The God Who Is There* (Downers Grove, Ill.: Inter-Varsity Press, 1968), 166.

19. The culmination of this type of research may have been reached in the work of an English Jesuit, Fr. Herbert Thurston (1856 – 1939). He continued the Bollandists' task and began the work of discerning spiritual from psychic phenomena, a most difficult task. See especially his *The Physical Phenomenon of Mysticism*, ed. J. H. Crehan (London: Burns Oates, 1952). For a biography and complete bibliography of this saintly scholar's massive output, see Joseph Crehan, *Father Thurston: A Memoir With a Bibliography of His Writings* (London: Sheed & Ward, 1952).

20. This is brilliantly documented in Peter Gay, "Beyond the Holy Circle," chap. 7 in *The Enlightenment: An Interpretation* (New York: Alfred A. Knopf, 1973).

Chapter 6
The Reformers Overreact to Catholic Error

1. Geddes MacGregor, *Introduction to Religious Philosophy* (Boston: Houghton Mifflin Co., 1953), 173, and Kelsey, *Tongue Speaking,* 186ff.

2. Kelsey, *Healing*, 220-223.

3. Calvin, *Institutes*, b. 5, chap. 19, sect. 18.

4. Ibid., sects. 19 and 21.

5. Ibid., sect. 6.

6. On the Reformers' suspicion of Catholic mysticism, see Bengt R. Hoffman, *Luther and the Mystics* (Minneapolis: Augsburg Publishing House, 1976).

7. Calvin, *Institutes*, b. 1, chap. 15, sect. 6.

8. For a wonderfully readable presentation of this serious defect in Calvinist-Puritan theology and its consequences, see Edmund S. Morgan, *The Puritan Dilemma* (Boston: Little, Brown and Company, 1958).

9. John Dillenberger and Claude Welch, *Protestant Christianity Interpreted Through Its Development* (New York: Charles Scribner's Sons, 1954), 97.

10. Ibid., 166-167. See also Jerald C. Brauer, *Protestantism in America: A Narrative History*, rev. ed. (London: SCM Press, 1966). See especially 146ff.

11. On the importance of analogous knowledge in spiritual matters, see James D. Foster and Glenn T. Moran, "Piaget and Parables: The Convergence of Secular and Scriptural Views of Learning," *Journal of Psychology and Theology* 13 (summer 1985): 97-103.

12. Rex Gardner, "Miracles of healing in Anglo-Celtic Northumbria as recorded by Venerable Bede and his contemporaries: a reappraisal in the light of twentieth century experience," *British Medical Journal* 257 (December 1983): 24-31.

Chapter 7
The Fall of Christianity in Europe

1. For a magnificent study of the relationship between the denial of miracles (cessationism) and the decline of Protestantism, see Ernst Keller and Marie-Luise Keller, *Miracles in Dispute: A Continuing Debate*, trans. Margaret Kohl (Philadelphia: Fortress Press, 1969).

2. Jon Ruthven, *On the Cessation of the Charismata: The Protestant Polemic on Postbiblical Miracles* (Sheffield, England: Sheffield Academic Press, 1993), 34-39.

3. See Gay, *The Enlightenment*, for an understanding of the central role anti-Christian thinking played in the Enlightenment philosophers.

4. David Hume, "On Miracles," *An Enquiry Concerning Human Understanding*.

5. For a survey of the Hume controversy see R. M. Burns, *The Great Debate on Miracles: From Joseph Glanwell to David Hume* (London: Associated University Press, 1981).

6. Rudolf Bultmann, "A Reply to the Thesis of J. Schniewind," in *Kerygma and Myth: A Theological Debate,* ed. Hans Werner Bartsch, trans. R. H. Fuller (London: Society for Promoting Christian Knowledge, 1957).

7. Kelsey, *Healing,* 236-237.

8. For a study by a liberal scholar who is uneasy with the faithlessness of the seminaries but only vaguely understands the origins of the problems, see Edward Farley, *Theologia: The Fragmentation and Unity of Theological Education* (Philadelphia: Fortress Press, 1983).

9. Steven Meyerhoff, "Andover Seminary: The Rise and Fall of an Evangelical Institution," *Presbyterian* 8, no. 2 (fall 1982), 13-24.

10. John H. S. Kent, *The End of the Line? The Development of Christian Theology in the Last Two Centuries* (Philadelphia: Fortress Press, 1982).

11. See Dave Hunt's letter, *CIB Bulletin* (October 1987). The bulletin is available from the Christian Information Bureau, P.O. Box 7349, Bend, Oregon 97708.

12. Hilaire Belloc, *The Great Heresies* (London: The Catholic Book Club, n.d.).

13. See Mark A. Noll, ed., *The Princeton Theology, 1812-1921* (Grand Rapids, Mich.: Baker Book House, 1983).

14. The literature of natural law is vast since the concept has been a major element in traditional Catholic theology. For a brief history of natural law see Charles Grove Haines, *The Revival of Natural Law Concepts*, vol. 4 of *Harvard Studies in Jurisprudence* (New York: Russell and Russell, 1965), and especially John Warwick Montgomery, *The Law Above the Law* (Minneapolis: Bethany House, 1975).

15. Immanuel Kant, *Religion Within the Limits of Reason Alone*, trans. Theodore M. Greene and Hoyt H. Hudson (LaSalle, Ill.: Open Court, 1960).

16. See a non-Christian understanding of this in Karl R. Popper's classic work, *The High Tide of Prophecy: Hegel, Marx, and the Aftermath*, vol. 2 of *The Open Society and Its Enemies* (New York: Harper & Row, 1963).

17. I have relied on three principal sources for this important but technical section. The most succinct was Sydney E. Ahlstrom's article, "The Scottish Philosophy and American Theology," *Church History* 24 (September 1955): 257-272. Longer and more detailed is the book by Theodore Dwight Bozeman, *Protestants in an Age of Science: The Baconian Ideal and Antebellum American Religious Thought* (Chapel Hill, N.C.: University of North Carolina Press, 1977). Also useful was Herbert Hovenkamp's study, *Science and Religion in America, 1800 – 1860* (Philadelphia, Pa.: University of Pennsylvania Press, 1978).

18. The information in the following paragraphs is taken mostly from Bozeman, *Protestants*, 21ff.

19. Herbert Hovenkamp calls Scottish realism the "evangelical world view" in his *Science and Religion*, 5.

20. For a survey of the enormous influence that Witherspoon's Scottish realism had on American evanglicalism, see Mark A. Noll, *Princeton and the Republic, 1768 – 1822* (Princeton, N.J.: Princeton University Press, 1989).

21. Bozeman, *"The Presbyterian Old School,"* chap. 2 in *Protestants*.

22. Ironically, Scottish realism was also taken over by the liberal Protestantism which quite logically extended its materialism to discredit the miraculous in the Bible and affirm the demythologizing hermeneutic. By 1810 the Harvard faculty had abandoned Trinitarian Christianity and adopted both Unitarianism and Scottish realism. See the discussion of this in Sydney E. Ahlstrom's, "Scottish Philosophy," 257-272.

23. Ibid., 257-258.

Chapter 8
The Rise of Dispensationalism

1. See, for example, F. Roy Coad, *A History of the Brethren Movement* (Grand Rapids, Mich.: William B. Eerdmans, 1968), chaps. 8 and 9, and Clarence B. Bass, *Backgrounds to Dispensationalism* (Grand Rapids, Mich.: William B. Eerdmans, 1960), chap. 2.

2. The parallels between Darby's and Marcion's understanding of the Old Testament are pointed out in Brown's *Heresies*, 61ff.

3 Brown, *Heresies*, 63. See also Larry E. Dixon, "Have the 'Jewels of the Church' Been Found Again? The Irving-Darby Debate on Miraculous Gifts," *Evangelical Journal* 5 (fall 1987): 78-92. It is a useful but poorly written and edited piece.

4. See Knox, *Enthusiasm.*

5. Coad, *History,* chaps. 8-10.

6 William E. Cox, *An Examination of Dispensationalism* (Phillipsburg, N.J.: Presbyterian and Reformed Publishing Company, 1980), 10.

7. Angus Kinnear, *Against the Tide* (Wheaton, Ill.: Tyndale House, 1978), 153-154.

8. Norman C. Kraus, *Dispensationalism in America* (Richmond, Va.: John Knox Press, 1958), 135.

9. The following insights are taken from the superb book on revivals by Lovelace, *Dynamics of Spiritual Life,* especially chap. 12.

10. Much has been made by antidispensationalist writers of Scofield's lack of character. That is not really the point. We are all sinners and incomplete in our sanctification, and theology should be judged by its biblical compatibility, not by the personality of the theologian. Jerome, the translator of the Latin Bible, was an irascible and intolerant character too. See John D. Hannah, review of *The Incredible Scofield and His Book,*" *Bibliotheca Sacra* 147 (July-September 1990): 351-364.

11. See the note to Matthew 5 in *The Scofield Reference Bible,* copyright © 1909, 1917.

12. Ibid., prefatory note to Ruth.

Chapter 9
Evangelical Healers of the 1800s

1 For more information about the "evolution" of Pentecostal theology, as opposed to the myth that Pentecostalism birthed instantly after 1900, see the work of Donald W. Dayton, *Theological Roots of Pentecostalism* (Metuchen, N.J.: The Scarecrow Press, 1987).

2. Asa Mahan, *The Baptism of the Holy Spirit* (New York: George Hughes, 1870).

3. A recent biography has resuscitated the important role that Phoebe Palmer played in American religious history: Charles Edward White, *The Beauty of Holiness: Phoebe Palmer as Theologian, Revivalist, Feminist, and Humanitarian* (Grand Rapids, Mich.: Francis Asbury Press, 1986). An article by the same author summarized his findings: "The Beauty of Holiness: The Career of Phoebe Palmer," *Fides et Historia* 19 (February 1987): 22-34. Thankfully, a splendid selection of her writings has been recently published: *Selected Writings of Phoebe Palmer,* ed. Thomas C. Oden (New York: Paulist Press, 1988).

4. Palmer, *Writings,* 114-115.

5. Ibid., 118-121.

6. Charles Edward White, "Phoebe Palmer and the Development of Pentecostal Pneumatology," *Wesleyan Theological Journal* 23 (spring/fall, 1988): 198-212.

7. Phoebe Palmer, *The Way of Holiness,* with *Notes by the Way* (New York: Piercy and Reed, 1843). Thankfully reprinted in *The Devotional Writings of Phoebe Palmer* (New York: Garland, 1986).

8. Synan, *Holiness-Pentecostal Movement.*

9. White, *Beauty of Holiness,* 158.

10. Chappell, *Divine Healing,* chap. 2.

11. Ethan O. Allen, *Faith Healing: Or, What I Have Witnessed of the Fulfilling of James 5:14, 15, 16* (Philadelphia: G. W. McCall, 1881), 3-4.

12. Michael Weiner and Kathleen Goss, *The Complete Book of Homeopathy* (Toronto, Ont.: Bantam Books, 1982). See also Gail Vines, "Ghostly Antibodies Baffle Scientists," *New Scientist* (14 July 1988): 39, and David Concar, "Ghost Molecules Theory Back From the Dead," *New Scientist* (16 March 1991): 10, which has a summary of the homeopathic controversy.

13. Charles Cullis, *Dr. Cullis and His Work: Twenty Years of Blessing in Answer to Prayer,* ed. W. H. Daniels (Boston: Willard Tract Repository, 1885), 339-340.

14. For Dr. Cullis' method of healing see: Charles Cullis, *Faith Cures; or, Answers to Prayer in the Healing of the Sick* (Boston: Willard Tract Repository, 1879).

15. Ibid., 342-344 and Chappell, *Divine Healing,* 135.

16. W. E. Boardman, *Faith Work Under Dr. Cullis in Boston* (Boston: Willard Tract Repository, 1874).

17. Cullis, *Faith Cures,* preface.

18. See, for example, the influence of Dr. Cullis and A. J. Gordon in Andrew Murray's *Divine Healing,* thankfully reissued as a current paperback (Springdale, Pa.: Whitaker House, 1982).

19. A fine biography of A. J. Gordon was written by his son, Ernest B. Gordon, *Adoniram Judson Gordon: A Biography* (New York: Fleming H. Revell, 1896). More accessible is the excellent article by Russell C. Allyn, "Adoniram Judson Gordon: Nineteenth-Century Fundamentalist," *American Baptist Quarterly* 4 (March 1985), 61-89, and the same author's chapter on Gordon in *Voices of American Fundamentalism* (Philadelphia: Westminster Press, 1976).

20. A. J. Gordon, *The Ministry of the Spirit* (1894; reprint, Minneapolis: Bethany House, 1985), and A. J. Gordon, *The Holy Spirit in Missions* (New York: Fleming H. Revell, 1893; reprint, Harrisburg, Pa.: Christian Publications, 1968).

21. E. Gordon, *A Biography,* 110.

22. For a discussion of A. J. Gordon's dispensational theology and his differences with Darby, see Allyn, "Adoniram Judson Gordon," 61-89.

23. Note the theology of the television evangelist Jimmy Swaggart for a contemporary example of combining healing and dispensationalism. See Jimmy Swaggart, *God's Plan for the Ages* (Baton Rouge, La.: Jimmy Swaggart Ministries, 1986).

24. E. Gordon, *A Biography,* chap. 11.

25. A. J. Gordon, *Ministry of Healing.*

26. Ibid., chap. 7.

27. Ibid., chap. 5. For a full description on Bushnell's theological stand, see Chappell, *Divine Healing,* chap. 1. Bushnell's beliefs were theoretical since he had no experience with healing prayer.

28. A. J. Gordon, *Ministry of Healing,* chap. 10, see especially 203-206.

29. Carrie Judd Montgomery's tri-movement influence was stressed in the scholarly article by Daniel E. Albrecht, "Carrie Judd Montgomery: Pioneering Contributor to Three Religious Movements," *Pneuma* 8 (fall 1986), 101-119.

30. Carrie F. Judd, *The Prayer of Faith* (Buffalo, N.Y.: H. H. Otis, 1882).

31. Because *Triumphs of Faith* included articles and reprints from such a wide variety of denominations and personalities, it remains a magnificent source of knowledge of anticessationist thought and activities for the turn of the century American evangelicals.

32. Judd, *Prayer of Faith,* 14-15.

33. Ibid., 26ff.

34. Ibid., 42-43.

35. Ibid., 97-98.

36. "Faith Without Works," *Triumphs of Faith,* October 1881, 145.

37. Information about George Montgomery and his role as prominent turn-of-the-century Christian businessman and leader is found in a two-part series by Jennifer Stock, "George S. Montgomery; Businessman for the Gospel," parts 1 and 2, *Assemblies of God Heritage* 9 (spring/summer 1989).

38. See Chappell, *Divine Healing,* chap. 4, and Dayton, "Rise," 13ff.

39. Allen, *Faith Healing.*

40. Cited in Dayton, "Rise," 12. Used by permission. Dayton obtained the quotation from A. B. Simpson, *The Gospel of Healing,* rev. ed. (New York: Christian Alliance Publishing Co., 1920), 64. On Simpson's role also see Cunningham, "From Holiness to Healing: the Faith Cure in America, 1872 – 1892," 507.

41. Cited in Dayton, "Rise," 13. Used by permission.

42. William G. Rothslein, "Medical Education," chap. 5 in *American Physicians in the Nineteenth Century: From Sect to Science* (Baltimore: Johns Hopkins University Press, 1972).

43. Ibid., 36.

44. As a child I was treated in New York City by a reputable doctor who prescribed a mustard plaster for a persistent cold (cir. 1948). Thankfully I recovered without scarring.

45. Marvin R. Vincent, "Modern Miracles," *The Presbyterian Review* 4 (July 1884): 497.

Chapter 10
The Healing Revival Destroyed by Victorian Pharisees

1. For a full length biography of the Rev. Buckley see George Preston Mains, *James Monroe Buckley* (New York: The Methodist Book Concern, 1917); and for a chapter-length biography see Harry C. Howard, "James Monroe Buckley," chap. 12 in *Princes of the Christian Pulpit and Pastorate,* 2d ser. (Nashville: Cokesbury Press, 1918).

2. James M. Buckley, *Constitutional and Parliamentary History of the Methodist Episcopal Church* (New York: The Methodist Book Concern, 1914).

3. Mains, *Buckley,* 172.

4. James M. Buckley, *Christian Science and Other Superstitions* (New York: The Century Co., 1899), 1-2.

5. The tragic story of the Methodists' retreat from the edge of Pentecostalism is told in Synan, *Holiness-Pentecostal Movement,* chaps. 1 and 2.

6. John Nevius, *Demon Possession and Allied Themes* (New York: Fleming H. Revell, 1896).

7. James M. Buckley, "Editorial: Primitive Traits in Religious Revivals," *The Christian Advocate* (9 August 1906).

8. Howard, *Princes,* 2d ser., 445.

9. James M. Buckley, *Faith-Healing, Christian Science, and Kindred Phenomenon* (New York: The Century Co., 1892, 1st ed., 1886), chaps. 3 and 4. See also Mains, *Buckley,* 174.

10. Buckley, *Other Superstitions,* 14.

11. There is much being written on power evangelism in the Third World. See, for example, C. Peter Wagner, *Spiritual Power and Church Growth* (Lake Mary, Fla.: Creation House, 1986).

12. Buckley, *Other Superstitions*, 45-46.

13. Ibid., 121. See also the later work by James M. Buckley, *The Fundamentals and Their Contrasts* (Nashville: Publishing House of the Methodist Episcopal Church, 1906), pp. 139ff.

14. That James M. Buckley was an expert in the writings of Edwards is clear from his discussion in "Editorial: Primitive Traits in Religious Revivals, II," *The Christian Advocate* (16 August 1906).

15. Albrecht, "Montgomery": 101-119.

16. R. Kelso Carter, *"Faith Healing" Reviewed After Twenty Years* (Boston: The Christian Witness Co., 1897). Thankfully it was reprinted in 1985 (New York: Garland).

17. In tone, wisdom and even circumstances Carter's book parallels Charles Farah's work of a century later. See chapter 19.

18. See T. J. McCrossan, *Bodily Healing and the Atonement*, ed. R. Hicks and Kenneth Hagin (Tulsa, Okla.: Faith Library Publications, 1982).

19. Dayton, "Rise," 18.

20. Benjamin B. Warfield, *Counterfeit Miracles* (New York: Charles Scribner's Sons, 1918). For a superb new work on Warfield see Ruthven, *Cessation*.

21. For a recent overview of this school of theology see Noll, ed., *Princeton Theology*. Noll's book is especially good in drawing out the scientific attitude of these theologians. See also Ernest R. Sandeen, "The Princeton Theology," *Church History* 31 (September 1962), 307-321.

22. See, for example, C. Everett Koop, "Faith-Healing and the Sovereignty of God," in *The Agony of Deceit*, ed. Michael Horton (Chicago: Moody Press, 1990), 177.

23. For an introduction into the richness and theological sophistication of the Anglican healing pioneers, see the works of Charles W. Gusmer, especially *The Ministry of Healing in the Church of England* (Essex, England: Mayhew-McCrimmon, 1974), and "Anointing of the Sick in the Church of England," *Worship* 45 (May 1971), 262-272.

24. Warfield, *Counterfeit Miracles*, 61.

25. Ibid., 38-39. See also chap. 3.

26. Ibid., 238-239, n. 21.

27. For a balanced appraisal of this church see Knox, *Enthusiasm*.

28. Warfield, *Counterfeit Miracles*, chap. 4.

29. Ibid., chap. 5.

30. Ibid., 190-191.

31. Ibid., 172.

32. Ibid., 176.

33. Ibid., 21-29.

34. See Calvin, *Institutes*, b. 4, chap. 19, sect. 6.

35. For a detailed critique of Warfield's hermeneutics see Jon Ruthven, "On Cessation of the Charismata: The Protestant Polemic of Benjamin B. Warfield," *Pneuma* 12 (spring 1990): 14-31.

36. The problem of the poverty of coverage of American church history has been ably pointed out in the excellent work of James L. Ash Jr., "American Religion and the Academy in the Early Twentieth Century: The Chicago Years of William Warren Sweet," *Church History* 50 (December 1981): 450-464.

37. Chappell, *Divine Healing*, 358.
38. Elmer T. Clark, *The Small Sects in America* (Nashville: Cokesbury Press, 1937).
39. Ibid., 107.
40. Cunningham, "Faith Cure," 499-513.

Chapter 11
Materialism Versus the Real World

1. For readable introductions to the concepts discussed in this section see John Gribbin, *In Search of Schrodinger's Cat* (Toronto, Ont.: Bantam Books, 1984); Fred Alan Wolf, *Taking the Quantum Leap: The New Physics for Nonscientists* (San Francisco: Harper & Row, 1981); and Abner Shimony, "The Reality of the Quantum World," *Scientific American* 258 (January 1988), 46-53. For an historical overview see George Gamow, *Thirty Years That Shook Physics* (Garden City, N.Y.: Doubleday & Co., 1966).
2. This is explained clearly in Gribbin, *In Search*, 166ff.
3. See J. Leslie, "How to Draw Conclusions From the Fine-Tuned Universe," in Robert J. Russell et al., *Physics, Philosophy, and Theology* (Vatican City, Rome: Vatican Observatory, 1988), 297-312.
4. Robert Pool, "Quantum Pot Watching," *Science* 246 (17 November 1989), 888.
5. Lee Smolin, "What Is Quantum Mechanics Really About?" *New Scientist* (24 October 1985): 40; and Nick Herbert, "How to Be in Two Places at the Same Time," *New Scientist* (21 August 1986): 41-44.
6. Alastair Rae, "Extrasensory Quantum Physics," *New Scientist* (27 November 1986): 36-39.
7. Gribbin, *In Search*, 23ff.
8. See the lead article, "A Disorienting View of God's Creation: Faith in the Crucible of the New Physics," *Christianity Today*, 1 February 1985. The presentation was sketchy and timid.
9. Fritjof Capra, *The Tao of Physics* (Boulder, Colo.: Shambhala Publications, 1975), marketed as a paperback by Bantam Books.
10. See, for example, Gary Zukav, *The Dancing Wu Li Masters: An Overview of the New Physics* (New York: William Morrow, 1979).
11. Dawne McCance, "Physics, Buddhism, and Postmodern Interpretations," *Zygon* 21 (spring 1986): 287-296.
12. Tony Rothman, "A 'What You See Is What You Beget' Theory," *Discover* 8 (May 1987): 90-99.
13. Gribbin, *In Search*, chap. 11.
14. See, for example, a Jewish interpretation of quantum physics in Philip J. Bentley's "Uncertainty and Unity," *Journal of Judaism* 33 (spring 1984): 191-201.

Chapter 12
The Spiritual Side of Quantum Physics

1. Some of the complementarities of Christian doctrine have been noted in John C. Polkinghorne, *The Way the World Is* (Grand Rapids, Mich.: William B. Eerdmans, 1984), 67. Also, John Honner, S.J., has drawn attention to the fact that Karl Rahner, the preeminent theologian of the Catholic church, has used complementarity in his theology of Christ. See John Honner, "Unity-in-Difference: Karl Rahner and Niels Bohr," *Theological Studies* 46 (September 1985): 480-506.

2. Cited in Werner Schaafs, *Theology, Physics, and Miracles*, trans. Richard L. Renfield (Washington, D.C.: Canon Press, 1974), 81-83. This work is possibly the best single book on the relationship between quantum physics and Christian theology to date.

3. Charles Farah Jr., *From the Pinnacle of the Temple* (Plainfield, N.J: Logos International, 1979), especially 177-178.

4. John C. Polkinghorne, "One World," chap. 7 in *One World: The Interaction of Science and Theology* (London: Society for Promoting Christian Knowledge, 1986).

5. See Philip Yancey, "Insight on Eternity From a Scientific View of Time," *Christianity Today* (6 April 1984): 26.

6. Don H. Gross, *The Case for Spiritual Healing* (New York: Thomas Nelson & Sons, 1958).

7. Ibid., appendix C, "On the Creation and Annihilation of Matter."

8. Studies in the history of science have shown that intellectual inertia often combines with the fear of the unknown to maintain current views as a form of "guild orthodoxy." The classic work on this issue is Thomas S. Kuhn, *The Structure of Scientific Revolutions* (Chicago: University of Chicago Press, 1962).

9. William L. DeArteaga, "The Crisis of Confidence," *Ministries Today* (July/August 1991): 56-62.

10. In fairness we should note a contrary example, the resuscitation of Lazarus (John 11). In this miracle Jesus begins with the Old Testament pattern of declaring that Lazarus was "asleep," not dead. But His disciples do not understand the point; Jesus says plainly that he is dead, then He goes on to resuscitate Lazarus. Why did Jesus break His earlier pattern? Most probably because at this late stage of His ministry the principal concern of the Father was that Jesus be glorified. Unlike the resuscitation of Jairus's daughter, Jesus was not teaching His disciples about faith. Interestingly, Peter's resuscitation of Dorcas in Acts 9:36-43 and Paul's resuscitation of Eutychus in Acts 20:7-12 take a middle course between the traditional Elisha pattern and Jesus' resuscitation of Lazarus.

11. Stanley Howard Frodsham, *Smith Wigglesworth, Apostle of Faith* (Springfield, Mo.: Gospel Publishing House, 1990), 68.

Chapter 13
What Does a Heretic Know About Truth?

1. Jo Ann Hackett, "Some Observations on the Balaam Tradition of Deiv cAlla," *Biblical Archaeologist* 49 (December 1986): 216-221.

2. See the excellent description of this dilemma in Don Richardson, *Eternity in Their Hearts* (Ventura, Calif.: Regal Books, 1981).

3. Werner Jaeger, *Early Christianity and Greek Paideia* (Cambridge, Mass.: Harvard University Press, 1961).

4. Brown, *Heresies*. Brown is a professor at Trinity Evangelical Divinity School.

5. Dom Odo Casel, *The Mystery of Christian Worship and Other Writings*, ed. Berkhard Neunheuser (Westminster, Md.: The Newman Press, 1962).

6. See the recent account of how early heresies forced the formation of the biblical canon in "The Canon: How God Gave His Word to the Church," *Christianity Today* (5 February 1988): 23-26.

7. For an excellent study of how the "radical" Reformers influenced modern Christianity see Leonard Verduin, *The Reformers and Their Stepchildren* (Grand Rapids, Mich.: William B. Eerdmans, 1964).

8. Brown, *Heresies*, 4.

9. Ibid., chap. 6.

10. For an example of Origen's work against heresy, see his dialogue "On the Soul" in *A Treasury of Early Christianity*, ed. Anne Fremantle (New York: New American Library, Mentor, 1960), 290-299.

Chapter 14
A Critique of New Thought and New Age

1. Of course, the Spirit also flowed mightily through more orthodox groups such as the Faith-Cure movement. These groups were shunned by the mainline churches.

2. Walter Martin, *The Kingdom of the Cults*, rev. ed. (Minneapolis: Bethany Fellowship, 1968), p. 17.

3. For an elaboration of the allegorical hermeneutic see the second half of the Christian Science bible, Mary Baker Eddy's *Science and Health,* with *Key to the Scriptures* (Boston: First Church of Christ, Scientist, 1906).

4. W. F. Evans, *Mental Medicine: A Theoretical and Practical Treatise* (Boston: Carter and Pettee, 1874), iv.

5. Many evangelicals believe that any form of hypnotism is sinful and contrary to the Bible. The biblical evidence for this position is ambiguous at best. Note the balanced position on this issue by the noted evangelical psychologist Gary Collins in "The Hypnotic Mind," chap. 15 in *The Magnificent Mind* (Waco, Tex.: Word Books, 1985). Early in my Christian life I attempted to minister through hypnotic-like states. With the benefit of hindsight I have come to the conclusion that there is no spiritually safe form of hypnotic ministry.

6. The literature on Gnosticism is vast and growing. For a review of it see Robert Haardt, *Gnosis: Character and Testimony*, trans. J. F. Hendry (Leiden, Germany: E. J. Brill, 1971).

7. Schmithals, *Gnosticism in Corinth;* Schmithals, *Paul and the Gnostics;* and Martin*, Kingdom.*

8. R. M. Grant, "Nature of Gnosticism," chap. 1 in *Gnosticism and Early Christianity* (New York: Columbia University Press, 1957).

9. Eddy, *Science and Health,* chap. 12.

10. See Raymond J. Cunningham, "The Impact of Christian Science on the American Churches, 1880 – 1910," *The American Historical Review* 72 (April 1967): 887-892.

11. Ibid., 891.

12. Among the best surveys of New Thought are Charles S. Braden, *Spirits in Rebellion: The Rise and Development of New Thought* (Dallas: Southern Methodist University Press, 1963), and J. Stillson Judah, *The History and Philosophy of the Metaphysical Movements in America* (Philadelphia: Westminster Press, 1967). The evangelical perspective is given in Martin's *Kingdom of the Cults.*

13. See, for example, Ralph Waldo Trine, *The Power That Wins: Henry Ford and Ralph Waldo Trine in an Intimate Talk on Life* (Indianapolis: Bobbs-Merrill Co., 1929).

14. Braden, *Spirits in Rebellion*, 138.

15. Finding a fair description of Unity is almost impossible. Evangelical sources treat Unity as a form of Christian Science, while the published biographies of Charles Fillmore are disciples' works with little critical evaluation. See James Dillet Freeman, *The Household of Faith: The Story of Unity* (Lee's Summit, Mo.: Unity, 1951) and Hugh D'Andrade, *Charles Fillmore: Herald of the New Age* (New York: Harper & Row, 1974). More objective and useful are the chapters on Unity found in Braden's *Spirits in Rebellion* and Judah's *Metaphysical Movements*.

16. Braden, *Spirits in Rebellion*, chap. 7.

17. I owe this analogy to my reading of Gay's classic work, *The Enlightenment*.

18. Donald Meyer, in his *Positive Thinkers: Religion as Pop Psychology From Mary Baker Eddy to Oral Roberts* (New York: Pantheon Books, 1980), relates Mind-Cure to the rise of psychosomatic medicine (chaps. 6 and 7).

19. Watchman Nee, *The Latent Power of the Soul* (New York: Christian Fellowship Publishers, 1972).

20. Richardson, *Eternity*.

21. For an explanation of the traditional Catholic theology of the preternatural powers of the mind, see the controversial book on Catholic exorcism by Malachi Martin, *Hostage to the Devil* (New York: Reader's Digest Press, 1976), especially the case of the "Rooster and the Tortoise."

22. Collins, *Magnificent Mind*, 42-63.

23. See a brief, popular account of this in Signe Hammers, "The Mind as Healer," *Science Digest* (April 1984): 47-49,100; and Collins, *Magnificent Mind*, chap. 5.

24. Elliot Miller, "Unity School of Christianity," in *Cults Reference Bible*, ed. Walter Martin (Santa Ana, Calif.: Vision House, 1981), 69.

25. Mr. Clark's autobiography is still in print: Glenn Clark, *A Man's Reach: The Autobiography of Glenn Clark* (1949; reprint, St. Paul, Minn.: MacAlester Park, 1977).

26. The remarkable story of Professor Moseley of Mercer University (Baptist), who became a Christian Scientist "practitioner" and after a vision of our Lord, a recommitted Christian, and after that a Pentecostal preacher, is told in his J. Rufus Moseley, *Manifest Victory: A Quest and a Testimony* (New York: Harper and Brothers, 1941).

27. Mrs. Sanford's autobiography clearly traces the influence that New Thought, and especially Emmet Fox, had on her thought. Agnes Sanford, *Sealed Orders* (Plainfield, N.J.: Logos International, 1972).

28. My forthcoming book, *From New Thought to the Charismatic Renewal* (working title). I should note that my knowledge of the Metaphysical movement comes partly out of personal experience. Like Kenyon, I too spent a season of my spiritual life within metaphysical circles. In my case it was in the 1970s. The Lord led me out of that entrapment step by step as I began to realize that fundamental discernment flaws lay at the root of the New Age cults.

Chapter 15
The Revival of Prosperity Teaching

1. Gail Thain Parker, "The Dream of Success," chap. 1 in *Mind Cure in New England: From the Civil War to World War I* (Hanover, N.H.: University Press of New England, 1973).

2. Clement of Alexandria, *Christ the Educator*, trans. Simon P. Wood (Washington, D.C.: Catholic University of America Press, 1953).

3. Ibid., 227.

4. Spanish literature contains a genre of novels (*novelas picarescas*) which revolve around the ruined *hidalgo* who lives by bluff and wits to avoid work.

5. The information in this section was mostly derived from the excellent study by Louis B. Wright, "The Whole Duty of the Citizen," part 2 in *Middle-Class Culture in Elizabethan England* (Chapel Hill, N.C.: University of North Carolina Press, 1935).

6. Cited in ibid., 161-162.

7. Ibid., 246.

8. Ibid., 247.

9. William Perkins, *A Treatise of the Vocations or Callings of Man*, in *The Work of William Perkins,* ed. Ian Breward (Appleford, England: The Sutton Courteney Press, 1970), 450.

10. Ibid., 458.

11. Cited in Whitney A. Griswold, "Three Puritans on Prosperity," *The New England Quarterly* 7 (September 1934), 479.

12. Ibid., 480.

13. Max Weber, *The Protestant Ethic and the Spirit of Capitalism* (London: n.p., 1930). The Weber work first appeared as articles during 1904 and 1905. The volume of literature generated by the Weber thesis is enormous. Among the best is R. H. Tawney's *Religion and the Rise of Capitalism* (London: n.p., 1929).

14. Stephen R. Covey, *The Seven Habits of Highly Effective People* (New York: Simon and Schuster, 1989).

15. Richard Weiss, "The Christian Novel and the Success Myth," chap. 3 in *The American Myth of Success: From Horatio Alger to Norman Vincent Peale* (New York: Basic Books, 1969).

16. Whitney A. Griswold, "New Thought: A Cult of Success," *The American Journal of Sociology* 60 (November 1934): 312. See also Weiss, *American Myth*, 150-153.

17. Orison Swett Marden, *Pushing to the Front: Or, Success Under Difficulties* (New York: Thomas Y. Crowell, 1894).

18. Orison Swett Marden, *Every Man a King: Or, Might in Mind-Mastery* (New York: Thomas Y. Crowell, 1906).

19. Ralph Waldo Trine, *In Tune With the Infinite* (Indianapolis: Bobbs-Merrill Co., 1897).

20. Ibid., 176.

21. Ibid., 181.

22. Ibid., 177.

23. Ibid., 180, 183.

24. Charles Fillmore, *Prosperity* (Kansas City, Mo.: Unity School of Christianity, 1938), 16-21.

25. Ibid., 16.

26. Ibid., 137-138. Chapter 9, "Tithing, the Road to Prosperity," is biblically sound.

Chapter 16
The Resurrection of Spiritual Laws

1. Emanuel Swedenborg, *Earth in the Universe*, 1st ed. (n.p., 1758), sect. 85.
2. Ibid., sect. 111.
3. C. G. Montefiore and H. Lowe, *A Rabbinic Anthology* (Cleveland: The World Publishing Co., 1963), xxxv.
4. Cited in ibid., 222.
5. See Gerhard Von Rad, *Wisdom in Israel* (Nashville: Abingdon Press, 1972), 124-137.
6. For a fair critique of the allegorical method see the hermeneutical classic by Frederic W. Farrar, *History of Interpretation* (London: Macmillan & Co., 1886), or the more modern work by R. M. Grant, *The Letter and the Spirit* (New York: Macmillan & Co. 1957).
7. Loring T. Swaim, *Arthritis, Medicine and the Spiritual Laws: The Power Beyond Science* (Philadelphia: Chilton Co., 1962).
8. There has not yet appeared any biographical article or book on either John or Paula Sandford. Autobiographical details of their lives appear with great candor throughout their works as they willingly expose their own failures in order to demonstrate how the Lord heals.
9. John Sandford and Paula Sandford, *Healing the Wounded Spirit* (South Plainfield, N.J.: Bridge, 1985), 19,21.
10. John Sandford and Paula Sandford, *The Transformation of the Inner Man* (South Plainfield, N.J.: Bridge, 1982), 4-5.
11. John Sandford and Paula Sandford, *The Elijah Task* (Tulsa, Okla.: Victory House, 1977), 111-112,116-117. Used by permission. Compare with comments in Sandford, *Transformation*, 74-75,86-87.
12. John Sandford and Paula Sandford, *Inner Vows* (Spokane, Wash.: Elijah House, n.d.), audiocassette.
13. Sandford, *Transformation*, 204-205.
14. Ibid., 262.
15. See Calvin, *Institutes*, b. 2, chaps. 7-8. For a brilliant exposition of moral law, see John Warwick Montgomery, *The Suicide of Christian Theology* (Minneapolis: Bethany Fellowship, 1970). See especially the chapter titled "Wisdom, Love and Law."
16. John Sandford and Paula Sandford, "The Lord's Kindness Leads to Repentance," *Voice 2* (September 1991): 1-2.

Chapter 17
Visualization and the Christian

1. The structure and many of the insights of this chapter were suggested by Brooks Alexander's masterful article, "Mind Power and the Mind's Eye," *SCP Journal* 9, no. 3 (1990): 8-20, which will be discussed in the text. (*SCP Journal* is published by Spiritual Counterfeit Projects, Inc., P.O. Box 4308, Berkeley, CA 94704; 415-540-0300; material used by permission.) Another key article was John K. La Shell's "Imagination and Idol: A Puritan Tension," *Westminster Theological Journal* 49 (1987): 305-334.

2. Eswyn Beven, "Lecture 3" in *Holy Images: An Inquiry into Idolatry and Image-Worship in Ancient Paganism and in Christianity* (London: George Allen & Unwin, 1940), 84-112.

3. Catholic literature is full of accounts of the appearances of Christ to His saints, yet this is not uncommon among Protestants either; for example, the critically important role that Jesus' appearance made in the life of the famous nineteenth-century evangelist Charles Finney. See Charles G. Finney, *Memoirs* (New York: A.S. Barnes, 1876), 19-20.

4. Ernst Kitzinger, "The Cult of Images in the Age Before Iconoclasm," chap. 5 in *The Art of Byzantium and the Medieval West* (Bloomington, Ind.: Indiana University Press, 1976), 90-156. See also the fine article by Stephen Gero, "Byzantine Iconoclasm and the Failure of a Medieval Reformation," in *The Image and the Word: Confrontations in Judaism, Christianity and Islam,* ed. Joseph Gutmann (Missoula, Mont.: Scholars Press, 1977), 28-59.

5. See Carl C. Christenson, "Pattern of Iconoclasm in the Early Reformation: Strasburg and Basil," in *The Image and the Word: Confrontations in Judaism, Christianity and Islam,* ed. Joseph Gutmann (Missoula, Mont.: Scholars Press, 1977), 107-148.

6. Calvin, *Institutes,* b. 1, chap. 11, sect. 9.

7. Ibid., sect. 3.

8. On this point see David Morgan, "The Protestant Struggle with the Image," *The Christian Century* 106 (22-29 March 1989): 308-311.

9. La Shell, "Imagination and Idol," 311.

10. Calvin, *Institutes,* book I, chap. xv, sect. 6.

11. Ibid., chap. xi, sect. 8.

12. Cited in La Shell, "Imagination and Idol," 316. Used by permission.

13. Edwards, *The Distinguishing Marks,* in La Shell, "Imagination and Idol," 317. Used by permission.

14. Ibid., 325-326.

15. Saint Bonaventura, *Meditations on the Life of Christ,* trans. Isa Ragusa and Rosalie B. Green (Princeton, N.J.: Princeton University Press, 1961), 38.

16. An excellent account of the famous exercises is found in Hugo Rahner, *The Spirituality of St. Ignatius Loyola: An Account of Its Historical Development,* trans. Francis John Smith (Westminster, Md.. The Newman Press, 1953); and, of course, St. Ignatius of Loyola, *The Spiritual Exercises of St. Ignatius,* trans. Anthony Mottola (Garden City, N.Y.: Doubleday & Co., 1964).

17. William T. MacArthur, *Ethan O. Allen,* cited in Chappell, *Divine Healing,* 99-104. Unfortunately Dr. Chappell cannot recall where he read the Allen biography, and that book has not been found even after extensive interlibrary efforts. I would appreciate any information on the whereabouts of MacArthur's book.

18. Tim Stafford, "The Kingdom of the Cult Watchers," *Christianity Today* (7 October 1991): 18-23.

19. Alexander, "Mind Power," 8-20.

20. Ibid., 11. Used by permission.

21. Ibid., 20. Used by permission.

Chapter 18
E. W. Kenyon and His Faith Theology

1. Dale Simmons, "The Postbellum Pursuit of Peace, Power and Plenty: As Seen in the Writings of Essek William Kenyon" (Ph.D. diss., Drew University, 1990).

2. When I was writing the first edition of *Quenching the Spirit,* the only published sources on Kenyon's life were the biographical sections in D. R. McConnell's *A Different Gospel: A Historical and Biblical Analysis of the Modern Faith Movement* (Peabody, Mass.: Hendrickson, 1988), a book which, in spite of its interpretive errors, was based on good original research. Some materials were gleaned from Kenyon's obituary in *Herald of Life* (April 1948). Kenyon's own writings also yielded additional biographical incidents. An excellent short article on Kenyon by R. M. Riss appeared in the *Dictionary of Pentecostal and Charismatic Movements,* ed. Stanley M. Burgeses and Gary B. McGee (Grand Rapids, Mich.: Zondervan, 1988).

In preparing this revised edition, I was able to consult the superb doctoral dissertation by Dr. Dale Simmons, mentioned earlier. Simmons' work definitively places Kenyon in the Faith-Cure and Higher Life camp rather than in New Thought circles. This work has been updated and will be released as a book. Unfortunately, Scarecrow Press, its intended publisher, has been sold, and there will be some additional delay before Simmons' scholarly work is available to the public.

Concurrently, two other scholars have been fruitfully laboring in the Kenyon field. Joe McIntyre, pastor of Word of His Grace Fellowship in Kirkland, Washington, who has access to the Kenyon papers and library, is preparing a popular biography on Kenyon, *E. W. Kenyon and His Message of Faith.* McIntyre has privately circulated a seven-page fact sheet, "E. W. Kenyon and His Critics," which summarizes his important findings. Cooperating and coordinating with these scholars and myself has been a Norwegian charismatic divinity student, Geir Lie. He wrote his master's thesis on Kenyon, "E. W. Kenyon: *Sekstifter eller kristen lederskikkelse? En historisk undersøkelse av Kenyons teologi med sãerlig nenblikk pâ deus historiske rotter og innflytelsen pâ samtid og ettertid*" (Norwegian Lutheran School of Theology, October 1994). Lie has been a special blessing to those in Kenyon studies and has been much grieved by the dispute over interpreting Kenyon's theology. I have had the privilege of assisting Lie in translating his materials into acceptable English. Lie has a knack for unearthing important documents and facts, and his contribution to Kenyon scholarship will hopefully see print in the future.

3. E. W. Kenyon, *The Hidden Man* (Lynnwood, Wash.: Kenyon's Gospel Publishing Society, 1970), 144.

4. E. W. Kenyon, *Sign Posts on the Road to Success* (1938; reprint, Lynnwood, Wash.: Kenyon's Gospel Publishing Society, 1966).

5. E. W. Kenyon, "Justification," *Reality,* November 1909, 133. Cited in Lie's manuscript.

6. McConnell cites evidence that even in his later years Kenyon read Mary Baker Eddy's *Science and Health* (see *A Different Gospel,* p. 25). While this point may be entirely true, it must be viewed in light of our discussion in the preceding chapters on the possibility that heresy often contains hidden truth.

7. E. W. Kenyon, *Two Kinds of Faith* (Lynnwood, Wash.: Kenyon's Gospel Publishing Society, 1969), 17. Used by permission.

8. Kenyon, *Hidden Man,* 183.

9. Evva Lydia Spurling Kenyon, "God's Leadings," *Tabernacle Trumpet* (January 1901): 131. Cited in Lie's manuscript.

10. E. W. Kenyon, "The Walk of Faith," *Reality* (January 1907): 163. Cited in Lie's manuscript.

11. McIntyre, "E. W. Kenyon and His Critics," 3.

12. Evva Kenyon, "God's Leadings," 131-136.

13. Kenyon, *Hidden Man,* 182. Used by permission.

14. E. W. Kenyon, *New Creation Realities* (1945; reprint, Lynnwood, Wash.: Kenyon's Gospel Publishing Society, 1964), 146.

15. Kenyon was elected president emeritus by the board following his departure. Bethel Bible Institute became Bethel College in 1923 and, after several name changes and relocations, became Barrington College, one of the finest evangelical colleges in the nation. That school merged with Gordon College, which had been founded by A. J. Gordon.

16. F. F. Bosworth, *Christ the Healer* (1924; reprint, Old Tappan, N.J.: Fleming H. Revell, 1973).

17. McConnell, *A Different Gospel,* 23. On the post-World War II healing revival see David Edwin Harrell, Jr., *All Things Are Possible: The Healing and Charismatic Revivals in Modern America* (Bloomington: Indiana University Press, 1975).

18. Ruth A. Kenyon, "He Is at Rest," *Herald of Life* (April 1948). Cited from a copy provided to the author by Kenyon's daughter, Mrs. Ruth A. Kenyon Houseworth.

19. For a current catalog of the Kenyon writings, write to: Kenyon's Gospel Publishing Society, P.O. Box 973, Lynnwood, WA 98046.

20. Kenyon's writings are repetitive. The reader does not need to read every one of them to understand his teachings. *The Hidden Man* contains the major elements of Kenyon's theology. Also, the reader may be confused by the way the Kenyon books are printed. The copyright dates show years in the 1960s and 1970s. These represent the dates when the copyrights were *renewed*. Also the books are often labeled as "tenth edition" or "thirteenth edition," etc., but this really means a numbered reprinting since the text was unchanged.

21. Kenyon, *New Creation Realities,* 16ff.

22. E. W. Kenyon, *Two Kinds of Knowledge* (Lynnwood, Wash.: Kenyon's Gospel Publishing Society, 1966).

23. Ibid., 11-12, 25-26.

24. E. W. Kenyon, *Identification: A Romance in Redemption* (Lynnwood, Wash.: Kenyon's Gospel Publishing Society, 1968).

25. Kenyon, *Two Kinds of Faith,* 7-8. Used by permission.

26. Ibid., 7. Used by permission.

27. Kenyon, *The Hidden Man,* 96.

28. Ibid., 99. Used by permission.

29. Ibid., 108.

30. Frodsham, *Smith Wigglesworth,* 63.

31. Kenyon, *Two Kinds of Faith,* 42-45.

32. Kenyon, *The Hidden Man,* 201-212.

33. Ibid., 91.

34. Kenyon, *New Creation Realities,* 66, 150.

35. Kenyon, *The Hidden Man,* 139.

36. Kenyon, *New Creation Realities,* 126-127.

37. McConnell, *A Different Gospel*, 175. See also Charles Farah Jr., "A Critical Analysis: The 'Roots and Fruits' of the Faith-formula Theology," *Pneuma* 3 (spring 1981): 15.

Chapter 19
Reproof for the Charismatic Renewal: Charles Farah Jr.

1. Harold Hill, *How to Live Like a King's Kid* (Plainfield, N.J.: Logos International, 1974).

2. Farah, *From the Pinnacle*, 14-17.

3. Ibid., 9-13.

4. Ibid., 37-39.

5. Ibid., 1-4.

6. Ibid., 20ff.

7. Ibid., 19-45.

8. Farah, "Roots and Fruits," 4.

9. Ibid., 17.

10. Ibid., 13-14.

11. Ibid., 10.

12. For more information write to Presbyterian and Reformed Renewal Ministries, 115 Richardson Blvd., P.O. Box 428, Black Mountain, NC 28711.

13. Charles Farah Jr., "Faith Theology: The Sovereignty of Man?" *Logos Journal* (May/June 1980): 50-55.

14. Farah, "Roots and Fruits," 3-21. The society is made of Christian scholars from many denominations who not only speak in tongues, but they often speak in footnotes! See also Charles Farah Jr., "Faith or Presumption?" in Francis MacNutt, *The Power to Heal* (Notre Dame, Ind.: Ave Maria Press, 1974), 226-236.

15. Farah, *From the Pinnacle*, 206.

16. Farah, "Roots and Fruits," 12.

17. Ibid., 7.

18. Ibid., 15,6. The confusion had begun earlier with some of the Faith-Cure leaders.

19. Ibid., 10.

20. Thankfully, after a lapse of more than a decade, Farah's book has been reprinted and is now widely available again.

21. I was informed of this in a memo from Dr. Dale Simmons to me, 16 August 1995.

22. Kenneth E. Hagin, *Must Christians Suffer?* (Tulsa, Okla.: Rhema Bible Church, 1982). Compare Hagin's book with Smith Wigglesworth, *Faith That Prevails* (1938; reprint, Springfield, Mo.: Gospel Publishing House, 1966), 46.

23. Letter from Charles Farah to Geir Lie (undated); copy supplied to author by Mr. Lie.

24. Kenneth E. Hagin, "Suffering Unto Perfection: Part 3," *Word of Faith* (November 1995): 16

25. Hagin's worldwide ministry and influence have been astonishing. For a hint of the extent see the interview of the South African pastor, the Rev. Ray McCauley, "A Pastor Dares to Face Apartheid," *Charisma & Christian Life* (June 1988): 63-66.

Chapter 20
Mistaken Critique: The Work of D. R. McConnell

1. McConnell, *A Different Gospel*. The inspiration, as well as the title, for McConnell's work was supplied by Farah's "Roots and Fruits."

2. McConnell, *A Different Gospel*, 50.

3. Ibid., xii.

4. D. R. McConnell, "The Kenyon Connection: A Theological and Historical Analysis of the Cultic Origins of the Faith Movement" (master's thesis, Oral Roberts University, 1982).

5. Dave Hunt, *Beyond Seduction* (Eugene, Oreg.: Harvest House, 1987), 269, n. 21.

6. McConnell, *A Different Gospel*, 21.

7. Ibid., 18.

8. Ibid., chaps. 2 and 3.

9. Telephone conversation between author and Dale Simmons, 4 September 1995.

10. See the Riss article on Kenyon in the *Dictionary of Pentecostal and Charismatic Movements*. R. M. Riss had authored several scholarly works on revival, including his most recent *A Survey of Twentieth Century Revival Movements in North America* (Peabody, Mass.: Hendrickson, 1988).

11. McConnell, *A Different Gospel*, 105.

12. The distinction between Paul's theology and dualism is clarified in the wonderful book by the Christian scholar W. D. Davies, *Paul and Rabbinic Judaism: Some Rabbinic Elements in Pauline Theology* (New York: Harper & Row, 1967), especially chap. 2, "The Old Enemy: Flesh and Sin," 17-35.

13. McConnell, *A Different Gospel*, 107.

14. Frodsham, *Smith Wigglesworth*, 68.

15. This passage is cited in Montgomery, *Christian Theology,* 289. Montgomery is a Lutheran scholar and priest, a legal expert and one of the finest theologians of the charismatic renewal.

16. McConnell, *A Different Gospel*, 108-109.

17. Watchman Nee, *The Normal Christian Life*, 3d rev. ed. (Fort Washington, Pa.: Christian Literature Crusade, 1973).

18. E. W. Kenyon, "What Happened During the Three Days and Three Nights," chap. 9 in *What Happened From the Cross to the Throne* (Seattle, Wash.: Kenyon's Gospel Publishing Society, 1945).

19. McConnell, *A Different Gospel*, 128-129.

20. Hank Hanegraaff, "Atonement Atrocities," part 4 in *Christianity in Crisis* (Eugene, Oreg.: Harvest House, 1993).

21. The multiple atonement theories are well summarized in an article by the anticult writer James R. Spencer, "How Jesus Provides Hope" *Through the Maze* #9-95, (1995), and in his book, *Heresy Hunters: Character Assassination in the Church* (Lafayette, Ind.: Huntington House, 1993), 101-104.

22. The moral example theory, though biblical, can lead to heresy, as it does in modern liberal theology, unless it is taught in conjunction with one of the other theories of the atonement.

23. J. Paterson Smyth, *The Gospel of the Hereafter* (New York: Fleming H. Revell, 1910), 59.

24. Mary Rakow, "Christ's Descent into Hell: Calvin's Interpretation," *Religion in Life* 42 (summer 1974): 218-226.

25. Calvin, *Institutes,* b. 2, chap 16, sects. 8-12.

26. Ibid., sect. 8.

27. Ibid., sect. 10.

28. Ibid., sect. 11.

29. Henry C. Mabie, *The Divine Reason of the Cross* (New York: Fleming H. Revell, 1911).

30. Joe McIntyre, "E. W. Kenyon and His Critics" (Kirkland, Wash.: privately printed, 1995), 7.

31. For a good perspective on this change see John Warwick Montgomery, In *Defense of Martin Luther* (Milwaukee, Wisc.: Northeastern Publishing House, 1970), 142-157.

32. McConnell, *A Different Gospel,* 3-14.

33. For instance, Leon D. Stump, *Metaphysical Elements in the Faith Movement* (Joplin, Mo.: privately printed, 1987), 78-116. Interestingly, Stump is a Rhema graduate.

34. Vinson Synan, "The Faith of Kenneth Hagin," *Charisma & Christian Life,* (June 1990): 68.

35. Correspondence from Geir Lie to author, 22 August 1995.

36. I have been much critized for my apologetic stand on Hagin's plagiarism. See for example, James A. Beverley, *Holy Laughter and the Toronto Blessing: An Investigative Report* (Grand Rapids, Mich.: Zondervan, 1996), 62-63. After publishing the first edition of *Quenching the Spirit* I discovered an example of an earlier church leader who had unintentionally plagiarized. Elwood Worcester was the cofounder of the Emmanuel Movement, an influential healing movement of the 1920s and 1930s. He had a photographic memory for the data of his readings but not the source of his readings. As an honest scholar he was embarrassed by discovering that some of his writings were in fact plagiarized versions of his previous readings. (see Elwood Worcester, *Life's Adventure: The Story of a Varied Career* (New York: Charles Scribner's Sons, 1932), 2. Similarly, I discovered that a section of the first book I ever wrote was a plagiarism lifted unintentionally from one of Agnes Sanford's works, although I have a far from a photographic memory.

37. Pointed out by Dennis Hollinger in his "Enjoying God Forever: An Historical/Sociological Profile of the Health and Wealth Gospel," *Trinity Journal* 9 (fall 1988): 144.

38. Synan, "The Faith of Kenneth Hagin," 68.

39. For Hagin's description of how he came to his basic understanding of healing faith see Kenneth E. Hagin, *I Believe in Visions* (Old Tappan, N.J.: Fleming H. Revell, 1972), 9-40.

40. Hagin, *Visions.*

41. At this point I should recognize McConnell's critique of my discussion of his work in *Quenching the Spirit.* It is found in the "Afterword" in the revised edition of *A Different Gospel* (Peabody, Mass.: Hendrickson Publishers, 1995). As always McConnell's work was well thought out and well researched. It saddened me that McConnell took offense where no offense was intended, and I have amended certain phrases in this current edition to make my respect for his scholarship clearer.

I consider his analysis of Kenyon *mistaken.* I believe that McConnell's basic origins argument against Kenyon is a weak one and one *prone to those who are pharisaical.*

However, using the origins argument by no means makes McConnell a Pharisee. McConnell did not have an iota of meanness toward others or slander against the Holy Spirit in his text and is therefore disqualified as a Pharisee.

The Simmons and Lie scholarship (cited earlier) indicates that both McConnell and I erred, overestimating the Metaphysical content of Kenyon's theology and underestimating its Faith-Cure elements. I have sought to correct that in this edition. McConnell also believed I used the word *polemical* in a negative way, implying that as a Christian he should not have been polemical (*A Different Gospel*, 211ff). That is also an unwarranted interpretation of what I wrote. *Polemical* was intended as a descriptive attribute of his writings. I would apply the same word to my writing, which is polemical in the defense of the faith-idealism insights of the Faith-Cure movement, Kenyon and the charismatic renewal.

On a more fundamental issue McConnell critiques my use of Harold O. J. Brown's *Heresies.* He believes I misinterpreted Brown by claiming too strong a role for heresy in the formation of orthodoxy. Brown is clear that although orthodoxy is present in the Christian community before heresy, it is heresy that makes its first *public* appearance and forces the public discussion of orthodoxy (Brown, *Heresies,* 4-5). Further, my argument is not merely based on the Brown work but on the equally scholarly works by Leonard Verduin and Dom Odo Casel (see notes 5 and 7 to chapter 13). Both of these authors made a stronger case for the symbiotic relationship between heresy and orthodoxy than Brown made. Note also the fundamental structure of *Quenching the Spirit.* It showed that the orthodox Christian healers of the Faith-Cure movement were rejected by the Pharisees of the nineteenth century, and it was *then* that New Thought and the Metaphysical movement became more influential in America. This fits the Brown description perfectly.

McConnell asserts that I have "lambasted" dissenting charismatics such as himself (p. 201) and am trying to silence charismatic and Pentecostal dissent. I find that incomprehensible. Let the reader judge. The last part of McConnell's appendix forms a theological discourse on how I have negated the virtue of hope by an unbiblical expansion of the concept of faith and how I have accepted extremist views that healing and the miraculous will be total and complete in this world. I thus confuse the partial kingdom that is here with us now with the fulfilled kingdom that will arrive after the second coming. Significantly all of the citations and notes relate to other authors. I do not believe any reading of *Quenching the Spirit* confuses my position with McConnell's caricature of it.

Chapter 21
A Pharisee's Assault on the Charismatic Renewal: Dave Hunt

1. Dave Hunt and T. A. McMahon, *The Seduction of Christianity: Spiritual Discernment in the Last Days* (Eugene, Oreg.: Harvest House, 1985). Apparently McMahon was Hunt's research assistant, not a major contributor, since practically all opinions and ideas were foreshadowed in Hunt's earlier works.

2. "The 1980s: Trends, Triumphs, Tragedies, Transitions," *Charisma & Christian Life*, December 1989, 49.

3. Dave Hunt, *Peace, Prosperity and the Coming Holocaust* (Eugene, Oreg.: Harvest House, 1983).

4. Hunt, *Beyond Seduction.* Significantly, McMahon's name does not appear as co-author in *Beyond Seduction.*

5. For example, Robert Wise et al., *The Church Divided* (South Plainfield, N.J.: Bridge, 1986); Terry C. Muck, "Open Season," *Christianity Today* (21 November

1986): 16-17; and "Four Knowledgeable Looks at *The Seduction of Christianity*," *Ministries Today* (Summer 1986): 70-74.

6. The biographical information for this section is taken from Hunt's spiritual autobiography which was written in the late 1960s and which is unfortunately out of print: Dave Hunt, *On the Brink* (Plainfield, N.J.: Logos International, 1972). Note also a brief description of his strict Brethren upbringing in Dave Hunt, *The Seduction of Christianity*, 1 (Dallas: Christian Information Bureau, n.d.), audiocassette #TH501.

7. Hunt, *On the Brink*, 77.

8. Ibid., 20.

9. Ibid., 59.

10. Ibid., chaps. 22 and 23.

11. Ibid., 203-206.

12. Ibid., 208.

13. Ibid., 223.

14. For an excellent modern biography of Murray, see Leona Choy, *Andrew Murray: Apostle of Abiding Love* (Fort Washington, Pa.: Christian Literature Crusade, 1978).

15. William Law, *The Power of the Spirit*, ed. Dave Hunt (Fort Washington, Pa.: Christian Literature Crusade, 1971).

16. Ibid., 11-12.

17. Hunt, *Beyond Seduction*, 190-192.

18. Hunt and McMahon, *Seduction of Christianity*, 194, 216.

19. Ibid., 43.

20. Hunt, *Beyond Seduction*, 17.

21. Hunt and McMahon, *Seduction of Christianity*, 174-175.

22. Kevin N. Springer, "Applying the Gifts to Everyday Life," *Charisma & Christian Life* (September 1985): 26-34.

23. See Wagner, *Spiritual Power and Church Growth*. Power evangelism is not only for the Third World. American charismatic and Pentecostal churches are doing very well in contrast to mainline cessationist churches.

24. Hunt, *Beyond Seduction*, 78.

25. Hunt and McMahon, *Seduction of Christianity*, for example, 38.

26. Ibid., 21, 73.

27. Hunt, *Beyond Seduction*, 103.

28. Ibid., see especially chap. 3, 44-61.

29. Dave Hunt, *Coming Holocaust*, 245.

30. Kenneth E. Hagin, "Having Faith in Your Faith," *The Word of Faith* (September 1980): 2-3,10.

31. Hunt and McMahon, *Seduction of Christianity*, 90.

32. Kenneth E. Hagin, *Plead Your Case* (Tulsa, Okla.: Faith Library Publications, 1979).

33. The critique of spiritual laws is found in Hunt and McMahon, *Seduction of Christianity*, 97-103; and Hunt, *Beyond Seduction*, chap. 3.

34. It is significant that in the seventeenth century Lutheran theologians accused the Calvinists of having Islamic tendencies. See Brown, *Heresies*, 372.

35. Hunt and McMahon, *Seduction of Christianity*, 103.

36. Ibid., chap. 10, 137ff.

37. Ibid., 160,163,172-173

38. Let me challenge the reader to acquire Mrs. Sanford's classic book *The Healing Light* (St. Paul, Minn.: Macalester Park, 1947) and test to see if the visualizations suggested by her pass the criteria developed by Brooks Alexander for valid Christian prayer-visualizations (chap. 17).

39. Hunt and McMahon, *Seduction of Christianity*, chaps. 1 and 2.

40. Paul [David] Yonggi Cho, *The Fourth Dimension: Volume Two* (South Plainfield, N.J.: Bridge, 1983).

41. Hunt and McMahon, *Seduction of Christianity*, 16.

42. Brooks Alexander, "Idol/Image/Imagination," *SCP Journal* 9, no. 3 (1990): 18.

43. Ibid., 20.

44. Hunt, *Beyond Seduction*, 223.

45. Hunt's pharisaical definition of prayer has been noted before; see Bob Passantino and Gretchen Passantino, *Witch Hunt* (Nashville: Thomas Nelson, 1990), 92.

46. Dave Hunt, *Global Peace and the Rise of the Antichrist* (Eugene, Oreg.: Harvest House, 1990), 276-278.

47. Schaeffer, *The God Who Is There*, note to sect. 2, chap. 2, p. 182.

48. In this severe reproof of Hunt's views we have not used the Pharisees' origins argument. Our disagreement with Hunt's theology and techniques of argumentation are not *because* of their historical roots. Rather, in pointing out the continuity with Darby's theology we are saying that *both* Darby's and Hunt's approaches are wrong from their fundamental assumptions. Had Hunt started from Darby and taken from his theology what was useful and wise and avoided what was harmful and exaggerated and gone on to new insights, we would be celebrating him instead.

49. For a clear description of Böhme's confusing system, see A. Keith Walker, "Jakob Böhme," chap. 10 in *William Law: His Life and Thought* (London: Society for Promoting Christian Knowledge, 1973). Walker's book gives an excellent evaluation of Böhme's influence on William Law.

50. Law, *The Power of the Spirit*, 7-14; and Dave Hunt, "A Serious Call Re-Echoed," *Christian Life* (May 1986): 48-50.

51. In an ironic turn of events, Dave Hunt has complained in a recent newsletter that a certain Canadian couple have taken it upon themselves to travel about the United States and warn evangelical churches that Hunt's writings are infected with heresy. They say Hunt has been influenced by the Böhme-inspired heresies of William Law. Truly this proves that the spiritual law of tit-for-tat works. See the *CIB Bulletin* (January 1992), 4.

Chapter 22
The Tragedy of Hank Hanegraaff and the CRI

1. James Spencer, *Heresy Hunters: Character Assassination in the Church* (Lafayette, La.: Huntington House Publishers, 1993).

2. "Through the Maze" Ministries, P.O. Box 9017, Boise, ID 83707.

3. Spencer, *Heresy Hunters*, 17.

4. The biblical office of *episkopos* is cited in Acts 20:28, Philippians 1:1 and 1 Peter 5:2. The King James version translates it as "bishop," while the New International Version uses the term *overseer*. It means "one in authority."

5. John Lawson, *The Biblical Theology of Saint Irenaeus* (London: The Epworth Press, 1948).

6. There are, of course, some bishops throughout the mainline denominations fighting against heresy. They have been mostly outmaneuvered. Interestingly, a new denomination, the Charismatic Episcopal Church, founded by Pentecostal ministers who were attracted to the *Book of Common Prayer* (but repelled by liberal Episcopal theology), has consciously resurrected the biblical function of bishop as apologist and defender of orthodoxy. Its monthly newsletter, *Sursum Corda,* recently featured two articles on the subject: "House of Bishops to Be House of Prayer," (December 1994), and "Earnestly Contend for the Faith," Ken Turner (October 1994). The newsletter is available through the Charismatic Episcopal Church, 107 West Marquita, San Clemente, CA 92672.

7. On the tragic story of the effects of liberalism in the seminaries, see the recent book by Thomas C. Oden, *Requiem: A Lament in Three Movements* (Nashville: Abingdon Press, 1995). There are, of course, a minority of biblically faithful seminaries.

8. A good history of the anticult ministries is sorely needed. The recent newsletter "Through the Maze," gave a brief sketch of their history in an article by James Spencer, "Why We Need Pop-Apologists," *Update* (95#8): 1-4.

9. Robert M. Bowman, Jr., *Orthodoxy and Heresy* (Grand Rapids, Mich.: Baker Book House, 1992). An anticult ministry that attempts to understand the transdenominational dimension of orthodoxy is the Watchman Fellowship, based in Birmingham, Alabama.

10. For a good popular presentation of Knox as a flawed but effective Reformer, see "John Knox: The Thundering Scot," *Christian History* 14 (1995).

11. This point is repeated in Spencer's new book: James R. Spencer, *Bleeding Hearts and Propaganda: The Fall of Reason in the Church* (Lafayette, La.: Huntington House, 1995).

12. Besides a seminary degree, Dr. Martin had advanced degrees from New York University and California Western University.

13. *Bible Answer Man* (radio program), 10 March 1995 (hereafter cited as *BAM*).

14. On the issue of anti-intellectualism among evangelicals see Mark A. Noll, *The Scandal of the Evangelical Mind* (Grand Rapids, Mich.: William B. Eerdmans, 1994), and Og Guinness, *Fit Bodies, Fat Minds* (Grand Rapids, Mich.: Baker Books, 1994).

15. The series on Catholicism began with the winter 1993 article by Kenneth Samples, "What Think Ye of Rome?" in *Christian Research Journal.* In the October 12 and 13 broadcasts of the *BAM.* Hanegraaff hosted a debate between a Roman Catholic and a Protestant evangelical. The Catholic scholar, James Aiken, seemed to have come out better in the debate, further infuriating Hanegraaff's conservative evangelical listeners!

16. Bob and Gretchen Passantino, "Psychology and the Church," parts 1, 2 and 3, *Christian Research Journal* (winter/spring/summer 1995).

17. James R. White, *The King James Only Controversy* (Minneapolis: Bethany House, 1995). White was interviewed on the *BAM,* 16-18 August 1995.

18. Doug LeBlanc, "The Worldwide Church of God: Resurrected into Orthodoxy," *Christian Research Journal* (winter 1996): 6-7,44-45.

19. Marilyn Hickey, whose teachings are generally excellent, has recently taught that while Jesus hung on the cross, every disease of humanity appeared on His body. Certainly the evangelists, and especially Luke the physician, would have recorded such an unusual phenomenon. The pious intention of proclaiming the power of Jesus' "stripes" to enable healing is thus made somewhat ridiculous by this unreproved hypothesis.

20. Walter Martin, "You Shall Be as Gods," in *The Agony of Deceit*, ed. Michael Horton (Chicago: Moody Press, 1990).

21. Hanegraaff, *Crisis*. To my knowledge the best critique of this work is found in Spencer, *Heresy Hunters*, and Spencer, *Bleeding Hearts and Propaganda*, chap. 11.

22. Raised in the dogmatic certainty of the 1950s, I recall (and have repented of) one instance in which I persuaded my father not to listen to a Billy Graham sermon because the man was a "heretic."

23. William L. DeArteaga, *Martin Luther: The Jerk!* (New York: Burnheretics Press, 1997). Gotcha! Well, this citation looks scholarly, doesn't it?

24. Some Christians may question my use of James, an unbeliever, as a source. I would cite the Passantino's fine articles on the Christian use of secular wisdom which appeared in the recent issues of *Christian Research Journal* (see note 16 above).

25. Various editions of this work are available to the modern reader. The book was delivered originally as the Gifford Lectures in 1901-1902.

26. James, "The Value of Saintlyness," lectures 14 and 15 in *Varieties*.

27. Hanegraaff, *Crisis*, chaps. 13-16.

28. Hank Hanegraaff, "A Summary Critique," *Christian Research Journal* (fall 1992): 38.

29. Hanegraaff, *Crisis*, 165.

30. Ibid., 119.

31. The information on the rabbinical exaltation of Adam and the influence of this literature on Paul is taken from this masterful work: W. D. Davies, *Paul and Rabbinic Judaism: Some Rabbinic Elements in Pauline Theology* (New York: Harper and Row, 1967), chap. 3, especially 44ff.

32. *BAM* 6 October 1992. This section on Hanegraaff versus Copeland is taken from Spencer's detailed analysis found in his *Bleeding Hearts*, chapter 11.

33. Hanegraaff, *Crisis*, 137-139. The sections in *Christianity in Crisis*, and the earlier article in *Christian Research Journal* on Copeland were ghostwritten for Hanegraaff by CRI staffer Erwin de Castro according to pages 8-9 in a letter from Robert Bowman to CRI Board, 1 June 1994. A copy of his letter and other pertinent documents can be received from: Robert Bowman, P.O. Box 450068, Atlanta, GA 31145. Hanegraaff may not have reviewed the Copeland tape upon which the distorted accusations are made, but he is responsible for what appeared under his name.

34. Kenneth Copeland, *The Incarnation* (Fort Worth: Kenneth Copeland Ministries, n.d.), audiocassette #01-0402, cited in Spencer, *Bleeding Hearts*, 180.

35. This refers to the major ministries. Countless local preachers can be found to teach heresy within any tradition.

36. James Beverley, "Toronto's Mixed Blessing," *Christianity Today* (11 September 1995): 24-25. I noticed that in the Rodney Howard-Browne revival I witnessed (Gatlinburg, Tennessee, July 1995), hundreds came forward for salvation and rededication.

37. For an insider's history of the revival at the Toronto Airport Christian Fellowship see Guy Chevreau, *Catch the Fire* (London: Marshall Pickering, 1994) and John Arnott, *The Father's Blessing* (Lake Mary, Fla.: Creation House, 1995).

38. Vineyard churches consciously avoid traditional church buildings and often set up in a rented warehouse or office building. In these unobstructed areas there is room to set up folding chairs (which can be quickly removed at "ministry time") and a large band area for their lively contemporary music.

39. Compare the beginnings of this revival in England as reported in Clive Price, "British Cautiously Embrace Renewal" *Charisma & Christian Life* (April 1995): 58-59, with the report of less than a year later, Clive Price, "A Revival Without Walls," *Charisma & Christian Life* (November 1995): 54-58.

40. Beverley, "Mixed," 24.

41. Lawrence J. Berber, "How I Was Blessed," *Christianity Today* (11 September 1995): 26.

42. Hanegraaff has avoided claiming that the Laughing Revival is demonic; rather, he claims it opens the public to the demonic (*BAM*, 30 November 1994.)

43. Hank Hanegraaff, "The Counterfeit Revival" (San Juan Capistrano: CRI International, 1995), audiocassette C-179. Hanegraaff is currently expanding this talk into a book by the same name which he anticipates to be on the market in early 1996. A superb rebuttal to Hanegraaff's attack on the Laughing Revival is Don Williams, *Revival: The Real Thing* (La Jolla, Calif.: privately printed, 1995). Available by writing Don Williams, P.O. Box 1302, La Jolla, CA 92038.

44. For example, *BAM* of 5, 15, 21 October and 29, 30 November 1994; and 26 May, 1995.

45. *BAM*, 1 September 1994.

46. *BAM*, 22 August 1995.

47. Can the "analogous" hermeneutic be mistaken or misleading? Yes. On the other hand it was through analogy with experience that turn-of-the-century Christians discovered a theology for the gift of tongues!

48. James A. Beverley has an excellent and evenhanded presentation of the interpretations of this verse in his *Holy Laughter,* 90-91.

49. This point is well documented in Williams, *Revival,* 27-34. We have pointed to various manifestations ("exercises") associated with revivals in chapters 2 and 3.

50. *BAM*, 29 November 1995 and other dates.

51. *BAM*, 4 May 1995. Hanegraaff's erroneous point is elaborated in an article by another anticult researcher: Byron Koch, "The Force — or Pumped, Scooped, Charged and Slain: Thoughts on the Theology of the 'Toronto Blessing'," *SCP Newsletter* (spring 1995): 1-13.

52. One reason why the writings of Agnes Sanford have been labeled cultic by Dave Hunt and others is because she had a keen understanding of God's *energies* as a healing source. It is the central motif of her pioneer book, *The Healing Light.*

53. *BAM,* 9 March 1995.

54. See this point covered extensively in John Arnott, *The Father's Blessing* (Lake Mary, Fla.: Creation House, 1995).

55. *BAM,* 23 June 1995. I must be clear and express my appreciation of both the *Christian Research Journal* and the *Bible Answer Man* program. My disagreement with them is limited to specific issues, and my criticism of Hanegraaff and Miller is not a general slam to the *Bible Answer Man.*

56. About July 1994. This broadcast took place before I had begun taking careful notes from the *Bible Answer Man.*

57. Christianity Today, Inc. has access to the best evangelical thinkers in practically any field. They publish *Christian History, Leadership, Books and Culture, Campus Life, Christian Reader, Marriage Partnership, Today's Christian Woman, Your Church* as well as *hristianity Today.*

58. "Camp Meetings and Circuit Riders," *Christian History* 45 (winter 1995). Thankfully, now reprinted and available by writing: *Christian History,* Past Issue Series, P.O. Box 550-A, Chestertown, MD 21690.

59. *BAM,* 28 December 1994.

60. James Beverley, *Holy Laughter and the Toronto Blessing: An Investigative Report* (Grand Rapids, Mich.: Zondervan, 1996).

61. Beverley, "Mixed," 24. In both article and book, Dr. Beverley cites me as calling all who oppose the Toronto Blessing "Pharisees." This is incorrect. The original edition of *Quenching the Spirit* came out before the revival broke out. In October 1994 I spoke at the Toronto Airport Vineyard's Catch the Fire conference, urging the ministers and lay leaders to avoid judging their critics as Pharisees. I pointed out that all new revivals have areas of immaturity, and the criticisms of some critics may indeed be correct (*What is Heresy?* 13 October 1994, tape or video available from the Toronto Airport Christian Fellowship). Dr. Beverley has demonstrated this very point — giving strong reproof that is certainly not Pharisaical. Dr. Beverley and I have communicated in a positive and Christian manner, and he will correct the next printing of *Holy Laughter.*

62. Beverley, "Mixed," 24-25.

63. Ibid., 27.

64. Ibid., 25-26.

65. Richard Lovelace, "The Surprising Works of God," *Christianity Today* (11 September 1995), 28-32.

66. Ibid., 32.

Chapter 23
The Renewal of the Spirit as "Messy" Revivals

1. See the excellent coverage of this television episode in *Charisma & Christian Life* (February 1992): 26-34.

2. Edwards, *The Distinguishing Marks* in Goen, *The Great Awakening*, 241, 244. See sections 6-8 of *The Distinguishing Marks* on the failure of revival leadership.

3. Ibid., 248.

4. Ibid., 249ff.

5. The exception was the controversies concerning Kenyon's speculations about Jesus' descent into Sheol, discussed in chapter 20. Note that even Kenyon's wrong-headed speculation does not in any way detract from the deity of Jesus or of His ultimate atoning work.

6. Edwards, *The Distinguishing Marks* in Goen, *The Great Awakening*, 250.

7. See, for example, Henry Ansgar Kelly, *The Devil, Demonology and Witchcraft: The Development of Christian Belief in Evil Spirits* (Garden City, N.Y.: Doubleday & Co., 1974).

8. We touched on this issue in James Buckley's dismissal of the pioneer discoveries of possession and exorcism by the missionary John Nevius (see chapter 10).

9. The problems of an immature and overzealous deliverance ministry are described in John Sandford, *A Sensible View of Exorcism* (Post Falls, Idaho: Elijah House, n.d.), audiocassette. For examples of the current literature on exorcism and spiritual warfare, see Matthew Linn and Dennis Linn, *Deliverance Prayer: Experiential, Psychological and Theological Approaches* (New York: Paulist Press, 1981); and C. Peter Wagner and F. Douglas Pennoyer, *Wrestling With Dark Angels: Toward a Deeper Un-*

derstanding of the Supernatural Forces in Spiritual Warfare (Ventura, Calif.: Regal Books, 1990).

10. We would note that Farah's critique, examined in chapter 19, although centered on healing abuses also criticized the prosperity doctrine.

11. Richard Foster, *Money, Sex and Power* (San Francisco: Harper & Row, 1985).

12. Kenneth Copeland, "The Purpose of Prosperity," *Charisma & Christian Life* (September 1990): 138-140.

13. Edwards, *The Distinguishing Marks*, in Goen, *The Great Awakening*, 253.

14. Marvin R. Wilson, *Our Father Abraham: Jewish Roots of the Christian Faith* (Grand Rapids, Mich.: William B. Eerdmans, 1989); and Terrance Callan, *Forgetting the Root: The Emergence of Christianity from Judaism* (New York: Paulist Press, 1986).

15. Even other Jewish feasts are getting attention from many Christian churches. See, for example, Mitch Glaser and Zhava Glaser, *The Fall Feasts of Israel* (Chicago: Moody Press, 1987).

16. Edwards, *The Distinguishing Marks*, in Goen, *The Great Awakening*, 254.

17. Ibid., 253.

18. Lovelace, *Dynamics of Spiritual Life*.

19. For example, churches in South Africa that are affiliated with Kenneth Hagin have made major inroads against apartheid. See Irving Hexham and Karla Poewe-Hexham, "Charismatics and Apartheid," *Charisma & Christian Life* (May 1990): 62-70.

20. Paul Thigpen, "What's the Fuss About 'Kingdom Now'?" *Ministries Today* (July/August 1988): 33-39. Earl Paulk has drawn the criticism of some mainline theologians because of his strong stand against liberation theology.

21. For example Francis Frangipane, Holiness, Truth and the Presence of God (Marion, Iowa.: Advancing Church, 1986), and John Wimber's quarterly magazine, *Equipping the Saints* (Winter 1990). See especially Wimber's lead article "Freed to Be Holy," pp. 4-7.

22. John Dawson, *Taking Our Cities for God* (Lake Mary, Fla.: Creation House, 1989); and George Otis Jr., *The Last of the Giants* (Tarrytown, N.Y.: Fleming H. Revell, Chosen Books, 1991).

Chapter 24
An Evaluation of Modern Pharisaism

1. Bob Passantino and Gretchen Passantino, *Witch Hunt* (Nashville: Thomas Nelson, 1990).

2. Ibid., 124.

3. Stafford, "Cult Watchers," 18-23.

4. John F. MacArthur Jr., *Charismatic Chaos* (Grand Rapids, Mich.: Zondervan Publishing House, 1992).

5. John F. MacArthur Jr., *The Charismatics: A Doctrinal Perspective* (Grand Rapids, Mich.: Zondervan Publishing House, 1978).

6. Millard J. Erickson, "Lordship Theology: The Current Controversy," *Southwestern Journal of Theology* 33, (spring 1991): 5-15; and Darrell L. Bock, review of *The Gospel According to Jesus*, by John F. MacArthur Jr., *Bibliotheca Sacra* 146 (January-March 1989): 20-23.

7. Erickson, "Lordship Theology," 13.

8. MacArthur, *Charismatic Chaos*, 31.

9. Ibid., 24.

10. Ibid., 163-165.

11. Ibid., 32.

12. Ibid., 109.

13. Ibid.,114ff.

14. Ibid., chap. 9, especially 201-203.

15. Buckley, *Other Superstitions,* 45-46.

16. Dorothy Kern, *The Living Touch* (London: Courier, 1914).

17. David Lewis, *Healing: Fiction, Fantasy or Fact?* (London: Hodder & Stoughton, 1989).

18. MacArthur, *Charismatic Chaos*, 194ff. Note that it was Freeman's ministry which triggered Charles Farah's reproof of faith theology (see chapter 19).

19. Ibid., 37-39.

20. Ibid., 112

21. Ibid., 130.

22. Ibid., chap. 6, 128-151.

23. Wimber with Springer, *Power Evangelism,* 47.

24. Richard V. Pierard, "Anti-Jewish Sentiments in an Unexpected Content: Evangelical Bible Expositor John MacArthur," *The Covenant Quarterly* 45 (November 1987): 182.

25. See "Hauled to Court," *Leadership* 6 (winter 1985): 127-138; and "The Nation's First 'Clergy Malpractice' Suit Goes to Trial Late This Month," *Christianity Today* (19 April 1985): 60-61.

26. MacArthur, *Charismatic Chaos*, 98-99.

27. John MacArthur, *Reckless Faith: When the Church Loses Its Will to Discern* (Wheaton, Ill.: Crossway Books, 1994) contains a long section (pp. 160-175) rebutting *Quencing the Spirit.* Its central assertion is an incredible interpretive inversion. MacArthur claims I asserted that Edwards was an Arminian and Charles Chauncy a Calvinist. Although I affirmed that Chauncy was dependent on Calvin for his theology of cessationism, nowhere did I even imply Edwards was Arminian. The reader may well satisfy himself on how ridiculous MacArthur's assertion is by reading pp. 30, 32 and 41 of the first edition. In this revised edition I made word changes to assure that no such interpretation is even remotely possible. The most unfortunate aspect of MacArthur's wild misinterpretation is that Hank Hanegraaff picked it up and broadcast it as true on his *Bible Answer Man* program (21 April and 11 May 1995).

28. *CIB Bulletin* (September 1987): 2.

29. It is significant that D. R. McConnell has refused to write a sequel to *A Different Gospel*, a sign that he did not cross the line into Pharisaism.

30. Dave Hunt, "Serious Call," 48-50.

31. A. W. Tozer, *Tragedy in the Church: The Missing Gifts* (Harrisburg, Pa.: Christian Publications, 1978).

32. See, for instance, how A. W. Tozer admires and quotes St. Teresa of Avila, the greatest of Catholic mystics in *Tragedy in the Church,* 87.

GLOSSARY

Anabaptist movement. A movement of the Reformation, radical for its time, which advocated adult baptism and the separation of church and state. Some Anabaptists set up communistic communities and fell into sexual immorality.

Analogous evidence, Analogy. The manner of learning in which an idea is learned by comparison with an idea or experience that is already known.

Arminianism. A form of Protestant theology which rebelled against Calvin's theory of predestination and affirmed that man could "appropriate" the grace of salvation.

Asceticism. A way of life which stresses poverty and the denial or restriction of bodily desires as a way to holiness.

Biblical Orthodoxy. Those doctrines which accurately reflect biblical doctrine (which may not be *perfectly* known this side of heaven).

Bollandists. A group of Catholic (Jesuit) priests and scholars who attempted to separate legend from fact in the lives of the saints.

Calvinism. The theological system developed by John Calvin (1505–1564), who was the first great systematic theologian of the Reformation. His theology stressed man's predestination and salvation by faith alone.

Cessationism. The belief that miracles occurred only in biblical times and that after the death of the last apostle God's special grace for healing and the miraculous was withdrawn.

Charismatic renewal. A movement of the Holy Spirit, dating from 1960, in which many believers in the mainline churches, including the Catholic church, began to manifest the gifts of the Spirit.

Christian Science. The major Gnostic and radical idealist cult. Founded by Mary Baker Eddy in the 1870s, its doctrines include the belief that matter is an illusion.

Complementarity. A concept in physics used to describe how certain phenomena can have different manifestations, as in light appearing as either a wave or particle.

Congregational church. These churches established the theology (Calvinism) and governing pattern for the churches in New England. In congregational churches the power to retain or dismiss a pastor lay with the individual congregation.

Consensus orthodoxy. A term used to refer to the theological interpretations accepted by the majority of religious people during a given time period.

Corresponding action. An action taken in faith which indicates that a healing or a miraculous event has taken place before there is direct evidence of the miracle.

Deism. A religious belief which says God created the universe and set it in motion but is not directly involved in its continuous operation.

Demonization. A term that covers both direct demonic activity on individuals and groups (as in demonic possession) and the tendency of ideas and institutions to become extreme and harmful in spite of their original good intentions.

Demythologizing. A form of biblical interpretation, based on philosophical materialism, which denies the possibility of miracles either in biblical times or in the current age.

Discernment (spiritual). The graced ability to understand an idea or phenomenon in terms of its relationship with either the kingdom of God or the demonic realm.

Dispensationalism. A system of biblical interpretation which divides human history into distinct periods. It has most often been used to deny the possibility of miracles in the "current dispensation."

Doceticism. An early form of Gnosticism which asserts that Jesus appeared on earth as an apparition. Therefore, His blood atonement was a dreamlike illusion.

Dualism. A philosophical and religious view which believes that the universe is divided between good and evil, with matter being inherently evil.

Enlightenment. A philosophical movement (1688 – 1789) which sought to counter "superstition" and "revealed religion" with reason and science. Enlightenment philosophers established the goals of what today is called "secular humanism."

Evangelicals. Christians who emphasize the importance of spreading the gospel and bringing people to an opportunity to choose salvation.

Faculties psychology. The system of psychology developed during the Middle Ages which stressed the ruling power of the will to regulate and direct the mind.

Faith-Cure movement. The first sustained healing revival of modern Christendom which occurred in the late nineteenth century among American evangelicals. The father of the Faith-Cure movement was Charles Cullis, a homeopathic physician from Boston.

Faith-doctrine. That component of biblical faith which focuses on the essential doctrines of biblical truth, such as the resurrection of Jesus Christ.

Faith-expectancy. That component of biblical faith which focuses on God's power to meet the specific needs of the believer, especially in response to prayer.

Faith-idealism. An understanding of Scripture in which the believer may anticipate the fulfilling of a promise of God for which there is no sensory evidence.

Fencing. The practice of devising overly restrictive rules in order to keep people away from the possibility of sinning.

Fundamentalism. A form of Protestant evangelicalism that arose to counter various forms of skepticism about the veracity of the Bible. It is now associated with the literal interpretation of the biblical text.

Galatian bewitchment. The recurring and false belief that the gifts of the Holy Spirit are earned by ascetical practices or special codes of holiness.

Gnosticism. One of the primary heresies of the Bible. In its many forms it always affirms the importance of direct revelation and personal experiences over the truth of Scripture. It also asserts that special knowledge is the key to salvation.

Hermeneutic. Any system of biblical interpretation that has its own rules and philosophical assumptions.

Holiness movement. A movement started among Protestants in the 1860s which produced outbursts of the gifts of the Spirit and emphasized a strict code of morals. Most of the early Pentecostal leaders came from this tradition.

Iconoclast. A person who opposes devotion toward paintings, statues or icons in worship as forbidden by the Old Testament injunction against images.

Idealism. The philosophical position that mind and matter interact, with mind having some influence over matter. It is the opposite of philosophical realism.

Karma. An Eastern doctrine, imported into Western occultism, which maintains that moral acts of one life are returned in kind in another incarnation.

Materialism. A philosophy which affirms that the material world seen by the five senses is the fullness of the universe and that the spiritual realm does not exist or is not significant.

Metaphysical movement. A philosophical and religious movement that began in the nineteenth century which combined philosophical idealism with Eastern and biblical religious doctrines.

Mind-Cure movement. A part of the Metaphysical movement, Mind-Cure centered on using the powers of the mind for healing. The Christian Science cult, founded by Mary Baker Eddy, is the best known of the Mind-Cure sects.

Natural theology. Those ideas about God and the moral order that can be discovered by most persons without the aid of biblical revelation.

New Thought. A development of the Metaphysical movement which stressed the doctrine of prosperity and healing and which moved away from the authoritarian dogmatism of Christian Science.

Origins fallacy. The belief that an idea can be discredited if its originating source is unorthodox.

Orthodoxy. See **Biblical Orthodoxy** and **Consensus Orthodoxy.**

Pentecostalism. A revival movement of Christianity, dating from 1900, which affirmed the present-day manifestations of the gifts of the Spirit as normative to Christians.

Perfectionist movement. Based on the teachings of Charles Finney, this movement sought a deeper understanding and higher standards of Christian life than that to which evangelicals had been accustomed. It produced the most sophisticated theology of the Holy Spirit of the era.

Pharisaism. A religious attitude and heresy that so affirms the role of tradition that a new move of the Holy Spirit is often identified as demonic.

Premillenialism. The theory that the second coming of Christ occurs before the thousand-year reign of Christ and that the rapture of the church occurs before the tribulation.

Protestantism. Those Christians who derive their theological legacy from the Reformation. Historically, Protestants rejected the sacramental system and authoritarian structure of Roman Catholicism.

Realism. The opposite of idealism, realism is the philosophical view that mind has no direct influence on matter. Realism is often associated with materialism.

Scottish common sense realism. A form of realist philosophy that originated in Scotland and eventually became the philosophical base of evangelical theology.

Spiritual law. The term given to the relationship between moral acts and attitudes and their consequences on earth.

Stoicism. A religious philosophy popular among pagans in New Testament times which stressed the fatherhood of God and a gracious acceptance of fate.

Swedenborgism. A religion established by the Swedish scientist Emanuel Swedenborg. Based on trance revelations, it gave detailed "revelations" about life in the solar system, views of heaven and hell, and a demonized variety of spiritual laws.

Syncretism. A term used to denote a philosophical or religious system that is made up of incompatible elements.

Talmud. A body of rabbinical commentaries on the Bible that has acquired special authority among pious Jews.

Tit-for-tat. The biblical principle that an individual's moral actions will incur consequences in this world as well as after death. The term was first used in rabbinical commentaries.

Torah. The name given to the first five books of the Bible where the Old Testament law is revealed. The word also signifies the law of God as revealed in Scripture.

Transcendentalism. A nineteenth-century philosophical movement which introduced philosophical idealism and concepts from Eastern religions into America.

Unitarianism. A deist cult that developed in America. Unitarians denied the divinity of Jesus and the Holy Spirit and quickly slid into universalism and other forms of theological liberalism.

Unity Christianity. A New Thought group established by Charles Fillmore at the turn of the century which had several unbiblical doctrines but which contained some truths.

Visualization. The use of the imagination in forming mental images of those things or events one desires.

BIBLIOGRAPHY

(Those books marked by an * have been particularly
important in the writing of this work.)

Ahlstrom, Sydney E. "The Scottish Philosophy and American Theology."
Church History 24 (September 1955): 257-272.

* Albrecht, Daniel E. "Carrie Judd Montgomery: Pioneering Contributor to
Three Religious Movements." *Pneuma* 8 (fall 1986): 101-119.

* Alexander, Brooks. "Idol/Image/Imagination." *SCP Journal* 9, no. 3 (1990):
18.

* ———. "Mind Power and the Mind's Eye." *SCP Journal* 9, no. 3 (1990):
8-20.

Allen, Ethan O. *Faith Healing: Or, What I Have Witnessed of the Fulfilling
of James 5: 14, 15, 16.* Philadelphia: G. W. McCall, 1881.

Allyn, Russell C. *Voices of American Fundamentalism.* Philadelphia: Westminster Press, 1976.

———. "Adoniram Judson Gordon: Nineteenth-Century Fundamentalist."
American Baptist Quarterly 4 (March 1985): 61-89.

Arnott, John. *The Father's Blessing.* Lake Mary, Fla.: Creation House,
1995.

Ash, James L., Jr. "American Religion and the Academy in the Early Twentieth Century: The Chicago Years of William Warren Sweet." *Church
History* 50 (December 1981): 450-464.

* ———. "The Decline of Ecstatic Prophecy in the Early Church." *Theological Studies* 37 (June 1976): 227-252.

Athanasius. *Life of St. Anthony the Great.* N.d; Reprint, Willits, Calif.:
Eastern Orthodox Press, n.d.

Augustine. *On the True Religion.*

———. *The Advantage of Believing the Fathers of the Church.* Translated
by Luanne Meagher. New York: Cima Publishing, 1947.

* ———. *The City of God.* In *The Fathers of the Church*, vol. 24. Translated
by Gerald G. Walsh. Washington D.C.: Catholic University of America
Press, 1968.

———. *The Lord's Sermon on the Mount.*

———. *The Retractions,* In *The Fathers of the Church*, vol. 60, bk. 1,
translated by Sister Mary Inez. Washington D.C.: Catholic University of
America Press, 1968.

Bass, Clarence B. *Backgrounds to Dispensationalism.* Grand Rapids,
Mich.: William B. Eerdmans, 1960.

Belloc, Hilaire. *The Great Heresies*. London: The Catholic Book Club, n.d.

Bentley, Philip J. "Uncertainty and Unity." *Journal of Judaism* 33 (spring 1984): 191-201.

Berber, Lawrence J. "How I Was Blessed." *Christianity Today* (11 September 1995): 26.

Beven, Eswyn. *Holy Images: An Inquiry into Idolatry and Image-Worship in Ancient Paganism and in Christianity*. London: George Allen & Unwin, 1940.

* Beverley, James A. *Holy Laughter and the Toronto Blessing: An Investigative Report*. Grand Rapids, Mich.: Zondervan, 1996.

———. "Toronto's Mixed Blessing." *Christianity Today* (11 September 1995): 24-25.

Boardman, W. E. *Faith Work Under Dr. Cullis in Boston*. Boston: Willard Tract Repository, 1874.

Bock, Darrell L. Review of *The Gospel According to Jesus*, by John F. MacArthur Jr. *Bibliotheca Sacra* 146 (January-March 1989).

Bonaventura, Saint. *Meditations on the Life of Christ*. Translated by Isa Ragusa and Rosalie B. Green. Princeton, N.J.: Princeton University Press, 1961.

Bosworth, F. F. *Christ the Healer*. 1924. Reprint, Old Tappan, N.J.: Fleming H. Revell, 1973.

* Bowker, John. *Jesus and the Pharisees*. Cambridge, England: Cambridge University Press, 1973.

* Bowman, Robert M., Jr. *Orthodoxy and Heresy*. Grand Rapids, Mich.: Baker Book House, 1992.

Bozeman, Theodore Dwight. *Protestants in an Age of Science: The Baconian Ideal and Antebellum American Religious Thought*. Chapel Hill, N.C.: University of North Carolina Press, 1977.

Braden, Charles S. *Spirits in Rebellion: The Rise and Development of New Thought*. Dallas: Southern Methodist University Press, 1963.

Bradley, James E. "Miracles and Martyrdom in the Early Church: Some Theological and Ethical Implications." *Pneuma* 13, no. 1 (spring 1991): 65-81.

Brauer, Jerald C. *Protestantism in America: A Narrative History*. Rev. ed. London: SCM Press, 1966.

* Brown, Harold O. J. *Heresies: The Image of Christ in the Mirror of Heresy and Orthodoxy From the Apostles to the Present*. Garden City, N.Y.: Doubleday & Co., 1984.

* Buckley, James M. *Christian Science and Other Superstitions*. New York: The Century Co., 1899.

———. *Constitutional and Parliamentary History of the Methodist Episcopal Church*. New York: The Methodist Book Concern, 1914.

———. *Faith-Healing, Christian Science, and Kindred Phenomenon*. New York: The Century Co., 1892. 1st ed., 1886.

————. *The Fundamentals and Their Contrasts*. Nashville: Publisning House of the Methodist Episcopal Church, 1906.

————. "Editorial: Primitive Traits in Religious Revivals," parts 1 and 2 *The Christian Advocate* (9 August 1906/16 August 1906).

Bultmann, Rudolf. "A Reply to the Thesis of J. Schniewind." In *Kerygma and Myth: A Theological Debate*. Edited by Hans Werner Bartsch. Translated by R. H. Fuller. London: Society for Promoting Christian Knowledge, 1957.

Burns, R. M. *The Great Debate on Miracles: From Joseph Glanwell to David Hume*. London: Associated University Press, 1981.

Callan, Terrance. *Forgetting the Root: The Emergence of Christianity from Judaism*. New York: Paulist Press, 1986.

Calvin, *Institutes*.

"The Canon: How God Gave His Word to the Church." *Christianity Today*. (5 February 1988): 23-26.

Capra, Fritjof. *The Tao of Physics*. Boulder, Colo.: Shambhala Publications, 1975 (marketed as a paperback by Bantam Books).

* Carter, R. Kelso. *"Faith Healing" Reviewed After Twenty Years*. Boston: The Christian Witness Co., 1897; New York: Garland, 1985.

Casel, Dom Odo. *The Mystery of Christian Worship and Other Writings*. Edited by Berkhard Neunheuser. Westminster, Md.: The Newman Press, 1962.

Chauncy, Charles. "The Heat and Fervour of Their Passions." In David S. Lovejoy, *Religious Enthusiasm and the Great Awakening*.

Chevreau, Guy. *Catch the Fire*. London: Marshall Pickering, 1994.

Chitty, Derwas J. *The Desert a City*. Crestwood, N.Y.: St. Vladimer's Seminary Press, 1977.

Cho, Paul [David] Yonggi. *The Fourth Dimension: Volume Two* (South Plainfield, N.J.: Bridge, 1983).

Choy, Leona. *Andrew Murray: Apostle of Abiding Love*. Fort Washington, Pa.: Christian Literature Crusade, 1978.

Christenson, Carl C. "Pattern of Iconoclasm in the Early Reformation: Strasburg and Basil." In *The Image and the Word: Confrontations in Judaism, Christianity and Islam*, edited by Joseph Gutmann. Missoula, Mont.: Scholars Press, 1977.

Clark, Elmer T. *The Small Sects in America*. Nashville: Cokesbury Press, 1937.

Clark, Glenn. *A Man's Reach: The Autobiography of Glenn Clark*. (1949. Reprint, St. Paul, Minn.: MacAlester Park, 1977.

Clement of Alexandria. *Christ the Educator*. Translated by Simon P. Wood. Washington, D.C.: Catholic University of America Press, 1953.

Cleveland, Catherine C. *The Great Revival in the West, 1797 – 1805*. Chicago: University of Chicago Press, 1916.

Coad, F. Roy. *A History of the Brethren Movement*. Grand Rapids, Mich.: William B. Eerdmans, 1968.

Coleman, William. *Those Pharisees*. New York: Hawthorn Books, 1977.

* Collins, Gary. *The Magnificent Mind*. Waco, Tex.: Word Books, 1985.

Concar, David. "Ghost Molecules Theory Back From the Dead." *New Scientist* (16 March 1991): 10.

* Conkin, Paul. *Cane Ridge: America's Pentecost*. Madison: University of Wisconsin Press, 1990.

Copeland, Kenneth. "The Purpose of Prosperity." *Charisma & Christian Life*. (September 1990): 138-140.

Covey, Stephen R. *The Seven Habits of Highly Effective People*. New York: Simon and Schuster, 1989.

Cox, William E. *An Examination of Dispensationalism*. Phillipsburg, N.J.: Presbyterian and Reformed Publishing Company, 1980.

* Crehan, Joseph. *Father Thurston: A Memoir With a Bibliography of His Writings*. London: Sheed & Ward, 1952.

Cullis, Charles. *Dr. Cullis and His Work: Twenty Years of Blessing in Answer to Prayer*. Edited by W. H. Daniels. Boston: Willard Tract Repository, 1885.

————. *Faith Cures: or, Answers to Prayer in the Healing of the Sick*. Boston: Willard Tract Repository, 1879.

Cunningham, Raymond J. "The Impact of Christian Science on the American Churches, 1880 – 1910." *The American Historical Review* 72 (April 1967): 887-892.

————. "From Holiness to Healing: the Faith Cure in America, 1872 – 1892." *Church History* 43 (1974): 499-513.

D'Andrade, Hugh. *Charles Fillmore: Herald of the New Age*. New York: Harper & Row, 1974.

Dallimore, Arnold A. *George Whitefield*. Wheaton, Ill.: Crossway Books, 1990.

* Davies, W. D. *Paul and Rabbinic Judaism: Some Rabbinic Elements in Pauline Theology*. New York: Harper & Row, 1967.

Dawson, John. *Taking Our Cities for God*. Lake Mary, Fla.: Creation House, 1989.

* Dayton, Donald W. *Theological Roots of Pentecostalism*. Metuchen, N.J.: The Scarecrow Press, 1987.

Dearmer, Percy. *Body and Soul*. New York: E. P. Dutton, 1908.

DeArteaga, William L. "The Crisis of Confidence." *Ministries Today*, (July/August 1991): 56-62.

————. "Pharisaism: A Pneumatological Perspective." Paper presented at the Twenty-first Annual Meeting of the Society for Pentecostal Studies, Lakeland, Fla., 1991.

Dictionary of Pentecostal and Charismatic Movements. Edited by Stanley M. Burgess and Gary B. McGee. Grand Rapids, Mich.: Zondervan, 1988.

340

Dillenberger, John and Claude Welch. *Protestant Christianity Interpreted Through Its Development.* New York: Charles Scribner's Sons, 1954.

"A Disorienting View of God's Creation: Faith in the Crucible of the New Physics." *Christianity Today* (1 February 1985).

Dixon, Larry E. "Have the 'Jewels of the Church' Been Found Again? The Irving-Darby Debate on Miraculous Gifts." *Evangelical Journal* 5 (fall 1987): 78-92.

Eddy, Mary Baker. *Science and Health,* with *Key to the Scriptures.* Boston: First Church of Christ, Scientist, 1906.

Edwards, Jonathan. *Distinguishing Marks.* In *The Great Awakening,* edited by C. C. Goen. New Haven, Conn.: Yale University Press, 1972.

———. *Religious Affections.* Edited by John E. Smith. New Haven, Conn.: Yale University Press, 1959.

———. "Faithful Narrative." In *The Great Awakening,* edited by C. C. Goen. New Haven, Conn.: Yale University Press, 1972.

———. "Personal Narrative, I, 13." In Iain H. Murray. *Jonathan Edwards: A New Biography.* Edinburgh, Scotland: The Banner of Truth Trust, 1987.

———. "The Terror of the Law." In David S. Lovejoy. *Religious Enthusiasm and The Great Awakening.* Englewood Cliffs, N.J.: Prentice Hall, 1969.

Enroth, Ronald M. *Churches That Abuse.* Grand Rapids, Mich.: Zondervan, 1992.

Erickson, Millard J. "Lordship Theology: The Current Controversy.' *Southwestern Journal of Theology* 33 (spring 1991): 5-15.

Eusebius. *Ecclesiastical History.*

Evans, W. F. *Mental Medicine: A Theoretical and Practical Treatise.* Boston: Carter and Pettee, 1874.

* Farah, Charles, Jr. *From the Pinnacle of the Temple.* Plainfield, N.J: Logos International, 1979.

* ———. "A Critical Analysis: The 'Roots and Fruits' of the Faith-formula Theology." *Pneuma* 3 (spring 1981): 15.

———. "Faith or Presumption?" In Francis MacNutt, *The Power to Heal.* Notre Dame, Ind.: Ave Maria Press, 1974.

———. "Faith Theology: The Sovereignty of Man?" *Logos Journal* (May/June 1980): 50-55.

Farley, Edward. *Theologia: The Fragmentation and Unity of Theological Education.* Philadelphia: Fortress Press, 1983.

Farrar, Frederic W. *History of Interpretation.* London: Macmillan & Co., 1886.

Fawcett, Arthur. *The Cambuslang Revival: The Scottish Evangelical Revival of the Eighteenth Century.* London: Banner of Truth, 1971.

Fillmore, Charles. *Prosperity.* Kansas City, Mo.: Unity School of Christianity, 1938.

Finney, Charles G. *Memoirs*. New York: A.S. Barnes, 1876.

Foster, James D. and Glenn T. Moran. "Piaget and Parables: The Convergence of Secular and Scriptural Views of Learning." *Journal of Psychology and Theology* 13 (summer 1985): 97-103.

Foster, Richard. *Money, Sex and Power*. San Francisco: Harper & Row, 1985.

"Four Knowledgeable Looks at *The Seduction of Christianity*." *Ministries Today* (summer 1986): 70-74.

Frangipane, Francis. *Holiness, Truth and the Presence of God*. Marion, Iowa.: Advancing Church, 1986.

Freeman, James Dillet. *The Household of Faith: The Story of Unity*. Lee's Summit, Mo.: Unity, 1951.

Frodsham, Stanley Howard. *Smith Wigglesworth, Apostle of Faith*. Springfield, Mo.: Gospel Publishing House, 1990.

Frost, Evelyn. *Christian Healing*. London: Bradford & Dickens, 1940.

* Gamow, George. *Thirty Years That Shook Physics*. Garden City, N.Y.: Doubleday & Co., 1966.

* Gardner, Rex. "Miracles of healing in Anglo-Celtic Northumbria as recorded by Venerable Bede and his contemporaries: a reappraisal in the light of twentieth century experience." *British Medical Journal* 257 (December 1983): 24-31.

* Gay, Peter. *The Enlightenment: An Interpretation*. New York: Alfred A. Knopf, 1973.

Gero, Stephen. "Byzantine Iconoclasm and the Failure of a Medieval Reformation." In *The Image and the Word: Confrontations in Judaism, Christianity and Islam*, edited by Joseph Gutmann. Missoula, Mont.: Scholars Press, 1977.

Glaser, Mitch and Zhava Glaser. *The Fall Feasts of Israel*. Chicago: Moody Press, 1987.

* Goen, C. C. ed. *The Great Awakening*. New Haven, Conn.: Yale University Press, 1972.

Gordon, A. J. *The Holy Spirit in Missions*. New York: Fleming H. Revell, 1893. Reprint, Harrisburg, Pa.: Christian Publications, 1968.

* ———. *The Ministry of Healing: Miracles of Cure in All Ages*. Boston: H. Gannett, 1882. Reprint, Harrisburg, Pa.: Christian Publications, 1961.

———. *The Ministry of the Spirit*. 1894. Reprint, Minneapolis: Bethany House, 1985.

Gordon, Ernest B. *Adoniram Judson Gordon: A Biography*. New York: Fleming H. Revell, 1896.

* Grant, R. M. *Gnosticism and Early Christianity*. New York: Columbia University Press, 1957.

———. *The Letter and the Spirit*. New York: Macmillan & Co. 1957.

* Greenspahn, Frederick E. "Why Prophecy Ceased." *Journal of Biblical Literature* 108, no. 1 (1989): 37-49.

Gregory of Nyssa. *On the Christian Mode of Life.* In *Ascetical Works,* translated by Virginia Woods Callahan. Washington, D.C.: Catholic University of America Press, 1967.

Gribbin, John. *In Search of Schrodinger's Cat.* Toronto, Ont.: Bantam Books, 1984.

Griffin, Edward M. *"Old Brick": Charles Chauncy of Boston, 1705 – 1787.* Minneapolis: University of Minnesota Press, 1980.

Griswold, Whitney A. "New Thought: A Cult of Success." *The American Journal of Sociology* 60 (November 1934): 312.

* ———. "Three Puritans on Prosperity." *The New England Quarterly* 7 (September 1934): 479.

* Gross, Don H. *The Case for Spiritual Healing.* New York: Thomas Nelson & Sons, 1958.

Guinness, Og. *Fit Bodies, Fat Minds.* Grand Rapids, Mich.: Baker Books, 1994.

Gusmer, Charles W. *The Ministry of Healing in the Church of England.* Essex, England: Mayhew-McCrimmon, 1974.

———. "Anointing of the Sick in the Church of England." *Worship* 45 (May 1971): 262-272.

Haardt, Robert. *Gnosis: Character and Testimony.* Translated by J. F. Hendry. Leiden, Germany: E. J. Brill, 1971.

Hackett, Jo Ann. "Some Observations on the Balaam Tradition of Deiv cAlla." *Biblical Archaeologist* 49 (December 1986): 216-221.

Hagin, Kenneth E. *I Believe in Visions.* Old Tappan, N.J.: Fleming H. Revell, 1972.

———. *Must Christians Suffer?* Tulsa, Okla.: Rhema Bible Church, 1982.

———. Plead Your Case (Tulsa, Okla.: Faith Library Publications, 1979).

———. "Suffering Unto Perfection: Part 3." *Word of Faith* (November 1995): 16.

———. "Having Faith in Your Faith," *The Word of Faith,* September 1980.

Haines, Charles Grove. *The Revival of Natural Law Concepts.* Vol. 4 of Harvard *Studies in Jurisprudence.* New York: Russell and Russell, 1965.

Hammers, Signe. "The Mind as Healer." *Science Digest* (April 1984): 47-49, 100.

* Hanegraaff, Hank. *Christianity in Crisis.* Eugene, Oreg.: Harvest House, 1993.

———. "A Summary Critique." *Christian Research Journal* (fall 1992): 38.

Hannah, John D. Review of *The Incredible Scofield and His Book. Bibliotheca Sacra* 147 (July-September 1990).

Harlan, David. *The Clergy and the Great Awakening.* Ann Arbor, Mich.: UMI Research Press, 1980.

Harrell, David Edwin, Jr. *All Things Are Possible: The Healing and Charismatic Revivals in Modern America.* Bloomington: Indiana University Press, 1975.

Hatch, Nathan O., ed. *Jonathan Edwards and The American Experience.* New York: Oxford University Press, 1988.

Herbert, Nick. "How to Be in Two Places at the Same Time." *New Scientist* (21 August 1986): 41-44.

Heron, Alasdair I. C. *The Holy Spirit.* Philadelphia: Westminster Press, 1983.

Hexham, Irving and Karla Poewe-Hexham. "Charismatics and Apartheid." *Charisma & Christian Life* (May 1990): 62-70.

Hill, Harold. *How to Live Like a King's Kid.* Plainfield, N.J.: Logos International, 1974.

Hoffman, Bengt R. *Luther and the Mystics.* Minneapolis: Augsburg Publishing House, 1976.

Holifield, E. Brooks. *A History of Pastoral Care in America: From Salvation to Self-Realization.* Nashville: Abingdon Press, 1983.

Hollinger, Dennis. "Enjoying God Forever: An Historical/Sociological Profile of the Health and Wealth Gospel." *Trinity Journal* 9 (fall 1988): 144.

Honner, John, S. J. "Unity-in-Difference: Karl Rahner and Niels Bohr." *Theological Studies* 46 (September 1985): 480-506.

Hoopes, James. "Jonathan Edwards' Religious Psychology." *The Journal of American History* 69 (March 1983): 849-865.

* Hopkins, Samuel. *The Life and Character of the Late Reverend Mr. Jonathan Edwards.* In *Jonathan Edwards: A Profile,* edited by David Levin. New York: Hill & Wang, 1969.

Hovenkamp, Herbert. *Science and Religion in America, 1800 – 1860.* Philadelphia, Pa.: University of Pennsylvania Press, 1978.

Howard, Harry C. *Princes of the Christian Pulpit and Pastorate,* 2d ser. Nashville: Cokesbury Press, 1918.

Hume, David. "On Miracles." *An Enquiry Concerning Human Understanding.*

* Hunt, Dave, *Beyond Seduction.* Eugene, Oreg.: Harvest House, 1987.

———. *The Cult Explosion.* Eugene, Oreg.: Harvest House, 1980.

———. *Global Peace and the Rise of the Antichrist.* Eugene, Oreg.: Harvest House, 1990.

———. *On the Brink.* Plainfield, N.J.: Logos International, 1972.

———. *Peace, Prosperity and the Coming Holocaust.* Eugene, Oreg.: Harvest House, 1983.

———. "A Serious Call Re-Echoed." *Christian Life* (May 1986): 48-50.

Hunt, Dave and T. A. McMahon. *The Seduction of Christianity: Spiritual Discernment in the Last Days.* Eugene, Oreg.: Harvest House, 1985.

Ignatius of Loyola, Saint. *The Spiritual Exercises of St. Ignatius.* Translated by Anthony Mottola. Garden City, N.Y.: Doubleday & Co., 1964.

Irenaeus. *Against Heresies.* In Evelyn Frost, *Christian Healings.*

Jaeger, Werner. *Early Christianity and Greek Paideia.* Cambridge, Mass.: Harvard University Press, 1961.

James, William. *The Varieties of Religious Experience.* Longmans, Gree..,
1903.

John of the Cross, Saint. *Ascent of Mount Carmel.*

"John Knox: The Thundering Scot." *Christian History* 14 (1995).

* Judah, J. Stillson. *The History and Philosophy of the Metaphysical Movements in America.* Philadelphia: Westminster Press, 1967.

* Judd, Carrie F. *The Prayer of Faith.* Buffalo, N.Y.: H. H. Otis, 1882.

Justin Martyr. "Dialogue With Trypho." In Ronald Kydd, *Charismatic Gifts in the Early Church.* Peabody, Mass.: Hendrickson, 1984.

Kant, Immanuel. *Religion Within the Limits of Reason Alone.* Translated by Theodore M. Greene and Hoyt H. Hudson. LaSalle, Ill.: Open Court, 1960.

* Keller, Ernst and Marie-Luise Keller. *Miracles in Dispute: A Continuing Debate.* Translated by Margaret Kohl. Philadelphia: Fortress Press, 1969.

Kelly, Henry Ansgar. *The Devil, Demonology and Witchcraft: The Development of Christian Belief in Evil Spirits.* Garden City, N.Y.: Doubleday & Co., 1974.

* Kelsey, Morton T. *Healing and Christianity.* New York: Harper & Row, 1976.

———. *Tongue Speaking: An Experiment in Spiritual Experience.* London: Hodder and Stoughton, 1968.

Kent, John H. S. *The End of the Line? The Development of Christian Theology in the Last Two Centuries.* Philadelphia: Fortress Press, 1982.

Kenyon, E. W. *The Hidden Man.* Lynnwood, Wash.: Kenyon's Gospel Publishing Society, 1970.

* ———. *Identification: A Romance in Redemption.* Lynnwood, Wash.: Kenyon's Gospel Publishing Society, 1968.

———. *New Creation Realities.* 1945. Reprint, Lynnwood, Wash.: Kenyon's Gospel Publishing Society, 1964.

———. *Sign Posts on the Road to Success.* 1938. Reprint, Lynnwood, Wash.: Kenyon's Gospel Publishing Society, 1966.

———. *Two Kinds of Faith.* Lynnwood, Wash.: Kenyon's Gospel Publishing Society, 1969.

———. *Two Kinds of Knowledge.* Lynnwood, Wash.: Kenyon's Gospel Publishing Society, 1966.

———. *What Happened From the Cross to the Throne.* Seattle, Wash.: Kenyon's Gospel Publishing Society, 1945.

———. "God's Leadings." *Tabernacle Trumpet* (January 1901).

———. "Justification." *Reality* (November 1909).

———. "The Walk of Faith." *Reality* (January 1907).

Kenyon, Evva Lydia Spurling. "God's Leadings." *Tabernacle Trumpet* (January 1901): 131.

Kenyon, Ruth A. "He Is at Rest." *Herald of Life* (April 1948).

Kern, Dorothy. *The Living Touch.* London: Courier, 1914.

Kinnear, Angus. *Against the Tide.* Wheaton, Ill.: Tyndale House, 1978.

Kitzinger, Ernst. *The Art of Byzantium and the Medieval West.* Bloomington, Ind.: Indiana University Press, 1976.

* Knox, R. A. *Enthusiasm: A Chapter in the History of Religion.* New York: Oxford University Press, 1950.

Koch, Byron. "The Force — or Pumped, Scooped, Charged and Slain: Thoughts on the Theology of the 'Toronto Blessing'." *SCP Newsletter* (spring 1995): 1-13.

Koop, C. Everett. "Faith-Healing and the Sovereignty of God." In *The Agony of Deceit,* edited by Michael Horton. Chicago: Moody Press, 1990.

Kraus, Norman C. *Dispensationalism in America.* Richmond, Va.: John Knox Press, 1958.

Kuhn, Thomas S. *The Structure of Scientific Revolutions.* Chicago: University of Chicago Press, 1962.

* La Shell, John K. "Imagination and Idol: A Puritan Tension." *Westminster Theological Journal* 49 (1987): 305-334.

LeBlanc, Doug. "The Worldwide Church of God: Resurrected into Orthodoxy." *Christian Research Journal* (winter 1996): 6-7,44-45.

Lang, Amy Schrager. "A Flood of Errors: Chauncy and Edwards in the Great Awakening." In *Jonathan Edwards and the American Experience,* edited by Nathan O. Hatch. New York: Oxford University Press, 1988.

Law, William. *The Power of the Spirit.* Edited by Dave Hunt. Fort Washington, Pa.: Christian Literature Crusade, 1971.

Lawson, John. *The Biblical Theology of Saint Irenaeus.* London: The Epworth Press, 1948.

Leslie, J. "How to Draw Conclusions From the Fine-Tuned Universe." In Robert J. Russell et al. *Physics, Philosophy, and Theology.* Vatican City, Rome: Vatican Observatory, 1988, 297-312.

Levin, David, ed. *Jonathan Edwards: A Profile.* New York: Hill Wang, 1969.

* Lewis, David. *Healing: Fiction, Fantasy or Fact?* London: Hodder & Stoughton, 1989.

Lie, Geir. "E. W. Kenyon: *Sekstifter eller kristen lederskikkelse?* En historisk undersøkelse av Kenyons teologi med sāerlig nenblikk på deus historiske rotter og innflytelsen på samtid og ettertid." Master's thesis, Norwegian Lutheran School of Theology, October 1994.

Linn, Matthew and Dennis Linn. *Deliverance Prayer: Experiential, Psychological and Theological Approaches.* New York: Paulist Press, 1981.

* Lovejoy, David S. *Religious Enthusiasm and the Great Awakening.* Englewood Cliffs, N.J.: Prentice-Hall, 1969.

———. *Religious Enthusiasm in the New World: Heresy to Revolution.* Cambridge, Mass.: Harvard University Press, 1985.

* Lovelace, Richard F. *Dynamics of Spiritual Life: An Evangelical Theology of Renewal.* Downers Grove, Ill.: InterVarsity Press, 1979.

———. "The Surprising Works of God." *Christianity Today* (11 September 1995): 28-32.

Mabie, Henry C. *The Divine Reason of the Cross.* New York: Fleming H. Revell, 1911.

* MacArthur, John F., Jr. *Charismatic Chaos.* Grand Rapids, Mich.: Zondervan Publishing House, 1992.

———. *The Charismatics: A Doctrinal Perspective.* Grand Rapids, Mich.: Zondervan Publishing House, 1978.

———. *Reckless Faith: When the Church Loses Its Will to Discern.* Wheaton, Ill.: Crossway Books, 1994.

MacArthur, William T. *Ethan O. Allen.* N.p., n.d.

MacGregor, Geddes. *Introduction to Religious Philosophy.* Boston: Houghton Mifflin Co., 1953.

* MacNutt, Francis. *Overcome by the Spirit.* Old Tappan, N.J.: Fleming H. Revell, 1990.

———. *The Power to Heal.* Notre Dame, Ind.: Ave Maria Press, 1977.

Mahan, Asa. *The Baptism of the Holy Spirit.* New York: George Hughes, 1870.

* Mains, George Preston. *James Monroe Buckley.* New York: The Methodist Book Concern. 1917.

Maloney, George. *Uncreated Energy.* Amity, N.Y.: Amity Hour, 1987.

Marden, Orison Swett. *Every Man a King: Or, Might in Mind-Mastery.* New York: Thomas Y. Crowell, 1906.

———. *Pushing to the Front: Or, Success Under Difficulties.* New York: Thomas Y. Crowell, 1894.

Martin, Malachi. *Hostage to the Devil.* New York: Reader's Digest Press, 1976.

* Martin, Walter. *The Kingdom of the Cults.* Rev. ed. Minneapolis: Bethany Fellowship, 1968.

———. "You Shall Be as Gods." In *The Agony of Deceit,* edited by Michael Horton. Chicago: Moody Press, 1990.

McCance, Dawne. "Physics, Buddhism, and Postmodern Interpretations." *Zygon* 21 (spring 1986): 287-296.

McCauley, Ray. "A Pastor Dares to Face Apartheid." *Charisma & Christian Life* (June 1988): 63-69.

* McConnell, D. R. *A Different Gospel.* Peabody, Mass.: Hendrickson, 1988.

———. "The Kenyon Connection: A Theological and Historical Analysis of the Cultic Origins of the Faith Movement." Master's thesis, Oral Roberts University, 1982.

McCrossan, T. J. *Bodily Healing and the Atonement.* Edited by R. Hicks and Kenneth Hagin. Tulsa, Okla.: Faith Library Publications, 1982.

McManus, Jim. *The Healing Power of the Sacraments.* Chawtaon, England: Redemptorist Publications, 1984.

Merton, Thomas. *The Wisdom of the Desert*. New York: New Directions, 1970.

* Meyer, Donald. *Positive Thinkers: Religion as Pop Psychology From Mary Baker Eddy to Oral Roberts*. New York: Pantheon Books, 1980.

* Meyerhoff, Steven. "Andover Seminary: The Rise and Fall of an Evangelical Institution." *Presbyterian* 8, no. 2 (fall 1982): 13-24.

Miller, Elliot. "Unity School of Christianity." In *Walter Martin's Cults Reference Bible*, edited by Walter Martin. Santa Ana, Calif.: Vision House, 1981.

Miller, Perry. *Jonathan Edwards*. N.p.: William Sloane Assoc., 1949; New York: Meridian, 1959.

———. "The Rhetoric of Sensation." In *Errand into the Wilderness*. New York: Harper & Row, 1964.

Montefiore C. G. and H. Lowe. *A Rabbinic Anthology*. Cleveland: The World Publishing Co., 1963.

Montgomery, John Warwick. *In Defense of Martin Luther*. Milwaukee, Wisc.: Northeastern Publishing House, 1970.

———. *The Law Above the Law*. Minneapolis: Bethany House, 1975.

* ———. *The Suicide of Christian Theology*. Minneapolis: Bethany Fellowship, 1970.

Morgan, David. "The Protestant Struggle with the Image." *The Christian Century* 106 (22-29 March 1989): 308-311.

Morgan, Edmund S. *The Puritan Dilemma*. Boston: Little, Brown and Company, 1958.

Moseley, J. Rufus. *Manifest Victory: A Quest and a Testimony*. New York: Harper and Brothers, 1941.

Muck, Terry C. "Open Season." *Christianity Today* (21 November 1986): 16-17.

Mumper, Sharon E. "Where in the World Is the Church Growing?" *Christianity Today* (11 July 1986): 17-21.

Murray, Andrew. *Divine Healing*. Springdale, Pa.: Whitaker House, 1982.

* Murray, Iain H. *Jonathan Edwards: A New Biography*. Edinburgh, Scotland: The Banner of Truth Trust, 1987.

Nee, Watchman. *The Latent Power of the Soul*. New York: Christian Fellowship Publishers, 1972.

———. *The Normal Christian Life*. 3d rev. ed. Fort Washington, Pa.: Christian Literature Crusade, 1973.

* Nevius, John. *Demon Possession and Allied Themes*. New York: Fleming H. Revell, 1896.

New Catholic Encyclopedia. New York: McGraw-Hill, 1967.

Nissenbaum, Stephen, ed. *The Great Awakening at Yale College*. Belmont, Calif.: Wadsworth Publishing Co., 1972.

Noll, Mark A. *Princeton and the Republic, 1768 – 1822*. Princeton, N.J.: Princeton University Press, 1989.

* ———, ed.. *The Princeton Theology, 1812 – 1921* Grand Rapids, Mich.: Baker Book House, 1983.

* ———. *The Scandal of the Evangelical Mind.* Grand Rapids, Mich.: William B. Eerdmans, 1994.

Oden, Thomas C. *Requiem: A Lament in Three Movements.* Nashville: Abingdon Press, 1995.

Origen. "On the Soul." In *A Treasury of Early Christianity,* edited by Anne Fremantle. New York: New American Library, Mentor, 1960.

Otis, George, Jr. *The Last of the Giants.* Tarrytown, N.Y.: Fleming H. Revell, Chosen Books, 1991.

Palladius. *Lausiac History.* Translated by Robert T. Meyer. Westminister, Md.: The Newman Press, 1965.

Palmer, Phoebe. *The Devotional Writings of Phoebe Palmer.* New York: Garland, 1986.

———. *The Way of Holiness, with Notes by the Way.* New York: Piercy and Reed, 1843.

———. *Selected Writings of Phoebe Palmer.* Edited by Thomas C. Oden. New York: Paulist Press, 1988.

* Parker, Gail Thain. *Mind Cure in New England: From the Civil War to World War I.* Hanover, N.H.: University Press of New England, 1973.

* Passantino, Bob and Gretchen Passantino. *Witch Hunt.* Nashville: Thomas Nelson, 1990.

———. "Psychology and the Church." Parts 1, 2 and 3. *Christian Research Journal* (winter/spring/summer 1995).

Perkins, William. *A Treatise of the Vocations or Callings of Man.* In *The Work of William Perkins,* edited by Ian Breward. Appleford, England: The Sutton Courteney Press, 1970.

Pierard, Richard V. "Anti-Jewish Sentiments in an Unexpected Content: Evangelical Bible Expositor John MacArthur." *The Covenant Quarterly* 45 (November 1987): 182.

* Polkinghorne, John C. *One World: The Interaction of Science and Theology.* London: Society for Promoting Christian Knowledge, 1986.

———. *The Way the World Is.* Grand Rapids, Mich.: William B. Eerdmans, 1984.

Pool, Robert. "Quantum Pot Watching." *Science* 246 (17 November 1989): 888.

* Popper, Karl R. *The Spell of Plato.* Vol. 1. *The High Tide of Prophecy: Hegel, Marx, and the Aftermath.* Vol. 2 of *The Open Society and Its Enemies.* New York: Harper & Row, 1963.

* Poulain, Fr. A., S. J. *The Graces of Interior Prayer: A Treatise on Mystical Theology.* Translated by L. L. Yorke-Smith. St. Louis, Mo.: B. Herder Book Co., 1950.

Price, Clive. "British Cautiously Embrace Renewal." *Charisma and Christian Life* (April 1995): 58-59.

———. "A Revival Without Walls," *Charisma and Christian Life* (November 1995): 54-58.

Proudfoot, Wayne. "From Theology to a Science of Religions: Jonathan Edwards and William James on Religious Affections." *Harvard Theological Review* 82 (April 1989): 149-168.

* Puller, Frederick William. *The Anointing of the Sick: Scripture and Tradition.* London: Society for Promoting Christian Knowledge, 1904.

Rae, Alastair. "Extrasensory Quantum Physics." *New Scientist* (27 November 1986): 36-39.

Rahner, Hugo. *The Spirituality of St. Ignatius Loyola: An Account of Its Historical Development.* Translated by Francis John Smith. Westminster, Md.: The Newman Press, 1953.

* Rakow, Mary. "Christ's Descent into Hell: Calvin's Interpretation." *Religion in Life* 42 (summer 1974): 218-226.

* Richardson, Don. *Eternity in Their Hearts.* Ventura, Calif.: Regal Books, 1981.

* Riss, R. M. *A Survey of Twentieth Century Revival Movements in North America.* Peabody, Mass.: Hendrickson, 1988.

———. "E. W. Kenyon." In *Dictionary of Pentecostal and Charismatic Movements.* Edited by Stanley M. Burgeses and Gary B. McGee. Grand Rapids, Mich.: Zondervan, 1988.

Rothman, Tony. "A 'What You See Is What You Beget' Theory." *Discover* 8 (May 1987): 90-91.

Rothslein, William G. *American Physicians in the Nineteenth Century: From Sect to Science.* Baltimore: Johns Hopkins University Press, 1972.

* Ruthven, Jon. *On the Cessation of the Charismata: The Protestant Polemic on Postbiblical Miracles.* Sheffield, England: Sheffield Academic Press, 1993.

———. "On Cessation of the Charismata: The Protestant Polemic of Benjamin B. Warfield." *Pneuma* 12 (spring 1990): 14-31.

Sandeen, Ernest R. "The Princeton Theology." *Church History* 31 (September 1962): 307-321.

* Sandford, John and Paula Sandford. *The Elijah Task.* Tulsa, Okla.: Victory House, 1977.

———. *Healing the Wounded Spirit.* South Plainfield, N.J.: Bridge, 1985.

* ———. *The Transformation of the Inner Man.* South Plainfield, N.J.: Bridge, 1982.

———. "The Lord's Kindness Leads to Repentance." *Voice* 2 (September 1991): 1-2.

* Sanford, Agnes. *The Healing Light.* St. Paul, Minn.: MacAlester Park, 1947.

———. *Sealed Orders.* Plainfield, N.J.: Logos International, 1972.

* Schaafs, Werner. *Theology, Physics, and Miracles.* Translated by Richard L. Renfield. Washington, D.C.: Canon Press, 1974.

Schaeffer, Francis A. *The God Who Is There*. Downers Grove, Ill.: InterVarsity Press, 1968.

* Schmithals, Walter. *Gnosticism in Corinth: An Investigation of the Letters to the Corinthians*. Translated by John E. Steely. Nashville: Abingdon Press, 1971.

———. *Paul and the Gnostics*. Translated by John E. Steely. Nashville: Abingdon Press, 1972.

Shimony, Abner. "The Reality of the Quantum World." *Scientific American* 258 (January 1988): 46-53.

* Simmons, Dale. "The Postbellum Pursuit of Peace, Power and Plenty: As Seen in the Writings of Essek William Kenyon." Ph.D. diss., Drew University, 1988.

Simpson, A. B. *The Gospel of Healing*. Rev. ed. New York: Christian Alliance Publishing Co., 1920.

Smolin, Lee. "What Is Quantum Mechanics Really About?" *New Scientist*, (24 October 1985): 40.

Smyth, Paterson J. *The Gospel of the Hereafter*. New York: Fleming H. Revell, 1910.

Spencer, James R. *Bleeding Hearts and Propaganda: The Fall of Reason in the Church*. Lafayette, La.: Huntington House, 1995.

* ———. *Heresy Hunters: Character Assassination in the Church*. Lafayette, La.: Huntington House Publishers, 1993.

———. "How Jesus Provides Hope." *Through the Maze* #9-95 (1995).

———. "Why We Need Pop-Apologists." *Update* (95#8): 1-4.

Springer, Kevin N. "Applying the Gifts to Everyday Life." *Charisma & Christian Life* (September 1985): 26-34.

Stafford, Tim. "The Kingdom of the Cult Watchers." *Christianity Today* (7 October 1991): 18-23.

Stock, Jennifer. "George S. Montgomery; Businessman for the Gospel." Parts 1 and 2. *Assemblies of God Heritage* 9, spring/summer 1989.

Stube, Edwin B. *According to the Pattern....* Baltimore: The Holy Way, 1982.

Stump, Leon D. *Metaphysical Elements in the Faith Movement*. Joplin, Mo.: privately printed, 1987.

Swaggart, Jimmy. *God's Plan for the Ages*. Baton Rouge, La.: Jimmy Swaggart Ministries, 1986.

Swaim, Loring T. *Arthritis, Medicine and the Spiritual Laws: The Power Beyond Science*. Philadelphia: Chilton Co., 1962.

Swedenborg, Emanuel. *Earth in the Universe*, 1st ed. N.p., 1758.

* Synan, Vinson. *The Holiness-Pentecostal Movement in the United States*. Grand Rapids, Mich.: William B. Eerdmans, 1971.

———. "The Faith of Kenneth Hagin," *Charisma & Christian Life*. (June 1990): 68.

————. "The Role of the Holy Spirit and the Gifts of the Spirit in the Mystical Tradition," *One in Christ* 10, no. 2 (1974).

Tawney, R. H. *Religion and the Rise of Capitalism.* London: n.p., 1929.

Thigpen, Paul. "What's the Fuss About 'Kingdom Now'?" *Ministries Today* (July/August 1988): 33-39.

* Thurston, Fr. Herbert. *The Physical Phenomenon of Mysticism.* Edited by J. H. Crehan. London: Burns Oates, 1952.

Tillich, Paul. *My Search for Absolutes.* New York: Simon and Schuster, 1967.

Tozer, A. W. *Tragedy in the Church: The Missing Gifts.* Harrisburg, Pa.: Christian Publications, 1978.

Trine, Ralph Waldo. *In Tune With the Infinite.* Indianapolis: Bobbs-Merrill Co., 1897.

————. *The Power That Wins: Henry Ford and Ralph Waldo Trine in an Intimate Talk on Life.* Indianapolis: Bobbs-Merrill Co., 1929.

* Tydings, Judith. *Gathering a People: Catholic Saints in Charismatic Perspective.* Plainfield, N.J.: Logos International, 1977.

* Verduin, Leonard. *The Reformers and Their Stepchildren.* Grand Rapids, Mich.: William B. Eerdmans, 1964.

Vincent, Marvin R. "Modern Miracles." *The Presbyterian Review* 4 (July 1884): 497.

Vines, Gail. "Ghostly Antibodies Baffle Scientists." *New Scientist.* (14 July 1988): 39.

Von Hugel, Friedrich. *The Mystical Element of Religion: As Studied in Saint Catherine of Genoa and Her Friends.* London: J.M. Kent, 1908.

* Von Rad, Gerhard. *Wisdom in Israel.* Nashville: Abingdon Press, 1972.

Wagner, C. Peter. *Spiritual Power and Church Growth.* Lake Mary, Fla.: Creation House, 1986.

Wagner, C. Peter and F. Douglas Pennoyer. *Wrestling With Dark Angels: Toward a Deeper Understanding of the Supernatural Forces in Spiritual Warfare.* Ventura, Calif.: Regal Books, 1990.

Walker, A. Keith. *William Law: His Life and Thought.* London: Society for Promoting Christian Knowledge, 1973.

Ward, William Reginald. *The Protestant Evangelical Awakening.* Cambridge, England: Cambridge University Press, 1992.

Warfield, Benjamin B. *Counterfeit Miracles.* New York: Charles Scribner's Sons, 1918.

Weber, Max. *The Protestant Ethic and the Spirit of Capitalism.* London: n.p., 1930.

Weiner, Michael and Kathleen Goss. *The Complete Book of Homeopathy.* Toronto, Ont.: Bantam Books, 1982.

Weiss, Richard. *The American Myth of Success: From Horatio Alger to Peale Norman Vincent.* New York: Basic Books, 1969.

* White, Charles Edward. *The Beauty of Holiness: Phoebe Palmer as*

Theologian, Revivalist, Feminist, and Humanitarian. Grand Rapids, Mich.: Francis Asbury Press, 1986.

————. "The Beauty of Holiness: The Career of Phoebe Palmer." *Fides et Historia* 19 (February 1987): 22-34.

————. "Phoebe Palmer and the Development of Pentecostal Pneumatology." *Wesleyan Theological Journal* 23 (spring/fall 1988): 198-212.

White, James R. *The King James Only Controversy.* Minneapolis: Bethany House, 1995.

Whitefield, George. "The Grand Itinerant." In David S. Lovejoy, *Religious Enthusiasm and the Great Awakening.*

Wigglesworth, Smith. *Faith That Prevails.* 1938. Reprint, Springfield, Mo.: Gospel Publishing House, 1966.

Williams, Don, *Revival: The Real Thing.* La Jolla, Calif.: privately printed, 1995.

Wilson, Marvin R. *Our Father Abraham: Jewish Roots of the Christian Faith.* Grand Rapids, Mich.: William B. Eerdmans, 1989.

Wimber, John and Kevin N. Springer. *Power Evangelism.* San Francisco: Harper & Row, 1986.

Wise, Robert. et al. *The Church Divided.* South Plainfield, N.J.: Bridge, 1986.

Wolf, Fred Alan. *Taking the Quantum Leap: The New Physics for Nonscientists.* San Francisco: Harper & Row, 1981.

Worcester, Elwood. *Life's Adventure: The Story of a Varied Career.* New York: Charles Scribner's Sons, 1932.

* Wright, Louis B. *Middle-Class Culture in Elizabethan England.* Chapel Hill, N.C.: University of North Carolina Press, 1935.

Yancey, Philip. "Insight on Eternity From a Scientific View of Time." *Christianity Today* (6 April 1984): 26.

Zimany, Roland. "The Divine Energies in Orthodox Theology." *Diakonia* 11. no. 3 (1976): 281-285.

Zukav, Gary. *The Dancing Wu Li Masters: An Overview of the New Physics.* New York: William Morrow, 1979.

INDEX